lonely planet

D0469217

Seattle

"All you've got to do is decide to go
and the hardest part is over.

So go!"

TONY WHEELER, COFOUNDER – LONELY PLANET

THIS EDITION WRITTEN AND RESEARCHED BY
Brendan Sainsbury,
Celeste Brash

Contents

Plan Your Trip — 4

Welcome to Seattle......... 4
Seattle's Top 10 6
What's New..................... 13
Need to Know 14
Top Itineraries 16

If You Like..................... 18
Month by Month 20
With Kids 22
Eating 24
Drinking & Nightlife ... 27

Entertainment.............. 29
Sports & Activities 31
Shopping....................... 34

Explore Seattle — 36

**Neighborhoods
at a Glance.................... 38**

Downtown, Pike Place
& Waterfront 40

Pioneer Square &
International District 63

Belltown &
Seattle Center 76

Queen Anne
& Lake Union................. 93

Capitol Hill &
First Hill 105

The CD, Madrona
& Madison Park 120

U District 130

Fremont & Green Lake 139

Ballard &
Discovery Park 149

Georgetown &
West Seattle 159

**Day Trips
from Seattle 168**

Sleeping 179

Understand Seattle — 189

Seattle Today.............. 190
History.......................... 192

The Way of Life 196
Music 200

Survival Guide — 203

Transportation 204

Directory A–Z 208

Index 214

Seattle Maps — 222

(left) EMP Museum (p82)

(above) The gum wall at Pike Place Market (p43)

(right) In-line skating in Discovery Park (p151)

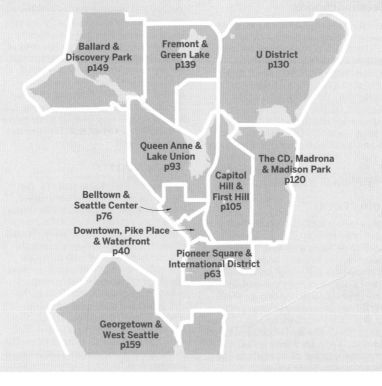

Ballard & Discovery Park p149

Fremont & Green Lake p139

U District p130

Queen Anne & Lake Union p93

The CD, Madrona & Madison Park p120

Capitol Hill & First Hill p105

Belltown & Seattle Center p76

Downtown, Pike Place & Waterfront p40

Pioneer Square & International District p63

Georgetown & West Seattle p159

Welcome to Seattle

Seattle is America's Cinderella city. Founded in 1851 and overlooked until the 1960s, it's been making up for lost time ever since.

A Confederation of Neighborhoods

Since it's less a city and more a loose alliance of jostling neighborhoods, getting to know Seattle is like hanging out with a family of affectionate but sometimes errant siblings. There's the aloof, elegant one (Queen Anne), the cool, edgy one (Capitol Hill), the weird, bearded one (Fremont), the independently minded Scandinavian one (Ballard), the bruised, weather-beaten one (Pioneer Square) and the precocious adolescent still carving out its identity (South Lake Union). You'll never fully understand Seattle until you've had a microbrew in all of them.

Going Local

Make a beeline for Seattle's proverbial pantry: Pike Place Market. It was founded in 1907 to ply locals with fresh Northwest produce, and its long-held mantra of 'meet the producer' is still echoed enthusiastically around a city where every restaurateur worth their salt knows the first name of their fishmonger and the biography of the cow that made yesterday's burgers. Welcome to a city of well-educated palates and experimental chefs who are willing to fuse American cuisine with just about anything – as long as the ingredients are local.

Coffee & Beer

The city that invented Starbucks coffee and Rainier beer has gone back to the drawing board in recent years and come up with an interesting alternative – a new wave of small, independent micro-businesses that are determined to put taste over global reach. Imbibe the nuances of a home-roasted Guatemalan coffee and check out the latest in nano-breweries in the city that has put a coffee shop on every street corner and created a different craft beer for every night of the year.

Music & Art

Imagine: a rocket sticking out of a shoe shop and a museum built to resemble a smashed-up electric guitar; wooden boats stacked with glass orbs and a statue of Lenin caught in a vengeful Bolshevik-era grimace; a waterside sculpture park and a Saturday-evening art walk through a blue-collar warehouse district; indie bands playing in grungy pubs and hip-hop artists eschewing bling for thrift shops. No, you haven't just over-indulged in some powerful (legal) marijuana. The city that inspired Dale Chihuly, Kurt Cobain, Jimi Hendrix and Macklemore has a lot to offer in the way of music and art – and it's never remotely dull.

Why I Love Seattle

By Brendan Sainsbury, Author

Since I grew up in England, Seattle lured me from afar. For a brief period in the early 1990s it was = to me at least = the center of the musical universe. When I had the chance to visit for the first time in the early 2000s, I discovered a city of diverse neighborhoods and shifting moods that inspired me with its arty subcultures and appetite for innovation. The atmosphere was infectious; and, as a Nirvana-loving, craft-beer-appreciating, outdoors-embracing, art-admiring, bus-utilizing coffee addict, I've never had a problem fitting in.

For more about our authors, see p248.

Top: The Space Needle (p80) and waterfront skyline

Seattle's
Top 10

Pike Place Market (p42)

1 Way more than just a market, century-old Pike Place is a living community, a cabaret show, a way of life and an intrinsic piece of Seattle's soul. Strolling through its clamorous, sometimes chaotic thoroughfares, you simply couldn't be in any other city. There's fish flying through the air, an artistic 'gum wall,' shops that look like they've sprung from a Harry Potter movie, and a multitude of classic old buskers jamming acoustic versions of AC/DC songs outside the world's oldest Starbucks. Pure magic!

⊙ *Downtown, Pike Place & Waterfront*

Space Needle (p80)

2 The city icon that is as synonymous with Seattle as the letters S-E-A-T-T-L-E was bu for the 1962 World's Fair, and its novel revolv-ing restaurant and bold futuristic design have proved durable. Although it's no longer Seattle's tallest structure, one million annual visitors still squeeze into the Space Needle's slick, speedy elevators to enjoy views that are best described as sublime. Granted, tickets ar expensive and you might have to fight off the odd tourist or three, but stop complaining and get in line: this is an essential Seattle pilgrimag

⊙ *Belltown & Seattle Center*

Capitol Hill *(p105)*

3 Other neighborhoods have their tourist shrines; Capitol Hill has its people – and a thoroughly eclectic lot they are too. Anything goes in this factory of hip, as long as it's not from the mainstream. There's beer-flavored ice cream and coffee-flavored beer, transvestites on in-line skates and dogs with dyed pink streaks in their fur, smoke shops selling hookah pipes, and enough vinyl and books to make you think that Amazon.com never happened. Welcome to Seattle's most colorful 'hood. Visiting isn't an option, it's a duty.

⊙ *Capitol Hill & First Hill*

EMP Museum *(p82)*

4 Paying homage to the left-handed, guitar-burning musical genius that was Jimi Hendrix, Paul Allen's architecturally bizarre EMP Museum is an apt memorial to a region that has been a powerful musical innovator since the days of Bing Crosby (born in Tacoma, WA). Come and see the legends and how they were created, from Hendrix to Kurt Cobain, or experiment with your own riffs in the interactive Sound Lab. Marrying Captain Kirk with Nirvana Kurt is the on-site 'Icons of Science Fiction' exhibit, where *Star Trek* meets *Doctor Who*.

⊙ *Belltown & Seattle Center*

Coffee Culture *(p27)*

5 Welcome to the new Vienna. Seattle practically invented modern North American coffee culture, thanks to a small store in Pike Place Market that went global: Starbucks. But, while the rest of the world has been quick to lap up the green mermaid logo and its multiple coffee-related inventions, Seattle has moved on. Starbucks is merely the froth on the cappuccino in a city where hundreds of small-scale micro-roasteries, cafes, baristas and knowledge-able caffeine connoisseurs continue to point the way to what's next in coffee.

VICTROLA COFFEE ROASTERS (P113)

🍷 *Drinking & Nightlife*

Public Art *(p141)*

6 Seattle likes to display its art out in the open with no holds barred. Sculptures and statues decorate parks, streets and squares, from the weird (a stone troll underneath a bridge), to the iconic (Hendrix in classic rock-and-roll pose), to the downright provocative (a statue of Vladimir Lenin). The city even has its own sculpture park, an outpost of the Seattle Art Museum that spreads its works across a beautifully landscaped outdoor space overlooking glassy Elliott Bay. FREMONT ROCKET (P142)

◉ *Fremont & Green Lake*

Museum of Flight *(p161)*

7 Even people with absolutely no interest in aviation have been known to blink in quiet astonishment at the remarkable Museum of Flight, which tells the tale of how humankind got from the Wright Brothers to the first moon landing in less than 66 years. Get ready for an exciting jet-propelled journey through war, peace, space rockets and inspired engineering, eloquently related with the aid of film, words, flight simulators, famous decommissioned aircraft, and a man called William E Boeing.

◉ *Georgetown & West Seattle*

Belltown Dining

(p84)

8 Belltown, the high-spirited neighborhood where flannel-shirted grunge groupies once practiced their stage-dives, is now better known for its restaurants – cramming more than 100 of them into a strip abutting downtown. Considered a microcosm of Seattle's gastronomic scene, this United Nations of food places a strong emphasis on 'locavore' cuisine, showcasing ingredients from Seattle's adjacent waters and farms. Look out for artisan bakeries, sushi, creative pizzas, Basque-style tapas, Greek fusion, seafood from Pike Place Market, and homemade pasta, served around communal tables.

🍴 **Belltown & Seattle Center**

Puget Sound Ferries (p169)

9 Tap the average Seattleite about their most cherished weekend excursion and they could surprise you with a dark horse – a cheap and simple ride on the commuter ferry across Puget Sound to Bainbridge Island. There's nothing quite like being surrounded by water and seeing Seattle's famous skyline disappearing in the ferry's foamy wake, the only commentary the cry of the seagulls and the only entertainment the comedic antics of escaping families bound for a day out on the Olympic Peninsula.

🏃 *Day Trips*

Discovery Park (p151)

10 Seattle justifies its 'Emerald City' moniker in the rugged confines of 534-acre Discovery Park, a one-time military installation reborn as a textbook example of urban sustainability. Speckled with Douglas fir trees, swooping eagles, log-littered beaches and wild meadows, it resembles a lonely tract of Pacific Northwestern wilderness picked up and dropped into the middle of a crowded metropolitan area. Come here for breathing space, coexistence with nature, and a chance to slow down and reflect on what lured people to Seattle in the first place.

◉ *Ballard & Discovery Park*

What's New

South Lake Union

South Lake Union continues to be the city's fastest-growing neighborhood, thanks in part to new occupant Amazon, the world's largest online retailer, which moved its HQ over from Beacon Hill in 2012. Techies and tourists can enjoy a new lakeside park embellished with the relocated Museum of History & Industry, along with sparkling condos, coffee bars, food carts and restaurants run by some of Seattle's finest chefs. (p93)

Chihuly Garden & Glass

Providing yet *another* reason to visit the eclectic Seattle Center is this spectacular homage to Dale Chihuly, the master of glass art, which captures an astounding array of his greatest work. (p78)

Seattle Great Wheel

With Ferris wheels now gracing the skylines of numerous cities around the globe, Seattle has jumped on the bandwagon with its own lofty Great Wheel, designed to lure visitors toward the city's waterfront. (p48)

Tom Douglas

The 2012 winner of the prestigious James Beard Award for Best Restaurateur now has 10 Seattle eating establishments, including the recently opened Brave Horse Tavern in South Lake Union. (p102)

Hotel Five & Maxwell Hotel

These two new boutique hotels in Belltown and Lower Queen Anne are run by Pineapple Hospitality, meaning they're modern, economical and chic. (p184) (p186)

Bill & Melinda Gates Foundation

Native son Mr Gates showcases his generous philanthropic work in a new visitor center at his $500-million foundation building opposite the Seattle Center. (p83)

Cheshiahud Loop

This well-signposted loop around the shores of Lake Union – an amalgamation of sidewalks, backstreets and preexisting trails – provides a vehicle-free thoroughfare through half a dozen of Seattle's northern neighborhoods. (p104)

The Rise of Ethan Stowell

Providing some friendly competition for Tom Douglas, chef Ethan Stowell now has seven Seattle eateries, including the new Rome-inspired Rione XIII in Capitol Hill. (p112)

Alaskan Way Viaduct

Digging for a new tunnel to redirect noisy SR 99 underground began in summer 2013. When it's finished the ugly Alaskan Way Viaduct will be demolished, leaving Seattle's waterfront a quieter and more salubrious place. (p59)

New Streetcar

Complementing the existing South Lake Union line, Seattle's second streetcar is due to open in 2014 and will run from Pioneer Square to Capitol Hill via First Hill. (p110)

For more recommendations and reviews, see **lonelyplanet. com/seattle**

Need to Know

For more information, see Survival Guide (p203)

Currency
US dollar ($)

Language
English

Visas
Visa requirements vary widely for entry to the US. For information, check http://travel.state.gov/visa/.

Money
ATMs are widely available. Credit cards are accepted at most hotels, restaurants and shops.

Cell Phones
The US uses GSM 850 and GSM 1900 bands. SIM cards are relatively easy to obtain.

Time
Pacific Standard Time (GMT/UTC minus eight hours)

Tourist Information
The Seattle Visitor Center & Concierge Services (Map p224; ☑206-461-5840; www.visit seattle.org; ◷9am-5pm) is in downtown's Washington State Convention Center on E Pike St. There is also a helpful Market Information Booth (Map p224; ☑206-682-7453; Pike St & 1st Ave) at the entrance to Pike Place Market.

Daily Costs

Budget:
Less than $100

➡ Dorm bed in hostel $20–30

➡ Pike Place Market take-out snacks $2–5

➡ Choose free public art and museums

Midrange:
$100–250

➡ Double room in no-frills Belltown hotel $100–150

➡ Eat in pubs, bakeries or funky sandwich bars

➡ Save 50% on sights with Seattle CityPass

➡ Walk or hire a bike for $30 a day

Top End:
More than $250

➡ Stay in a downtown hotel for more than $200

➡ Eat in innovative Capitol Hill restaurants from $50 per head

➡ Tickets to the theater or a concert from $40

Advance Planning

One month before Start looking at options for car rental, accommodations, tours and train tickets.

Two weeks before If you're hoping to see a particular performance or game, whether it's the Mariners or the opera, it's wise to buy tickets in advance.

One to two days before Book popular restaurants in advance. Search the *Stranger* and the *Seattle Times* for upcoming art and entertainment listings.

Useful Websites

➡ **Stranger** (www.thestranger. com) Seattle's best newspaper for entertainment listings – and it's free.

➡ **Not for Tourists** (www. notfortourists.com/seattle) Irreverent reviews and neighborhood commentaries.

➡ **Seattle Post-Intelligencer** (www.seattlepi.com) Online-only newspaper.

➡ **Lonely Planet** (www. lonelyplanet.com/seattle) Succinct summaries on traveling, and the Thorn Tree bulletin board.

WHEN TO GO

Winter is dreary. Spring brings a few gorgeous days. July to September is dry and sunny. Early fall brings Bumbershoot and Oktoberfest.

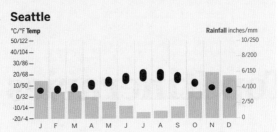

Seattle

Arriving in Seattle

Sea-Tac International Airport (SEA) Link Light Rail connects to downtown Seattle in 30 minutes; shuttle buses stop on the 3rd floor of the airport garage and cost from $18 one way; taxis are $42 to downtown (25 minutes).

King Street Station Amtrak *Empire Builder* to Chicago has one arrival/departure daily; *Coast Starlight* to Los Angeles via Portland, OR, and Oakland, CA, runs once daily each way; Amtrak *Cascades* runs twice daily each way to Vancouver, Canada, and four times daily to Portland and Eugene, OR.

Pier 52 Washington State Ferries runs regular daily passenger/vehicle ferries to Bainbridge Island and Bremerton, WA. The pier is on the downtown waterfront.

Kenmore Air Seaplane flights from Lake Union to the San Juan Islands and Victoria, Canada.

For much more on **arrival**, see p204.

Getting Around

There is a large and growing network of public transportation in Seattle.

➡ **Bus** Run by Metro Transit on a wide number of routes. They are pay-as-you-enter and cost a peak-time flat fee of adult/child $2.50/1.25.

➡ **Link Light Rail** Regular all-day service on one line between Sea-Tac airport and downtown. New line connecting to Capitol Hill and U District to open in 2016.

➡ **Streetcar** Runs from Westlake Hub (by Westlake Center) to South Lake Union every 15 minutes. New line from Pioneer Square to Capitol Hill opens 2014.

➡ **Water Taxi** Runs between Pier 50 on waterfront to West Seattle daily in summer, weekdays only in winter.

➡ **Taxi** $2.50 initial charge, then $2.70 per mile.

For much more on **getting around**, see p205.

Sleeping

Seattle has a trio of reputable hostels, one in downtown, one in Belltown and a new one in Fremont. Aside from dorms, they also offer economical private rooms. You'll find few good hotels for under $100 a night unless you're willing to share a bathroom/toilet. For some good bargains in the $100 to $120 range, look around in Belltown and Lower Queen Anne. There has been a recent increase in boutique hotels, especially those run by Pineapple Hospitality. Capitol Hill has some excellent B&Bs. Big chains and more expensive options characterize downtown.

Useful Websites

➡ **Visit Seattle** (www.visitseattle.org) Deals available through the 'hotel concierge' page of official Seattle/King County website.

➡ **Seattle Bed & Breakfast Association** (www.lodginginseattle.com) Portal of city's 20 best B&Bs.

For much more on **sleeping**, see p179.

Top Itineraries

Day One

Pike Place Market (p40)

Early birds catch more than worms at Pike Place Market. Arrive promptly at 9am for some real-life street theater at **market roll call** before wandering over to the Main Arcade to see the lippy **fish throwers** warming up. Spend the morning getting lost, browsing, tasting, buying and bantering with the producers, but don't miss the **gum wall** or **Rachel the pig**. To complement your own wanderings, consider a market tour with **Seattle Free Walking Tours**.

 **Lunch** Join the queue at Russian bakery Piroshky Piroshky (p52).

Waterfront & Downtown (p40)

Duck under the soon-to-be-demolished Alaskan Way Viaduct to access Seattle's waterfront. Be a tourist and head for the **Seattle Aquarium** on Pier 59, then become a local and jump on a **Puget Sound ferry** just for the ride. Save a good hour to browse the latest exhibits at **Seattle Art Museum** (SAM) on the western edge of downtown.

Dinner SAM's Taste Restaurant (p50) themes dishes around its art displays.

Pioneer Square (p63)

Head to Pioneer Square for a drink in positively ancient **J&M Café** before hitting the **Comedy Underground**, where even poker-faced misérables have been known to break into uncontrollable giggles.

Day Two

Seattle Center (p76)

Resist the lure of the Seattle Center no longer. After a cursory orientation of the complex, opt first for its newest and (arguably) best sight, **Chihuly Garden & Glass**. If you buy a joint-admission ticket you can zip up the adjacent **Space Needle** afterwards for equally dazzling views.

 Lunch Divert into Belltown for lunch at Seattle's best bakery, Macrina (p84).

Seattle Center (p76)

After lunch, enjoy glittering Elliott Bay views and giant, imaginative art at the **Olympic Sculpture Park** before returning to the Seattle Center for an afternoon of rock-and-roll nostalgia at **EMP Museum**. Anyone who has ever picked up an instrument will require at least an hour to twiddle guitar knobs in the Sound Lab on the 3rd floor. Stroll along 5th Ave to your dinner venue. If you can walk past **Top Pot Hand-Forged Doughnuts** without going inside you deserve an abstinence medal.

Dinner Arrive early for happy hour and Italian food at Barolo Ristorante (p87).

Belltown (p76)

Start off with a game of pinball in **Shorty's**. If you like your bars divey, stay put. To up the hipster rating a touch, head north for cocktails at **Black Bottle** before checking out what band's playing at the **Crocodile**.

Theo Chocolate Factory (p143)

Day Three

Pioneer Square (p63)

 Start the morning like a true Seattleite with a latte in **Zeitgeist**, possibly the city's best indie coffee shop. Cross the road, admiring 1890s redbrick architecture, and visit the entertaining, educational and free museum, the **Klondike Gold Rush National Historical Park**. If there's time, take a gilded-age elevator up the **Smith Tower** before lunch.

> **Lunch** Hit the International District for Vietnamese food at Green Leaf (p71).

International District (p63)

 In the Asian-flavored ID, call in on its most famous sight, the **Wing Luke Asian Museum**, and its most esoteric, the **Pinball Museum** (for a quick game), before imbibing tea and Japanese-American history in the **Panama Hotel Tea & Coffee House**. From here, climb up through genteel First Hill to Capitol Hill.

> **Dinner** Join Seattle's locavore culture at Capitol Hill's Sitka & Spruce (p112).

Capitol Hill (p105)

Spontaneous evenings in Capitol Hill start early and go on till late. Work up the Pike–Pine corridor with an espresso in **Victrola Coffee Roasters**, a martini in **Sun Liquor Distillery** and a microbrew in **Elysian Brewing Company**. If the entertainment hasn't already found you, check out what's on at **Neumo's** (live music), **R Place** (drag shows) or **Northwest Film Forum** (cinema).

Day Four

Lake Union (p93)

Time for a journey through Seattle's outer neighborhoods. Start the morning in South Lake Union, where a lakeside park hosts the **Museum of History & Industry**, a roller-coaster journey through Seattle's past. If there's time afterwards, pop into the **Center for Wooden Boats** to plan future sailing sorties.

> **Lunch** Dine at Serious Biscuit (p101), owned by celebrity chef Tom Douglas.

Fremont (p139)

 Stroll through Westlake along the **Cheshiahud Loop**, or flag a bus to take you to Fremont. Soon after crossing the Fremont Bridge, you'll spy *Waiting for the Interurban* and, within the space of a few blocks, several other whimsical sculptures. It would be foolish to leave Fremont without a visit to **Theo Chocolate Factory**. Get to know the locals afterwards at **Fremont Brewery** before hitting the **Burke-Gilman Trail** (or getting a bus) to Ballard.

> **Dinner** Go French at Bastille Cafe & Bar (p153) on Ballard Ave NW.

Ballard (p149)

If weather permits, stroll out to the **Hiram M Chittenden Locks** for sunset, before returning to Ballard Ave to experience the neighborhood's self-contained nightlife. Whiskey flows in new bar **Sexton**, and epic beer can be procured in **Noble Fir**. Of Ballard's two small music venues, the **Tractor Tavern** is legendary. Check the schedules on the door.

If You Like...

Views

Columbia Center The highest human-made view in Seattle can be scaled for just $9. (p52)

Space Needle The (expensive) rite of passage for every tourist since 1962. (p80)

Kerry Park Climb up to this steep park in Seattle's salubrious Queen Anne quarter and watch the sun set over the city. (p96)

Mt Rainier Fitness, bravery and a decent pair of crampons are required to scale this 14,411ft volcano with killer views. (p176)

Sculpture & Statues

Olympic Sculpture Park The alfresco outpost of Seattle Art Museum sets modern sculpture against the natural backdrop of Elliott Bay. (p83)

Pioneer Square Park Totem Pole This icon of Native American culture replaced an earlier pole put here in 1899 after being stolen from a Tlingit village. (p66)

Fremont Troll The scary stone monster that lives under a bridge. (p141)

Chihuly Garden & Glass Dale Chihuly's intricate glass art blends seamlessly with flowers and reeds in Seattle's newest museum. (p78)

Hendrix Statue A hallowed shrine for anyone who has ever picked up an electric guitar. (p107)

Flower-carpeted meadows at the foot of Mt Rainier (p176)

Offbeat Stuff

Gum Wall Get rid of your chewing gum and contribute your own creativity to Seattle's biggest (and most unhygienic) art wall. (p43)

Fish Throwers Watch huge salmon flying through the air at Pike Place Market. (p44)

Statue of Lenin Come and pay your respects, or hurl a few insults, at Vladimir Ilyich Ulyanov, aka Lenin, in Fremont. (p141)

Solstice Cyclists Off-kilter Fremont offers a June fair with live music, food and crafts, and the overtly artsy Solstice Parade, where nude cyclists traipse through the neighborhood in a lively tribute to quirkiness.

Freebies

Boat Rides on Lake Union Free 45-minute sailing trips at 10am Sunday at the Center for Wooden Boats; first come, first served. (p96)

Music in Pike Place Concert violinists have been known to busk for free in Pike Place Market. (p42)

Borrow a Bike Numerous hotels now offer free bikes. Grab some wheels and hit the beautiful Burke-Gilman Trail. (p133)

Public Art Viewing all of Seattle's alfresco art, including the Olympic Sculpture Park, costs precisely zero dollars. (p83)

Museums

Seattle Art Museum A leading player in modern and ethnic art, SAM's main gallery has an enviable Native American collection. (p46)

Klondike Gold Rush National Historical Park Interactive museum run by the National Park Service that details Seattle's role in the 1897 gold fever that gripped the Yukon. (p66)

Museum of History & Industry The whole spread of Seattle's boom-bust history laid out in plush new digs on the south shore of Lake Union. (p95)

Chihuly Garden & Glass Seattle honors Tacoma-born Dale Chihuly (at last) in a dazzling display of glass art tucked beneath the Space Needle. (p78)

Green Spaces

Green Lake Park Amateur athletics track? Body-beautiful competition? Giant alfresco community center? Green Lake Park is where it all happens – out in the open. (p144)

Volunteer Park Follow Millionaires Row to this elegant park on the posher side of Capitol Hill, where a water tower offers panoramic views. (p107)

Discovery Park This former military installation that became a park in the 1970s retains an element of wilderness lacking elsewhere. (p151)

Washington Park Arboretum Pleasant green corridor that bisects Seattle's eastern neighborhoods with multiple paths and a Japanese garden. (p122)

Romance

Kerry Park Favorite spot for poetry-inspiring views, marriage proposals and a late-night snog. (p96)

Benaroya Concert Hall Impress your date with Dale Chihuly's opulent chandeliers and the sophisticated sounds of the Seattle Symphony Orchestra. (p47)

For more top Seattle spots, see the following:
➡ Eating (p24)
➡ Drinking & Nightlife (p27)
➡ Entertainment (p29)
➡ Sports & Activities (p31)
➡ Shopping (p34)

PLAN YOUR TRIP IF YOU LIKE...

Fairmont Olympic Hotel Shack up for a night of expensive passion at Seattle's poshest hotel. (p182)

Georgian Old-school culinary elegance still reigns supreme in this well-mannered bastion of taste. (p52)

Orcas Island Ply the elysian land and waters of the San Juan Islands and ponder lucid summer sunsets. (p173)

Architecture

Pioneer Square The homogenous historic quarter where Seattle was born in the 1850s guards the city's most valuable architectural legacy. (p65)

Queen Anne Stroll this hilly, well-to-do neighborhood to see fine residential houses designed in the elegant Queen Anne revivalist style popular in the 1890s. (p96)

Seattle Public Library Looking like a giant diamond dropped from outer space, this 21st-century architectural marvel has proved that libraries can prosper in the internet age. (p47)

EMP Museum Some love it. Some hate it. Few are indifferent. Frank Gehry allegedly designed the building to resemble one of Hendrix's smashed guitars. (p82)

Month by Month

TOP EVENTS

Bumbershoot
September

Seattle International Film Festival May to June

Northwest Folklife Festival May

Fremont Street Fair June

Seafair July

January

The year starts with a hangover and occasional flurries of snow. Plan indoor activities or bring your skis and head to the nearby mountains.

Chinese New Year

Beginning end of January or start of February and lasting for two weeks, the year's first big ethnic festival takes place in the International District with parades, firecrackers, fireworks and plenty of food.

February

Those who haven't jetted off to Hawaii hunker down for another overcast month. Scour the internet for hotel deals and book a night at the theater.

Northwest Flower & Garden Show

Usually held the second week of February, this popular event (www.gardenshow.com) held in the Washington State Convention Center includes lectures, seminars, demo gardens and children's activities.

March

The odd warm day can see restaurants opening up their patios, but more often than not rain persists. St Patrick's Day provides a good excuse to shrug off the long, hard winter.

Moisture Festival

The Moisture Festival (www.moisturefestival.com) has developed from a little-known quirkfest into something that locals look forward to each year. Comedy, variety, theater and burlesque events are held at the Hale's Ales Palladium (at the Fremont brewpub).

April

Bargain-hunters still seek deals as the aroma of spring is detected in Seattle's parks and gardens.

Cherry Blossom & Japanese Cultural Festival

Usually held in late April, this celebration of Japanese heritage includes performances of music, dance and drama. It's part of the Seattle Center's series of multicultural festivals, dubbed Festál.

May

People start hitting the waterside attractions. Last chance of a hotel deal as the shoulder season begins.

Northwest Folklife Festival

This humungous festival takes over Seattle Center during Memorial Day weekend. More than 5000 performers and artists from over 100 countries present music, dance, crafts and food in celebration of the rich cultural heritage of the Pacific Northwest.

★☆ Seattle International Film Festival

Held from late May to mid-June, this festival (www.seattlefilm.com), the largest of its kind in the nation, brings nearly a month's worth of international film premieres to Seattle. Its HQ is the SIFF Theater in Seattle Center.

June

Showers can linger in the early part of June, but summer's in the post.

★☆ Fremont Street Fair

Off-kilter Fremont offers a June fair with live music, food and crafts, and the overtly artsy Solstice Parade, where human-powered floats traipse through the neighborhood in a lively tribute to quirkiness.

★☆ Seattle Pride Festival

Seattle's lesbian- and gay-pride event (www.seattlepride.org) usually falls on the last Sunday in June and includes a film festival, art exhibit, parade and the requisite food and entertainment.

July

Peak temperatures (75°F/24°C) and peak prices mark Seattle's peak season, when you'd be wise to book ahead for pretty much everything.

★☆ Seafair

A month-long extravaganza, the city's biggest festival (www.seafair.com) includes a torchlight parade, an air show, lots of music, a carnival and even the arrival of the naval fleet.

August

Salmon bakes, neighborhood street fairs and lazy beach afternoons give August a laid-back feel. But school's out, so expect ubiquitous cries of excited kids.

★☆ Viking Days

Citizens of Ballard rediscover their inner Viking and celebrate Seattle's Scandinavian heritage in the grounds of the Nordic Heritage Museum.

September

The best month to visit? Possibly. Once Bumbershoot's over, the tourists go home and hotel prices deflate, but the weather usually remains sunny and relatively warm until early October.

☆ Bumbershoot

Seattle's biggest arts and cultural event (www.bumbershoot.org) takes over Seattle Center on Labor Day weekend (the first Monday in September) with hundreds of musicians, artists, theater troupes and writers coming from all over the country to perform on the festival's two-dozen stages.

October

There's the possibility of an Indian summer in the first half of the month when the start of the shoulder season brings cheaper prices. As the clouds roll in, people get out to celebrate Halloween.

☆ Seattle Lesbian & Gay Film Festival

Held the third week of October, this festival (www.threedollarbillcinema.org) brings mainstream and underground queer films to theaters around town.

November

November can be a dismal month for weather, but most sights stay open and, with low season kicking in, some hotels slash their prices to half summer rates,

◉ Best of the Northwest

Art and fine-art show (www.nwartalliance.com) bivouacked at the Smith Cove Cruise Terminal in Magnolia that showcases artists and designers of all genres from jewelry to glass.

December

Seattle's surrounding ski resorts open up, making the city a good urban base for snow-related activities. Hotel prices continue to drop along with the temperatures.

★☆ Winterfest

Seattle Center holds a month-long celebration of holiday traditions from around the globe, starting with Winter Worldfest, a massive concert and dance performance, and continuing with exhibits, dances, concerts and ice skating.

With Kids

Take it easy, overworked parent. Seattle will entertain, pacify and often educate your energetic kid(s) without them even realizing it. Some attractions are obvious (a children's theater and a zoo). Others are more serendipitous: don't miss the Pinball Museum or the urban theater of Pike Place Market.

JOHN ELK / GETTY IMAGES ©

Seattle Aquarium (p48)

Where to Eat

Most restaurants in Seattle are kid-friendly. The only places where you're likely to see 'No Minors' signs is in pubs, gastropubs and dive bars (notwithstanding, many pubs will serve families as long as you don't sit at the bar). Some places introduce a no-kids policy after 10pm.

Pike Place Market has the widest selection of cheap, immediately available food and is a fun place to hang out and eat. You'll struggle to find anyone (kid or adult) who doesn't fall instantly in love with the mac 'n' cheese cartons sold at Beecher's Handmade Cheese (p53) or the flaky pastries rolled before your eyes at Piroshky Piroshky (p52). Elsewhere, Pie (p145) in Fremont cooks up some excellent crusty fare, and Belltown's La Vita é Bella (p86) is a traditional family-friendly Italian trattoria. Every youthful visitor to Seattle should be allowed at least one 'treat' from Top Pot Hand-Forged Doughnuts (p84) – preferably for breakfast. Ivar's Acres of Clams (p55) makes a good post-aquarium fish-and-chips lunch. Watch out for the hungry seagulls!

Seattle Center

The Seattle Center has the most concentrated stash of kid-friendly activities including the professional Seattle Children's Theater (p91) and the Children's Museum (p83; better for the under 10s). In the summer, balloon-twisters, singers and dancers entertain the crowds alfresco.

Aside from the interesting and educational permanent displays, the Pacific Science Center (p84) has some excellent touring exhibits. Recent showings have included Harry Potter movie memorabilia and King Tutankhamen's jewels. In the EMP Museum (p82) you could fill an afternoon in the Sound Lab, where adults and kids can requisition drum kits, guitars and keyboards, and even form their own band for the special 'On Stage' feature. The elevator ride in the Space Needle (p80)is an adventure and there are plenty of things to press at the top.

Outdoor Activities

Discovery Park

There are sometimes organized nature walks in the park; check schedules at the Environmental Learning Center. Otherwise this giant green space has a kids play area, wonderful beachcombing opportunities and several miles of safe trails. (p151)

Hiram M Chittenden Locks

Watch the boats traverse the locks and see the fish ladder. The adjacent park is good for a picnic, weather permitting. (p153)

Center for Wooden Boats

You can sail model boats on the pond in Lake Union Park at weekends from 11am to 2pm. The center also offers free sailboat rides (first come, first served) on Lake Union on Sunday (sign-ups at 10am). (p96)

Cycling the Burke-Gilman Trail

Recycled Cycles (p133) in the U District rents trail-a-bikes or trailers (chariots) so you can cycle safely with your kids.

Alki Beach

The main part of West Seattle's beach is sandy – ideal for sandcastle building and all of those other timeworn seaside pleasures. There are good tide pools further west around the lighthouse. (p163)

Shops for Kids

Zanadu

Comics, toys and superhero paraphernalia in Belltown. (p92)

Market Magic

Pike Place Market's resident joke-and-magic shop. (p60)

Card Kingdom

Ballard games emporium with on-site board games to buy or just play. (p157)

Once Upon a Time

Specialist kids shop in Queen Anne. (p103)

Animal Viewing

Woodland Park Zoo

Considered one of the best zoos in the US, with 300 species including snow leopards, lions and tigers. (p144)

Seattle Aquarium

Designed with kids in mind, the aquarium has a fish 'touching tank' and daily feeding shows. (p48)

Rainy-Day Activities

Seattle Pinball Museum

Pay $7 for unlimited use of several dozen pinball machines (stools are available for the vertically challenged). The catch: getting your kid out afterwards! (p68)

Museum of Flight

Huge museum with plenty of interactive exhibits including a flight simulator. (p161)

Museum of History & Industry

Learn about Seattle's past through film, music, quizzes and questions. (p95)

Tours

Seattle by Foot

Offers a special Seattle Kids Tour that lasts two hours and strolls for a handful of blocks around Pike Place and downtown, taking in the market, the music room at Benaroya Hall, the art area at Seattle Art Museum, the gum wall, and a chocolate shop. Educational and engaging! (p49)

Ride the Ducks of Seattle

A local version of a popular national brand famous for its use of amphibious buses on land and water. Its standard 90-minute Seattle tour takes in Pike Place, Pioneer Square, the waterfront and Seattle Center, before going for a quick dip in Lake Union. Drivers add humorous commentary. (p207)

Clam chowder makes great use of local seafood

 **Eating**

If you want to get a real taste for eating in Seattle, dip your metaphorical finger into Pike Place Market. This clamorous confederation of small-time farmers, artisan bakers, cheese producers, fishers, and family-run fruit stalls is the gastronomic bonanza that every locavore dreams about, and its cheap, sustainable, locally produced food ends up on the tables of just about every Seattle restaurant that matters.

Northwest Cuisine

A lot of Seattle's gourmet restaurants describe their food as 'Northwest cuisine.' Its cornerstone is high-quality regional ingredients: seafood so fresh it squirms, fat berries freshly plucked, mushrooms dug out of the rich soil, and cornucopias of fruit and vegetables. Another distinguishing feature is pan-Asian cooking, often referred to as Pacific Rim cuisine or fusion food. The blending of American or European standards with ingredients from Asia, it results in some unusual combi-

nations – don't be surprised if you get wasabi on your French fries.

Things Seattle Does Well

Surrounded by water, Seattle is an obvious powerhouse of fresh seafood. Local favorites include Dungeness crab, salmon, halibut, oysters, spot prawns, and clams. Although it's not one of the US's most cosmopolitan cities, Seattle has a sizable Chinese population and a strong selection of dim sum restaurants in the International District. The ID also harbors a good cluster of Vietnamese restaurants in its

'Little Saigon' quarter. Seattle's Italian restaurants are often highly progressive, many of them specializing in regional food such as Roman or Piedmontese. Chef Ethan Stowell has successfully married Italian cuisine with Northwest traditions and popularized the use of homemade pasta.

Other genres in which Seattle excels are bakeries (a by-product of its cafe culture), Japanese food (the sushi is unwaveringly good) and – perhaps surprisingly – spicy Ethiopian food; the bulk of the East African restaurants are in the Central District (CD). Many visitors from the south comment on the dearth of Mexican restaurants (though there are a handful of good'uns) and, while the Indian fare can't compete with that found in Vancouver, the appearance of Shanik restaurant (from Canada's Vikram Vij) has upped the ante somewhat. Seattle also loves a good steak – especially one that's led a happy, grass-fed life on a farm just outside of town. The city's latest food fashion is crusty sweet or savory pies, with several new restaurants dedicating themselves exclusively to the genre.

Mold-Breaking Chefs

Tom Douglas The biggest name on the Seattle food scene, Douglas helped define what people mean when they talk about Northwest cuisine. He opened his first restaurant, Dahlia, in 1989 and has since followed it with nine more. Douglas won the prestigious James Beard Award for Best Restaurateur in 2012 and once battled Masaharu Morimoto in an episode of *Iron Chef America* – and won.

Ethan Stowell With seven Seattle restaurants, Stowell is considered a rising star. His specialty is marrying creative Italian cuisine with classic Northwest ingredients, especially seafood.

Matt Dillon Seattle's most devotedly sustainable chef owns a farm on Vashon Island and is a strong proponent of food foraging. In 2012 he shared James Beard honors with Tom Douglas when he won the Best Northwest Chef award. His don't-miss restaurant is Sitka & Spruce, where pretty much all the ingredients are local.

Eating by Neighborhood

➡ **Downtown, Pike Place & Waterfront** Enjoy fine dining in downtown; grab cheap, on-the-go, artisan food at Pike Place Market.

NEED TO KNOW

Price Ranges

These guides reflect the average cost of a main dish.

$	under $10
$$	$10–20
$$$	over $20

Opening Hours

Specific opening hours are listed in reviews if they differ from the norm; otherwise, we simply note which meals each restaurant serves. Breakfast is typically served from 7am to 11am, brunch from 7am to 3pm, lunch from 11:30am to 2:30pm and dinner from 5:30pm to 10pm.

Booking Tables

Most Seattle restaurants don't require bookings, but the hot new places fill up quickly so it's best to call ahead if you want to be sure to avoid disappointment.

Tipping

Tips are not figured into the check at a restaurant. In general, 15% is the baseline tip, but 20% is usually more appropriate, 25% if you enjoyed the service.

➡ **Pioneer Square & International District** Old-school steakhouses dot Pioneer Square; Vietnamese food and dim sum characterize the ID.

➡ **Belltown & Seattle Center** Vies with Capitol Hill for Seattle's best selection of restaurants covering every genre and budget.

➡ **Capitol Hill & First Hill** All over the map, with Seattle's hottest chefs competing alongside the next big thing.

➡ **The CD, Madrona & Madison Park** A plateful of surprises that'll satisfy everyone from French haute cuisine snobs to diehard vegans.

➡ **U District** Cheap, no-frills, ethnic food that's kind to vegetarians.

➡ **Fremont & Green Lake** Fremont specializes in unusual non-corporate fast food; Green Lake exhibits warm, family-friendly restaurants.

➡ **Ballard & Discovery Park** Seafood, with some cool bistros playing an interesting cameo.

Lonely Planet's Top Choices

Cascina Spinasse (p112) Could be the best Italian food you taste outside Italy.

Sitka & Spruce (p112) If you had to sum up Seattle cuisine in three words, this is it.

Bakery Nouveau (p164) Destination bakery that's worth crossing town to West Seattle for – and there's now a new branch in Capitol Hill!

Serious Pie (p86) And the prize for the most original pizza goes to...Tom Douglas.

Best by Budget

$

Pike Place Chowder (p54) Entered a chowder competition in New England – and won!

Piroshky Piroshky (p52) Russian buns are rolled in the window of this Pike Place Market hole-in-the-wall.

Top Pot Hand-Forged Doughnuts (p84) The champagne of doughnuts.

Bakery Nouveau (p164) Best bakery this side of...Paris.

$$

Serious Pie (p86) Seriously good pizzas with novel toppings.

Wild Ginger (p50) Asian fusion with style and a kick.

Portage Bay Cafe (p135) Astoundingly good brunch.

$$$

Cascina Spinasse (p112) Italian nosh that's worth the extra investment.

Sitka & Spruce (p112) The shrine for all locavores.

Madison Park Conservatory (p127) New place creating waves on the shores of Lake Washington.

Rover's (p127) French culinary perfection in the Gallic Madison Valley neighborhood.

Best Italian

Cascina Spinasse (p112) Relaxed but classy purveyor of Piedmontese food.

La Vita é Bella (p86) Traditional Italian trattoria with gregarious staff.

How to Cook a Wolf (p100) Northwest meets Italian cuisine atop Queen Anne Hill.

Barolo Ristorante (p87) Worth visiting for the Piedmontese wine alone.

Best Seafood

Walrus & the Carpenter (p154) Ballard oyster bar where they serve 'em raw with white wine.

Steelhead Diner (p54) Located in Pike Place Market, with fresh fish bought yards from your plate.

Ivar's Acres of Clams (p55) Fish and chips the old-fashioned way.

Best Asian

Wild Ginger (p50) All kinds of Asian cuisine under the same downtown roof.

Green Leaf (p71) Vietnamese hole-in-the-wall that's become something of a city legend.

Shiro's Sushi Restaurant (p87) Japanese food as art in the heart of Belltown.

Jade Garden (p71) The best in dim sum in the International District.

Best New Restaurants

Cascina Spinasse (p112) Rustic but classy Italian food arrives in Capitol Hill.

Shanik (p101) Seattle gets its first taste of Indian-fusion food – already a legend in Vancouver.

Bar Sajor (p71) Another chance to taste the delicious foraged ingredients of chef Matt Dillon.

Drinking & Nightlife

It's hard to complain too much about Seattle's crappy weather when the two best forms of rainy-day solace – coffee and beer – are available in such abundance. No doubt about it, Seattle's an inviting place to enjoy a drink, whatever your poison: hearty, European-style craft-brewed beer, or a micro-roasted post-Starbucks pour-over made by one of a growing band of coffee guerrillas.

Coffee Culture

When the first Starbucks opened in Pike Place Market in 1971, Seattle was suddenly the center of the coffee universe. It still is, although these days Starbucks is loved and loathed in equal measure.

After Starbucks came the 'third wave': coffee shops that buy fair-trade coffee with traceable origins and concoct it through a micro-managed in-house roasting process that pays attention to everything from the coffee's bean quality to its 'taste notes.' These shops are now as ubiquitous as Starbucks, though they remain independent and adhere strictly to their original manifesto: quality not quantity.

Macro Amounts of Microbrews

The microbrew explosion rocked the Northwest around the same time as the gourmet-coffee craze – not coincidentally, Seattle's Redhook Brewery was cofounded in 1981 by Gordon Bowker, one of the guys who founded Starbucks.

Most local microbreweries started out as tiny craft breweries that produced European-style ales. Many of these small producers initially lacked the capital to offer their brews for sale anywhere but in the brewery building itself, hence the term brewpub – an informal pub with its own on-site brewery.

Though you can find microbrews at practically every bar in town, brewpubs often feature signature beers and ales not available anywhere else. It's worth asking about specialty brews or seasonal beers on tap. Most of the brewpubs listed offer a taster's selection of the house brews. Pints range in price from $4 to $6, so a sampler can be good value if you're not sure what you like.

Drinking & Nightlife by Neighborhood

⇒ **Downtown, Pike Place & Waterfront** Hotel bars and pleasant old-school drinking nooks tucked away in Pike Place.

⇒ **Pioneer Square & International District** Gritty saloons in Pioneer Square; bubble tea and restaurant lounges in the ID.

⇒ **Belltown & Seattle Center** Belltown's bar-hopping, late-night drinking scene is not as grungy as it once was.

⇒ **Capitol Hill & First Hill** *The* place for a night out, with gay bars, dive bars, cocktail lounges and third-wave coffee shops.

⇒ **U District** No-frills dives and a plethora of coffee shops designed for the laptop crowd.

⇒ **Fremont & Green Lake** Mix of new-ish brewpubs and old-school neighborhood pubs.

⇒ **Ballard & Discovery Park** Bar-crawl heaven, with old-fashioned pubs sitting alongside whiskey bars and cocktail perches.

⇒ **Georgetown & West Seattle** Blue-collar pubs reborn as bohemian Georgetown bars.

NEED TO KNOW

Opening Hours

This is caffeine-addicted Seattle, so some coffee bars open as early as 5am and close at around 11pm, but 7am until 6pm is more standard. Bars usually serve from lunchtime until 2am (when state liquor laws demand they stop selling booze), although some don't open until 5pm and others start as early as 7am. Variations from the norm are noted in individual reviews.

Ha-Ha-Happy Hours

The term 'happy hour' is a misnomer: most Seattle bars run their happy hours from around 3pm until 6pm. As well as reductions in drink prices, some bars also offer happy-hour deals on bar snacks, appetizers or even full-blown meals.

Lonely Planet's Top Choices

Zeitgeist (p72) Best coffee in Seattle? Go and find out!

Owl & Thistle (p55) No one does pubs like the Irish.

Pike Pub & Brewery (p56) The secret's in the hops.

Bookstore Bar (p56) Buy a scotch; snuggle down with a great novel.

Best Coffee Bars

Espresso Vivace (p113) Drink coffee, listen to the Ramones, see the latest in lopsided haircuts.

Zeitgeist (p72) At Zeitgeist it's all about the coffee – and the gorgeous almond croissants.

Victrola Coffee Roasters (p113) When hipsters go to heaven they probably get teleported to Victrola in Capitol Hill.

Caffè Umbria (p73) Coffee culture with Italian affiliations.

Best Brewpubs

Pike Pub & Brewery (p56) One of the oldest and most cherished brewpubs in Seattle.

Fremont Brewing (p146) New old-school brewery where you can taste beer at wooden tables on the factory floor.

Elysian Brewing Company (p114) Good beer and even better people-watching in Capitol Hill.

Hale's Ales Brewery (p146) Fine ales make up for the uncozy feel of this large brewpub on the Fremont–Ballard border.

Best Dive Bars

Five Point Café (p89) That stale-beer smell has been there since 1929.

Shorty's (p88) Pinball, hot dogs, punk rock and beer = a devastating combination in Belltown.

Monkey Pub (p136) A dive by nature not design in the U District.

Blue Moon (p136) Romanticism with a rough edge in former poets haven in the U District.

Comet (p115) Hosted loud grunge gigs in the '90s with audiences numbering in the low 30s. Still does.

Best GLBT Bars

Wildrose (p115) Lesbian pub in Capitol Hill.

Re-Bar (p89) What? A gay club that's not in Capitol Hill?

R Place (p115) Flamboyant performers and tactile regulars.

Best Old-Fashioned Pubs

Owl & Thistle (p55) Genuine Irish pub with good music and cheap old-country food.

Canterbury Ale & Eats (p115) Old-school haven in trendy Capitol Hill.

George & Dragon Pub (p146) Seattle's most Anglophile pub, with a high percentage of limeys.

☆ Entertainment

Quietly aggrieved that it was being bypassed by big-name touring acts in the 1980s, Seattle shut itself away and created its own live-music scene. This explosive grassroots movement is backed up by independent cinema, burlesque theater, bookstore poetry readings and some high-profile opera, classical music and drama.

Live Music

Seattle's music venues can be stacked in a triangle. At the top sits the 17,000-capacity Key Arena. Below this is a trio of medium-sized historic theaters: the 2807-capacity Paramount, the 1420-capacity Moore (dating from 1907) and the 1137-capacity Showbox (dating from 1939).

Next is a handful of more clamorous venues, small enough to foster the close band-audience interaction that was so crucial in the development of Seattle's 1990s music revolution. Some of these '90s bastions still exist, though in a more sanitized form. Still pulling less mainstream big-name acts are the 475-capacity Crocodile in Belltown, and 650-capacity Neumo's in Capitol Hill.

Hosting lesser-known local talent are various neighborhood venues such as Ballard's 360-capacity Tractor Tavern and Fremont's High Dive. Right at the bottom of the triangle are the ubiquitous pubs, clubs and coffee bars that showcase small-time local talent from Irish fiddlers to Bjork-like singers.

Seattle has two jazz venues, Tula's and Dimitriou's Jazz Alley. For an altogether swankier scene, hit downtown's Triple Door.

The Arts

Seattle is a book-loving town and there's a literary event practically every night. Film is also big news these days. The Seattle International Film Festival is among the most influential festivals in the country, and a thriving independent scene has sprung up in a handful of underground venues. Theater runs the gamut from big productions, such as Ibsen at the Intiman, to staged readings of obscure texts in cobbled-together venues or coffee shops. The Seattle Symphony has become nationally known and widely respected, primarily through its excellent recordings. For current entertainment listings, scour the *Stranger* (p210) or *Seattle Weekly* (p210).

Entertainment by Neighborhood

➡ **Downtown, Pike Place & Waterfront** Classical music and historic Showbox theater in downtown.

➡ **Pioneer Square & International District** Comedy shows and a few tough pubs peddling punk and metal.

➡ **Belltown & Seattle Center** Alt-rock and jazz venues in Belltown; opera, ballet and theater in Seattle Center.

➡ **Queen Anne & Lake Union** Fringe theater and hallowed rock venues such as El Corazón.

➡ **Capitol Hill & First Hill** Everything outside the mainstream, including alt-rock and electronica.

➡ **U District** Small pub strummers and stand-up comedy plus name acts at revived Neptune Theater.

➡ **Fremont & Green Lake** Intimate High Dive and Nectar Lounge book small-name live acts.

➡ **Ballard & Discovery Park** Pubs and clubs plus the Sunset and Tractor Taverns cement a good live-music scene.

NEED TO KNOW

Opening Hours

Typically, live music starts between 9pm and 10pm and goes until 1am or 2am. For most venues you can pay admission at the door; for a small to medium-size venue, the cover charge can be anywhere from $5 to $15.

Tickets & Reservations

Tickets for big events are available through **Ticket-Master** (www.ticketmaster.com). **Brown Paper Tickets** (www.brownpapertickets.com) handles sales for a number of smaller and quirkier venues, from theater to live music. Alternatively, you can often book via the venue website.

Lonely Planet's Top Choices

Crocodile (p90) Even 25 years on, it hasn't lost its ability to rock and roll.

Dimitriou's Jazz Alley (p90) Be-bopping the crowds in Belltown since 1985.

Seattle International Film Festival (p21) One of the best and most multifarious film festivals in the US.

Benaroya Concert Hall (p47) The spectacular HQ for Seattle's prestigious symphony orchestra.

Best Live-Music Venues

Crocodile (p90) Nationally renowned midsize live venue that helped promote grunge.

Neumo's (p115) The other pillar of Seattle's dynamic scene has updated and remains relevant.

McCaw Hall (p91) Go and hear the Seattle Opera raise the roof.

Chop Suey (p115) Diverse selection of live acts, with indie alternating with hip-hop.

Tractor Tavern (p157) The anchor of Ballard's live scene specializes in alt-country.

Best Cinemas

Fremont Almost Free Outdoor Cinema (p147) Hedonistic summer cinema with lots of audience participation.

Cinerama (p91) This unique curved screen is the best place to see the latest blockbuster.

Northwest Film Forum (p116) Arts-club feel lends expertise to this film geeks' heaven.

Harvard Exit (p116) Come here for best independent and foreign-language showings.

Grand Illusion Cinema (p137) Tiny U District nook run by passionate film buffs.

Best Theaters

A Contemporary Theater (p57) With its central stage and gilded decor, this is Seattle's best all-round theater.

On the Boards (p102) Cutting-edge contemporary drama in Queen Anne.

Jewel Box Theater (p89) Small gem specializing in burlesque hidden in a Belltown cocktail bar.

Paramount Theater (p58) Touring Broadway shows.

Best Small Live Venues

High Dive (p147) Small Fremont dive for up-and-coming bands.

Espresso Vivace (p113) Hip coffee bar where local bands play regular laid-back sets.

Black Coffee (p114) Readings, rants, street poets and punk soloists in this new Pine St coffee bar.

Owl & Thistle (p55) Downtown Irish pub with fine fiddlers and folk music.

CenturyLink Field (p75), home to the Seattle Seahawks

Sports & Activities

Never mind the rain – that's why Gore-Tex was invented. When you live this close to the mountains, not to mention all that water and a stunning range of parks, it's just criminal not to get outdoors, come rain, hail or shine. Seattle is rare for a large city in that many forms of outdoor recreation are available within the city itself.

Spectator Sports

With state-of-the-art stadiums and teams that flirt with glory, Seattle is a great town in which to watch the pros play. College games, too, are hugely popular with locals and a fun way to spend an afternoon.

Formed in 1977 and former tenants of the erstwhile Kingdome, the beloved **Seattle Mariners** (Map p228; www.mariners.org; tickets $7-60) baseball team play in Safeco Field. They have yet to win a World Series title.

The Northwest's only National Football League (NFL) franchise, the **Seattle Seahawks** (Map p228; www.seahawks.com; tickets $42-95) play in 72,000-seat CenturyLink Field. Their only Superbowl appearance was in 2006, when they lost out to the Pittsburgh Steelers.

The **University of Washington Huskies** (Map p242; ✆206-543-2200; www.gohuskies.com; tickets $38-72) football and basketball teams are another Seattle obsession. The Huskies football team plays at 72,500-capacity Husky Stadium and you'll find the men's

NEED TO KNOW

Tickets

You can buy tickets for Seattle's main sports teams through **TicketMaster** (www.ticketmaster.com) or on the individual team's website.

Rental

Bike rental goes from between $30 and $45 per day. Single kayak rental starts at around $17 per hour. Paddleboards are slightly more at $20 per hour.

Internet Resources

Cascade Bicycle Club www.cascade.org

Disc Northwest www.discnw.org

Seattle Frontrunners www.seattlefront runners.org

Washington Kayak Club www.washing tonkayakclub.org

Washington Water Trails Association www.wwta.org

and women's basketball teams at the Hec Edmundson Pavilion, both of which are on campus. The women's basketball team draws massive crowds.

Reincarnated in 2008, soccer team the Seattle Sounders (p75) has fanatical supporters and lots of 'em: 67,000 once attended a friendly against Manchester United. Highly successful, they share digs at CenturyLink Field with the Seahawks. The soccer season runs May to mid-September.

Activities

ON THE WATER

Seeing Seattle from the water is one of the best ways to fall in love with the city. A number of places rent kayaks and canoes, or you can arrange a guided tour through the Northwest Outdoor Center (p104), the Aqua Verde Paddle Club (p138) or the Moss Bay Rowing Club (p104). The Center for Wooden Boats (p96) offers sailing lessons, sailboat rentals and free 45-minute sailboat rides every Sunday morning (first come, first served).

The calmest, safest places to launch are Green Lake, Lake Union or near the water-taxi dock in Seacrest Park in West Seattle. If you're not confident, take a lesson. Several of the rental companies in Green Lake,

Westlake (Lake Union) and the U District offer instruction from around $60 per hour.

Seattle's chilly waters are good for diving, with regular sightings of octopus, huge ling cod, cabezon, cathedral-like white anemones and giant sea stars. Most of the area's best dive sites are outside of Seattle, in sheltered coves and bays up and down the coast. Popular spots include Alki Cove, on the eastern side of Alki Point; Saltwater State Park, south of Seattle in Des Moines; and Edmonds Underwater Park near the Edmonds Ferry Dock, north of Seattle.

BICYCLING

Despite frequent rain and hilly terrain, cycling is still a major form of both transportation and recreation in the Seattle area.

In the city, commuter bike lanes are painted on many streets, city trails are well maintained, and the friendly and enthusiastic cycling community is happy to share the road. The wildly popular 20-mile **Burke-Gilman Trail** winds from Ballard to Log Boom Park in Kenmore on Seattle's Eastside. There, it connects with the 11-mile long **Sammamish River Trail**, which winds past the Chateau Ste Michelle winery in Woodinville before terminating at Redmond's Marymoor Park.

Other good places to cycle are around Green Lake (congested), at Alki Beach (sublime) or, closer to downtown, through scenic Myrtle Edwards Park. The Myrtle Edwards Park trail continues through Interbay to Ballard, where it links with the Burke-Gilman.

Anyone planning on cycling in Seattle should download or pick up a copy of the *Seattle Bicycling Guide Map,* published by the City of Seattle's Transportation Bicycle & Pedestrian Program (p205).

GOLF

Seattle Parks & Recreation (p148) operates four public golf courses in Seattle, along with a short (nine-hole) pitch-and-putt course located at **Green Lake** (☑206-632-2280; 5701 W Green Lake Way N), a fun spot to go if you're just learning or lack the patience or experience to go a full round. Green fees for the **Jefferson Park Golf Course** (☑206-762-4513; 4101 Beacon Ave S) in Beacon Hill and **West Seattle Golf Course** (☑206-935-5187; 4470 35th Ave SW) are $34 per person on weekdays and $39 on weekends. When they're not booked, the courses also offer reduced rates in the evenings.

HIKING

In Seattle, it's possible to hike (or run) wilderness trails without ever leaving the city. **Seward Park**, east of Georgetown, offers several miles of trails in a remnant of the area's old-growth forest, and an even more extensive network of trails is available in 534-acre **Discovery Park**, northwest of downtown. At the northern edge of Washington Park Arboretum, **Foster Island** offers a 20-minute wetlands trail winding through marshlands created upon the opening of the Lake Washington Ship Canal. This is also a great place for bird-watching, fishing and swimming.

RUNNING

With its many parks, Seattle provides a number of good trails for runners. If you're in the downtown area, the trails along **Myrtle Edwards Park** – just north of the waterfront along Elliott Bay – make for a nice run, affording views over the sound and of the downtown skyline. **Green Lake** includes two paths, the 2.75-mile paved path immediately surrounding the lake and a less-crowded, unpaved path going around the perimeter of the park. The **Washington Park Arboretum** is another good choice for running, as the trails lead through some beautiful trees and flower gardens. The trails in the arboretum connect to the Lake Washington Blvd trail system, which extends all the way south to Seward Park, just in case you happen to be training for a marathon.

SWIMMING

When summer temperatures rise, there's no more popular place to be than on one of Seattle's beaches. One of the most visited is **Alki Beach** in West Seattle, a real scene with beach volleyball, acres of flesh and teenagers cruising in their cars. **Green Lake Park** has two lakefront swimming and sunbathing beaches, as do several parks along the western shores of Lake Washington, including Madison Park, Madrona Park, Seward Park, Magnuson Park and Mt Baker Park. Lifeguards are on duty at public beaches between 11am and 8pm mid-June to Labor Day (beginning of September).

Sports & Activities by Neighborhood

➡ **Downtown, Pike Place & Waterfront** Bike-tour companies and rental points.

➡ **Pioneer Square & International District** Home of Seattle's two pro sports stadiums.

➡ **Belltown & Seattle Center** Free yoga classes in the Olympic Sculpture Park during summer months.

➡ **Queen Anne & Lake Union** Multiple water activities available on Lake Union; new multipurpose path now circumnavigates the lake.

➡ **The CD, Madrona & Madison Park** Parks, beaches and waterside attractions on Lake Washington.

➡ **U District** Cycling on the Burke-Gilman Trail; boating access on Lake Union; Husky Stadium for college football.

➡ **Fremont & Green Lake** Jogging, cycling and boating bonanza around Green Lake.

➡ **Ballard & Discovery Park** Two wild waterside parks and a climbing center.

➡ **Georgetown & West Seattle** Cycling, kayaking, swimming and in-line skating along Alki Beach.

Shopping

Seattle, like any big US city, has a whole range of big-name stores. You won't have to look for them; they'll find you. More interesting, unique and precious are the quirky, one-of-a-kind shops hidden away in some half-forgotten back alley with a spray-painted sign. The city's tour de force is its bookstores and record stores, surely some of the best in the nation.

Independent Bookstores

A striking irony in the city that spawned Amazon is the continued relevance of bookstores. It's no wonder that Seattle is ranked as one of the most literate populaces in the US. While some of the chain brands may have gone the way of the dodo, many indie booksellers are fighting a brave rearguard action. Elliott Bay Book Company, Seattle's nationally revered book emporium, now based in Capitol Hill, is often mentioned in the same breath as City Lights in San Francisco and Powell's in Portland. The other big 'un is University Bookstore in the U District, while mega-retailer Barnes & Noble maintains a store downtown. Smaller shops lie scattered around the individual neighborhoods. Most of them offer author signings, book readings and staff reviews.

Viva Vinyl

Vinyl dead? Think again. The word on the street is that Seattle has more record stores that any other US city, and with such a weighty musical legacy to call upon, who's arguing? Every neighborhood has its favorite independent dealer and three Seattle stores recently appeared in a list in *Rolling Stone* magazine of the 'Best Record Stores in the USA' – namely West Seattle's Easy Street Records, Ballard's Sonic Boom and Fremont's tiny Jive Time. What record stores offer over online deals is atmosphere, expertise and extras. Easy Street has long been a destination store for collectors and has its own cafe, Sonic Boom hosts live in-house bands, publishes a weekly top 25 chart and sells gig tickets, while Jive Time is geek heaven, selling bargain secondhand rarities and old, yellowed music magazines.

Shopping by Neighborhood

⇒ **Downtown, Pike Place & Waterfront** Big-name brands in downtown; small-time no-brands in Pike Place; tourist kitsch on the waterfront.

⇒ **Pioneer Square & International District** Expensive antiques and carpets in Pioneer Square; cheap Asian supermarkets in the ID.

⇒ **Capitol Hill & First Hill** Huge selection of indie boutiques, esoterica, sex toys, and one of the nation's best bookstores.

⇒ **U District** Cheap vintage clothing for tight student budgets and abundant bookstores for fact-hungry undergraduates.

⇒ **Fremont & Green Lake** Junk stores and vintage-clothing shops being gradually pushed out by fancier boutiques.

⇒ **Ballard & Discovery Park** Card-game emporium, weird T-shirt prints, rare vinyl and artsy Sunday-market stalls.

Lonely Planet's Top Choices

Elliott Bay Book Company (p116) Great books, top readings, and snug on-site cafe.

Bop Street Records (p157) Every musical genre, overseen by passionate staff.

Market Magic (p60) Classic Pike Place Market throwback.

REI (p104) The original and best of the outdoor outfitters.

Best Shopping Strips

Pike Place Market (p42) Support your local farmer/craftsperson/third-generation store owner in Seattle's bustling heart.

Downtown (p58) Big-name stores deliver the goods in the city's retail core.

Broadway (p116) Check your hipster rating by going shopping on Capitol Hill's main strip.

'The Ave' (p137) A dearth of designer labels but an abundance of welcome bargains beckon in the U District.

Best Bookstores

Elliott Bay Book Company (p116) Best bookstore in the nation? Add it to the list of contenders.

University Bookstore (p137) Everything you need to pass your degree.

Magus Books (p137) Beautiful old-fashioned secondhand bookstore in the U District.

Left Bank Books (p60) Just in case you lost your copy of *Das Kapital.*

Best Record Stores

Easy Street Records & Café (p166) Drink coffee, imbibe beer, eat snacks and...oh...browse excellent records.

Georgetown Records (p166) Rare picture-cover 45s and vintage LPs next door to Fantagraphics comic shop.

Bop Street Records (p157) Astounding array of every musical genre known to *Homo sapiens.*

Singles Going Steady (p92) If this name means anything to you, this punkish record shop is your nirvana.

Best Esoterica

Market Magic (p60) Everything the young aspiring magician could dream of.

Tenzing Momo (p60) Atmospheric apothecary where you expect to see Professor Snape jump out from behind the counter.

Card Kingdom (p157) Interactive games emporium in Ballard that could delay you for...oh... hours.

Babeland (p116) Classy sex-toy boutique in – where else? – Capitol Hill.

Best Vintage Clothes

Red Light (p117) Uber-trendy Capitol Hill store showcasing latest retro looks.

NEED TO KNOW

Opening Hours

Shops are usually open from 9am or 10am to 5pm or 6pm (9pm in shopping malls) Monday to Friday, as well as noon to 5pm or so (later in malls) on weekends. Some places, like record stores and bookstores, may keep later hours, such as from noon to 8pm or 9pm.

Taxes & Refunds

A 9.5% sales tax is added to all purchases except food to be prepared for consumption (ie groceries). Unlike the European VAT or Canadian GST, the sales tax is not refundable to tourists.

Throwbacks NW (p117) Novel vintage-sportswear shop.

Crossroads Trading Co (p117) Used-clothing store with lower hipster quotient.

Best Markets

Pike Place Market (p42) No intro required – lose yourself for a day, at least!

U District Farmers Market (p137) Produce-only market that's been running since 1993.

Ballard Farmers Market (p152) With food and some crafts, this is *the* place to go on a Sunday.

Explore Seattle

**Neighborhoods
at a Glance** 38

**Downtown, Pike
Place & Waterfront ..40**
Top Sights 42
Sights...................47
Eating...................49
Drinking & Nightlife.......55
Entertainment 57
Shopping 58
Sports & Activities........ 61

**Pioneer Square &
International District..63**
Top Sights 65
Sights...................66
Eating...................70
Drinking & Nightlife.......72
Entertainment 73
Shopping 74
Sports & Activities........75

**Belltown &
Seattle Center 76**
Top Sights 78
Sights...................83
Eating...................84
Drinking & Nightlife.......88
Entertainment 90
Shopping 91
Sports & Activities........92

**Queen Anne &
Lake Union..........93**
Top Sights 95

Sights...................96
Eating...................97
Drinking & Nightlife......102
Entertainment 102
Shopping 103
Sports & Activities.......104

**Capitol Hill &
First Hill 105**
Sights..................107
Eating.................. 110
Drinking & Nightlife...... 113
Entertainment 115
Shopping 116
Sports & Activities....... 117

**The CD, Madrona &
Madison Park 120**
Sights..................122
Eating..................123
Drinking & Nightlife......128
Shopping 128
Sports & Activities.......129

U District 130
Sights..................132
Eating..................133
Drinking & Nightlife......136
Entertainment 137
Shopping 137
Sports & Activities.......138

**Fremont &
Green Lake 139**
Top Sights 141
Sights..................143

Eating..................145
Drinking & Nightlife......146
Entertainment 147
Shopping 147
Sports & Activities.......148

**Ballard & Discovery
Park 149**
Top Sights 151
Sights..................152
Eating..................153
Drinking & Nightlife......156
Entertainment 157
Shopping 157
Sports & Activities.......158

**Georgetown &
West Seattle 159**
Top Sights 161
Sights..................162
Eating..................163
Drinking & Nightlife......165
Entertainment 166
Shopping 166
Sports & Activities.......167

**Day Trips from
Seattle 168**
Puget Sound...........169
San Juan Islands 172
Snoqualmie Valley 175
Mt Rainier 176

Sleeping...........179

SEATTLE'S
TOP SIGHTS

Pike Place Market 42

Seattle Art Museum
(SAM) 46

Pioneer Square
Architecture.......................65

Chihuly Garden & Glass ...78

Space Needle 80

EMP Museum....................82

Museum of History
& Industry 95

Fremont Public
Sculpture 141

Discovery Park 151

Museum of Flight.............161

Neighborhoods at a Glance

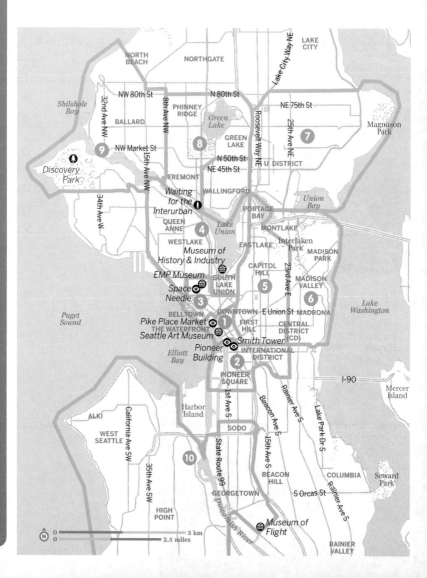

① Downtown, Pike Place & Waterfront (p40)

Downtown is a standard American amalgam of boxy skyscrapers and brand-name shopping opportunities that's given welcome oomph by Pike Place Market, the city's number-one must-see. The waterfront, blemished since the 1950s by the soon-to-be-demolished Alaskan Way Viaduct, is undergoing a slow regeneration.

② Pioneer Square & International District (p63)

Seattle's birthplace retains the grit of its 'Skid Row' roots with historic redbrick architecture and rambunctious street life. The ID is a scruffy quarter known for its dim sum restaurants and Little Saigon.

③ Belltown & Seattle Center (p76)

Where industry once fumed, glassy condos now rise in the thin, walkable strip of Belltown. The neighborhood gained a reputation for trendsetting nightlife (read: grunge) in the 1990s, but these days it's more renowned for its 100-plus restaurants. The adjacent Seattle Center's frequent makeovers have kept it vital and relevant.

④ Queen Anne & Lake Union (p93)

Salubrious Queen Anne hoards old money in beautiful fin-de-siècle mansions. Lake Union's southern shores are changing more quickly than the fresh-faced influx of techies can tweet about them, with celebrity chefs, a traffic-lightening streetcar and the sprawling new Amazon offices.

⑤ Capitol Hill & First Hill (p105)

Capitol Hillers congregate in cafes to drink fair-trade coffee while trying to work out how to keep their neighborhood edgy in the face of gentrification. But this is still Seattle's best quarter for a spontaneous night out, a locavore lunch or an evening drag show. More straitlaced First Hill is home to an art museum and multiple hospitals.

⑥ The CD, Madrona & Madison Park (p120)

Seattle's Central District (CD), traditionally an African American neighborhood, has been augmented by an influx of Ethiopian immigrants, creating what some have dubbed Little Ethiopia. Madison Park and Madrona are upscale lakeside communities with popular beaches.

⑦ U District (p130)

This neighborhood of young, studious out-of-towners places the beautiful, leafy University of Washington campus next to the shabbier 'Ave,' an eclectic strip of cheap boutiques, dive bars and ethnic restaurants.

⑧ Fremont & Green Lake (p139)

Fremont pitches young hipsters among old hippies in an unlikely urban alliance, and vies with Capitol Hill as Seattle's most irreverent neighborhood, with junk shops, urban sculpture and a healthy sense of its own ludicrousness. Family-friendly Green Lake is a more affluent suburb favored by fitness devotees.

⑨ Ballard & Discovery Park (p149)

A former seafaring community, with Scandinavian heritage, Ballard still feels like a small town engulfed by a bigger city. Gritty, no-nonsense and uncommercial, it's slowly being condo-ized but remains a good place to down a microbrew or see a band.

⑩ Georgetown & West Seattle (p159)

Acquiring a veneer of trendiness has worked wonders for Georgetown's street cred – its ice-cool mix of bars, galleries and post-industrial architecture tends to be called 'bohemian chic.' West Seattle is the city's Coney Island: good for beaches and cheap shopping.

Downtown, Pike Place & Waterfront

DOWNTOWN | PIKE PLACE MARKET | WATERFRONT

Neighborhood Top Five

1 Seeing, smelling and tasting the unique energy of **Pike Place Market** (p42), from the charismatic fish throwers to the creative – but disgusting – gum wall.

2 Seeing how nine suspended cars can be made into spectacular modern art at **Seattle Art Museum** (p46).

3 Riding on the **Bainbridge Island ferry** just for the hell of it (and admiring the amazing views).

4 Viewing Seattle's ongoing waterfront regeneration from the brand new **Seattle Great Wheel** (p48).

5 Joining the line for a cheap take-out pastry at Pike Place Market baking phenomenon **Piroshky Piroshky** (p52).

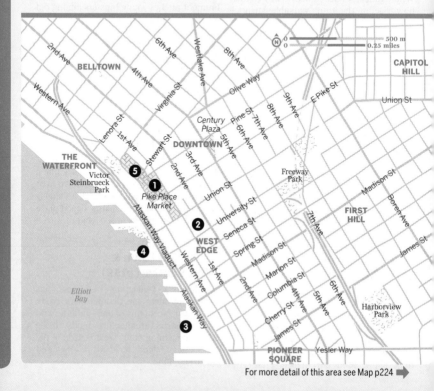

For more detail of this area see Map p224 ➡

Explore: Downtown, Pike Place & Waterfront

You don't have to search long to find Seattle's soul: head directly to Pike Place Market and throw away any map you might have acquired; your nose, eyes and ears are the only compasses you'll need here.

It's particularly important to get to the market early if you want to avoid that cattle-truck feeling (40,000 visitors per day!): weekdays and before 10am on weekends are best. That said, many enjoy the organized chaos of the arcades at Saturday lunchtime. The waterfront is more weather dependent; a sunny weekend afternoon finds it swarming, while on a misty weekday morning you'll have the place pretty much to yourself.

Downtown Seattle, though impressive from a distance, is a bit of an anomaly. Instead of being the beating heart of the city, it's a fairly quiet, functional business district adjacent to Seattle's twin hearts: Pike Place Market and Pioneer Square. What most people mean by 'downtown' is the collection of office buildings, hotels and retail shops between 2nd and 7th Aves. It's best to visit on a weekday, when throngs of people are working and shopping in the area. At night and on weekends it can feel rather desolate.

Downtown is home to much of the city's important architecture – follow the Downtown Architecture walking tour (p50) for a closer look. Seattle's retail heaven extends from the corner of 5th Ave and Pike St a few blocks in all directions. A block north, on 5th Ave at Pine St, is the flagship store of Nordstrom, the national clothing retailer that got its start in Seattle. Just to the west is Westlake Center.

Local Life

➡ **Early-Morning Market** Get to Pike Place early and listen to the vendors chitchat as they set up their stalls. Witness the unique 'market roll call' in the North Arcade when day-stall vendors are allocated their spaces.

➡ **Ferry Across the Sound** Pretend you're a Puget Sound commuter and stow away on a Bainbridge Island ferry just for the ride.

Getting There & Away

➡ **Light Rail** Sound Transit's Link Light Rail from Sea-Tac Airport has two downtown stations: Westlake, and University Street and 3rd Avenue.

➡ **Streetcar** Service to South Lake Union from Westlake.

➡ **Bus** You can get downtown easily from any part of Seattle by bus.

➡ **Ferry** Car ferries dock at Pier 52 on the waterfront. Water taxis to West Seattle leave from Pier 50.

Lonely Planet's Top Tip

Look down! Seattle's public art extends to its hatch covers (manholes). Nineteen of them have been emblazoned with an imprint of a downtown map with your location marked. It's impossible to get lost.

✗ Best Places to Eat

➡ Wild Ginger (p50)

➡ Pink Door Ristorante (p54)

➡ Ivar's Acres of Clams (p55)

➡ Piroshky Piroshky (p52)

For reviews, see p49 ➡

🍷 Best Places to Drink

➡ Pike Pub & Brewery (p56)

➡ Kells (p57)

➡ Seattle Coffee Works (p55)

➡ Owl & Thistle (p55)

For reviews, see p55 ➡

✗ Best Pike Place Market Takeouts

➡ Piroshky Piroshky (p52)

➡ Beecher's Handmade Cheese (p53)

➡ Pike Place Chowder (p54)

➡ Mee Sum Pastries (p54)

➡ Cinnamon Works (p54)

For reviews, see p52 ➡

DOWNTOWN, PIKE PLACE & WATERFRONT

TOP SIGHT
PIKE PLACE MARKET

Take a bunch of small-time businesses and sprinkle them liberally around a spatially challenged waterside strip amid crowds of old-school bohemians, new-wave restaurateurs, tree huggers, bolshie students, artists, urban buskers and artisans. The result: Pike Place Market, a cavalcade of noise, smells, personalities, banter and urban theater that's almost London-like in its cosmopolitanism. In operation since 1907, Pike Place is Seattle in a bottle, a wonderfully local experience that highlights the city for what it really is: all-embracing, eclectic and proudly singular.

Some History

Pike Place Market is the oldest continuously operating market in the nation. It was established in 1907 to give local farmers a place to sell their fruit and vegetables and bypass the middleman. Soon, the greengrocers made room for fishmongers, bakers, ethnic groceries, butchers, cheese sellers and purveyors of the rest of the Northwest's agricultural bounty. The market wasn't exactly architecturally robust – it's always been a thrown-together warren of sheds and stalls, haphazardly designed for utility – and was by no means an intentional tourist attraction. That came later.

An enthusiastic agricultural community spawned the market's heyday in the 1930s. Many of the first farmers were immigrants, a fact the market celebrates with annual themes acknowledging the contributions of various ethnic groups; past years have featured Japanese Americans, Italian Americans and Sephardic Jewish Americans.

By the 1960s, sales at the market were suffering from suburbanization, the growth of supermarkets and the move away from local, small-scale market gardening. Vast tracts of agricultural land were disappearing, replaced by such ventures as the Northgate Mall

DON'T MISS...

➡ The fish throwers
➡ Gum wall
➡ Market roll call
➡ World's oldest Starbucks

PRACTICALITIES

➡ Map p224
➡ www.pikeplace market.org
➡ btwn Virginia St & Union St & 1st Ave & Western Ave
➡ ⏰9am-6pm Mon-Sat, to 5pm Sun
➡ 🚇Westlake

and the Sea-Tac airport. The internment of Japanese American farmers during WWII had also taken its toll. The entire area became a bowery for the destitute and a center for prostitution and peep shows.

In the wake of the 1962 World's Fair, plans were drawn up to bulldoze the market and build high-rise office and apartment buildings on this piece of prime downtown real estate. Fortunately, public outcry prompted a voter's initiative to save the market. Subsequently, the space was cleaned up and restructured, and it has become once again the undeniable heart and soul of downtown; some 10 million people mill through the market each year. Thanks to the unique management of the market, social-services programs and low-income housing mix with commerce, and the market has maintained its gritty edge. These initiatives have prevented the area from ever sliding too far upmarket. A market law prohibits chain stores or franchises from setting up shop and ensures all businesses are locally owned. The one exception is, of course, Starbucks, which gets away with its market location because it is the coffee giant's first outlet (it opened in 1971).

Orientation

If you're coming from downtown, simply walk down Pike St toward the waterfront; you can't miss the huge **Public Market sign** etched against the horizon. Incidentally, the sign and clock, installed in 1927, constituted one of the first pieces of outdoor neon on the West Coast. From the top of Pike St and 1st Ave, stop and survey the bustle and vitality. Walk down the cobblestone street, past perpetually gridlocked cars (don't even think of driving down to Pike Pl) and, before walking into the market, stop and shake the bronze snout of **Rachel the Market Pig**, the de facto mascot and presiding spirit of the market. This life-size piggy bank, carved by Whidbey Island artist Georgia Gerber and named after a real pig, collects about $10,000 each year. The funds are pumped back into market social services. Nearby is the **information booth** (Pike St & 1st Ave), which has maps of the market and information about Seattle in general. It also serves as a ticket booth, selling discount tickets to various shows throughout the city.

Economy Market Building

Once a stable for merchants' horses, the Economy Market Building on the south side of the market entrance has a wonderful Italian grocery store, DeLaurenti's – a great place for any aficionado of Italian foods to browse and sample. There's also Tenzing Momo, one of the oldest apothecaries on the West Coast, where you can pick up herbal remedies,

CHEWING GUM ART

Seattle's oddest and most unhygienic sight is the bizarre **gum wall** situated at the southern end of Post Alley, a once venerable redbricked facade now covered in used pieces of chewing gum originally stuck there by bored theater-goers standing in line for a nearby ticket office in the 1990s. Despite early attempts by the city council to sanitize the wall, the gum-stickers persevered, becoming ever more creative in their outlandish art arrangements and, in 1999, the wall was declared a tourist attraction. Feel free to add your own well-chewed morsels to the Jackson Pollock–like display.

Anyone can busk in the market as long as they register with the market office, pay a $30 annual fee and perform in one of 13 designated spots. With a guaranteed annual audience of 10 million people passing through, pitches are understandably popular. Well-known market performers include Johnny Hahn, who has been tickling the keys of an upright piano for nearly 30 years, and Emery Carl, who plays guitar while spinning a Hula-Hoop.

incense, oils and books. Tarot readings are available here on occasion. Look down at the Economy Market floor and you'll see some of its 46,000 tiles, sold to the public in the 1980s for $35 apiece. If you bought a tile, you'd get your name on it and be proud that you helped save the market floor. Famous tile owners include Cat in the Hat creator Dr Seuss and former US president Ronald Reagan.

Main & North Arcades

Rachel the Market Pig marks the main entrance to the **Main & North Arcades** (Map p224; Western Ave), thin shed-like structures that run along the edge of the hill; these are the busiest of the market buildings. With banks of fresh produce carefully arranged in artful displays, and fresh fish, crab and other shellfish piled high on ice, this is the real heart of the market. Here you'll see fishmongers tossing salmon back and forth like basketballs (many of these vendors will pack fish for overnight delivery). You'll also find cheese shops, butchers, tiny grocery stalls and almost everything else you need to put together a meal. The end of the North Arcade is dedicated to local artisans and craftspeople – products must be handmade to be sold here. It's also abloom with flower sellers, most of them of Vietnamese Hmong origin. The Main Arcade was built in 1907, the first of Frank Goodwin's market buildings.

Down Under

As if the levels of the market that are above ground aren't labyrinthine enough, below the Main Arcade are three lower levels called the Down Under. Here you'll find a fabulously eclectic mix of pocket-size shops, from Indian spice stalls to magicians supply shops and military-button booths.

South Arcade

If you continue past DeLaurenti's, you'll come into the South Arcade, the market's newest wing, home to upscale shops and the lively Pike Pub & Brewery. It's not technically part of the historic market but is with it in spirit and rambunctious energy.

Corner & Sanitary Market Buildings

Across Pike Pl from the Main Arcade are the 1912 **Corner & Sanitary Market Buildings** (Map p224; Pike Pl & Pike St), so named because they were the first of the market buildings in which live animals were prohibited. It's now a maze of ethnic groceries and great little eateries, including the Three Girls Bakery, which has a sit-down area (it's always packed) and a take-out window with some of the best breads and sandwiches around. This is also the home of Left Bank Books, an excellent source for all your radical reading needs.

Post Alley

Between the Corner Market and the Triangle Building, tiny Post Alley (named for its hitching posts) is lined with more shops and restaurants. Extending north across Stewart St, this street offers two of the area's best places for a drink: the Pink Door Ristorante, an Italian hideaway with a cool patio, and Kells, an Irish pub. In Lower Post Alley beside the market sign is the LaSalle Hotel, which was the first bordello north of Yesler Way. Originally the Outlook Hotel, it was taken over in 1942 by the notorious Nellie Curtis, a woman with 13 aliases and a knack for running suspiciously profitable hotels with thousands of lonely sailors lined up nightly outside the door. (She's the inspiration for the Pike Pub & Brewery's equally tempting Naughty Nellie's Ale.) The building, rehabbed in 1977, now houses commercial and residential space.

Market fishmonger

Triangle Building

All in a row in the diminutive Triangle Building, sandwiched between Pike Pl, Pine St and Post Alley, are Mr D's Greek Delicacies, Mee Sum Pastries (try the steamed pork bun), a juice bar and Cinnamon Works – all great choices for a quick snack.

First Avenue Buildings

The market's newest buildings, added mainly in the 1980s, blend seamlessly into the older hive. Here you'll find Pike Pl's only two accommodations – Pensione Nichols and Inn at the Market – a couple of classic pubs and community resources such as a medical center.

North End

The market's North End stretches along Pike Pl from Pine St to Victor Steinbrueck Park – a popular meeting point for daily walking tours. The 1918 Soames-Dunn building, once occupied by a seed and a paper company, is now home to the world's oldest Starbucks. Beware of crowds and errant elbows knocking over your mermaid-logo coffee cup.

MARKET ROLL CALL

Watching Pike Place's daily market roll call, rung in by an old-fashioned hand bell promptly at 9am (10am on Sunday), is like watching a boisterous rural cattle auction conducted in an indecipherable foreign language. The purpose of roll call is to allocate where the market's temporary craft-sellers will set up on any particular day. As Pike Place has over 200 registered vendors but only 130 available trading spots, each day is a nail-biting lottery. Not everyone gets lucky, but by 9:30am clipboards have been signed, a large whiteboard has been filled out, and people are industriously going about their business. Roll call is held at the north end of the North Arcade and is a great way to imbibe the true spirit of the market and its workings. Anyone can watch. Just don't be late!

Pike Place is home to approximately 350 people, who are supported by a proper neighborhood infrastructure that includes a clinic, a senior center, a preschool, childcare facilities and a food bank.

TOP SIGHT
SEATTLE ART MUSEUM (SAM)

While not comparable with the big guns in New York and Chicago, Seattle Art Museum (SAM) is no slouch. Over the last decade, it has added more than 100,000 sq ft to its gallery space and acquired about $1 billion worth of art. It's known for its extensive **Native American** artifacts and work from the local **Northwest school**.

Entrance Lobby

Progressing across the entire lobby and down to the level below is Chinese artist Cai Guo-Qiang's *Inopportune: Stage One* – a simulation of a car bombing, made up of a series of tumbling cars exploding with neon. Between the two museum entrances is the 'art ladder,' with various installations cascading down a hallway.

Modern & Contemporary Art

Level 3 is home to Andy Warhol's *Double Elvis*, a silk-screen image of a young Presley firing a gun right at the viewer, and Jackson Pollack's *Sea Change*.

Native American Art

The Hauberg Gallery is dedicated to the museum's impressive collections of items from Northwest coastal peoples, as well as Australian Aboriginal art and American and Native American textiles. Groups such as the Tlingit, Haida and Kwakwaka'wakw are all well represented.

Top Floor

Level 4 has a rather scattered collection of world art from Greek pottery to the Italian renaissance. Stand-out pieces include *Pomponne Il de Bellièvre* by Van Dyck, *Last Supper* by Rubens, and a huge glass and porcelain showroom.

DON'T MISS...

➡ *Inopportune: Stage One*

➡ Art ladder

➡ Native American art

➡ Van Dyck's *Pomponne Il de Bellièvre*

PRACTICALITIES

➡ Map p224

➡ www.seattleart museum.org

➡ 1300 1st Ave

➡ adult/child $17/11

➡ ⊙10am-5pm Tue, Wed, Sat & Sun, to 9pm Thu & Fri

➡ Ⓡ University St

◉ SIGHTS

The waterfront is the thin strip of land between Elliott Bay and the soon-to-be-dismantled Alaskan Way Viaduct. Downtown is bounded east–west by I-5 and the Alaskan Way Viaduct along with (by most estimations) Olive Way to the north and Cherry St to the south. Pike Place Market sits to the northwest of the downtown core.

The entire western portion of downtown (including Pike Place Market) between 2nd Ave and the Viaduct is sometimes referred to as the West Edge, although, on the ground, it's hard to differentiate between the two neighborhoods.

◉ Downtown

PIKE PLACE MARKET   MARKET
See p42.

SEATTLE ART MUSEUM   MUSEUM
See p46.

HAMMERING MAN   MONUMENT
Map p224 (⎆University St) Although not unique to Seattle, *Hammering Man,* the 48ft-high metal sculpture that guards the entrance to the Seattle Art Museum on the corner of 1st Ave and University St, has become something of a city icon since it was raised in 1992.

The sculpture, whose moving motor-powered arm silently hammers four times per minute, 364 days a year (he has Labor Day in September off), is supposed to represent the worker in all of us. It was conceived by Jonathan Borofsky, an American artist from Boston, who has designed similar hammering men for various other cities. There are taller and heavier models in Frankfurt, Germany, and Seoul, South Korea.

SEATTLE PUBLIC LIBRARY   LIBRARY
Map p224 (☏206-386-4636; www.spl.org; 1000 4th Ave; ⊙10am-8pm Mon-Thu, 10am-6pm Fri & Sat, noon-6pm Sun; ℗; ⎆Pioneer Sq) FREE There's not much chance you'll miss glimpsing the Seattle Public Library, but it's worth going inside for a closer look. Conceived by Rem Koolhaas and LMN Architects, the $165.5-million sculpture of glass and steel was designed to serve as a community gathering space, a tech center, a reading room and, of course, a massive book-storage facility. The main room, on Level 3, has especially high ceilings, a teen center, a small gift shop and a coffee stand.

There's an underground level for parking. Near the top is the **Seattle Room**, a 12,000-sq-ft reading room with 40ft glass ceilings. It has amazing light, nice views of downtown and seating for up to 400 people.

But the importance of the building's function certainly hasn't cost it anything in the form department. In short, it looks brilliant, as striking as any other building in the city including the Space Needle. The overall style of the place is as far from stodgy as you can possibly get – sort of like when that sexy librarian finally takes off her spectacles. Lemon-yellow escalators, hot-pink chairs and zippy wi-fi connections make for a modern, tech-friendly experience. There are also 132 research computers available in the **Mixing Chamber,** where librarians in teams help with in-depth research. And the **Book Spiral**, spanning several floors, holds most of the library's nonfiction books, organized by the Dewey Decimal Classification system with numbers marked on small mats on the floor. Guests can take free one-hour group tours (for a schedule, see the website) or a self-guided podcast tour.

BENAROYA CONCERT HALL   CONCERT HALL
Map p224 (☏206-215-9494; 200 University St; ⎆University St) With a hefty bill of almost $120-million in construction costs, it's no wonder the Benaroya Concert Hall, Seattle Symphony's primary venue, oozes luxury. From the minute you step into the glass-enclosed lobby of the performance hall you're overwhelmed by views of Elliott Bay; on clear days you might be lucky enough to see the snowy peaks of the Olympic Range far in the distance.

Even if you're not attending the symphony, you can walk through the foyer and marvel at the 20ft-long chandeliers, specially created by Tacoma glassmaker Dale Chihuly.

SEATTLE TOWER   LANDMARK
Map p224 (1218 3rd Ave; ⎆University St) Formerly the Northern Life Tower, this 26-story art-deco skyscraper, built in 1928, was designed to reflect the mountains of the Pacific Northwest. The brickwork on the exterior blends from dark at the bottom to light on top, the same way mountains

appear to do. Check out the 18-karat-gold relief map in the lobby.

SAFECO PLAZA LANDMARK

Map p224 (University St) Built in 1969, and originally known as 1001 Fourth Avenue Plaza, this was one of the city's first real skyscrapers. At the time, 1001 Fourth Ave Plaza was a darling of the architectural world, though nowadays the 50-story bronze block looks dated. Locals nicknamed it 'the box that the Space Needle came in.'

In the plaza outside is the **Three Piece Sculpture: Vertebrae**, a sculpture by Henry Moore – a result of Seattle's '1% for art' clause, under which 1% of the construction cost of the building is invested in public art.

ARCTIC BUILDING LANDMARK

Map p224 (700 3rd Ave, at Cherry St; Pioneer Sq) The Arctic Building, completed in 1917, is unique for its intricate terra-cotta ornamentation and 25 walrus heads peeking out from the building's exterior.

Though the walruses' tusks were originally authentic ivory, an earthquake in the 1940s managed to shake a few of them loose to the ground. To protect passersby from the unusual urban hazard of being skewered by falling tusks, the ivory was replaced with epoxy.

TIMES SQUARE BUILDING LANDMARK

Map p224 (cnr Olive Way & Stewart St; Westlake) This terra-cotta and granite structure, guarded by eagles perched on the roof, was designed by the Paris-trained architect Carl Gould (who also did the Seattle Asian Art Museum and the University of Washington's Suzzallo Library). It housed the *Seattle Times* from 1916 to 1931.

WASHINGTON STATE CONVENTION & TRADE CENTER CONVENTION CENTER

Map p224 (206-447-5000; main entrance cnr 7th Ave & Pike St; Westlake) It's hard to miss this gigantic complex decked out with ballrooms, meeting rooms, space for exhibitions and the Seattle Convention and Visitors Bureau (p211). An arched-glass bridge spans Pike St between 7th and 8th Aves, with what looks like a giant eye in the middle of it.

Freeway Park provides a leafy, fountain-laden downtown oasis.

WESTLAKE CENTER MALL

Map p224 (cnr 4th Ave & Pine St; Westlake) Scorned by locals, this cheeseball shopping mall is useful these days primarily as a land-

mark. The courtyard-like area outside has become a favorite place for activist gatherings and political protests, and it offers rich if sobering opportunities for people-watching. (Keep tabs on your wallet.)

This is also where the **monorail** stops and starts on its 1.2-mile trip to and from Seattle Center.

Waterfront

SEATTLE AQUARIUM AQUARIUM

Map p224 (www.seattleaquarium.org; 1483 Alaskan Way, at Pier 59; adult/child $19/12; 9:30am-5pm; University St) While not comparable to Seattle's nationally lauded Woodland Park Zoo, the aquarium – situated on Pier 59 in an attractive wooden building – is probably the most interesting site on the waterfront, and it's a handy distraction for visiting families with itchy-footed kids.

The entry lobby instantly impresses, with a giant fish-filled tank called Window on Washington Waters grabbing your attention; background music is sometimes provided by live string quartets. While there are no large sea mammals such as whales and dolphins, Seattle does have harbor seals and resident sea and river otters who float comically on their backs. An underwater dome on the lower level gives a pretty realistic glimpse of the kind of fish that inhabit the waters of Puget Sound, and the daily diver show here is probably the best of the aquarium's live events. For kids there are plenty of hands-on exhibits, including a pool where you can stroke starfish and caress sea urchins.

SEATTLE GREAT WHEEL FERRIS WHEEL

Map p224 (www.seattlegreatwheel.com; 1301 Alaskan Way; adult/child $13/8.50; 11am-10pm Mon-Thu, to midnight Fri & Sat, 10am-10pm Sun; University St) With the Alaskan Way Viaduct soon to be confined to the history books, Seattle has started work on beautifying its often neglected waterfront. Leading the way is this 175ft Ferris wheel that was installed in June 2012 with 42 gondolas, each capable of carrying eight people on a 12-minute ($13!) ride.

The wheel sticks out over the water on Pier 57 and is the tallest of its type on the west coast, though it pales in comparison with other behemoths such as the London Eye. So far, it has fulfilled its role as a popular Space Needle–like attraction primarily aimed at tourists.

GUIDED WALKING TOURS

Downtown Seattle, and in particular Pike Place Market, is awash with good, independent walking tours of many types, but with a strong bias towards food and drink. As a rule, the tours are organized by small private individuals or companies who offer professional but highly personal service. All of them will give you a candid view of Seattle, its market and its people. With wet weather rarely off the menu, tours usually go ahead rain or shine.

Public Market Tours (www.publicmarkettours.com) To get an quick insider's view of Pike Place's confusing labyrinth, join a one-hour market tour that leaves from the corner of Western Ave and Virginia St daily at 10am or 2pm. A percentage of the $15 ticket price goes to the Pike Place Market Foundation.

Seattle Free Walking Tours (www.seattlefreewalkingtours.org) A nonprofit set up by a couple of world travelers and Seattle residents in 2012 who were impressed with the free walking tours offered in various European cities, these tours meet daily at 11am on the corner of Western Ave and Virginia St. The intimate two-hour walk takes in Pike Place, the waterfront, and Pioneer Square. If you have a rip-roaring time (highly likely), there's a suggested $15 donation. No bookings required.

Seattle by Foot (206-508-7017; www.seattlebyfoot.com; tours $20-25) This company runs a handful of tours including the practically essential (this being Seattle) Coffee Crawl, which will ply you liberally with caffeine while explaining the nuances of latte art and dishing the inside story of the rise (and rise) of Starbucks. It costs $25 including samples. Registration starts at 9:50am Thursday to Sunday at the Hammering Man outside Seattle Art Museum. The same company also offers a unique Seattle Kids Tour, two hours of educational fun involving art, music and chocolate. Prices are $10 to $15 depending on age. Tours run weekends at 1pm. Reserve ahead.

Savor Seattle (206-209-5485; www.savorseattletours.com) These guys lead a handful of gastronomic tours, the standout being the two-hour Booze-n-Bites that runs daily at 4pm from the corner of Western Ave and Virginia St. It costs $59.99 and visits such culinary bastions as Cutter's Crabhouse and Taste inside the Seattle Art Museum. Prepare yourself for some sublime cocktails, wine and food.

Seattle Bites (425-888-8837; www.seattlebitesfoodtours.com) Try Lummi Island salmon, Nutella crepes, clam chowder, Washington wine and German sausage all in one market tour. This 2½-hour stroll costs $39.99 and leaves at 10:30am, so go easy on breakfast. Participants are given listening devices enabling them to wander off and still hear the guide's words of wisdom.

VICTOR STEINBRUECK PARK PARK

Map p224 (cnr Western Ave & Virginia St; Westlake) When you've had enough of the market and its crowds, wander out the end of the North Arcade and cross Western Ave to Victor Steinbrueck Park, a small grassy area designed in 1982 by Steinbrueck and Richard Haag.

A historic armory building once stood on the site, but it was knocked down in 1968, much to the disgust of Steinbrueck, a major preservationist who worked hard to save both Pike Place and Pioneer Square from the wrecking ball. As consolation, this small breathing space between the waterfront and downtown was created. Perched over Elliott Bay, it has benches, a couple of totem poles carved by Quinault tribe members James Bender and Marvin Oliver, and great views over the waterfront and Elliott Bay. Rallies and political demonstrations are often held here.

 EATING

You'll have to dig deep to fill your stomach in the central downtown area, but this is the place to find classic Northwest food in old-fashioned oyster bars and cavernous steakhouses. Happy hours are your best bet for affordable bar snacks, small plates and oysters less than $2. Plenty of the top-notch hotels in the area have posh dining rooms and bars inside their opulent interiors.

Save for a couple of old stalwarts, Pike Place is where you go for cheap on-the-go grub invariably sold to you by the person who picked/made/reared it. Explore the market on an empty stomach and commit to a few hours of snacking; you'll be full by the time you leave, and it won't have cost you much. Food styles are all over the map, but the words 'fresh,' 'local' and 'sustainable' are a given. Many stalls have been owned and operated by the same families since before you (and your grandma) were born.

The waterfront is where to go for oysters, clams and fish. Most of the chips seem to end up in the beaks of the resident seagulls.

✗ Downtown

CYBER-DOGS   VEGETARIAN $
Map p224 (909 E Pike St; dogs $2-5; ⊙10am-midnight; ✐ 🖒; 🖳10) 'Free hot dog if you're David Bowie,' says the sign inside the door at this quirky cyber cafe that sells all kinds of 'not dogs' (ie they're exclusively vegetarian). Dress up as Ziggy Stardust, Aladdin Sane or the Thin White Duke and try your luck. Internet is $6 per hour.

★ WILD GINGER   ASIAN $$
Map p224 (www.wildginger.net; 1401 3rd Ave; mains $15-28; ⊙11am-3pm & 5-11pm Mon-Sat, 4-9pm Sun; 🖳University St) All around the Pacific Rim – via China, Indonesia, Malaysia, Vietnam and Seattle, of course – is the wide-ranging theme at this highly popular downtown fusion restaurant. The signature fragrant duck goes down nicely with a glass of Riesling. The restaurant also provides food for the swanky Triple Door (p58) club downstairs.

TASTE RESTAURANT   NORTHWEST $$
Map p224 (✆206-903-5291; www.tastesam.com; 1300 1st Ave; mains $15-25; ⊙11am-close, to 5pm Tue & Sun; 🖳University St) Inside the Seattle Art Museum, Taste changes its menu to honor the gallery's various temporary exhibitions. British bangers and mash were doffing a cap to Gainsborough on our last visit. The venue is popular among city workers for its 3pm-to-6pm happy hour, when red-eyed bankers wash down oysters with cocktails. Aside from the rather chic sit-down space there's also a take-out counter.

🏃 Neighborhood Walk
Downtown Architecture

START ARCTIC BUILDING
END WESTLAKE CENTER
LENGTH 2 MILES; ONE HOUR

Downtown Seattle isn't the city's most buzzing or creative neighborhood, but its tall, modern edifices contain some interesting architectural details rarely spared a glance by the suited office workers who hurry from building to building at street level.

Start this walk at the south end of downtown at the ❶ **Arctic Building** (p48). Crane your neck to get a look at the walrus heads on the building's exterior. Then walk up Cherry St and take a left onto 4th Ave.

The ❷ **Columbia Center** (p52), formerly the Bank of America Tower and the Columbia Seafirst Center, takes up the block between 4th and 5th Aves and Columbia and Cherry Sts. This is the tallest building on the West Coast. If you have time, check out the observation deck on the 73rd floor.

Follow 4th Ave to Madison St, to ❸ **Safeco Plaza** (p48). Built in 1969, this was one of the city's first real skyscrapers, and it ended the Space Needle's short seven-year reign at the top. The building ushered in a era of massive downtown growth – most of it in a vertical direction. It is now Seattle's fifth tallest skyscraper.

Just across 4th Ave, hop into the ❹ **Seattle Public Library** (p47) and take a quick ride up the lime-green escalators to see how good architecture can combine practicality and beauty. There are good views from the top levels.

Continue north on 4th Ave to University St and take a left, walk half a block and look up. Formerly the Northern Life Tower, the ❺ **Seattle Tower** (p47), an art-deco skyscraper built in 1928, was designed to reflect the mountains of the Pacific Northwest.

Continue down University St across 3rd Ave. The beauty of the Seattle skyline is reflected in the blue-and-cream ❻ **1201 Third Avenue** at 3rd Ave at

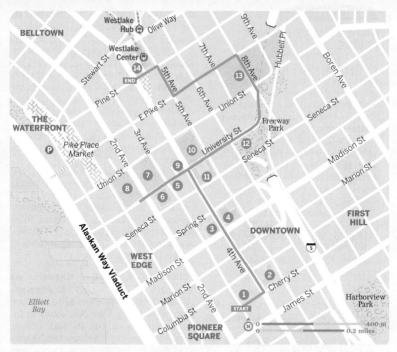

Seneca St, which changes colors with the clouds and sunsets. Enter off 3rd Ave to explore the building's stunning interior.

Cross University St to **7** **Benaroya Concert Hall** (p47). Walk into the glass-enclosed lobby of the performance hall, where you can take in excellent views of Elliott Bay. Check out Dale Chihuly's 20ft-long chandeliers.

Since you're this close, continue along University to get an eyeful of the **8** **Seattle Art Museum** (p46). It may not be one of the seven wonders of the architecture world, especially from the outside, but it is a clever solution to the problem of finding more and better gallery space in the crowded downtown core.

Walk back up University St, across 3rd Ave to the corner of 4th Ave. Look up at the 1910 **9** **Cobb Building** and see remnants of an older Seattle. Peering out from the building is the dour terra-cotta head of a Native American chief.

Continue on University St across 4th Ave to **10** **Rainier Tower**. Taking up an entire block between 4th and 5th Aves and University and Union Sts is Rainier Sq, a shopping center connected to the top-heavy tower.

Cross University St and gaze in wonder at the **11** **Fairmont Olympic Hotel** (p182), undoubtedly one of the classiest remnants of Seattle's early-20th-century heyday. The block-square building looks sober and unrevealing on the outside, but journey through the revolving doors to discover a plush lobby dominated by chandeliers, marble walls and exotic carpets.

Continue northeast on University St past 6th Ave; look ahead to **12** **Freeway Park**. Meander through it, then follow signs to the **13** **Washington State Convention & Trade Center** (p48) and the visitor center inside. Leave the convention center through its front doors on Pike St. Follow Pike (you'll see Pike Place Market at the end of the street) to 5th Ave.

Take a right on 5th Ave to Pine St; turn left, toward the specter of the **14** **Westlake Center** (p60). Stop for a latte and park yourself in front of the entrance for some entertaining amateur street theater.

DOWNTOWN, PIKE PLACE & WATERFRONT EATING

HIGHER THAN THE SPACE NEEDLE

Everyone makes a rush for the iconic Space Needle, but it's neither the tallest nor the cheapest of Seattle's glittering viewpoints. That honor goes to the sleek, tinted-windowed **Columbia Center** (Map p224; 701 5th Ave; adult/concession $9/6; ⊙8:30am-4:30pm Mon-Fri), built between 1982 and 1985, which at 932ft high is the loftiest building in the Pacific Northwest. The tower sports 76 floors. An elevator in the lobby takes you up to the free-access 40th floor, where there's a Starbucks. From here you must take another elevator to the plush observation deck on the 73rd floor, from where you can look down on ferries, cars, islands, roofs and – ha, ha – the Space Needle!

VON'S 1000 SPIRITS　　NORTHWEST, FUSION **$$**
Map p224 (☑206-621-8667; www.vons1000 spirits.com; 1225 1st Ave; frics $11-17; ⊙11am-midnight Sun-Thu, to 1am Fri & Sat; ☒University St) ✐ It's almost worth coming to this new place opposite Seattle Art Museum to read the footnotes on the menu; invaluable nuggets that tell you who made the chocolate cake (the executive chef's mother), how Henry II of France inspired modern French cooking, and what kind of grain was used to feed the cows that made the meat that made the burgers.

Once you've deciphered all of this, try one of the de rigueur cocktails ($5 martinis!) and plump for a frics – a sourdough French country pizza.

IL FORNAIO　　ITALIAN **$$**
Map p224 (☑206-264-0994; www.ilfornaio.com; 600 Pine St, No 132; pasta & pizza $15-17; ⊙11:30am-10pm Sun-Thu, to 11pm Fri & Sat; ☒; ☒Westlake) Split over two levels (upstairs is more formal), this is where to come for quick, hearty, relatively authentic Italian cucina. The open kitchen puts on a good show, and the food (fairly standard Italian dishes) comes with ample focaccia and a good kids menu. It abuts the Pacific mall. You can enter via the mall or from a separate street-side entrance at ground level.

GEORGIAN　　CONTINENTAL **$$$**
Map p224 (☑206-621-7889; 411 University St; express lunch $15, mains $20-35; ⊙6:30am-2:30pm Sun & Mon, 6:30am-2:30pm & 5:30-9:30pm Tue-Sat; ☒University St) A treat above treats, the Georgian at the Fairmont Olympic Hotel is one of the most imposing restaurants in the city – the ornate high ceilings and dripping chandeliers, shiny silver and gilt details will have you swooning. The food is equally eye-catching, and it's inspired by regional ingredients, such as scallops with truffles or roasted sea bass.

Service is tops, and it's one of the few places where Seattleites tend to be sharply dressed; jackets aren't required, but they're certainly not discouraged. Reservations are recommended. Bargain hunters or those short of time should try the express lunch, which includes soup, salad, sandwich and dessert delivered all at once.

PURPLE CAFE & WINE BAR　　INTERNATIONAL **$$$**
Map p224 (☑206-829-2280; www.thepurple cafe.com; 1225 4th Ave; mains $20-32; ⊙11am-11pm, to midnight Fri & Sat; ☒University St) Instantly impressive with its high ceiling, lofty mezzanine floor and spectacular tower of wine bottles, the Purple Cafe almost always seems to fill its ostentatious interior, providing an atmosphere not unlike King Street Station five minutes after the Chicago train has just pulled in. The multifarious menu reads like *War and Peace*.

To save time, opt for the lobster mac 'n' cheese and a bottle of wine pulled from the collection of 5000 stashed in that tower.

MCCORMICK'S FISH HOUSE & BAR　　STEAK, SEAFOOD **$$$**
Map p224 (☑206-682-3900; www.mccormickand schmicks.com; 722 4th Ave; mains $17-36; ⊙11am-10pm Mon-Fri, 4-10pm Sat & Sun; ☒Pioneer Sq) A mainstay of traditional Seattle dining and the flagship of a small Northwest chain, this classy, wood-lined place is a network of cubbyholes that looks like an old boys club (it was built as a hotel in 1927). The food is consistently good, with daily fresh fish specials (mostly grilled with zesty sauces) and a fine selection of local oysters, chops and steak.

✖ Pike Place Market

★**PIROSHKY PIROSHKY**　　BAKERY **$**
Map p224 (www.piroshkybakery.com; 1908 Pike Pl; snacks $2-7; ⊙8am-6:30pm Oct-Apr, from

7:30am May-Sep; ⓇWestlake) Proof that not all insanely popular Pike Place holes-in-the-wall go global (à la Starbucks), Piroshky is still knocking out its delectable mix of sweet and savory Russian pies and pastries in a space barely big enough to swing a small kitten. Join the melee and order one 'to go.'

CRUMPET SHOP CRUMPETS $

Map p224 (1503 1st Ave; crumpets $3-6; Ⓣ7am-5pm; ⓇWestlake) Take a treasured British culinary invention (the crumpet) and give it a distinct American twist (ridiculously lavish toppings) and you've got another reason to have your breakfast or lunch in Pike Place Market.

Join the queue (there always is one) for crumpets made before your eyes and embellished with ricotta, almond butter, marmalade, pesto and – for Brits and brave Americans only – Marmite (yeast extract).

BEECHER'S HANDMADE CHEESE SNACKS $

Map p224 (www.beechershandmadecheese.com; 1600 Pike Pl; snacks $3-5; Ⓣ9am-6pm; ⓇWestlake) Artisan beer, artisan coffee...next up, Seattle brings you artisan cheese and it's made as you watch in this always-crowded Pike Place nook, where you can buy all kinds

LOCAL KNOWLEDGE

COFFEE TALK

Sebastian Simsch, owner of Seattle Coffee Works, a local cafe and coffee roaster with branches in downtown and Ballard, is better placed than most to talk about Seattle's trendsetting coffee culture and he has some interesting thoughts about how it was established and why it is so important to the city's psyche.

Bad weather has long pushed people in Seattle to look for an escape from the rain, says Simsch, and coffee provides an ideal pick-me-up. Having retreated indoors, the coffee culture was shaped by a unique Seattle talent: its tech-minded workforce. In a city famous for Boeing airplanes, there's a strong engineering culture. Tech-savvy Seattleites didn't try to just recreate European coffee culture, they sought to re-invent it – quite literally. Local entrepreneurs, fascinated by the industry's machinery, started to take apart complex Italian espresso machines to see how they worked. And so began a process of betterment and refinement. Look around the coffee world these days, says Simsch, and you'll find that many of the best espresso machines such as Synesso and Slayer are made in Seattle. The same goes for grinders, scoops, cups and other coffee paraphernalia. Food culture is another important influence on coffee, he adds. There has always been a strong culinary tradition in the Pacific Northwest and this has had a knock-on effect in the cafes. Customers have refined taste buds and they demand high-quality products; you can't pull the wool over their eyes.

With this in mind, Simsch's Seattle Coffee Works sources its baked goods from local bakery Macrina in Belltown, and vegan doughnut producers Mighty O Doughnuts, who run a popular cafe in Green Lake. This process of sharing and networking has always been important among Seattle's tight-knit independent businesses, where many talented coffee entrepreneurs began their careers working together. Indeed, three of the city's best cafes, Bauhaus, Zeitgeist and Top Pot Hand-Forged Doughnuts were conceived by the same people, a fact evident in each establishment's attractive woody decor and hip sense of style.

Simsch thanks the relatively low price of real estate for a lot of his own success, as well as the role networking has played in drawing in local talent to work for him. As with many third-wave coffee producers, he maintains direct relations with farmers in Guatemala, Costa Rica, Brazil, Honduras and El Salvador and he'll often pay them a visit in order to perfect the quality of his beans, primarily through the drying process.

Seattle Coffee Works roasts its beans at its downtown premises in Pike St in regular small batches. The aim is to produce a balanced drink that is both fruity and acidic, but not too dark. To experiment with the subtleties of taste, the cafe maintains an on-site 'slow bar' where customers can sample taster cups made by different methods. The cafe is best known for its Obama blend, a mix of beans that are drawn from the president's heritage lands in Indonesia and Kenya. However, despite all the intricate experimentation, Seattle's favorite drink, according to Simsch, is still the good old 12oz latte.

of cheese-related paraphernalia. As for that long, snaking, almost permanent queue – that's people lining up for the wonderful homemade mac 'n' cheese that comes in two different-sized tubs and is simply divine.

PIKE PLACE CHOWDER
SEAFOOD $

Map p224 (206-267-2537; www.pikeplacechowder.com; 1530 Post Alley; medium chowder $6.25; 11am-5pm; Westlake) Proof that some of the best culinary ideas are almost ridiculously simple, this Pike Place hole-in-the-wall takes that old New England favorite (clam chowder) and gives it a dynamic West Coast makeover. You can choose from four traditional chowders in four different sizes accompanied by four different salads. Then you can fight to eat it at one of four indoor tables.

The chowder has been voted the nation's best more than once – in competitions held in New England!

LOWELLS
DINER $

Map p224 (www.eatatlowells.com; 1519 Pike Pl; mains $6-9; 7am-6pm; Westlake) Fish and chips is a simple meal often done badly – but not here. Slam down your order for Alaskan cod at the front entry and take your food up to the top floor for delicious views over Puget Sound. Lowells also serves corned-beef hash and an excellent clam chowder.

CINNAMON WORKS
BAKERY $

Map p224 (206-583-0085; www.cinnamonworks.com; 1536 Pike Pl; baked goods from $1; 10am-5pm Mon-Sat; Westlake) It's hard to walk past this bakery in Pike Place that has been part of the market's furniture since the early 1980s and not stop. Not surprisingly, the cinnamon buns are warm and delicious (and not too sweet), but the bakery also does other stuff – cookies, for instance – and, this being Seattle, anything comes in gluten-free or vegan versions.

PROCOPIO GELATI
GELATO $

Map p224 (206-622-4280; 1501 Western Ave; gelato $2-5; 9am-6pm; Westlake) If the Pike Place Hillclimb wears you out – or even if it doesn't – stop for an authentic Italian-style gelato. The owner learned his trade from a Milanese gelato maker, and he uses only super-fresh ingredients for completely undiluted flavors.

MEE SUM PASTRIES
ASIAN $

Map p224 (206-682-6780; 1526 Pike Pl; bao $2.95; 9am-6pm; Westlake) This little storefront window is famed for its giant *hum bao* – eminently portable meat- or vegetable-filled steamed buns that make a great snack or small meal. The steamed pork *bao* is tops. Next door is a smoothie stand, where you can round out your tidy little meat bomb with some fresh fruits and vegetables.

PINK DOOR RISTORANTE
ITALIAN $$

Map p224 (206-443-3241; 1919 Post Alley; mains $16-24; 11:30am-10pm Mon-Thu, to 11pm Fri & Sat, 4-10pm Sun; Westlake) A restaurant like no other, the Pink Door is probably the only place in the US (the world?) where you can enjoy fabulous *linguine alla vongole* (pasta with clams and pancetta) and other Italian favorites while watching live jazz, burlesque cabaret, or – we kid you not – a trapeze artist swinging from the 20ft ceiling.

LE PICHET
FRENCH $$

Map p224 (www.lepichetseattle.com; 1933 1st Ave; lunch/mains $9/18; 8am-midnight; Westlake) Say *bienvenue* to Le Pichet just up from Pike Place Market, a *très français* bistro with pâtés, cheeses, wine, *chocolat* and a refined Parisian feel. An economical way to impress a date.

STEELHEAD DINER
SEAFOOD $$

Map p224 (206-625-0129; www.steelheaddiner.com; 95 Pine St; sandwiches $9-13, mains $15-33; 11am-10pm Tue-Sat, 10am-3pm Sun; Westlake) Homey favorites such as fish and chips, grilled salmon or braised short ribs and grits become fine cuisine when they're made with the best of what Pike Place Market has to offer.

CAFÉ CAMPAGNE
FRENCH $$

Map p224 (206-728-2233; www.cafecampagne.com; 1600 Post Alley; dinner menu $29; 11am-10pm Mon-Fri, 8am-11pm Sat, 8am-10pm Sun; Westlake) Since the closure of the market's upscale Campagne restaurant, this more casual cafe has gone it alone. Compared to its erstwhile namesake, the prices are more manageable, and you don't have to dress up for dinner. The weekend brunch is a treat.

ETTA'S SEAFOOD
SEAFOOD $$

Map p224 (206-443-6000; www.tomdouglas.com; 2020 Western Ave; brunch $8-15, mains $12-25, happy-hour oysters $1; 11:30am-10pm Mon-Fri; 9am-3pm & 4-10pm Sat & Sun; Westlake)

Famous for its gourmet seafood brunch, which includes such mouth-waterers as poached eggs with Dungeness crab and chipotle hollandaise, Etta's is a reliable and classy place with a fish-focused dinner menu.

MATT'S IN THE MARKET   NORTHWEST $$$

Map p224 (☑206-467-7909; www.mattsinthe market.com; 94 Pike St, Suite 32; lunch $7-23, small plates $13-18, dinner mains $27-39; ☺11:30am-2:30pm & 5-10pm Mon-Sat; ⓡWestlake) ✐ A beloved spot that's been dramatically renovated, Matt's is deep in the heart of the market and draws from its surroundings. A pulled-pork sandwich is made with Stumptown coffee barbecue sauce; several dishes use locally grown potatoes and organic meats. The menu leans heavily toward seafood, and fresh fruit abounds, but you certainly won't be forced to endure a meal without pork belly.

CUTTER'S CRABHOUSE   SEAFOOD $$$

Map p224 (☑206-448-4884; www.cutterscrab house.com; 2001 Western Ave; mains $25-35; ☺11am-9pm, to 10pm Fri & Sat; ⓡWestlake) When you're 70 sailing miles from Dungeness Spit there's no avoiding the crabs. Recently refurbished Cutter's ain't cheap, but it delivers the freshest crab catch in Seattle in cakes, gnocchi or just steamed whole. Also recommended are the deep-fried curds from nearby Beecher's Handmade Cheese and the bread from Macrina bakery.

✗ Waterfront

IVAR'S ACRES OF CLAMS   SEAFOOD $

Map p224 (☑206-624-6852; www.ivars.com; 1001 Alaskan Way, Pier 54; fish & chips $8-9; ☺11am-10pm Sun-Thu, to 11pm Fri & Sat; ☒; ⓡUniversity St) Ivar Haglund was a beloved local character famous for silly promotional slogans ('Keep clam!'), but he sure knew how to fry up fish and chips. Ivar's is a Seattle institution that started in 1938, and its founder still stands sentinel at the door (albeit as a statue).

Forgo the dining room for the outdoor lunch counter; the chaotic ordering system involves a lot of yelling, but it seems to work, and then you can enjoy your clam strips or fish and chips outdoors on the pier. The tradition at Ivar's is to feed chips to the seagulls, who'll swoop down and take them out of your hand.

ELLIOTT'S OYSTER HOUSE   SEAFOOD $$

Map p224 (☑206-623-4340; www.elliottsoyster house.com; 1201 Alaskan Way, Pier 56; 6 oysters $12; ☺11am-10pm Sun-Thu, to 11pm Fri & Sat; ⓡUniversity St) One of the best oyster houses in Seattle overhangs the water on Pier 56. The oyster menu lists over 30 different varieties plucked from practically every inlet and bay in Puget Sound and they're nicely paired with Washington white wines. A progressive happy hour kicks off at 3pm with 75c per oyster; the price rises 50c an hour until 6pm.

🍷🍸 DRINKING & NIGHTLIFE

Hotel bars are your best bet for drinking here, as there aren't too many watering holes in the downtown commercial core. Oliver's Lounge in the Mayflower Park Hotel is a nice little oasis. Coffee shops abound, but those with character are scarce.

There are some extremely romantic and very cozy drinking spots tucked away among the warrenlike market buildings in this area, and many of them have incredible views across the water. Also here is atmospheric Irish pub Kells.

🍸 Downtown

OWL & THISTLE   IRISH PUB

Map p224 (☑206-621-7777; www.owlnthistle.com; 808 Post Ave; ☺11am-2am; ⓡPioneer Sq) One of the best Irish pubs in the city, the dark, cavernous Owl & Thistle is located slap-bang downtown but misses most of the tourist traffic (who home in on the more 'themed' Fado) because it's hidden in Post Alley.

Aside from hosting Celtic folk bands or acoustic singer-songwriters who make pleasant noises here most evenings, it serves excellent beer and possibly the cheapest fish and chips in the city (less than $4 during happy hour). Most importantly, it's run by an Irishman (and his wife).

SEATTLE COFFEE WORKS   CAFE

Map p224 (www.seattlecoffeeworks.com; 107 Pike St; ☺7am-6pm Mon-Fri, 8am-6pm Sat, 9am-5pm Sun; 🛜; ⓡWestlake) ✐ Amid the frenetic action of downtown is a cafe where they truly treat their coffee like wine. Seattle Coffe

WINE TASTING

Although it's a long way behind California in terms of annual grape yield, Washington state is the US's second-largest wine-producing region – and it's growing. Ninety-five percent of the state's grapes are grown on the eastern side of the Cascade Mountains in nine different AVAs (American Viticultural Areas) that support over 700 private wineries, many of which are small and family-run. Unlike other wine regions that have become famous for one particular type of grape, Washington is known as a good all-rounder whose youthful wines – in particular the reds – are trumpeted for their fruitiness and fresh acidity. Not surprisingly, Pike Place Market is a good place to sample the wares of some of Washington's best small producers, and there are few better places than the **Tasting Room** (Map p224; ☑206-770-9463; www.tastingroomseattle.com; 1924 Post Alley; ⊙noon-8pm Sun-Thu, to 10pm Fri & Sat), which offers daily tastings from $2 for 1oz pours. Friendly experts will talk you through the taste notes and tannins of prized vintages from Walla Walla, the Yakima Valley and the Columbia River region.

Works' woody interior is split in two, with a normal walk-up counter and a 'slow bar' where they'll brew your coffee to order and discuss its taste notes like enthusiastic oenologists.

The Obama blend (a mix of Kenyan and Indonesian beans), perfected in the wake of the 2008 election, is an old favorite (they also tried a McCain blend but it apparently didn't sell!).

BOOKSTORE BAR
BAR

Map p224 (☑206-624-4844; www.alexishotel.com; 1007 1st Ave; ⊙2pm-midnight Tue-Sat, to 10pm Sun & Mon; ⊛Pioneer Sq) Cementing downtown's reputation as a font of good hotel bars is the Bookstore, encased in the front window of the Alexis Hotel, which mixes books stacked on handsome wooden shelves with whiskey – an excellent combination (ask Dylan Thomas). There are over 100 varieties of Scotch and bourbon available, plus a full gamut of weighty literary tomes from Melville to Twain.

Should you be peckish, the curried crawfish mac 'n' cheese goes down a treat.

🍷 Pike Place Market & Waterfront

⭐ PIKE PUB & BREWERY
BREWPUB

Map p224 (www.pikebrewing.com; 1415 1st Ave; ⊙11am-midnight; ⊛University St) Leading the way in the microbrewery revolution, this brewpub was an early starter, opening in 1989 underneath Pike Place Market. Today it continues to serve high-palate pub food and hop-heavy beers in a neo-industrial multilevel space that's a beer nerd's heaven. The brewery runs free tours daily at 2pm.

Friendly bar staff will also help you to pair beer with your food.

ATHENIAN INN
BAR

Map p224 (☑206-624-7166; 1517 Pike Place Market; happy hour well drinks $3; ⊙11am-8pm Mon-Sat, 9am-4pm Sun; ⊛Westlake) There's nothing fancy about the Athenian, but it's a landmark and a bastion of unpretentious, frontier-era Seattle, a holdover from the days before Starbucks and Grand Central Bakery (*way* before – it opened in 1909, two years after the market itself).

It's been a bakery and a lunch counter, and now it seems to have settled in as a diner-bar combination where, especially in the off hours, you can snuggle into a window booth and gaze over Elliott Bay with a plate of fried fish and a frosty mug of Manny's Pale Ale.

ALIBI ROOM
COCKTAIL BAR

Map p224 (☑206-623-3180; 85 Pike Pl; cocktails from $7; ⊙3pm-2am Mon-Thu, noon-2am Fri-Sun, happy hour 3-6pm Mon-Thu, noon-6pm Fri-Sun; ⊛University St) The perfect place to hide from the perfect crime, the Alibi provides entertainment as well as a hideout, with regular DJ nights, art installations, stand-up performances and experimental-film screenings. Good eats, too, and the happy-hour menu includes $5 food items, $4 well drinks and $3 beers.

ZIG ZAG CAFÉ
COCKTAIL BAR

Map p224 (☑206-625-1146; www.zigzagseattle.com; 1501 Western Ave; cocktails from $8; ⊙5pm-2am; ⊛University St) For serious cocktails, this is the unmissable destination in town.

Classic and inventive drinks are made with precision by nattily attired alchemists – including some of the best bartenders in Seattle. These folks know how to sling a bottle of chartreuse; sitting at the bar on a quiet night and watching them command the stage is a treat.

You'll see all manner of potions behind the bar, most of which you've probably never heard of (and if you're nice, you might be offered a taste). Drinks start at $5 during happy hour.

CONTOUR CLUB

Map p224 (☎206-447-7704; www.clubcontour.com; 807 1st Ave; ⊙3-8pm Sun-Thu, 2-10pm Fri & Sat; ⓡPioneer Sq) This plush venue is open late and has a more extensive food menu than you might expect of a club whose top priority is clearly to keep your booty shaking until dawn. Contour hosts local and visiting DJs, with after-hours dance nights until 4:30am Thursday through Saturday.

VIRGINIA INN TAVERN PUB

Map p224 (☎206-728-1937; 1937 1st Ave; cocktails/beers $8.50/5; ⊙11:30am-11pm Mon-Thu & Sun, to 2am Fri & Sat; ⓡWestlake) Near Pike Place Market is one of Seattle's most likable bars. Lots of draft beers, a nice brick interior and friendly staff make this a good rendezvous point for forays elsewhere.

KELLS IRISH PUB

Map p224 (☎206-728-1916; www.kellsirish.com/seattle; 1916 Post Alley; ⊙11:30am-2am; ⓡWestlake) Part of a small West Coast chain of Irish pubs, this location is the most atmospheric and authentic, with its exposed-brick walls, multiple nooks and crannies, and rosy-cheeked crowd. The perfectly poured Imperial pints of Guinness are divine and there's live Irish (or Irish-inspired) music nightly (no cover charge).

☆ ENTERTAINMENT

☆ Downtown

★**A CONTEMPORARY THEATRE** THEATER

Map p224 (ACT; www.acttheatre.org; 700 Union St; ⓡUniversity St) One of the three big companies in the city, the theater fills its $30-million home at Kreielsheimer Place with performances by Seattle's best thespians and occasional big-name actors. Terraced seating surrounds a central stage and the interior has gorgeous architectural embellishments.

SHOWBOX LIVE MUSIC

Map p224 (☎206-628-3151; www.showboxonline.com/market; 1426 1st Ave; ⓡUniversity St) This cavernous 1137-capacity showroom –

LOCAL KNOWLEDGE

STARBUCKS: IT STARTED HERE (ALMOST)

It's practically impossible to walk through the door of **Starbucks** (Map p224; 1912 Pike Pl; ⊙6am-9pm) in Pike Place Market without appearing in someone's Facebook photo, so dense is the tourist traffic. But, while this hallowed business might be the world's oldest surviving Starbucks store, it is not – as many assume – the world's first Starbucks location, nor is it Seattle's oldest espresso bar. The original Starbucks opened in 1971 at 2000 Western Ave (at Western Ave's north end). It moved to its current location, a block away, in 1976. The honor of Seattle's oldest continuously running coffee bar goes to Café Allegro in the U District, which opened in 1975. Until the early 1980s Starbucks operated purely as a retail store that sold coffee beans and equipment (plus the odd taster cup). The company didn't open up its first espresso bar until 1984, after CEO Howard Shultz returned from an epiphanic trip to Italy. The Pike Place cafe is unique in that, in keeping with the traditional unbranded ethos of the market, it doesn't sell food or baked goods – just coffee.

Other interesting Starbucks facilities in Seattle include the cafe on the 40th floor of the Columbia Center (Seattle's tallest building); the company's first LEED-certified cafe that opened downtown on the corner of Pike St and 1st Ave in 2009 and sports the original brown logo, and Roy Street Coffee & Tea in Capitol Hill. The latter is sometimes known as a 'stealth Starbucks' as, despite being run by the company, it goes under a different name and is used as a testing ground for new ideas and products.

which hosts mostly national touring acts, ranging from indie rock to hip-hop – reinvents itself every few years and successfully rode the grunge bandwagon while it lasted. Between sets, hop over to the attached Green Room, the venue's smaller bar and restaurant.

TRIPLE DOOR
CLUB

Map p224 (✆206-838-4333; www.thetripledoor.net; 216 Union St; ◉University St) This club downstairs from Wild Ginger restaurant (p50) has a liberal booking policy that includes country and rock as well as jazz, gospel, R&B, world music and burlesque performances. There's a full menu and valet parking; the club is all-ages before 9:30pm.

5TH AVENUE THEATER
THEATER

Map p224 (✆206-625-1900; www.5thavenue.org; 1308 5th Ave; ◉box office 9:30am-5:30pm Mon-Fri; ◉University St) Built in 1926 with an opulent Asian motif, the 5th Avenue opened as a vaudeville house; it was later turned into a movie theater and then closed in 1979. An influx of funding and a heritage award saved it in 1980, and now it's Seattle's premier theater for Broadway musical revivals. It's worth going just for a look at the architecture.

Tickets are available by phone or at the theater box office.

PARAMOUNT THEATER
THEATER

Map p224 (✆206-682-1414; www.stgpresents.org; 911 Pine St; ◉10) A theater with a checkered history, the Paramount dates from 1928 and was originally conceived as a movie house with back-up from the popular vaudeville acts of the day. It continued as a cinema until 1971 (Bruce Lee was briefly an usher), whereupon it became a rock venue, lost money and degenerated into a tatty shadow of its former self (notwithstanding, Pink Floyd and the Grateful Dead both played legendary shows here).

Saved from demolition and listed as a historic monument in the mid-'70s, it was restored to its Jazz Age finery in 1995 and has since operated as an esteemed multi-performance venue (rock, comedy, theater), though its forte is touring Broadway shows.

SEATTLE SYMPHONY
CLASSICAL MUSIC

Map p224 (www.seattlesymphony.org; ◉University St) A major regional ensemble. It plays at the Benaroya Concert Hall, which you'll find downtown at 2nd Ave and University St.

☆ Pike Place Market & Waterfront

MARKET THEATER
THEATER

Map p224 (✆206-781-9273; www.unexpectedproductions.org; 1428 Post Alley; ◉Westlake) The Market Theater hosts improvisational comedy, called Theatersports, on Friday and Saturday nights at 10:30pm. Weekday shows are varied and usually start around 8:30pm. Buy tickets at www.brownpapertickets.com or call 800-838-3006.

🔒 SHOPPING

The main shopping area in Seattle is downtown between 3rd and 6th Aves and between University and Stewart Sts. If you're anywhere nearby, you can't miss it.

For the compulsive browser, amateur chef, hungry traveler on a budget, or anyone else with their five senses fully intact, Seattle has no greater attraction than Pike Place Market. This is shopping central in Seattle: dozens of market food stalls hawk everything from geoduck clams to fennel root to harissa. Locals shops here just as much as tourists.

For the full gamut of souvenirs, simply stroll up and down the boardwalk along the waterfront.

🔒 Downtown

LEGACY LTD GALLERY
ARTS & CRAFTS

Map p224 (✆206-624-6350; 1003 1st Ave; ◉11am-5:30pm Tue-Sat; ◉Pioneer Sq) Legacy Ltd is an internationally known and widely respected source of Northwest Coast Indian and Inuit art and artifacts, including baskets and jewelry. It's good for a browse even if you don't happen to be a museum curator or a millionaire.

SWAY & CAKE
CLOTHING

Map p224 (✆206-624-2699; 1631 6th Ave; ◉11am-6pm Mon-Sat; ◉Westlake) This cute little upscale boutique has cute little designer dresses and jeans from hot names like Rag & Bone, Diane von Fürstenberg and Helmut Lang. Sales staff are friendly, even if you're dressed down.

BURYING THE ALASKAN WAY VIADUCT

'Nice bay, shame about the flyover' is a comment you'll sometimes hear yelled above the din of traffic on Seattle's cacophonous waterfront. The flyover in question is the Alaskan Way Viaduct, an ugly elevated section of state Rte 99 built between 1949 and 1953 that carries over 100,000 vehicles a day through downtown Seattle. In the pioneering era of the motor car, the viaduct served its purpose, redirecting traffic away from Seattle's downtown grid and keeping the peace in Pike Place Market; but by the 1970s many Seattleites had started to view it as a noisy eyesore that was doing untold damage to the city's potentially idyllic waterfront. D Day came in February 2001, when the viaduct was significantly damaged by the 6.8-magnitude Nisqually earthquake. Although emergency repairs were quickly carried out, the structure was no longer considered safe in such an earthquake-prone city. What would happen if a really big one hit?

Long debates ensued about possible transport alternatives along Seattle's waterfront (the city even held a popular ballot on the issue) until it was finally agreed in 2009 that the viaduct should be dismantled and a 2-mile-long tunnel built in its place (the world's largest bored tunnel by diameter). After years of planning, a specially designed boring machine, made in Japan and nicknamed 'Bertha' after Seattle's first female mayor, began digging in the summer of 2013. The $3.1-billion tunnel is expected to be finished by 2015, whereupon the Alaskan Way Viaduct will be dismantled and consigned to the history books.

The Washington State Department of Transportation has set up a clever, interactive information center in Pioneer Square pertaining to the tunnel project called Milepost 31 (p67).

ALHAMBRA CLOTHING

Map p224 (www.alhambrastyle.com; 101 Pine St; ⏲10am-6:30pm Mon-Sat, 11:30am-6pm Sun; Ⓜ Westlake) Beautifully laid out designer boutique showcasing elegant women's clothing for those with fat wallets (or envious window-shoppers).

BELLA UMBRELLA ACCESSORIES

Map p224 (☎206-297-1540; www.bellaumbrella.com; 1535 1st Ave; ⏲10am-6pm Mon-Sat, 11am-5pm Sun; Ⓜ Westlake) Highly convenient pitstop on those 150 days of the year when you walk past and it's raining. If it's sunny, Bella Umbrella has a large collection of parasols, vintage umbrellas and wedding props.

NORTH FACE OUTDOORS

Map p224 (☎206-622-4111; 1023 1st Ave; ⏲10am-7pm Mon-Sat, 11am-6pm Sun; Ⓜ Pioneer Sq) For hardcore camping, climbing and hiking clothing and equipment, go to the North Face, downtown toward the waterfront.

MACY'S CLOTHING

Map p224 (☎206-344-2121; 1601 3rd Ave; ⏲10am-9pm Mon-Sat, 11am-7pm Sun; Ⓜ Westlake) Seattle's oldest and largest department store, this hard-to-miss classic – formerly Bon-Marché, but renamed Bon-Macy's in August 2003 when it was bought by Macy's, then shortened for convenience – is a mainstay of clothing and homewares shopping.

BARNES & NOBLE BOOKS

Map p224 (600 Pine St; ⏲9am-10pm Mon-Thu, to 11pm Fri-Sun; Ⓜ Westlake) Since the demise of Borders in 2011 and the relocation of Elliott Bay Books to Capitol Hill, Barnes & Noble remains downtown's main book emporium, with generous opening hours and helpful, well-read staff.

NIKETOWN CLOTHING

Map p224 (☎206-447-6453; 1500 6th Ave; ⏲10am-8pm; Ⓜ Westlake) The huge Niketown has its roots in the Northwest – it was founded by Phil Knight in Eugene, OR. The store sells all kinds of Nike clothing, shoes and accessories, and acts as a sort of museum for the company's marketing campaign, with posters and quotations from some of its endorsement stars covering the walls.

NORDSTROM CLOTHING

Map p224 (☎206-628-2111; Pine St btwn 5th & 6th Aves; ⏲9:30am-9pm Mon-Sat, 10am-7pm Sun; Ⓜ Westlake) Born and raised in Seattle by a Klondike gold-rush profiteer, this chain department store occupies a giant space in the former Frederick and Nelson Building. Closer to Pike Place Market, **Nordstrom Rack** (Map p224; ☑206-448-8522; 1601 2nd Ave) offers closeouts and returns from the parent store.

BROOKS BROTHERS   CLOTHING

Map p224 (☑206-624-4400; 1330 5th Ave; ⊙9:30am-7pm Mon-Fri, 10am-6pm Sat, noon-5pm Sun; ඹUniversity St) This is the undisputed destination for classy men's clothing in the neighborhood. The salespeople are total pros – they greet you at the door, take your measurements and avoid all signs of being pushy.

PACIFIC PLACE   MALL

Map p224 (www.pacificplaceseattle.com; 600 Pine St; ඹWestlake) Seattle's best-quality boutique mall feels a bit like the lobby of an upscale hotel – it's cylindrical, and the total lack of that hectic shopping-mall vibe makes it very pleasant to walk around.

Clothiers include **J Crew** (☑206-652-9788), **Club Monaco** (☑206-264-8001) and **BCBG** (☑206-447-3400). Large stores such as **Williams-Sonoma** (☑206-624-1422) are fun to look around in.

Take a moment to gape in the window at **Tiffany & Co** (☑206-264-1400) or saunter inside for a special gift. The mall's top level features a movie theater, a pub and a couple of restaurants. This is also where you'll find the nicest public restrooms in downtown Seattle.

WESTLAKE CENTER   MALL

Map p224 (☑206-467-3044; www.westlake center.com; cnr 4th Ave & Pine St; ඹWestlake) This 'boutique mall' – also the starting point for the monorail – has turned into a landmark, partly because of its location and the fact that its concrete patio and steps make a nice gathering point.

It's somehow heartening to see ragtag groups of antiwar protesters (and an inordinate number of cops) rallying in front of such a monument to the big American dollar.

Inside you'll find shops like **Lush** (☑206-624-5874) and **Made in Washington** (☑206-623-1063). Local stores include an outlet of **Fireworks** (☑206-682-6462), which offers inexpensive arty products by regional craftspeople – they make great gifts.

🏠 Pike Place Market & Waterfront

★DELAURENTI'S   FOOD

Map p224 (☑206-622-0141; cnr 1st Ave & Pike Pl; ⊙9am-6pm Mon-Sat, 10am-5pm Sun; ඹUniversity St) DeLaurenti's is a mandatory market stop for the Italian chef or continental food enthusiast. Not only is there a stunning selection of cheese, sausages, hams and pasta, but there's also the largest selection of capers, olive oil and anchovies that you're likely to find this side of Genoa. The wine selection is also quite broad.

TENZING MOMO   APOTHECARY

Map p224 (☑206-623-9837; www.tenzingmomo. com; Economy Market Bldg, Pike Place Market; ⊙10am-6pm; ඹUniversity St) Doing a good impersonation of one of the magic shops in Diagon Alley from the Harry Potter books, Tenzing Momo, is an old-school natural apothecary, with shelves of mysterious glass bottles filled with herbs and tinctures to treat any ailment.

MARKET MAGIC   MAGIC

Map p224 (☑206-624-4271; www.general rubric.com; 1501 Pike Pl, No 427; ⊙9:30am-5pm; ඹWestlake) Selling fake dog turds, stink bombs, water-squirting rings and magic tricks, this Pike Place magic shop is heaven for aspiring magicians, pranksters, school kids, and grown-ups who wish they still were school kids.

LA BUONA TAVOLA   FOOD

Map p224 (www.trufflecafe.com; 1524 Pike Pl; ⊙10am-6pm; ඹWestlake) If you're struggling to work out which fine Pike Place artisan product to take home with you, here's some friendly advice: proceed directly to La Buona Tavola and buy its truffle oil. Made from high-quality Italian truffles, this is a unique and hard-to-procure substance in North America and well worth the investment. Bonus: they'll let you sample it for free.

LEFT BANK BOOKS   BOOKS

Map p224 (www.leftbankbooks.com; 92 Pike St; ⊙10am-7pm Mon-Sat, 11am-6pm Sun; ඹWestlake) This 38-year-old collective displays 'zines in *español,* revolutionary pamphlets, a 'fuck authority' notice board and plenty of Chomsky. You're in Seattle, just in case you forgot.

SUR LA TABLE
COOKWARE

Map p224 (www.surlatable.com; 84 Pine St; ⊗9am-6:30pm; 🚇Westlake) It's hard to miss this gigantic cookware store. It's a chain, but a good one, and it started here in Seattle. The rich supply of cookware, books, gear and gadgets is bound to entice any foodie, gourmand or gourmet.

PURE FOOD FISH
FOOD

Map p224 (☎206-622-5765; www.freshseafood. com; 1511 Pike Pl; ⊗9am-5pm; 🚇Westlake) Perhaps the gift that says 'I heart Seattle' the most is a whole salmon or other fresh seafood from the fish markets. All the markets will prepare fish for transportation on the plane ride home, or you can just call and have them take care of the overnight shipping; Pure Food Fish has the best reputation locally for quality and value.

METSKER MAPS
MAPS

Map p224 (☎206-623-8747; www.metskers.com; 1511 1st Ave; ⊗9am-8pm Mon-Fri, 10am-6pm Sat & Sun; 🚇Westlake) In its high-profile location on 1st Ave, this legendary map shop sells all kinds of useful things for the traveler, from maps to guidebooks to various accessories. It also has a good selection of armchair-travel lit and pretty spinning globes for the dreamers.

MADE IN WASHINGTON
SOUVENIRS

Map p224 (☎206-467-0788; www.madeinwash ington.com; 1530 Post Alley; ⊗7am-5:30pm Mon-Fri, 10am-6pm Sat & Sun; 🚇Westlake) If you're looking for something authentically Northwest, head to Made in Washington. One of several locations around the city, it stocks arts and crafts, T-shirts, coffee and chocolate, smoked salmon, regional wines, books and handy creations like the 'Bite of Washington' gourmet-food gift basket.

YE OLDE CURIOSITY SHOP
SOUVENIRS

Map p224 (☎206-682-5844; Pier 54; ⊗9am-9pm; 🚇University St) This landmark shop, on Pier 54, now has a lesser sibling, Ye Olde Curiosity Shoppe Too – but never mind that. The original shop is where you'll find cabinets of shrunken heads, piglets in jars and dried puffer fish – not for sale, of course, just for atmosphere.

Also not for sale are the famous black diamond, Chief Seattle's hat, a variety of stalagmites and 'tites, and some pretty cool fortune-telling machines. The funniest souvenir available for purchase is a Mt St Helens 'snowglobe' – instead of snow, it has little gray particles meant to look like ash from the volcano's eruption.

SOUK
SPICES

Map p224 (☎206-441-1666; 1916 Pike Pl; ⊗10am-6pm; 🚇Westlake) Supplies here include Middle Eastern and North African spices and foods. Named after the Arabic word for marketplace, the shop sells everything you'll need to get from cookbook to curry – including cookbooks and curries.

READ ALL ABOUT IT
MAGAZINES

Map p224 (93 Pike St; ⊗10am-6pm; 🚇University St) Who said magazines are dead? You can read all about it at this Pike Place Market newsstand in *Jazz Times, Surfer Journal, Cigar Aficionado*, Spanish tattoo mags, Italian gossip tabloids, Russian comics and the good old *Buddhist Times*.

GOLDEN AGE COLLECTABLES
TOYS

Map p224 (☎206-622-9799; downstairs, 1501 Pike Place Market; 🚇Westlake) A haven for geeks, kids and, especially, geeky kids, this shop has comics and comic-book–inspired toys, novelty items (hopping nuns etc), costumes and loads of goth-friendly knickknacks.

OLD SEATTLE PAPERWORKS
POSTERS, MAGAZINES

Map p224 (www.oldseattlepaperworks.com; downstairs, 1501 Pike Place Market; ⊗10am-5pm; 🚇Westlake) If you like decorating your home with old magazine covers from *Life, Time*, and *Rolling Stone*, have a penchant for art-deco tourist posters from the 1930s, or are looking for that rare Hendrix concert flyer from 1969, this is your nirvana. It's in the market's Down Under section.

🏃 SPORTS & ACTIVITIES

🏃 Downtown

SEATTLE CYCLING TOURS
CYCLING

Map p224 (☎206-356-5803; www.seattle -cycling-tours.com; 714 Pike St; tours from $49; 🚌10) With Seattle mayor Mike McGinn an avid cyclist, it's not surprising that the city's bike culture is improving. Perhaps one of the best ways for new visitors to get oriented is with a bike tour. Seattle Cycling Tours

DOWNTOWN, PIKE PLACE & WATERFRONT SPORTS & ACTIVITIES

FUTURE OF FLIGHT AVIATION CENTER & BOEING TOUR

One of the Seattle area's most worthwhile outlying sights is the **Future of Flight Aviation Center & Boeing Tour** (☑1-800-464-1476; www.futureofflight.org; 8415 Paine Field Blvd; adult/child $18/12; ☺8:30am-5:30pm) in the city of Everett, 25 miles north of Seattle. Serving as a good complement to Georgetown's Museum of Flight, the Center, aside from its museum, offers something different: a tour of the real working Boeing factory where the famous airplanes are made. The huge complex is actually the world's most voluminous building, meaning the 90-minute tours involve plenty of traveling around, some of it by bus. Getting to the center without a car can be a pain, but you can save time by partaking in an organized tour with **Tours Northwest** (☑206-768-1234; www.toursnorthwest.com), which picks up from downtown hotels. It charges $65/49 per adult/child, including admission. No cameras are allowed.

organizes some corkers. Two tours leave daily from its downtown base, the best going all the way to Ballard Locks, avoiding Seattle's famous hills.

Another option is the longer weekend ride to Bainbridge Island. It also rents bikes ($24 for two hours). Book online.

SBR SEATTLE BICYCLE
RENTAL & TOURS
CYCLING

Map p224 (☑800-349-0343; www.seattlebicyclerentals.com; Pier 58; rental per hr/day $10/40; ☺11am-7pm Wed-Mon; 🚊University St) Bike-rental point offering reasonable rates and also daily tours. Book online.

DOWNTOWN SEATTLE YMCA
GYM

Map p224 (☑206-382-5010; www.seattleymca.org; 909 4th Ave; day pass $10-15; ☺5am-9pm

Mon-Fri, 7am-6:30pm Sat, 11am-6:30pm Sun; 🚊60) The Y is notably traveler-friendly, and this location has clean, classy, updated equipment including a pool, free weights, cardio equipment and child care.

GOLD'S GYM
GYM

Map p224 (☑206-583-0640; 1310 4th Ave, No 101; day pass $10-15; ☺5am-11pm Mon-Thu, 5am-9pm Fri, 7am-7pm Sat & Sun) The downtown branch of this chain has first-rate facilities for cardio and strength training, plus classes in aerobics, yoga, Pilates, dance, kickboxing and karate. Massage, personal training, a sauna and a women-only section are also available.

Pioneer Square & International District

PIONEER SQUARE | INTERNATIONAL DISTRICT

Neighborhood Top Five

1 Reliving the spirit of the gold rush at the inspiring **Klondike Gold Rush National Historical Park** (p66), set in one of the many redbrick Richardsonian Romanesque buildings that sprang up after the 1889 Great Fire.

2 Plugging into the spirit of the times and enjoying a damn fine cup of coffee at **Zeitgeist** (p72).

3 Searching for and finding a boisterous **dim sum restaurant** in the International District (p71).

4 Getting culturally tuned in on a **First Thursday Art Walk** (p74).

5 Taking an old-school elevator up to the 35th floor of the **Smith Tower** (p65).

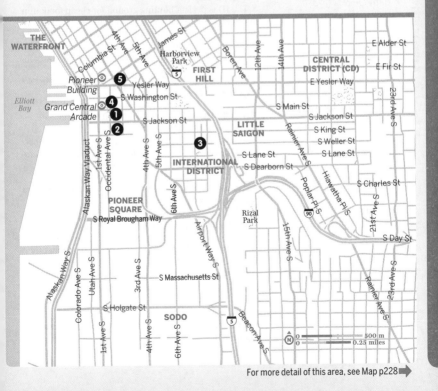

For more detail of this area, see Map p228 ➡

Lonely Planet's Top Tip

Pioneer Square social life is heavily affected by the sports events that go on at the two adjacent stadiums. If you like your pubs and restaurants loud and boisterous, come on a game day. If you don't, go elsewhere.

✖ Best Places to Eat

➡ Tamarind Tree (p72)

➡ Bar Sajor (p71)

➡ Green Leaf (p71)

➡ Delicatus (p71)

For reviews, see p70 ➡

🍷 Best Places to Drink

➡ Zeitgeist (p72)

➡ Caffè Umbria (p73)

➡ Panama Hotel Tea & Coffee House (p73)

➡ Pyramid Ale House (p73)

For reviews, see p72 ➡

👁 Best Architectural Gems

➡ Smith Tower (p65)

➡ King Street Station (p66)

➡ Pioneer Building (p65)

➡ Pioneer Square pergola (p66)

For reviews, see p66 ➡

Explore: Pioneer Square & International District

Browsing the Pioneer Square Historic District is rather like visiting a movie set of early-20th-century Seattle, except that the food and the shopping are better. This is the birthplace of Seattle, and the redbrick district of historical buildings, antique shops and musty bars is still a real crossroads of the modern city.

Some visitors arrive by long-distance bus or train at King Street Station, a good place to get oriented due to its proximity to a trio of local squares. Pioneer Square Park is an architectural showpiece, Occidental Park has a handy information booth, and just off Occidental Sq Zeitgeist will brew your first (and possibly best) Seattle coffee. Across the street from Zeitgeist is the fantastic, free Klondike Gold Rush National Historical Park, which will quickly make you an expert on Seattle's history. Take time to wander the streets afterwards to admire the handsome architecture.

Next door to Pioneer Square, but nothing like it architecturally, is the International District (ID) – Seattle's de facto Chinatown. The 'international' moniker has some merit: while predominantly Chinese, there is a strong Vietnamese presence and some interesting Japanese pioneer history.

The ID is perfect hunting ground for cheap food: dim sum and Vietnamese *pho* predominate. You'll also find the Wing Luke Asian Museum and the delectable Panama Hotel Tea & Coffee House. Hidden treasures include everything from sketchy pet shops to a pinball museum.

Local Life

➡**Uwajimaya** Shop for exotic fruit and vegetables in this giant Asian community market.

➡**Salami Talk** Exchange work grumbles, make dates or discuss the merits of *finocchiona* salami over *sopressata* in the perennial queue at sandwich bar Salumi.

Getting There & Away

➡**Bus** Pioneer Square is a few blocks from downtown, so any of the city buses that stop in downtown will get you pretty close. Metro bus 7 runs to the ID frequently from 3rd Ave downtown.

➡**Light Rail** Link Light Rail from Seattle-Tacoma Airport stops at Pioneer Square Station or International District/Chinatown Station. It carries on to Westlake Station in downtown.

➡**Streetcar** Runs from S Jackson St to First Hill and Capitol Hill.

TOP SIGHT
PIONEER SQUARE ARCHITECTURE

Some important heirlooms are concentrated in Pioneer Square, the district that sprang up after the 1889 Great Fire. Instantly recognizable by its handsome redbrick buildings, the neighborhood's predominant architectural style is Richardsonian Romanesque, strongly influenced by America's Chicago School.

DON'T MISS...

➡ Smith Tower
➡ Pioneer Building
➡ Grand Central Arcade

Pioneer Building

Built in 1891, the magnificent **Pioneer Building** (Map p228; 606 1st Ave S) facing Pioneer Square Park is one of the finest Victorian buildings in Seattle, and showcases many of the classic components of Richardsonian Romanesque; look for the Roman arches, a recessed main doorway, curvaceous bay windows and decorative flourishes, most notably the two frontal columns that frame some skillfully embellished bricks.

PRACTICALITIES

➡ Map p228
➡ btwn Alaskan Way S, S King St, 5th Ave S, 2nd Ave ext & Columbia St
➡ ℝPioneer Sq

Smith Tower

The 42-story neoclassical **Smith Tower** (Map p228; cnr 2nd Ave S & Yesler Way; observation deck adult/child $7.50/5; ⊙10am-dusk) was, for half a century after its construction in 1914, the tallest building west of Chicago. The beaux arts–inspired lobby is paneled in onyx and marble, while the brass-and-copper elevator is still manually operated. The public can access the 35th-floor Chinese Room, with its hand-carved ceiling.

Grand Central Arcade

This lovely meeting point was originally Squire's Opera House, erected in 1879. When the Opera House burned down, it was rebuilt as the Squire-Latimer Building in 1890 and later became the Grand Central Hotel. The hotel died during the Depression, but it underwent a major restoration in the 1970s and now contains two floors of shops.

◉ SIGHTS

◉ Pioneer Square

PIONEER SQUARE NEIGHBORHOOD
See p65.

**KLONDIKE GOLD RUSH
NATIONAL HISTORICAL PARK** MUSEUM
Map p228 (www.nps.gov/klse; 117 S Main St;
⊘9am-5pm; ⍟International District/Chinatown)
FREE This is a shockingly good museum eloquently run by the US National Park Service with exhibits, photos and news clippings from the 1897 Klondike gold rush, when a Seattle-on-steroids acted as a fueling depot for prospectors bound for the Yukon in Canada. It would cost $10 anywhere else; in Seattle it's free!

The best aspect of the museum is its clever use of storytelling. At the outset you are introduced to five local characters who became stampeders (Klondike prospectors) in the 1890s and you are invited to follow their varying fortunes and experiences periodically throughout the rest of the museum. Sound effects and interactive exhibits are used to good effect.

The museum is housed in the old Cadillac Hotel (built in 1889) that was rescued from a grisly fate after nearly being toppled in the 2001 Nisqually earthquake. It opened in 2006.

KING STREET STATION LANDMARK
Map p228 (303 S Jackson St; ⍟International District/Chinatown) One of the pillars upon which Seattle built its early fortunes, the old Great Northern Railroad depot has suffered a lot of neglect since the 1960s – although the tide is now turning. The western terminus of the famous *Empire Builder* train that still runs cross-country between Seattle and Chicago, this jewel of a train station was designed to imitate St Mark's bell tower in Venice.

It was originally constructed in 1906 by Reed & Stem, who also designed New York City's Grand Central Station, and is notable for many features, not least a fabulous Italianate plasterwork ceiling in the waiting room that is rich in period detail. The waiting room was covered up by a horrible suspended ceiling in the 1960s but, as part of a recent $26-million revamp, the entire interior and exterior of the station has been returned to its gilded age high watermark.

OCCIDENTAL PARK PARK
Map p228 (btwn S Washington & S Main Sts; ⍟Pioneer Sq) Notable in this cobblestone plaza, just off 1st Ave S, are the **totem poles** carved by Duane Pasco, a nationally respected Chinookan carver and artist from Poulsbo on the Kitsap Peninsula. The totems depict the welcoming spirit of Kwakiutl, a totem bear, the tall Sun and Raven, and a man riding on the tail of a whale.

Also eye-catching is the **Firefighters' Memorial**, featuring life-size bronze sculptures of firefighters in action. Engraved on the granite slabs surrounding the sculpture are the names of Seattle firefighters who have been killed in the line of duty since the department's inception after the Great Fire. The artist is Hai Ying Wu, a University of Washington graduate.

OCCIDENTAL SQUARE SQUARE
Map p228 (btwn S Main & S Jackson Sts; ⍟Pioneer Sq) Occidental Sq, another cobblestone space flanked by unusually handsome Victorian buildings, is one of the nicest places in this area. Visit **Glasshouse Studio** to see local artists' impressive works of blown, cast and lamp-worked glass.

If you need a shot of caffeine or a chance to catch your breath, make the pilgrimage to Zeitgeist. This coffeehouse is a local haunt of artists and architects. Along S Jackson St you'll find an excellent concentration of antique stores and some of the city's most prestigious galleries.

PIONEER SQUARE PARK SQUARE
Map p228 (cnr Cherry St & 1st Ave S) The original Pioneer Square is a cobbled triangular plaza where Henry Yesler's sawmill cut the giant trees that marked Seattle's first industry. Known officially as Pioneer Square Park, the plaza features a bust of **Chief Seattle** (Sealth, in the original language), an ornate pergola and a **totem pole**.

Some wayward early Seattleites, so the story goes, stole the totem pole from the Tlingit native people in southeastern Alaska in 1890. An arsonist lit the pole aflame in 1938, burning it to the ground. When asked if they could carve a replacement pole, the Tlingit took the money offered, thanking the city for payment for the first totem, and said it would cost $5000 to carve another one. The city coughed up the money and the Tlingit obliged with the pole you see today.

The decorative **pergola** was built in the early 1900s to serve as an entryway to an underground lavatory and to shelter those waiting for the cable car that went up and down Yesler Way. The reportedly elaborate restroom eventually closed due to serious plumbing problems at high tide. In January 2001, the pergola was leveled by a wayward truck, but it was restored and put back where it belonged the following year, looking as good as new.

WATERFALL PARK · PARK

Map p228 (cnr S Main St & 2nd Ave S; ☒Pioneer Sq) This unusual park is an urban oasis commemorating workers of the United Parcel Service (UPS), which grew out of a messenger service that began in a basement at this location in 1907. The artificial 22ft waterfall that flows in this tiny open-air courtyard is flanked by tables and flowering plants.

This is the perfect spot to eat a brown-bag lunch or to rest weary feet.

YESLER WAY · STREET

Map p228 (☒Pioneer Sq) Seattle claims its Yesler Way was the coining ground for the term 'skid road' – logs would 'skid' down the steeply sloped road linking a logging area above town to Henry Yesler's mill.

As for Henry Yesler himself, local historians paint him as an ambitious business zealot who clashed frequently with the wild-and-woolly Doc Maynard. These two men, who by all accounts were equally stubborn, both owned part of the land that would eventually become Pioneer Square. This resulted in a highly symbolic grid clash, in which Yesler's section of the square had streets running parallel to the river, while Maynard's came crashing in at a north–south angle. Yesler maintained, not unreasonably, that Doc was drunk when he submitted his portion of the plans.

ROQ LA RUE · GALLERY

Map p228 (www.roqlarue.com; 532 1st Ave S; ☒1-6pm Wed-Sat; ☒Pioneer Sq) **FREE** This gallery, recently relocated from Belltown, has secured its reputation by taking risks: the work on view here skates along the edge of urban pop-culture. Since opening in 1998, the gallery, which is owned and curated by Kirsten Anderson, has been a significant force in the pop surrealism field, and is frequently featured in *Juxtapoz* magazine.

MILEPOST 31 · MUSEUM

Map p228 (211 1st Ave S; ☒11am-5pm Tue-Sat; ☒Pioneer Sq) **FREE** A project as compre-

hensive and long-winded as the Alaskan Viaduct Replacement Program requires an explanatory museum, and this small but concise exhibit in Pioneer Square does a fine of job of relaying the facts – plus there are some fascinating nuggets of incidental Seattle history thrown in for good measure. Numerous old photos and a scale model of the drilling machine encourage lingering.

The exhibit will remain open as long as the program lasts – until 2016 at least.

FOSTER/WHITE GALLERY · GALLERY

Map p228 (☒206-622-2833; www.fosterwhite.com; 220 3rd Ave S; ☒10am-6pm Tue-Sat; ☒International District/Chinatown) **FREE** The famed Foster/White Gallery, which opened in 1968, features glassworks, paintings and sculpture by mainstream Northwest artists in a beautifully renovated 7000-sq-ft space. Some of the exhibits are for sale (if you're rich), but realistically, if you're from hoi polloi, this is more a contemporary art gallery – and a fine one too – that deserves half an hour of quiet contemplation.

SEATTLE METROPOLITAN POLICE MUSEUM · MUSEUM

Map p228 (www.seametropolicemuseum.org; 317 3rd Ave S; adult/child $5/3; ☒11am-4pm Tue-Sat; ☒International District/Chinatown) Riot-control gear, uniforms, a jail cell...welcome to the police museum, apparently the largest of its kind on the West Coast. Varied exhibits set out to 'demystify' the police force. There's an interactive play area for kids.

◉ International District

WING LUKE ASIAN MUSEUM · MUSEUM

Map p228 (www.wingluke.org; 719 S King St; adult/child $12.95/8.95; ☒10am-5pm Tue-Sun; ☒Chinatown/International District E) Relocated and refurbished in 2008, the Wing Luke examines Asian and Pacific American culture, focusing on prickly issues such as Chinese settlement in the 1880s and Japanese internment camps in WWII. There are also art exhibits and a preserved immigrant apartment. Guided tours are available and recommended.

UWAJIMAYA · MALL

Map p228 (☒206-624-6248; 600 5th Ave S; ☒9am-10pm; ☒Chinatown/International District West) Founded by Fujimatsu Moriguchi, one of the few Japanese to return here from the

THE ORIGINAL SKID ROW

Recognized as a byword for decrepit down-at-heel urban neighborhoods everywhere, the term 'skid row' originated in Seattle in the 1860s when greased logs were skidded down First Hill to a timber mill on the shores of Elliott Bay owned by a local lumber entrepreneur named Henry Yesler. The mill road – known officially as Yesler Way but colloquially as Skid Row – was punctuated by a strip of bawdy bars that grew up to support a rambunctious population of itinerant mill workers. Famed for its drunken revelry and occasional fistfights, the area quickly acquired an unsavory reputation, causing Seattle's affluent classes to migrate north to the newer, more salubrious streets of what is now the downtown core. Meanwhile, 'Skid Row' was left to slip into a long and inglorious decline, and an infamous nickname was born.

After decades of poverty, Yesler Way finally came out of its coma in the 1970s after a vociferous community campaign saved the Pioneer Square Historic District from the demolition ball. Sandwiched amid the handsome redbrick edifices of Seattle's original downtown, it's a gritty but innocuous place these days where the only log you'll see is the lofty Native American totem pole that towers over nearby Pioneer Square Park.

WWII internment camps, this large department and grocery store – a cornerstone of Seattle's Asian community – has everything from fresh fish and exotic fruits and vegetables to cooking utensils, and you'll come face-to-face with those dim sum ingredients you've always wondered about.

The current location is a self-styled community that includes living quarters and occupies a whole block. There's a food court in addition to the grocery store. It's a great place to browse. Sharing the same building as Uwajimaya, Kinokuniya bookstore has an excellent collection of books about Asia and by Asian writers in several Asian languages and English, as well as imported CDs and DVDs.

SEATTLE PINBALL MUSEUM   MUSEUM, GAMES
Map p228 (508 Maynard Ave S; ⊘11am-5pm Sun & Mon, 6-9pm Thu, 2-10pm Fri, 1-10pm Sat; ⚑; ⚑Chinatown/International District E) Got kids? Got kid-like tendencies? Love the buzzers and bells of good old-fashioned games machines? Lay aside your iPad apps and become a pinball wizard for the day in this fantastic games room in the ID with antique machines from the 1960s onwards. Just $10 buys you unlimited games time. Sure plays a mean pinball!

HAU HAU MARKET   MARKET
Map p228 (☎206-329-1688; 412 12th Ave S; ⚑Little Saigon) Hau Hau is a modern and bustling Chinese and Vietnamese food market where you can get cheap produce, specialty meats such as pig's ears and chicken's feet, fireworks, and Asian gifts and knickknacks.

HING HAY PARK   SQUARE
Map p228 (cnr Maynard Ave S & S King St; ⚑Chinatown/International District E) If you need a tranquil spot to rest while wandering the ID, Hing Hay Park lends a little green to the otherwise austere district. The traditional Chinese pavilion was a gift from the people of Taipei. On Saturdays in August you can catch a free outdoor movie here beginning at sunset, sponsored by the Seattle Chinatown-International District, which also runs the summer Night Market here.

INTERNATIONAL CHILDREN'S PARK   PARK
Map p228 (cnr S Lane St & 7th Ave S; ⚑; ⚑Chinatown/International District E) If the kids aren't up for exploring the Asian markets or sitting still for a dim sum brunch, bring them here to work off some energy by playing on the bronze dragon sculpture, designed by George Tsutakawa, a Seattle native who spent much of his childhood in Japan, then returned to become an internationally renowned sculptor and painter and a professor at the University of Washington.

UNION STATION   LANDMARK
Map p228 (401 S Jackson St; ⚑International District/Chinatown) Another landmark to benefit from restoration fever is Union Station, the old Union Pacific Railroad depot (1911) that was unoccupied between 1971 and 1999. The restoration project included the preservation of the original tile floors, clocks and windows. More than 90 years of grime was hand-scrubbed off the exterior brick.

The Great Hall, half the size of a football field, remains an impressive space.

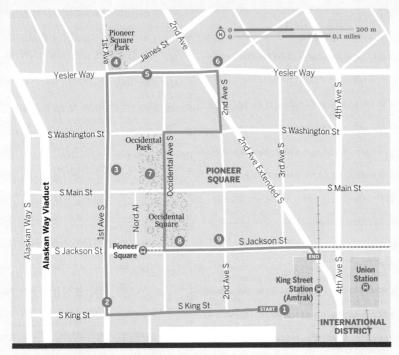

Neighborhood Walk
Historical Pioneer Square Circuit

START KING STREET STATION
FINISH KING STREET STATION
LENGTH 1 MILE; ONE HOUR

Start off at ❶ **King Street Station** (p66), recently returned to its 'gilded age' glory. Before the advent of cars this was most people's first impression of Seattle. Exiting via the side door, walk west along King St in the shadow of Safeco Field; the bars and restaurants here are packed with baseball supporters on match days. Turn right onto redbrick ❷ **1st Avenue South**, little altered since it rose in the aftermath of the 1889 fire. Galleries and antique shops will catch your eye, but be sure to descend, as President Obama recently did, to the ❸ **Grand Central Baking Co** (p70) for cakes and sandwiches. ❹ **Pioneer Square Park** (p66) is usually awash with tourists and homeless people, including local characters selling the newspaper *Real Change*. The small triangular park sports an Eiffel-esque iron pergola and the

Richardsonian Romanesque Pioneer Building. Leading east, ❺ **Yesler Way** (p67) holds the dubious distinction of being the nation's original 'skid row.' The appearance of the ugly concrete car park on James St convinced the city to introduce greater conservationist measures in the 1960s. You can divert on the corner with 2nd Ave for a quick glance at the neoclassical ❻ **Smith Tower** (p65), erected by LC Smith, a man who built his fortune on typewriters (Smith-Corona) and guns (Smith & Wesson). Head south on 2nd Ave S and go right on Washington St S; ❼ **Occidental Park** (p66), with its ivy-covered edifices, quickly opens out on your left. Cross Main St into Occidental Sq before heading left on ❽ **South Jackson Street**, the western terminus of Seattle's newest streetcar. In the 1890s S Jackson's stores outfitted prospectors heading for the Klondike, Canada. Fill in your historical gaps at the ❾ **Klondike Gold Rush National Historical Park** (p66) before pacing one block back to King Street Station.

RICHARDSONIAN ROMANESQUE

Pioneer Square's hallmark architecture is a revivalist style named after American architect Henry Richardson from Louisiana, who first popularized it in Boston and Chicago in the 1870s and '80s. It harked back to the medieval European genre of Romanesque in vogue from the 10th to the 12th centuries. Features of Richardsonian Romanesque include classic Roman arches, heavy rough-cut masonry, recessed doorways, and the use of decorative columns and bricks. Many of these features can still be spotted on Pioneer Square's historic buildings.

✖ EATING

Pioneer Square is the ideal place to be if you're looking for a meal in an old-school steak and seafood restaurant with loads of atmosphere and traditional service. It also has a good range of budget-friendly options that are inexpensive without lacking character.

The ID is a great neighborhood to grab cheap eats or go all-out on a sumptuous eight-course dinner banquet. It's also a good place to seek out decent food after the bars close. The many Vietnamese, Thai and Chinese restaurants that line S Jackson St between 6th and 12th Aves give you plenty of options. East of 8th Ave S and I-5, Little Saigon takes over and the flavor becomes decidedly Vietnamese.

Locals argue over which place does the best *pho* and, especially, the best dim sum, so ask around and try a bunch.

✖ Pioneer Square

★ SALUMI   SANDWICHES $
Map p228 (www.salumicuredmeats.com; 309 3rd Ave S; sandwiches $7-10; ⊙11am-4pm Tue-Fri; ☒International District/Chinatown) The queue outside Salumi has long been part of the sidewalk furniture. It's even formed its own community of chatterers, food bloggers, Twitter posters and gourmet-sandwich aficionados comparing notes. Being owned by the father of celebrity chef Mario Batali probably helps.

When you make it inside the sinuous three's-a-crowd shop, the sandwiches come with any of a dozen types of Italian-style cured meat and fresh cheese. Great for a picnic!

GRAND CENTRAL
BAKING CO   SOUP, SANDWICHES $
Map p228 (☎206-622-3644; Grand Central Arcade, 214 1st Ave S; sandwiches $4-10; ⊙7am-5pm Mon-Fri, 8am-4pm Sat; ☒Pioneer Sq) Already well established by the time President Obama popped in in 2011 and asked for a turkey-chutney sandwich, Grand Central (located in the eponymous building) is considered one of the best bakeries in Seattle. Its artisan breads can be bought whole or sliced up for sandwiches in its cafe. Beware the lunchtime queues.

There are nine other locations, seven of them in Portland, OR.

CAFE PALOMA   TURKISH $
Map p228 (☎206-405-1920; www.cafepaloma.com; 93 Yesler Way; meze $6-10; ⊙10am-9pm, to 2pm Sun; ☒Pioneer Sq) Various words spring to mind when thinking of Cafe Paloma... Bistro. Eggplant. Casual. Friendly. Turkish. Meze. Music. Lemonade. Falafel. If any of this sounds interesting, be sure to drop by this jewel of a restaurant in Pioneer Square where small Turkish miracles are concocted.

NEW ORLEANS
CREOLE RESTAURANT   SOUTHERN $
Map p228 (☎206-622-2563; www.neworleanscreolerestaurant.com; 114 1st Ave S; lunch $6-8, mains $7-13; ⊙11am-late Mon-Sat; ☒; ☒Pioneer Sq) Enjoy some live Dixieland jazz with your homemade gumbo or jambalaya in one of the coolest spaces in Pioneer Square. This bourbon-heavy institution serves unpretentious food in an attractive space (warm lighting and exposed-brick walls decorated with portraits of jazz greats) that's kid-friendly until 10pm. There's live music most nights, including blues and zydeco.

ZAINA   MIDDLE EASTERN $
Map p228 (☎206-624-5687; 108 Cherry St; gyros $8-11; ⊙10am-9pm Mon-Fri, 11am-9pm Sat; ☒Pioneer Sq) This friendly cafe, bejeweled with a mishmash of sparkly decorations and pulsing with Middle Eastern pop, dishes out juicy falafel sandwiches stuffed to overflowing, as well as shawarma, tabbouleh, hummus, great baklava and freshly squeezed lemonade. On weekend nights the

vibe goes clubbish, with hookahs and belly dancers in the house.

BAKEMAN'S
DINER $

Map p228 (☑206-622-3375; www.bakemans catering.com; 122 Cherry St; sandwiches $4.50; ⊙10am-3pm Mon-Fri; ⓡPioneer Sq) Legendary for its theatrical counter service and its roasted-fresh-daily turkey-and-cranberry sandwich, this subterranean diner demands that you know what you want and aren't afraid to ask for it.

★BAR SAJOR
MEDITERRANEAN $$

Map p228 (☑206-682-1117; www.sitkaand spruce.com; 323 Occidental Ave; plates $10-25; ⊙11am-8pm Mon, to late Tue-Fri; ⓡPioneer Sq) 🍴 Resembling a bright open-plan French country kitchen and claiming to serve Portuguese-inspired food created from the raw ingredients of Seattle's hinterland, Bar Sajor is another project from Matt Dillon, owner of Capitol Hill's hugely popular (and sustainable) Sitka & Spruce.

Both the atmosphere and the food (homemade bread, cheese and salami selections, and genuinely delicious vegetable plates) will have you living vicariously as a European without ever having to abandon your locavore instincts.

DELICATUS
DELI, SANDWICHES $$

Map p228 (☑206-623-3780; www.delicatussea ttle.com; 103 1st Ave S; sandwiches $9-12; ⊙11am-9pm Mon-Thu, to 10pm Fri & Sat, to 4pm Sun; ⓡPioneer Sq) It's a testament to a good eating joint when it is cited as an excuse to visit a whole neighborhood – and newly established Delicatus is certainly luring people to Pioneer Square. The reason is as simple as a sandwich, and Delicatus' are well stuffed and enlivened with interesting relishes. Go at lunchtime for the best atmosphere.

FX MCRORY'S STEAK, CHOP & OYSTER HOUSE
STEAK, SEAFOOD $$

Map p228 (☑206-623-4800; www.fxmcrorys.com; 419 Occidental Ave S; mains $12-35; ⊙11:30am-9pm Mon-Thu, to 10pm Fri & Sat; ⓡPioneer Sq) This vast Pioneer Square landmark across from the sports stadiums is a weird blend of class and ass – it's a majestic old space with a bar on one side, a fancy dining room on the other and an oyster bar in between, but the ballcap-jock quotient gets high on days when the Seahawks or Mariners play.

McRory's claims to have the largest selection of bourbon in the world – believable when you ogle the pyramid of booze behind the bar. Tuck into classic fare like prime rib or Dungeness crab, or share a seafood platter of oysters on the half-shell, smoked salmon, prawns, crab, Penn Cove mussels and scallops.

✖ International District

★GREEN LEAF
VIETNAMESE $

Map p228 (☑206-340-1388; www.greenleaf taste.com; 418 8th Ave S; pho $7.95, specials $11.95; ⊙11am-10pm; ⓢChinatown/International District E) As sinuous as a railway carriage and as crowded as a pub full of Sounders supporters, Green Leaf shoots out rapid-fire dishes from its tiny kitchen to its shiny black tables. People shout about the huge bowls of traditional or vegetarian *pho* and a swoon-inducing version of *bahn xeo* – sort of a cross between a pancake and an omelet.

PURPLE DOT CAFÉ
CHINESE $

Map p228 (☑206-622-0288; 515 Maynard Ave S; mains $7-14; ⊙9am-1am Sun-Thu, to 3:30am Fri & Sat; ⓢChinatown/International District E) The Purple Dot looks like the inside of an '80s video game (it is actually purple) and draws a late-night drunken-disco crowd on weekends, but most of the time it's a calm, quiet place to get dim sum and Macao-style specialties (meaning you can feast on baked spaghetti and French toast along with your Hong Kong favorites).

JADE GARDEN
CHINESE $

Map p228 (☑206-622-8181; 424 7th Ave S; dim sum items $2-3, mains $8-12; ⊙10am-10pm; ⓢChinatown/International District E) Usually mentioned near the top of the list of best places for dim sum in the ID, Jade Garden offers a good range of the delicacies, with everything from standard, newbie-friendly shrimp dumplings and steamed pork buns to the more exotic plates, like black cylinders of sesame-paste gel and, of course, chicken's feet. The more things you try, the more fun you'll have.

The Jade Garden's hot pots are also recommended.

PHO BAC
VIETNAMESE $

Map p228 (☑206-568-0882; 1240 S Jackson St; pho from $6.50; ⊙7am-9pm; ⓢLittle Saigon) It looks like the sort of place where you can follow last week's crumbs around the table, but you can get three sizes of *pho* at this

ℹ REAL CHANGE

Pioneer Square's large population of homeless people can be a shocking sight to the first-time visitor, although they are rarely threatening. In fact, some homeless Seattleites are genuine local characters. One of the best ways to help these people get back on their feet is to buy the weekly newspaper *Real Change*, sold on the street for $2 by vendors who are often homeless (vendors buy the paper for $0.60 a copy, thus making a 60% profit). The paper, founded in 1994, generates nearly $1 million a year for homeless causes and helps to alleviate panhandling.

well-established restaurant, with its huge windows gazing onto Little Saigon.

HOUSE OF HONG   CHINESE $$

Map p228 (☏206-622-7997; 408 8th Ave S; dim sum $2-3 per item, mains $12-15; ☺9am-11pm; 🛦; 🚇Chinatown/International District E) This huge mainstay of the neighborhood serves dim sum from 10am until 4:30pm every day – handy if your craving hits in the middle of the day.

SHANGHAI GARDEN   CHINESE $$

Map p228 (☏206-625-1688; www.theshanghai garden.com; 524 6th Ave S; lunch specials $8, dinner mains $10-16; ☺lunch & dinner; 🚇Chinatown/International District W) Hand-shaved barley noodles are the specialty of Shanghai Garden, and they frankly trounce all expectations you might ordinarily have of a noodle. They're wide and chewy, almost meaty, and just barely dressed with perky spinach and nicely integrated globs of chicken, tofu, beef or shrimp.

It might seem odd to get all rapturous about a plate of noodles, but these deserve it. The sugar-pea vines are also a favorite, and if neither of those options tempts you, there are about 75 other choices.

TAMARIND TREE   VIETNAMESE $$

Map p228 (☏206-860-1414; 1036 S Jackson St; pho $5-9, mains $10-16; ☺10am-10pm Sun-Thu, to midnight Fri & Sat; 🚇Little Saigon) Serving upscale food at lowbrow prices in a beautiful dining room, this elegant place has a *huge* menu, including everything from satays and salad rolls to big bowls of *pho* and a

tasty version of the traditional scallop-prawn-pork-mushroom fried crepe. It also donates some of its profits to the Vietnam Scholarship Foundation. Reservations are recommended on weekends.

🍷 DRINKING & NIGHTLIFE

Though it lends itself more to frenzied clubbing than casual pint-sipping, Pioneer Square is home to some of the city's oldest and most atmospheric bars. If you prefer a saloon to a salon, this historical part of town is your best bet.

The lounges inside many of the restaurants in the ID are good haunts for hiding away with a cocktail any time of day; many of them have afternoon happy-hour food specials, too. The ID is also the place to come for things like bubble tea and unusual herbal-tea concoctions. Hipster cachet roams the area freely, so explore on your own to find the current coolest spot.

🍸 Pioneer Square

ZEITGEIST   CAFE

Map p228 (www.zeitgeistcoffee.com; 171 S Jackson St; ☺6am-7pm Mon-Fri, from 8am Sat & Sun; 📶; 🚇Pioneer Sq) Listen: the comforting buzz of conversation! People actually talk in the attractive exposed-brick confines of Zeitgeist – they're not all glued to their laptops. Bolstered by tongue-loosening doses of caffeine, you can join them discussing the beautiful smoothness of your *doppio macchiato* or the sweet intensity of your to-die-for almond croissant in what could very well be Seattle's best indie coffee bar.

88 KEYS DUELING PIANO BAR   BAR

Map p228 (☏206-839-1300; www.ilove88keys.com; 315 2nd Ave S; ☺5pm-2am; 🚇Pioneer Sq) Reviving the almost lost art of dueling pianos, this sports bar–jazz haunt has two grands set up facing each other on a raised stage (so, strictly speaking, it's 176 keys). The time to come is Friday or Saturday night, when two talented musicians belt out piano classics in unison (everything from Fats Domino to Billy Joel) with plenty of audience interaction.

There's food and drink, of course. But this place is all about the music – and the electric atmosphere.

PYRAMID ALE HOUSE BREWPUB
Map p228 (📞206-682-3377; 1201 1st Ave S; pints $4-5; ⏰11am-10pm Mon-Thu, to 11pm Fri & Sat, to 9pm Sun; 🚉Stadium) Technically in SoDo by Safeco Field, this brewpub has the cleaned-up-industrial feel – all bricks and brass and designer lighting – that defines the Pacific Northwest brewpub. It's a nice and mainstream (but still appreciably Seattle-ish) place to take your parents or tenderfoot visitors. But don't even try on a game day, unless you want to squeeze into the standing-room-only beer tent outdoors.

CAFFÈ UMBRIA CAFE
Map p228 (www.caffeumbria.com; 320 Occidental Ave S; ⏰6am-6pm Mon-Fri, from 7am Sat, 8am-5pm Sun; 🚉Pioneer Sq) Umbria has a European flavor with its 8oz cappuccinos, chatty clientele (instead of the usual laptop gazers), pretty Italianate tiles, and baguettes so fresh they must have been teleported over from Milan. Ideal for Italophiles and Starbucks-phobes.

CENTRAL SALOON PUB
Map p228 (📞206-622-0209; 207 1st Ave S; ⏰11:30am-2am, happy hour 4-7pm Mon-Fri; 🚉Pioneer Sq) It may be two years younger than the official Oldest Bar in Seattle, the Jules Maes, but the Central isn't exactly new and shiny. More of a locals' hangout than an object of historical interest, this long, narrow joint makes grotty bathrooms and blah food seem charming, by virtue of cheap suds, friendly barkeeps and a comfortable, unfussy vibe.

Live music most nights means that anyone who disapproves of metal should get in and out fairly early.

FUEL SPORTS BAR
Map p228 (📞206-405-3835; www.fuelseattle.com; 164 S Washington St; ⏰11:30am-close; 🚉Pioneer Sq) TV-filled sports bar that is the favored meet-up for Seattle Sounders 'Emerald City Supporters' soccer fans on match days. Tuck your elbows in and inhale deeply as you enter.

LAST SUPPER CLUB CLUB
Map p228 (📞206-748-9975; www.lastsupperclub.com; 124 S Washington St; ⏰9pm-2am Wed-Sun; 🚉Pioneer Sq) Better for DJs, dancing and cocktails than supper, though there's a rather posh sit-down lounge here. The dance floor gets clamorous from 11pm onwards with the kind of snappily dressed people who spent plenty of time checking their reflection in the mirror before they came out. House and hip-hop music dominates.

J&M CAFÉ BAR
Map p228 (📞206-292-0663; www.thejmcafe.com; 201 1st Ave S; ⏰11am-2am; 🚉Pioneer Sq) Burgers, loud music, beer, soccer/football crowds, bags of Skid Row–era history: welcome to Pioneer Square and this old classic that's currently going through one of its less classic phases.

🍴 International District

PANAMA HOTEL TEA & COFFEE HOUSE CAFE
Map p228 (607 S Main St; ⏰8am-7pm Mon-Sat, from 9am Sun; 🚉Chinatown/International District W) The Panama, a historic 1910 building containing the only remaining Japanese bathhouse in the US, doubles as a memorial to the neighborhood's Japanese residents forced into internment camps during WWII. The beautifully relaxed cafe has a wide selection of teas and is one of the few places in Seattle to sell Lavazza Italian coffee. Board games and old photos encourage lingering.

☆ ENTERTAINMENT

☆ Pioneer Square

COMEDY UNDERGROUND COMEDY
Map p228 (📞206-628-0303; www.comedyunderground.com; 109 S Washington St; tickets $6-15; 🚉Pioneer Sq) The best comedy club in Seattle has an 8:30pm show most nights and a second 10:30pm show on Friday and Saturday. Talent is mainly local and there's a full bar plus a pizza-and-burger-style food menu. Under 21s are welcome Sunday to Thursday. Monday is open mic, a crapshoot of the surprisingly good or the skin-crawlingly bad.

Buy tickets through **TicketWeb** (www.ticketweb.com), preferably in advance.

SHOPPING

Not surprisingly, given its historical importance to the city, Pioneer Square is where to shop for antiques. It's also a good place to find reasonably priced artwork and crafts by local artists, particularly blown glass and traditional art by coastal Native American artists.

In addition to the behemoth Uwajimaya, it's worth exploring nooks and crannies in this neighborhood for odd shopfronts and imported wares.

Pioneer Square

PIONEER SQUARE ANTIQUE MALL ANTIQUES
Map p228 (☑206-624-1164; 602 1st Ave; ☒Pioneer Sq) The Antique Mall is a warren of little shops across from the Pioneer Square pergola; it's actually part of the Seattle 'underground' and can be somewhat claustrophobic, but if you're a patient gem hunter you'll definitely score. There are lots of vintage clothing, jewelry, photos, cameras, china and knickknacks.

GLASSHOUSE STUDIO ARTS & CRAFTS
Map p228 (☑206-682-9939; 311 Occidental Ave S; ☺demonstrations 10am & 1-5pm Mon-Sat; ☒Pio-

neer Sq) The Seattle area is known for its Pilchuck School of glassblowing art, and this is the city's oldest glassblowing studio. Stop by to watch the artists in action and pick up a memento right at the source.

SEATTLE MYSTERY BOOKSHOP BOOKS
Map p228 (☑206-587-5737; www.seattlemystery.com; 117 Cherry St; ☺10am-6pm Mon-Sat, noon-5pm Sun; ☒Pioneer Sq) The name gives it away – Seattle Mystery Bookshop is a specialty store for page-turners and whodunits.

CLOG FACTORY SHOES
Map p228 (217 1st Ave S; ☺10am-6pm Mon-Sat, 11am-5pm Sun; ☒Pioneer Sq) Surviving on the edges of popular fashion, it's only a matter of time before Seattle's anti-mainstream hipsters discover the retro value of clogs. Beat them to it by visiting this Pioneer Square store with unique footwear from Sweden, Denmark and Germany.

FLANAGAN & LANE ANTIQUES ANTIQUES
Map p228 (☑206-682-0098; www.flanagan-laneantiques.com; 165 S Jackson St; ☺11am-5pm; ☒Pioneer Sq) Since opening in the early 1990s, this shop has been devoted to American, English and Continental antiques. It's one of the neighborhood's more upmarket places, though you might find a bargain if you dig around long enough.

International District

PACIFIC HERB & GROCERY FOOD, HERBS
Map p228 (☑206-340-6411; 610 S Weller St, btwn 6th Ave & Maynard Ave S; ☒Chinatown/International District E) A good place to get a sense of Chinatown is along S Weller St. Apart from the many restaurants, there's Pacific Herb & Grocery, where the herbal-medicine specialists can tell you all about the uses of different roots, bones, flowers and teas. The shop next door is a great place to buy tofu at low prices – you can even watch them make it on the premises.

KINOKUNIYA BOOKS
Map p228 (☑206-587-2477; 525 S Weller St; ☺10am-9pm Mon-Sat, to 8pm Sun; ☒Chinatown/International District W) A great source for hard-to-find imported books and magazines in Asian languages (and in English about Asian culture), this bookstore inside Uwajimaya Village is also one of the few shops in the country where you can buy the

---

LOCAL KNOWLEDGE

FIRST THURSDAY ART WALK

Art walks are two a penny in US cities these days, but they were pretty much an unknown quantity when the pioneering artists of Pioneer Square instituted their first amble around the local galleries in 1981. The neighborhood's **First Thursday Art Walk** (www.firstthursdayseattle.com) claims to be the oldest in the nation and a creative pathfinder for all that followed (and there have been many). Aside from gluing together Pioneer Square's network of 50-plus galleries (only a few of which can be listed in this book), the walk is a good excuse to admire creative public sculpture, sip decent coffee (many cafes serve as de facto galleries), browse an array of stalls set up in Occidental Park, and get to know the neighborhood and its people. The Art Walk is self-guided, but you can pick up a map from the information booth in Occidental Park.

THE SOUND OF THE SOUNDERS

If you think soccer is a niche sport in the US inspiring little of the passion and noise of football and baseball, you obviously haven't been to Seattle. The **Seattle Sounders** (Map p228; ☑206-622-3415; www.seattlesounders.net; tickets from $37), the third incarnation of Seattle's main soccer club who launched in 2008, are the best supported Major League Soccer (MLS) team, garnering more than twice as many home supporters as local baseball team the Mariners. Indeed, in 2012 their average home gates topped out at 43,000, higher than European Champions League winners Chelsea.

Sounders fans, who are organized into half a dozen supporters groups, are famous for their highly musical 'March to the Match' which kicks off from Occidental Park in Pioneer Square. There's plenty to shout about. The team have won an unprecedented three US Open Cups since their inaugural MLS season in 2009.

lesser-known films of Kinji Fukasaku and other masters of Asian cinema on DVD.

UWAJIMAYA FOOD, GIFTS
Map p228 (☑206-624-6248; 600 5th Ave S; ◷9am-10pm Mon-Sat, to 9pm Sun; ⊠Chinatown/International District W) Dried squid? Yes. Sheets of seaweed? Absolutely. Dumpling steamers, teapots, chopsticks? All of the above. The enormous Asian grocery and supply store Uwajimaya, anchoring an eponymous shopping center, has everything needed to prepare Thai, Japanese, Chinese and just about any other type of Asian specialty.

You'll find fresh and frozen meat and fish, canned and dried produce, and intriguingly labeled treats of all kinds, as well as cooking tools, small appliances, spices and gift items. It also has a deli and bakery, and a number of hole-in-the-wall restaurants edge the building.

🏃 SPORTS & ACTIVITIES

🏃 Pioneer Square

SAFECO FIELD STADIUM
Map p228 (☑206-346-4241; 1250 1st Ave S; tours adult/child $10/8; ◷1hr tours 10:30am, 12:30pm

& 2:30pm nongame days Apr-Oct; ⊠Stadium) The Mariners' $517-million ballpark, Safeco Field, opened in July 1999. With its retractable roof, 47,000 seats and real grass, the stadium was funded in part by taxpayers and tourists; more than half the money came from taxes on food sold in King County restaurants and bars, and from taxes on rental cars. Money also came from profits on scratch-lottery tickets.

The Mariners coughed up most of the difference. The stadium's unique design means it commands fantastic views of the surrounding mountains, downtown and Puget Sound. There's no 2:30pm tour on game days and no tours if the game is before 6pm.

CENTURYLINK FIELD STADIUM
Map p228 (800 Occidental Ave S; ⊠Stadium) The late, mostly unlamented Kingdome, long Seattle's biggest eyesore, was once the home field for the city's professional baseball and football franchises. Then it was imploded spectacularly in 2000 and replaced by this 72,000-seat stadium, home of the Seattle Seahawks (NFL) and Seattle's soccer team, the Sounders.

Belltown & Seattle Center

BELLTOWN | SEATTLE CENTER

Neighborhood Top Five

❶ Pondering the shimmering glass art that sprang from the creative mind of Dale Chihuly in the newly opened **Chihuly Garden & Glass** (p78) underneath the Space Needle.

❷ Watching the sun slip behind faraway mountains from the grassy slopes of the **Olympic Sculpture Park** (p83).

❸ Discovering the next big thing in Seattle's music scene at the **Crocodile** (p90).

❹ Playing pinball while downing an alcoholic slushie in the dive bar **Shorty's** (p88).

❺ Taking a proverbial Seattle rite of passage and zipping up to the top of the **Space Needle** (p80).

For more detail of this area, see Map p230 ➡

Explore: Belltown & Seattle Center

Belltown's compact, walkable core is long on dining and entertainment options but relatively short on daytime attractions. The exception is the Olympic Sculpture Park, a grassy art garden that snares visitors strolling between Pike Place Market and the Seattle Center.

Capitol Hillers might disagree, but Belltown's main nightlife zone (1st and 2nd Aves between Blanchard and Battery Sts) is the best place in the city to string together a bar-hopping evening out. A few of the grunge-era landmarks are still in business, but these days distorted guitars compete with the chatter of the cocktail crowd. Whatever your fashion affiliations, Belltown's after-dark scene is hip and noisy and rarely stands still. Watch out for drunken hipsters and sidewalk vomit.

The Seattle Center, site of the highly successful 1962 World's Fair, is Belltown in reverse; sights and museums abound, but you'll struggle to find any memorable food. The solution: spend most of your sightseeing time in the Seattle Center (EMP Museum, Chihuly Garden & Glass and the Space Needle merit a day between them) and escape to adjacent Belltown for lunch, drinks and dinner.

Entertainment-wise, the Seattle Center offers plenty of sit-down plays, concerts and films. The McCaw Hall is home of the Seattle Opera and the Pacific Northwest Ballet, plus there's a cinema, a children's theater and a regional theater in the complex. It's also a fun place to just hang out, especially in summer when alfresco events and street performers take over.

Local Life

➡ **Serious Pie** It's all communal tables at Tom Douglas' riotously popular pizza restaurant, where you can discuss weird pizza toppings, microbrews and where Seattle's culinary maestro might open up next.

➡ **Five Point Café** Sit at the bar of this crusty dive and see who walks through the door next: Lou Reed? Captain Sparrow? The ghost of Charles Bukowski?

Getting There & Away

➡ **Bus** Nearly all Belltown buses go up and down 3rd Ave and originate in downtown.

➡ **Monorail** The famous train in the sky runs every 10 minutes between downtown's Westlake Center, at Pine St and 4th Ave, and the Seattle Center. Tickets cost $2.25/1 per adult/child. The journey takes two minutes.

➡ **Walking** Lacking busy arterial roads, Belltown is a highly walkable neighborhood and easily reachable on foot from downtown, Pike Place Market, the Seattle Center and Lower Queen Anne.

Lonely Planet's Top Tip

Many people – including a lot of locals – consider the Space Needle to be an expensive tourist trap. If you're on a budget, you might be better off investing your money in tickets for the EMP Museum or Chihuly Garden & Glass. You can get a better and far cheaper view of Seattle from the Columbia Center.

✕ Best Places to Eat

➡ Top Pot Hand-Forged Doughnuts (p84)
➡ 360 Local (p86)
➡ Serious Pie (p86)
➡ Macrina (p84)

For reviews, see p84 ➡

🍷 Best Places to Drink

➡ Shorty's (p88)
➡ Lava Lounge (p89)
➡ Five Point Café (p89)
➡ Bedlam (p89)

For reviews, see p88 ➡

☆ Best Live Music

➡ Crocodile (p90)
➡ Dimitriou's Jazz Alley (p90)
➡ Seattle Opera (p91)
➡ Rendezvous (p89)

For reviews, see p90 ➡

TOP SIGHT
CHIHULY GARDEN & GLASS

Opened in 2012 and reinforcing Seattle's position as the Venice of North America, this exquisite exposition of the life and work of dynamic local glass sculptor Dale Chihuly requires a sharp intake of breath on first viewing. It has quickly become a top city icon to rival the neighboring Space Needle.

Dale Chihuly

With his Long John Silver eye patch and shock of electric hair, Dale Chihuly looks every part the eccentric artist. Born in Tacoma, WA, in 1941, the world's best-known glass sculptor majored in interior design at the University of Washington before moving to Venice, where he enthusiastically immersed himself in the delicate art of glassblowing. Returning to the Seattle area in 1971, Chihuly founded a glass art school and gradually began to establish a reputation before two successive accidents in the 1970s left him with permanent injuries to his eye and shoulder and no longer able to contribute directly to the glassblowing process. Undeterred by the setback, Chihuly channeled his energies 100% into design, hiring vast teams of glassblowers to enact his lucid artistic visions. It was a highly successful formula. With Chihuly acting as both composer and conductor to a large orchestra of employees, the size and scale of his exhibits soared. Before long, his provocative glass art leaped onto the world stage. By the 1980s, Chihuly's opulent creations were being exhibited all over the globe, inspiring a mixture of awe and controversy in all who saw them but never failing to get a reaction.

Layout

The masterpieces are split between an eight-room exhibition center, a glasshouse filled with natural light, and a garden. Between them they showcase the full gamut of Chihuly's

DON'T MISS

➡ Sealife Tower
➡ Chandeliers
➡ Mille Fiori
➡ Glasshouse

PRACTICALITIES

➡ Map p230
➡ ☎206-753-3527
➡ www.chihulygarden andglass.com
➡ 305 W Harrison St
➡ adult/child $19/12
➡ ⊙11am-7pm Sun-Thu, to 8pm Fri & Sat
➡ Ⓜ Seattle Center

© 2013 CHIHULY STUDIO

Pacific Northwest influences, most notably Native American art, Puget Sound sea life, and wooden boats.

Exhibition Hall

The first standout exhibit is **Sealife Tower**, a huge azure structure of intricately blown glass that looks as if it has sprung straight out of Poseidon's lair. Look out for the small octopuses and starfish melded into the swirling waves and examine Chihuly's early sketches for the work that adorn the surrounding walls. The next exhibit, **Persian Ceilings**, creates a reflective rainbow of light in an otherwise unfurnished room, while the ambitious **Mille Fiori** presents glass as vegetation with multiple pieces arranged in an ethereal Wizard of Oz–like 'garden.' The **Ikebana & Float Boat** consists of several boats overflowing with round glass balls and was inspired by Chihuly's time in Venice: he casually threw luminous glass spheres into the canals and watched as local children enthusiastically collected them in boats. In the adjoining room lie the main objects of the *Chihuly Over Venice* project: rich, ornate **chandeliers** of varying sizes and colors that were hung artistically around the city in 1996.

Glasshouse

Sitting like a giant greenhouse under the Space Needle, the Glasshouse offers a nod to London's Crystal Palace, one of Chihuly's most important historical inspirations. You'll notice that the floor space of the glasshouse has been left empty (the area can be hired for wedding receptions), drawing your eye up to the ceiling where a huge medley of flower-shaped glass pieces imitate the reds, oranges and yellows of a perfect sunset. Adjacent to the glasshouse is the **Collections Café**, where numerous collected objects (accordions, bottle openers, toy cars) adorn the ceiling, tables and toilets. Nearby, a **theater** shows several revolving short films including *Chihuly Over Venice*.

Garden

Seattle's relatively benign climate means glass can safely be displayed outside year round. Chihuly uses the garden to demonstrate the seamless melding of glass art and natural vegetation. Many of the alfresco pieces are simple pointed shards of glass redolent of luminescent reeds, but the real eye-catcher is **The Sun**, a riot of twisted yellow 'flames' whose swirling brilliance erases the heaviness of the most overcast Seattle sky.

LEARN GLASSBLOWING

In the summer of 1971, Dale Chihuly co-founded **Pilchuck Glass School** (www.pilchuck.com) at a campus in Stanwood, WA, 50 miles north of Seattle on an old tree farm. Inhabiting rustic buildings constructed in typical Northwestern style, the school remains popular 40 years on, especially in the summer, when it offers intensive two-week courses in glassblowing.

Chihuly Garden & Glass has revitalized the Seattle Center after a tough five years. In 2008, the Key Arena (and Seattle) lost its pro basketball team the SuperSonics, who relocated to Oklahoma City, and then, in 2011, the Intiman Theater briefly disappeared after a financial crisis (it reopened in 2012). Other casualties have been the Funhouse, a much-loved live punk venue, and the Fun Forest, a kitschy amusement park and one of the 1962 World's Fair's original attractions that ran for 48 years until its closure in January 2011.

BELLTOWN & SEATTLE CENTER CHIHULY GARDEN & GLASS

TOP SIGHT
SPACE NEEDLE

You might be from Alabama or Timbuktu, but your abiding image of Seattle will probably be of the Space Needle, a streamlined, modern-before-its-time tower built for the 1962 World's Fair that has been the city's defining symbol for over 50 years. The needle anchors the fair site, now called the Seattle Center, and – despite its rather steep admission fee – still persuades over a million annual visitors to ascend to its flying-saucer-like observation deck.

Some History

The Space Needle (originally called 'The Space Cage') was designed by Victor Steinbrueck and John Graham Jr, reportedly based on the napkin scribblings of World's Fair organizer Eddie Carlson. Looking like a cross between a flying saucer and an hourglass, and belonging to an architectural subgenre commonly referred to as Googie (futuristic, space age and curvaceous), the Needle was constructed in less than a year and proved to be an instant hit; 2.3 million people paid $1 to ascend it during the World's Fair, which ran for six months between April and October 1962. The lofty revolving dome originally housed two restaurants (they were amalgamated in 2000) and its roof was initially painted a brilliant 'Galaxy Gold' (read: orange). After many color changes, it was repainted in the same shade for its 50th anniversary in 2012. The structure has had two major refurbishments since the '60s: the first in 1982 when the Skyline level was added, and the second in 2000 in a project that cost as much as the original construction. The tradition of holding fantastical New Year's Eve firework displays at the Needle began in 1992.

DON'T MISS...

➡ Observation deck
➡ Lunch in the SkyCity Restaurant
➡ Joint-ticket offers

PRACTICALITIES

➡ Map p230
➡ www.spaceneedle.com
➡ 400 Broad St
➡ adult/child $19/12
➡ ⊘10am-11pm Mon-Thu, 9.30am-11:30pm Fri & Sat, 9.30am-11pm Sun
➡ Ⓜ Seattle Center

Vital Statistics

Standing apart from the rest of Seattle's skyscrapers, the Needle often looks taller than it actually is. On its completion in 1962, it was the highest structure west of the Mississippi River, topping 605ft, though it has since been easily surpassed (it's currently the sixth-tallest structure in Seattle). The part of the Needle that's visible above ground weighs an astounding 3700 tons. Most visitors head for the 520ft-high observation deck on zippy elevators that ascend to the top in comfortably less than a minute. The 360-degree views of Seattle and its surrounding water and mountains are suitably fabulous.

Visiting

To avoid the queues, purchase your ticket from one of the self-service machines outside the Space Base (tourist shop) and proceed up the ramp. You'll undergo a friendly bag search and then enter the gold capsule elevators, where an attendant will give you a quick-fire 41-second précis of the Needle (basically, the time it takes to ascend). The elevators dock at the **observation deck**. To get to the **SkyCity Restaurant** you have to descend one level by stairs (or another lift). The observation deck has a reasonable cafe (with drinks and sandwiches), plenty of wall-mounted facts, free telescopes and some interesting touchscreens. One, a collection called 'local voices,' shows various Seattleites talking with affection about their city. Another is a high-powered telescope that you can move around and zoom in and out to see close-up images of the street below flashed up on a screen. It's all a little nosy and voyeuristic!

The alfresco part of the observation deck (open the same hours, weather permitting) is guarded by a Perspex screen and an enclosed wire fence, presumably to deter the overly depressed or the overly adventurous from jumping (there have been two illegal base jumps and four suicides in Needle history). The view is broad. On clear days, you can see three Cascade volcanoes (Mts Rainier, Baker and St Helen's), the Olympic range, the jagged coastline of Puget Sound and the sparkling surfaces of Lakes Union and Washington fanning out in the haze. Equally interesting is the complex topography of Seattle and its splayed neighborhoods that lie beneath you.

LUNCH AT 500FT

If you decide to ascend the Space Needle, it's more economical to tie it in with lunch. Standard Space Needle tickets cost $19 (just for the view). However, if you go up for lunch in the rotating **SkyCity Restaurant**, the standard entry will be waived as long as your order costs at least $25. The restaurant rotates fully every 47 minutes, ideal for a leisurely view-enhanced lunch. The menu is true to Seattle's locavore tradition with a strong emphasis on fish.

To cut your costs at the Space Needle you can combine it with a visit to Chihuly Garden & Glass, located at its base, on the same ticket. Joint tickets cost $33 (saving $5). Alternatively, the Needle is included on the $74 Seattle CityPass that grants access to five other sights, including the EMP Museum and the Pacific Science Center.

TOP SIGHT
EMP MUSEUM

This dramatic marriage of super-modern architecture and rock-and-roll history was inaugurated as the Experience Music Project (EMP) in 2000. Founded by Microsoft co-creator Paul Allen, it was inspired by the music of Seattle-born guitar icon Jimi Hendrix.

Architecture
The building was designed by renowned Canadian architect Frank Gehry, a strong proponent of deconstructivism. Gehry supposedly used one of Hendrix's smashed-up guitars as his inspiration.

Main Exhibits
The main exhibits are anchored by *If VI Was IX*, a tower of 700 instruments designed by German-born artist Trimpin. Many of the permanent exhibits center on Hendrix, including the Fender Stratocaster guitar that he played at Woodstock in 1969. Dominating proceedings is the **Sky Church**, a huge screen displaying musical and sci-fi films.

Sound Lab
On the 3rd floor is the interactive **Sound Lab**, where you can lay down vocal tracks, play instruments, fiddle with effects pedals and – best of all – jam in a mini studio. **On Stage** is an opportunity to belt out numbers under stage lights with a virtual audience.

Icons of Science Fiction
A separate Science Fiction Museum opened on the site in 2004 and, in 2012, was incorporated into EMP in a permanent 2nd-floor display called 'Icons of Science Fiction.' Expect to meet a *Doctor Who* Dalek, a *Terminator 2* skull and swarms of visiting *Star Trek* nerds.

DON'T MISS
→ Sound Lab
→ Sky Church
→ On Stage

PRACTICALITIES
→ Map p230
→ www.empsfm.org
→ 325 5th Ave N
→ adult/child $20/14
→ ⊙10am-7pm Jun–mid-Sep, to 5pm mid-Sep–May
→ Ⓜ Seattle Center

⊙ SIGHTS

⊙ Belltown

OLYMPIC SCULPTURE PARK   PARK, SCULPTURE
Map p230 (2901 Western Ave; ☉sunrise-sunset; 🚋13) **FREE** Hovering over train tracks, in an unlikely oasis between the water and busy Elliott Ave, is the 8.5-acre, $85-million Olympic Sculpture Park. Worth a visit just for its views of the Olympic Mountains over Elliott Bay, the park has begun to grow into its long-range plan.

Among the highlights is *The Eagle*, Alexander Calder's 39ft-tall red steel creation from 1971, which crouches along the horizon of the park. The thing probably weighs about a ton, but from where it's positioned, it looks like it's about to launch itself off the top of the hill and into the distant mountains.

The sculpture park is an excellent lesson in how to make the most out of limited urban space. Its Z-shaped path slinks back and forth between Belltown, busy Elliott Ave and the edge of the bay, rescuing three parcels of land and filling them with art and plant life.

Starting from the bottom, Tony Smith's *Wandering Rocks* zigzags up the hill in the Ketcham Families Grove, described on signs as 'a deciduous forest of quaking aspen' – well, eventually. It's just beginning to sprout now, but it's still pretty. More than 20 large pieces of sculpture dot the landscape, including Claes Oldenburg and Coosje van Bruggen's *Typewriter Eraser, Scale X*, with its weird blue sprouts bristling over Elliott Ave.

The glass building at the top of the park contains a small cafe, restrooms, a gift shop and visitor information.

MYRTLE EDWARDS PARK   PARK
(🚋13) Your best bet for an uninterrupted walk or jog if you're staying downtown is this fringe of lawn and trees along Elliott Bay that starts next to the Olympic Sculpture Park and continues as far as the Interbay area between Queen Anne and Magnolia.

The park (sometime erroneously called Elliott Bay Park) was named after a Seattle councilor and environmental campaigner in the 1960s and the path that runs through it is a favorite of joggers and power-walkers pursuing lunchtime fitness. In warm weather, the linked paths, with stupendous views over the Sound to the Olympic Mountains, make a good place for a picnic (eagles are sometimes spotted). Halfway through the park a large, distinctive grain terminal bridges the walkway.

CORNISH COLLEGE OF THE ARTS   COLLEGE
Map p230 (☏800-726-2787; 1000 Lenora St; 🚋Westlake & 9th) The south campus of the ornamental Cornish College of the Arts, built in 1921, has survived many bouts of debt and is now a top-notch school for music, art, dance and drama.

⊙ Seattle Center

CHIHULY GARDEN & GLASS   MUSEUM
See p78.

SPACE NEEDLE   LANDMARK
See p80.

EMP MUSEUM   MUSEUM
See p82.

BILL & MELINDA GATES FOUNDATION VISITOR CENTER   VISITOR CENTER
Map p230 (440 5th Ave N; ☉10am-5pm Tue-Sat; Ⓜ️Seattle Center) 🏃 **FREE** The generous actions of the world's most unselfish billionaire are eloquently displayed at this suitably high-tech visitor center (part of the larger foundation building), which opened opposite the Space Needle in February 2012.

Spread over five rooms with highly interactive exhibits, the center lays out the Gates' bios and shows examples of their work around the world (including fighting malaria in Africa and notable philanthropic activities inside the US). It also offers scope for plenty of visitor involvement. Various screens and notepads invite visitors to jot down ideas, help solve tricky problems and lend their own brainpower to the foundation's 'intellectual bank.'

The Gates Foundation transferred over to this new 900,000-sq-ft, $500-million campus in 2011. Over 1500 staff are accommodated in two sustainable LEED-certified buildings (with green roofs and recycled rainwater), where they coordinate the ongoing development work.

CHILDREN'S MUSEUM   MUSEUM
Map p230 (☏206-441-1768; www.thechildrens museum.org; 305 W Harrison St; adult & child/grandparent $8.25/7.25; ☉10am-5pm Mon-Fri, to

THE DENNY TRIANGLE

A proverbial no-man's land shoehorned between South Lake Union and Belltown, the Denny Triangle is positioning itself as Seattle's next big thing with ambitious plans for offices, condo towers and super-modern multi-use buildings that will create up to 25,000 new jobs. Ironically, the neighborhood sits on some important pioneer history. Seattle's first land claim was staked here by the Denny Party in 1852, though the weary, rain-lashed pioneers probably wouldn't recognize their fledgling settlement today. Until the 1890s, the area was occupied by a steep hill that covered 62 city blocks and had a summit at the intersection of modern-day 4th Ave and Blanchard St. Seen as an impediment to the continued expansion of downtown, the hill was gradually 'demolished' and sluiced into Elliott Bay in a massive public-works project known as the Denny Regrade that began in 1898 and took 32 years to complete.

Devoid of sights per se, the triangle is best known for its endless construction sites and annoying traffic diversions. Its most recognizable landmark is the gaudy neon **pink elephant sign** outside the Elephant Super Car Wash that has been revolving on the corner of Denny Way and Battery St since 1956. To local residents it's as quintessentially Seattle as the Space Needle.

6pm Sat & Sun; MSeattle Center) In the basement of Center House near the monorail stop, the Children's Museum is an anachronistic learning center that offers activities and displays seemingly imported from an earlier time; it's a museum that might itself belong in a museum. But it's all very charming, if lacking in modern-day bells and whistles.

INTERNATIONAL FOUNTAIN FOUNTAIN
Map p230 (light-show schedule 206-684-7200; MSeattle Center) This is the place to be on sunny days. With 287 jets of water (recycled, of course) pumping in time to a computer-driven music system, the International Fountain at the heart of the Seattle Center is a great place to rest your feet or eat lunch on a warm day. On summer nights there's a free light-and-music show.

PACIFIC SCIENCE CENTER MUSEUM
Map p230 (www.pacsci.org; 200 2nd Ave N; adult/child exhibits only $18/13, with Imax $22/17; 10am-5pm Mon-Fri, to 6pm Sat & Sun; MSeattle Center) This interactive museum of science and industry once housed the science pavilion of the World's Fair. Today the center features virtual-reality exhibits, a tropical butterfly house, laser shows, holograms and other wonders of science, many with hands-on demonstrations. Also on the premises is the vaulted-screen **Imax Theater**, a laserium and a planetarium.

✖ EATING

Formerly scruffy but now condo-clean, Belltown makes it easy to spend either a little or a lot and still get a fabulous meal. Among its rows of bars and cocktail lounges are a great variety of cafes, delis, top-of-the-line restaurants and low-budget noodle huts frequented by arty musicians and starving students. The other advantage of Belltown is that you're more likely to be able to find late-night dining, thanks to an active cocktail scene that encourages many restaurants to serve at least a bar menu until 2am.

★TOP POT HAND-FORGED DOUGHNUTS CAFE $
Map p230 (www.toppotdoughnuts.com; 2124 5th Ave; doughnuts from $1.50; 6am-7pm; 13) Top Pot is to doughnuts what champagne is to wine – a different class. And its cafes – especially this one in an old car showroom with floor-to-ceiling library shelves and art-deco signage – are equally legendary. The coffee's pretty potent too.

MACRINA BAKERY $
Map p230 (206-448-4032; 2408 1st Ave; pastries $2-3.75; 7am-7pm; 13) That snaking queue's there for a reason: damned good artisan bread (you can watch through the window as the experts roll out the dough). There are two options and two lines at Macrina. One is for the fantastic take-out bakery (possibly the best in Seattle); the other's

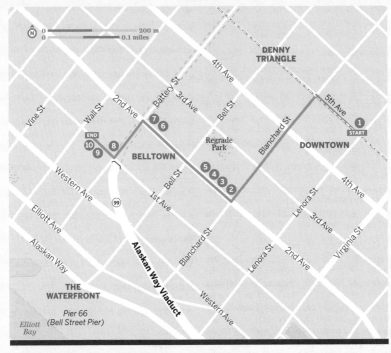

🏃 Neighborhood Walk
The Belltown Hustle

START TOP POT DOUGHNUTS
FINISH CYCLOPS
LENGTH 1 MILE; A FULL EVENING

Start the tour by fueling up with coffee and sugar at **①Top Pot Hand-Forged Doughnuts** (p84), whose book-lined cafe in an ex–car showroom sits under the concrete pillars of the monorail on 5th Ave.

Wander down Blanchard St to 2nd Ave where, on the corner, you'll spot the snakeskin-green sign of the **②Crocodile** (p90), a key venue in the rise of grunge. Check its windows for upcoming shows. The Crocodile marks the start of one of Seattle's best nightlife strips. **③Tula's** (p91) is a great jazz venue and home of some of Seattle's best-kept secrets. If you're after more active pursuits and you're thirsty, keep walking to **④Shorty's** (p88), otherwise known as pinball heaven. Grab a cheap beer or a slushy blue cocktail and head straight to the back room to test your reflexes.

When the pinball wears you out or simply beats you into submission, hop next door to the **⑤Lava Lounge** (p89), another groovy nightspot with comfy wooden booths. Continue on past legendary nosh spot Mama's Mexican Kitchen to **⑥Rendezvous** (p89), a classy place with a curvilinear bar and the adorable, recently gussied-up **⑦Jewel Box Theater** (p89) in the back.

Head toward the water on Battery St to 1st Ave: turn left and halfway down the block you'll see **⑧Macrina** (p84), one of Seattle's best bakeries. If it's gone 7pm and it's shut, make menu notes for tomorrow's hangover cure.

Hungry? Head toward the corner of 1st Ave and Wall St, where you can procure food in **⑨Cyclops** (p86), a prime location for observing the street's late-night dramas. If you're lucky enough to be staying at the **⑩Ace Hotel** (p184), you can chill at the Cyclops until your eyes match the bleary, bloodshot one hanging over the door, then stumble upstairs and fall into bed. End of tour.

for the sit-down cafe with its so-good-it-could-be-Paris sandwiches, soups and other such snacks. Join the pilgrimage.

CYCLOPS
AMERICAN $

Map p230 (www.cyclopsseattle.com; 2421 1st Ave; mains from $8; ⊙5pm-2am daily, plus 9am-2pm Sat & Sun; 🚇13) Sometimes when you're tramping the streets in search of food and drink (and a bathroom) after a day of arduous sightseeing, you just want somewhere cheap, unpretentious and comfortable to rest your weary legs.

Welcome to Cyclops, where a pint of Boundary Bay IPA and a good ole' burger can be consumed amid the to-ing and fro-ing of Belltown life and some rather eclectic decor (a swordfish, bullfighting portraits and a collection of metal crosses). Lap it up.

MAMA'S MEXICAN KITCHEN
MEXICAN $

Map p230 (📞206-728-6262; 2234 2nd Ave; burritos $7-9; ⊙11am-10pm, to 11pm Fri & Sat; 🚇13) An endearing Mexican restaurant on Belltown's noisy nightlife strip that's full of interesting paraphernalia (including a weird Elvis fixation) and equally interesting local characters; you're practically guaranteed to just talking to the people at the next table. Food is economical Mexican *comida* that arrives fast and goes down well with a Corona beer.

BLACK BOTTLE
MODERN AMERICAN $

Map p230 (www.blackbottleseattle.com; 2600 1st Ave; plates $8-12; ⊙4pm-2am Thu-Sat, 4pm-midnight Sun-Wed; 🚇13) This trendy minimalist bar-restaurant showcases the new Belltown of smart condo dwellers and well-coiffed wine quaffers. The food is mainly appetizers, but with menu items such as grilled lamb and sumac hummus, and braised artichoke heart and greens, even the nostalgic grunge groupies of yore will find it hard to resist.

BELLTOWN PIZZA
PIZZA $

Map p230 (📞206-441-2653; www.belltownpizza.net; 2422 1st Ave; pizzas $12-17; ⊙4pm-2am Mon-Fri, 11:30am-2am Sat & Sun; 🚇13) Pizza and beer is great, but pizza and hard liquor works quicker. Started as a tiny bar serving New York–style pizza, Belltown Pizza has expanded a lot since then but maintains its original mission of good food and good fun at grown-up hours (the bar's open until 2am). A large pie is enough to feed four hungry people.

You can also get salads, pasta and sandwiches.

★ SERIOUS PIE
PIZZA $$

Map p230 (www.tomdouglas.com; 316 Virginia St; pizzas $16-18; ⊙11am-11pm; 🚊Westlake) It's an audacious move to take the down-to-earth Italian pizza and give it a gourmet spin, but local culinary phenomenon Tom Douglas pulls off the trick with casual aplomb. In the crowded confines of Serious Pie you can enjoy beautifully blistered pizza bases topped by such unconventional ingredients as clams, kale, potato, apples, pistachio and more. It's seriously good!

LA VITA É BELLA
ITALIAN $$

Map p230 (www.lavitaebella.us; 2411 2nd Ave; pasta $10-14; ⊙11:30am-10pm Mon-Sat, 5-10pm Sun; 🚇13) As any Italian food snob will tell you, it's very hard to find authentic home-spun Italian cuisine this side of Sicily. Thus extra kudos must go to La Vita é Bella for trying and largely succeeding in a difficult field. The pizza margherita is a good yardstick, though the *vongole* (clams), desserts and coffee are also spot on.

As in all good Italian restaurants, the owners mingle seamlessly with the clientele with plenty of handshakes and good humor.

360 LOCAL
NORTHWEST $$

Map p230 (📞206-441-9360; www.local360.org; cnr 1st Ave & Bell St; mains $16-26; ⊙11am-late Mon-Fri, 8am-late Sat & Sun; 🚇13) 🍃 Snaring 90% of its ingredients from within a 360-mile radius, this new restaurant follows it ambitious 'locavore' manifesto pretty rigidly. The farms where your meat was reared are displayed on the daily blackboard menu and the restaurant's wood-finish interior looks like a rustic barn. With such a fertile hinterland to draw upon the food is pretty special; try the rabbit, the oysters or the chickpea cake.

Fresh vegetables supplement most meals, and even the whiskey is local.

FARESTART RESTAURANT
NORTHWEST $$

Map p230 (📞206-443-1233; www.farestart.org; 700 Virginia St; 3-course dinner $25; ⊙11am-2pm Mon-Fri, 5:30-8pm Thu; 🚊Westlake & 7th) 🍃 FareStart serves substantial meals that benefit the community. All proceeds from lunch and the popular Thursday-night Guest Chef dinners – when FareStart students work with a famous local chef to produce outstanding meals – go to support the FareStart program, which provides intensive job training, housing assistance and job placement for disadvantaged and homeless people.

The constantly changing lunch menu is pretty darn gourmet for the price – try the veggie Reuben, or a flatiron steak in blue-cheese sauce. Reservations are strongly recommended for dinner.

PALACE KITCHEN   NORTHWEST $$

Map p230 (206-448-2001; www.tomdouglas.com; 2030 5th Ave; starters $9-15, mains $15-26; 4:30pm-1am; Westlake) Owned by the Dahlia's Tom Douglas, the Palace is a see-and-be-seen hot spot that really picks up for the late-night cocktail scene. Daily dinner specials present such wonders as spaetzle-stuffed pumpkin or traditional pork loin.

Snack on appetizers – including a smoked-salmon-and-blue-cheese terrine or a sampler plate of regional cheeses – or go for the whole shebang with grilled trout, leg of lamb or roast chicken with blackberries and nectarines. There's a late-night happy hour starting at 11pm that includes barbecued short ribs and other awesome deals ($4 to $5), plus drink specials.

PINTXOS   TAPAS $$

Map p230 (www.pintxoseattle.com; 2207 2nd Ave; tapas $5-10; 11am-10pm, to 11pm Fri & Sat; 13) Say the word Basque these days and you might as well be saying 'gourmet' – the Spanish autonomous region has more Michelin stars per capita than anywhere in the world apart from Tokyo. Pinxtos are Basque tapas, and they serve them with panache in this ice-cool bar that could have you planning your next vacation to San Sebastian.

Honorable mentions should go to the lamb skewers with yogurt dip, and the cauliflower with garlic and olive oil.

QUEEN CITY GRILL   SEAFOOD $$

Map p230 (206-443-0975; www.queencitygrill.com; 2201 1st Ave; starters $8-17, salads $5-12, mains $12-33; 4:30-11pm Sun-Thu, to midnight Fri & Sat; 13) This longtime Belltown favorite specializes in grilled seafood from its daily menu and a solid selection of meats and chicken from its seasonal menu. The goat's cheese appetizer, crab cakes and rib eye are all highly rated, and the warm lighting makes the room feel cozy yet sophisticated. Reservations are recommended.

BAROLO RISTORANTE   ITALIAN $$$

Map p230 (206-770-9000; www.baroloseattle.com; 1940 Westlake Ave; pasta $16-22, mains $20-42; 11:30am-10:30pm, to 11pm Fri & Sat; Westlake & 7th) An upscale Italian place named after one of Italy's finest vinos, Barolo provides a good excuse to taste the deep, powerful 'king of wines' or – if your budget won't stretch that far – a supporting cast of half a dozen under-appreciated Barberas or Dolcettos (there's a generous and popular 'happy hour' that kicks off daily at 3pm).

If you're sitting down to eat, the rigatoni with lamb and Parmesan, followed by a *secondo* of lemony veal is as good as anything you'll find in Piedmont. The restaurant is located in the Denny Triangle, a five-minute walk from the Westlake Center.

DAHLIA LOUNGE   NORTHWEST $$$

Map p230 (206-682-4142; www.tomdouglas.com; 2001 4th Ave; lunch $10-22, dinner starters $9-15, mains $22-38; 11:30am-2:30pm, 5-10pm Mon-Fri, 9am-2pm, 5-11pm Sat & Sun; Westlake) Owner Tom Douglas started fusing flavors at this Seattle institution in the late 1980s and single-handedly made Seattleites more sophisticated; his empire has grown a lot since then, but the flagship restaurant remains a local favorite. There's a bakery next door where you can pick up one of the Dahlia's fabulous desserts to go. Reservations are recommended.

SHIRO'S SUSHI RESTAURANT   JAPANESE $$$

Map p230 (www.shiros.com; 2401 2nd Ave; mains $26.75; 5:30-9:45pm; 13) There's barely room for all the awards and kudos that cram the window in this sleek Japanese joint. Grab a pew behind the glass food case and watch the experts concoct delicate and delicious Seattle sushi.

TILIKUM PLACE CAFE   NORTHWEST, BRUNCH $$$

Map p230 (206-282-4830; www.tilikumplacecafe.com; 407 Cedar St; mains $20-30; 11am-10pm; 3) Sometimes old Belltown and new Belltown sit bumper to bumper, and the juxtaposition is never more marked than on Cedar St, where the suave, pseudo-Parisian Tilikum Place lies right next door to its polar opposite, the Five Point Café. Both serve a mean brunch.

In Tilikum you can enjoy your grilled eggplant sandwich with the yoga crowd. In Five Point tuck into 11oz fried chicken steaks alongside Charles Bukowski look-alikes.

LOLA   GREEK, MEDITERRANEAN $$$

Map p230 (206-441-1430; www.tomdouglas.com; 2000 4th Ave; mains $22-32; ; Westlake) Seattle's ubiquitous cooking maestro

IT HAPPENED AT THE WORLD'S FAIR

Known officially as the Century 21 Exposition, Seattle's 1962 World's Fair set out to depict the future, as envisaged through the eyes of an affluent Cold War generation still trapped in the rigid social mores of the 1950s. Looking back today, many of its exhibits look like relics from a Flash Gordon movie, although the expo's larger infrastructure has endured, most notably the monorail (an early experiment in mass transit that was way ahead of its time), the Space Needle (a distinctive city icon) and the Pacific Science Center.

Running for six months between April and October 1962, the fair attracted 10 million visitors, including a freshly demobbed Elvis Presley in the throes of a skin-crawlingly trite movie career. It Happened at the World's Fair was partly filmed in Seattle, and Presley's presence caused quite a stir – although not with the critics, who called the movie a lemon. The fair itself garnered more plaudits and turned a tidy profit (unusual for the time). It also helped cement Seattle as a top-tier American city.

Overshadowed by the Cold War, the fair's main themes were science, the future and 'outer space' (President Kennedy famously pledged to put a man on the moon, in a speech made in September 1962 while the fair was still running). The 'World of Science' exhibit hosted a fantastical Spacearium that took visitors on a virtual journey to the outer galaxies, while the 'World of Tomorrow' sported a Bubbleator, a hydraulic elevator that lifted visitors through a series of aluminum cubes and foretold the future. For all its playful predictions, Century 21 was more an end than a beginning. It closed under the shadow of the Cuban Missile Crisis with Kennedy crying off the closing ceremony to deal with more urgent affairs (ie possible nuclear annihilation). In little over a year, the president would be dead, US soldiers would be dispatched to Vietnam and America would be taking off its '50s straitjacket and embracing the hippie-dippie 1960s.

Tom Douglas goes Greek in this ambitious Belltown adventure and delivers once again with gusto. Stick in trendy clientele, some juicy kebabs, heavy portions of veg, shared meze dishes and pita with dips, and you'll be singing Socratic verse all the way home.

TAVOLÀTA
ITALIAN $$$

Map p230 (✆206-838-8008; 2323 2nd Ave; meals $40-75; ⊗5-11pm; ☐13) Eating around a large communal table was once something you did reluctantly in youth hostels, but lately it's been deemed trendy, which is why it's become a feature in cool Belltown restaurants like Italian-tinged Tavolàta, owned by top Seattle chef Ethan Stowell.

Tavolàta's decor is industrial Belltown, though the menu's more Italian trattoria (homemade pasta) with some Northwestern inflections (nettles). The 5pm happy hour's a laugh.

BUENOS AIRES GRILL
STEAKHOUSE $$$

Map p230 (✆206-441-7076; 2000 2nd Ave; starters $8.50-14, steaks $29-42; ⊗5-10:30pm Tue-Thu, 5pm-12:30am Fri-Sun; ☐13) Tucked into a Belltown side street, this Argentinean steakhouse serves minty-fresh cocktails, unusual salads (like hearts of palm) and huge portions of well-prepared steak. The cooking aromas will lure you in; the fun vibe and the staff's tendency to tango on request will make you linger.

🍷 DRINKING & NIGHTLIFE

For many people, this is the pinnacle of Seattle nightlife. Others say it's been completely ruined by an influx of hipsters who then departed, leaving frat boys in their wake. Whichever view you hold, Belltown is definitely not the sketchy grungeville it once was, but it still has the advantage of numerous bars lined up in tidy rows that lend themselves to all-night bar-hopping.

★SHORTY'S
DIVE BAR

Map p230 (www.shortydog.com; 2222 2nd Ave; ⊗noon-2am; ☐13) Shorty's is all about beer, pinball and music, which is punk and metal mostly. A remnant of Belltown's grungier days that refuses to become an anachronism, it keeps the lights low (to cover the grime?) and the music loud. Pinball machines are built into every table and very basic snacks (hot dogs, nachos) soak up the beer.

FIVE POINT CAFÉ
DIVE BAR, DINER

Map p230 (⏣206-448-9993; 415 Cedar St; ◷24hr; ⚇3) Not 'retro,' just old and endearingly grim, the Five Point Café in Tilikum Sq has been around since 1929, and so have many of its patrons. Half diner, half bar and too worn-in to be mistaken for hip, it's where seasoned barflies and young punks go to get wasted, any time of day.

Check out the men's bathroom: 'allegedly' the urinal offers a periscope view of the Space Needle.

RENDEZVOUS
BAR

Map p230 (⏣206-441-5823; www.rendezvous seattle.com; 2320 2nd Ave; ⚇13) This classy place has a curved bar up the front and a small theater in the back room. Emblematic of the chic makeover of Belltown, the **Jewel Box Theater** was once a slightly grubby venue for punk bands but now sparkles enough to live up to its name. It hosts a variety of music, film and theatrical performances.

LAVA LOUNGE
COCKTAIL BAR

Map p230 (⏣206-441-5660; 2226 2nd Ave; ◷3pm-2am; ⚇13) This tiki-themed dive has games of all kinds and over-the-top art on the walls (you can't miss the Mt St Helen's mural). High-backed booths encourage all-night lingering.

BEDLAM
CAFE

Map p230 (www.bedlamite.com; 2231 2nd Ave; ◷6am-8pm, to 9pm Fri & Sat; ⚇13) There's nothing mad about Bedlam, unless you count the wall-mounted bicycle and the Space Needle sculpture – made out of old junk – that guards the door. Welcome to a one-off coffee bar with no pretensions and a low geek count that specializes in decent lattes and ultra-thick slices of wholemeal toast loaded with peanut butter and jam.

FRONTIER ROOM
BAR

Map p230 (⏣206-441-3377; www.frontierroom. com; 2203 1st Ave; ◷to 2am Tue-Sat; ⚇13) Once an old-school holdover from Belltown's

gritty whiskey-drinkin' days, the Frontier Room went through a phase of being colonized by frat boys and par-tay-ers – sort of a microcosm of Belltown as a whole. It now seems to have calmed down some and is focused on serving pretty good barbecue to the late-night crowd.

ROB ROY
COCKTAIL BAR

Map p230 (⏣206-956-8423; www.robroyseattle. com; 2332 2nd Ave; ◷4pm-2am; ⚇13) A proper cocktail lounge, Rob Roy is dignified yet comfortable – there's a long, dark bar and sophisticated touches like cologne in the restroom, but there's also puffy wallpaper, squishy leather couches and a boar's head and antlers on the wall.

TWO BELLS BAR & GRILL
PUB

Map p230 (⏣206-441-3050; 2313 4th Ave; ◷11am-late Mon-Fri, 1pm-late Sat, 11:30am-late Sun; ⚇13) Flee the white-belt-and-skinny-jeans crowd and seek refuge in the Two Bells, a neighborhood pub with the friendliest barkeeps in town and a familiar crew of regulars whose intense discussions of the previous night's adventures are portable enough to be taken out back to the patio for a smoke. The house special is a meaty burger stacked thigh-high ($9).

Show up Sunday at 1pm for help with the *Times* crossword.

NITELITE LOUNGE
BAR

Map p230 (⏣206-443-0899; 1926 2nd Ave; ◷noon-2am; ⚇Westlake) This little place attached to the Moore Hotel has an outsize charm, thanks mostly to the seen-it-all-and-liked-most-of-it bartenders and regulars.

Some of its classic patina has been lost in a recent facelift, and there's a whole new section with its own look and feel, but the reasons to stop in are the same: it's never crowded and the drinks are strong and cheap. When you go in the door, turn right for the old-school regular crowd or left to see what the youngsters are up to.

RE-BAR
GAY

(www.rebarseattle.com; 1114 Howell St; ⚇70) This storied dance club, where many of Seattle's defining cultural events happened (such as Nirvana album releases), welcomes gay, straight, bi or undecided revelers to its lively dance floor. It's in the Denny Triangle.

⭐ ENTERTAINMENT

☆ Belltown

★CROCODILE   LIVE MUSIC
Map p230 (www.thecrocodile.com; 2200 2nd Ave; ▣13) Nearly old enough to be called a Seattle institution, the Crocodile is a clamorous 560-capacity music venue that first opened in 1991, just in time to grab the coattails of the grunge explosion. Everyone who's anyone in Seattle's alt-music scene has since played here, including a famous occasion in 1992 when Nirvana appeared unannounced supporting Mudhoney.

Despite changing ownership in 2009 and undergoing a grunge-cleansing refurbishment, the Croc remains plugged into the Seattle scene, though these days aspiring stage-divers are more likely to get kicked out than crowd-surfed on the arms of an adoring audience. There's a full bar, a mezzanine floor and a no-frills pizza restaurant on site. Shows kick off around 10pm.

DIMITRIOU'S JAZZ ALLEY   JAZZ
Map p230 (✆206-441-9729; 2033 6th Ave; ▣Westlake & 7th) Hidden in an unlikely spot behind a boring-looking office building is Seattle's most sophisticated and prestigious jazz club. Dimitriou's hosts the best of the locals and many national acts passing through.

BELLTOWN RELICS

Belltown was a featureless amalgam of dull warehouses and low-rise office blocks in the mid-1980s, and well off the radar of the city's condo-dwelling yuppies. Offering cheap rents and ample studio space, it became an escape hatch for underground musicians and hard-up artists whose arrival heralded a creative awakening and led, in part, to the spark that ignited grunge. But, while the grit and grime of '80s Belltown were crucial components in the rise of the Seattle sound, the music's runaway international success had a catalytic effect: Belltown – much to the chagrin of the hard-up rockers who created it – became cool.

So followed a familiar story: seedy inner-city neighborhood attracts artists, gets creative, becomes cool, attracts hipsters, gentrifies, and loses its edge. Belltown's rise, brief honeymoon and rapid decline largely mirrored that of grunge, which, in the eyes of many purists, died the day Nirvana's *Nevermind* hit No 1. By the 2000s, many locals thought the neighborhood was over. Condos were rising, wine bars were replacing exciting music venues, and the martini-and-cocktail set had suddenly decided it was the ideal place to live. But all was not lost. A handful of Belltown's more tenacious older businesses, despite frequent threats of closure, have put up a brave rearguard action. Bars such as Shorty's continue to attract a loyal clientele, old record shops have benefited from a resurgent interest in vinyl, and the neighborhood's most iconic club, the Crocodile, reopened in 2009 after a two-year hiatus. Add in the general air of excitement among the people that crowd the streets, restaurants and clubs every night (even if half of them now wear stilettos), and reports of Belltown's death have clearly been exaggerated. Sure, the bars no longer place cardboard boxes on their toilet floors to soak up the urine, but – rest assured – there's life in the old beast yet.

For a taste of the grittier Belltown of yore, check out the following survivors:

Mama's Mexican Kitchen (p86) In operation since 1975, Mama's has seen off punk, grunge and everything since.

Shorty's (p88) No-compromise dive bar with pinball machines.

Crocodile (p90) The live-music venue that opened at the height of grunge was recently reincarnated in slightly less grungy form.

Rendezvous (p89) Velvety bar with good burgers and an adjoining burlesque theater that's been around since 1927.

Singles Going Steady (p92) Memories of punk rock in a vinyl/CD store.

Five Point Café (p89) A bar that's older than your grandad and all the better for it.

CINERAMA
CINEMA

Map p230 (www.cinerama.com; 2100 4th Ave; 🚇13) Possibly Seattle's most popular theater, Cinerama is one of only three of its type (with a giant curved three-panel screen) left in the world and has a fun, sci-fi feel. Regular renovations, the last of them in 2010, have kept it up to date. It presents a good mix of new releases and 70mm classics.

MOORE THEATER
LIVE MUSIC

Map p230 (📞206-443-1744; www.stgpresents. org/moore; 1932 2nd Ave; 🚇Westlake) Bands love playing this 1800-seat borderline-downtown venue for its classy style and great acoustics. Attached to a stately old hotel, it's Seattle's most venerable operating theater (dating from 1907) and exudes a battered grace and sophistication whether the act is a singer-songwriter, a jazz phenomenon or a rock band.

TULA'S JAZZ
JAZZ

Map p230 (📞206-443-4221; www.tulas.com; 2214 2nd Ave; ⊗4pm-midnight; 🚇13) Tula's has live jazz seven nights a week, from big bands and Latin jazz to up-and-coming names on tour. It's a non-indie-rock oasis in the booze alley that is Belltown.

☆ Seattle Center

SEATTLE REPERTORY THEATER
THEATER

Map p230 (📞206-443-2222; www.seattlerep. org; 155 Mercer St; ⊗box office 10am-6pm Tue-Fri; 🚇Seattle Center) The Seattle Repertory Theater (the Rep) won a Tony Award in 1990 for Outstanding Regional Theater. The largest nonprofit resident theater outfit in the Pacific Northwest, it's known for elaborate productions of big-name dramas and second-run Broadway hits.

INTIMAN THEATER COMPANY
THEATRE

Map p230 (📞206-269-1900; www.intiman.org; 201 Mercer St; ⊗ticket office noon-5pm Tue-Sun; 🚇Seattle Center) In a move that shocked many, Seattle's Tony Award–winning Intiman Theater abruptly closed in April 2011, a victim of the financial crisis, cancelling its whole planned summer season in the process. But city icons aren't allowed to die. Emergency resuscitation was administered and the Intiman raised the $1 million necessary for a heroic reopening in 2012.

With a new artistic director (Andrew Russell) in place, the Intiman is back doing what it does best: magnificent stagings of Shakespeare and Ibsen. Time for another Tony?

SIFF FILM CENTER
CINEMA

Map p230 (📞206-324-9996; www.siff.net; Northwest Rooms, Seattle Center; 🚇Seattle Center) The new digs of the famous film festival runs movies in a small auditorium year round.

PACIFIC NORTHWEST BALLET
DANCE

Map p230 (www.pnb.org; 🚇Seattle Center) The foremost dance company in the Northwest puts on more than 100 shows a season from September through June at Seattle Center's McCaw Hall.

SEATTLE OPERA
CLASSICAL MUSIC

Map p230 (www.seattleopera.org; 🚇Seattle Center) Features a program of four or five full-scale operas every season at McCaw Hall, including a Wagner's *Ring* cycle that draws sellout crowds in summer.

VERA PROJECT
THEATER

Map p230 (📞206-956-8372; www.theveraproject.org; cnr Republican St & Warren Ave N; 🚇Seattle Center) An excellent nonprofit community center run by and for teenagers, the Vera Project books exclusively all-ages shows in a smoke-free and alcohol-free environment. It's also dedicated to giving youth a place to learn skills, make art and get involved in the community.

SEATTLE CHILDREN'S THEATER
THEATER

Map p230 (📞206-441-3322; www.sct.org; 201 Thomas St; tickets $10; ⊗Thu-Sun Sep-Jun; 🚇Seattle Center) Friday and Saturday matinees and evening performances run September to June. There's also a Drama School summer season.

🛍 SHOPPING

Belltown's shopping is patchy. Look hard and you'll find a punk-rock record store and the polar-fleece-happy Patagonia. Rich pickings it ain't.

PETER MILLER ARCHITECTURE & DESIGN BOOKS
BOOKS

Map p230 (www.petermiller.com; 2326 2nd Ave; ⊗10am-6pm Mon-Sat; 🚇13) This recently relocated store, whose window arrangements can make a bibliophile or a design fiend drool, specializes in luxurious architecture books, stationery and art supplies.

SINGLES GOING STEADY
MUSIC

Map p230 (📞206-441-7396; 2219 2nd Ave; ⊙11am-7pm Mon-Sat, noon-6pm Sun; 🚌13) Singles Going Steady – named after an album by those English punk pioneers the Buzzcocks – specializes in punk, hip-hop and ska, mostly in the form of 7in vinyl singles, as well as posters, patches and other accessories. There's a good little magazine selection, too.

ZANADU
COMICS

Map p230 (www.zanaducomics.com; 1923 3rd Ave; ⊙10am-6pm Mon-Sat, noon-5pm Sun; 🚇Westlake) Awash with superheroes and sci-fi geekdom, Zanadu specializes in comics (hundreds of them) and comic-related toys.

ELLIOTT BAY BICYCLES
BICYCLES

Map p230 (📞206-441-8144; www.elliottbay bicycles.com; 2116 Western Ave; ⊙10am-7pm Mon-Sat, 11am-4pm Sun; 🚇Westlake) This place aims itself toward pro or hardcore cyclists who are prepared to slap down big bucks for top-end road bikes. Custom-built Davidson cycles, renowned for their beauty and inventiveness, are assembled out the back. The shop also does repairs.

EXOFFICIO
OUTDOOR EQUIPMENT

Map p230 (📞206-283-4746; www.exofficio.com; 114 Vine St; ⊙10am-6pm Mon-Fri, to 5pm Sat, to 4pm Sun; 🚌13) Kit yourself out for the Sahara or – closer to home – Mt Rainier National Park at this handy alternative to Patagonia.

🏃 SPORTS & ACTIVITIES

🏃 Belltown

SEATTLE GLASSBLOWING STUDIO
GLASSBLOWING

Map p230 (www.seattleglassblowing.com; 2227 5th Ave; ⊙9am-6pm Mon-Fri, 10am-6pm Sat & Sun; 🚌13) If Dale Chihuly's decadent chandeliers have inspired you, try creating your own modest glass art at this blow-your-own glass studio a few blocks from the master's museum. One-off sessions cost $85 to $125, or there are four-hour group or private lessons most days. Alternatively, you can just watch the fascinating process (there's a cafe with a viewing window overlooking the workshop).

24-HOUR FITNESS
GYM

(📞206-624-0651; 1827 Yale Ave; initial fee about $150, monthly dues $35; ⊙24hr; 🚌70) Close to downtown, this gym has an indoor pool, spa, sauna and steam room, child care, classes and tanning, plus the usual weights and cardio equipment. Ask about specials or check online before you go; free 10-day passes are often available, and you can usually get around the joining fee if you time it right.

🏃 Seattle Center

SEATTLE STORM
BASKETBALL

Map p230 (📞206-217-9622; www.wnba.com/storm; single game tickets $20-200; Ⓜ️Seattle Center) With the demise of the SuperSonics, local basketball fans have turned to Seattle's female team, the WNBA championship–winning Storm. Boasting several star US and international players, they've consistently made the play-offs in recent years, taking the title in 2004 and 2010. They play at Key Arena in Seattle Center from May to September.

Queen Anne & Lake Union

QUEEN ANNE | LAKE UNION

Neighborhood Top Five

1 Riding the streetcar to Seattle's fabulously refurbished **Museum of History & Industry** (p95) for a first-class exposition of the city's grunge-playing, aircraft-building, computer-designing history.

2 Circumnavigating Lake Union on dry land on the new **Cheshiahud Loop** (p104).

3 Gawping at **opulent mansions** atop Queen Anne Hill (p96).

4 Sailing in an old wooden boat on placid **Lake Union** (p97).

5 Joining the growing number of celebrity chefs for haute cuisine in **South Lake Union** (p101).

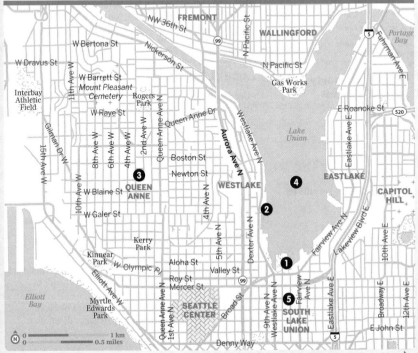

For more detail of this area, see Map p234 ➡

Lonely Planet's Top Tip

Hit a Queen Anne super-market or sandwich bar and take a picnic over to Kerry Park (weather permitting) to enjoy what many locals claim is Seattle's finest view.

✖ Best Places to Eat

➡ Toulouse Petit (p100)
➡ How to Cook a Wolf (p100)
➡ Shanik (p101)
➡ 5 Spot (p100)

For reviews, see p96 ➡

🍷 Best Places to Drink

➡ Uptown Espresso Bar (p102)
➡ El Diablo Coffee Co. (p102)
➡ Mecca Café (p102)
➡ Hilltop Ale House (p102)

For reviews, see p102 ➡

🏃 Best Sporty Activities

➡ REI (p104) indoor climbing wall
➡ Kayaking on Lake Union (p104)
➡ Jogging the Cheshiahud Loop (p104)

For reviews, see p104 ➡

Explore: Queen Anne & Lake Union

At some point during your Seattle sightseeing sojourn, you'll exit the tourist-heavy Seattle Center and be deposited on one of the busy thoroughfares of Lower Queen Anne, a lived-in urban locale good for a cheap meal or an eye-widening dose of Seattle coffee culture. To get a view of a posher side of the neighborhood, take a steep hike (or jump on a bus) up Queen Anne Ave N, aka 'The Counterbalance' to a markedly different neck of the woods.

Sitting on a 456ft hill above the Seattle Center, Queen Anne proper is an elegant collection of majestic redbrick houses and apartment buildings, sweeping lawns manicured to perfection, and gorgeous views of the city and Elliott Bay. Vistas aside (and, yes, they're worth the energy expenditure), the favorite pastime here is 'mansion-viewing,' ie wandering at will along the traffic-lite streets spying on an opulent array of fin de siècle architecture.

To the east, Lake Union – Seattle's watery playground – covers a large area that encompasses several neighborhoods including Fremont and the U District. To get an overview of its famous houseboats and various water-based activities, start in Lake Union Park and circumnavigate the lake on the new Cheshiahud Loop, a 6-mile walking circuit. If you have less time, head straight for the Museum of History & Industry, one of Seattle's best new sights. Across Mercer St there are enough restaurants and coffee bars in the burgeoning South Lake Union neighborhood to keep you fueled until dinner time. The handy streetcar will zap you back from lakeside to downtown in 10 minutes.

Local Life

➡**Uptown Espresso** Examine the velvet foam on your latte while eavesdropping on cell-phone conversations, yoga enthusiasts comparing breathing techniques, and 20-somethings bragging about how many Twitter followers they have.

➡**5 Spot** Find out about the party you missed last night while standing in line for brunch at 5 Spot.

➡**Cheshiahud Loop** Take an early-morning jog around Lake Union and watch the city waking up.

Getting There & Away

➡**Bus** Metro buses 2 and 13 run frequently to Queen Anne from downtown and Seattle Center. Buses 62 and 70 serve the Westlake and Eastlake neighborhoods of Lake Union from downtown.

➡**Streetcar** Seattle's premier streetcar runs between South Lake Union and the Westlake Center downtown every 10 minutes.

MUSEUM OF HISTORY & INDUSTRY

JOHN & LISA MERRILL / GETTY IMAGES ©

TOP SIGHT
MUSEUM OF HISTORY & INDUSTRY

Almost everything you need to know about Seattle is crammed into the refurbished Museum of History & Industry (MOHAI), recently relocated to new digs in South Lake Union. In operation since the 1950s, and with an archive of over four million objects, MOHAI displays its stash of historical booty in an impressively repurposed naval armory building.

Exhibits

The big eye-catcher as you walk in is a 1919 Boeing airplane hanging from the roof (the first commercial Boeing ever made). Indeed, the name 'Boeing' looms large over the whole museum, along with numerous other Seattle icons (Starbucks, Rainier beer, grunge). In the city that produced Microsoft, there is no shortage of interactive exhibits to enjoy (kids will have a ball), including a photo and comment booth, touchscreen TVs and an opportunity to explore railroad history by banging large mallets on railway sleepers. With so many artifacts to call upon, exhibits can change regularly, although the museum's overriding sentiment remains constant: an unashamed celebration of Seattle's short but action-packed history.

Upper Floors

In the upper-floor rooms, the exhibits unfold chronologically using various themes to paint a multilayered portrait of the city. Highlights include the 1889 Great Fire, the 1962 World's Fair, a focus on film and TV (covering everything from *Twin Peaks* to *Grey's Anatomy*), and an interesting dip into Seattle's counterculture – including a self-critical look at the 1999 WTO conference riots. On the top floor there's an ingenious periscope that offers visitors a 360-degree view of the world outside, dominated by the glistening waters of Lake Union.

DON'T MISS...

➡ Film & TV exhibit
➡ Main atrium
➡ Periscope

PRACTICALITIES

➡ Map p234
➡ ☎ 206-324-1126
➡ www.mohai.org
➡ 860 Terry Ave N
➡ adult/child under 14yr $14/free
➡ ⊙ 10am-5pm, to 8pm Thu
➡ 👶
➡ 🚊 Lake Union Park

◉ SIGHTS

◉ Queen Anne

KERRY PARK   PARK

Map p234 (211 W Highland Dr; 🚻; 🚌2) Amid the glittering Beverly Hills–like mansions of Highland Dr, mere commoners can enjoy eagle's-eye views of downtown Seattle and Elliott Bay (and Mt Rainier, should it take its cloudy hat off) from this spectacular lookout.

Binoculars (50c) are provided, so you can look back at the people at the top of the Space Needle looking over at you. The park is set on a steep incline of Queen Anne Hill (looking south) and is split in two, with a stairway linking to a popular children's playground below. This is a favorite spot to end a romantic date night – or make a proposal!

Going a little further west along W Highland Dr will take you to the lesser-known **Betty Bowen Park**, where views stretch west across Puget Sound to the Olympic Mountains. Across the way, check out **Parsons Garden**, a public garden that's especially popular for summer weddings.

GABLE HOUSE   LANDMARK

Map p234 (1 W Highland Dr, at Queen Anne Ave N; 🚌2) This 14-gabled house was built in 1901 by Harry Whitney Treat, a friend of William F 'Buffalo Bill' Cody. Treat also built the Golden Gardens Park. It's long since become an office building, but both the building and the hillside setting are worth a look.

QUEEN ANNE COUNTERBALANCE   STREET

Map p234 (Queen Anne Ave N, north of W Roy St; 🚌2) The streetcar that chugged up and down the steep grade along Queen Anne Ave started operating on overhead-wire electricity in 1900, but it still needed some help to manage the hill. So engineers designed a system of counterweights – a 16-ton train that ran in a tunnel beneath the street would go up when the cable car went down and vice versa.

The cable cars were retired in 1943, but the underground tunnels are still there.

TURRET HOUSE   LANDMARK

Map p234 (cnr W Halladay St & 6th Ave W; 🚌2) This adorable castle-like building, with gables and (appropriately enough) turrets galore, was once the home of the Love Israel Family, an ex-hippie commune turned religious cult. Love Family members were famous for huffing noxious gasses, refusing to cut their hair and believing they were each part of the body of Jesus Christ. The building has since been converted to apartments.

◉ Lake Union

MUSEUM OF HISTORY & INDUSTRY   MUSEUM

See p95.

CENTER FOR WOODEN BOATS   MUSEUM, SAILING

Map p234 (☎206-382-2628; www.cwb.org; 1010 Valley St; sailboat/rowboat rental per hr $30/25, beginner sailing course $375; ⊙12:30pm-dusk

---

QUEEN ANNE WHO?

Observant students of history might wonder why the Seattle neighborhood of Queen Anne is named after an undistinguished British queen who reigned between the years 1702 and 1714, 150 years before the city was even founded. The answer is rooted in architecture. The hill on which the Queen Anne neighborhood sits is embellished by a rather nebulous style of revivalist architecture first concocted in the UK in the 1860s and brought to North America in the early 1880s, where it remained in vogue until around 1910 (when the neighborhood was being laid out). Queen Anne architecture supposedly harked back to the English baroque buildings of the early 18th century (during the reign of Queen Anne), but the name quickly became something of a misnomer, as the revivalist Queen Anne style took on a life of its own, particularly in the US. Typical Queen Anne features in North America include large bay windows, wraparound porches, steep gabled roofs, polygonal towers, shingles, and lavish gardens. To see some of the more whimsical examples, wander at will among the large private houses on top of Queen Anne Hill. The mansions along Highland Dr are particularly opulent.

TOP SIGHT
LAKE UNION

Unifying Seattle's various bodies of water, freshwater Lake Union was carved by glacial erosion 12,000 years ago. Native American Duwamish tribes once subsisted on its then-isolated shores, but 21st-century Lake Union is backed by densely packed urban neighborhoods and is linked to both Lake Washington and Puget Sound by the Lake Washington Ship Canal (built as part of a huge engineering project in the 1910s). Not surprisingly, the lake is a nexus for water-sports enthusiasts – you'll regularly see kayakers, rowers and sailboats negotiating its calmish teal waters. It also acts as a runway for seaplanes. **Kenmore Air** (www.kenmoreair.com) operates services to Victoria (Canada) and the San Juan Islands from here. Houseboats have punctuated the lake since the 1890s, and it still hosts one of the largest houseboat populations in the US (around 500). The most famous houseboat is that of Sam, the fictional character played by Tom Hanks in the movie *Sleepless in Seattle*. Surrounding the lake on its eastern, western and southern shores are the neighborhoods of **Westlake**, **Eastlake** (dominated by the decommissioned City Light Steam Plant – now occupied by a biotech company) and **South Lake Union**, the city's fastest developing neighborhood-in-the-making.

DON'T MISS...

→ Houseboats
→ Kayaking
→ South Lake Union

PRACTICALITIES

→ Map p234
→ 🚊Lake Union Park

Sat & Sun & by appointment Oct-Apr, 12:30pm-dusk Tue-Sun May-Sep; 🚊Lake Union Park) If you have an interest in the history and craft of wooden boats then you'll definitely want to visit this place. A museum and enthusiast's center, it features vintage and replica boats and offers sailing lessons, including an excellent beginner course that gives you as many lessons as it offers in a four-month period (usually eight to 12).

Seasoned sailors who are a little rusty can take a one-on-one lesson for around $50 per hour, and there are also classes on sail repair and boat building. You can rent sailboats and rowboats, but one person in your party has to know how to sail and must do a checkout ($10 fee) before you'll be permitted to rent. It's pretty straightforward: you need to demonstrate tacking, jibing and docking. The center also offers free boat rides every Sunday afternoon.

LAKE UNION PARK   PARK

Map p234 (🏛; 🚊Lake Union Park) Opened in 2010, this welcome green patch occupies ex-Navy land on the southern tip of Lake Union and has a wading pond (with model sailboats you can use), an attractive bridge

and a boat launch. It hosts the Museum of History & Industry in the old naval armory building and the Center for Wooden Boats.

Various interpretive panels chronicle Seattle's maritime connections. The South Lake Union streetcar stops outside.

DENNY PARK   PARK

Map p234 (🚊Westlake & Denny) Seattle's oldest park was originally designated a cemetery – but that status ended up being rather temporary, and the land was rededicated as parkland. Formerly part of Denny Hill, the park was later flattened in the Denny Regrade of 1910, over protests by preservationists. Today it attracts homeless people and tentative tourists from the nearby Space Needle.

EATING

Many of the dining options in Lower Queen Anne, just west of Seattle Center, are geared toward the pre- or post-event crowd attending functions at Key Arena. If you head up the hill to Upper Queen Anne, you'll find the restaurants

Music & Nightlife

Detroit, New Orleans, Nashville...Seattle! There aren't many cities in the US that can claim to have redirected the path of modern music. But, while the angry firmament of grunge may have faded since the demise of Nirvana et al, the city's rambunctious nightlife scene remains varied and vital.

1. EMP Museum (p82)

The design of this museum was allegedly inspired by one of Jimi Hendrix's smashed-up guitars.

2. Music at the Seattle Center (p76)

The entertainment venues of the Seattle Center offer plenty of ways to get a culture fix.

3. Summer at the Seattle Center (p76)

Alfresco events and street performers take over the grounds of the Seattle Center in summer.

4. Comet (p115)

Capitol Hill's Comet is one of the city's longest-standing venues for live punk, grunge and rock.

have more of the neighborhood's quiet, grown-up, family-friendly atmosphere.

The area around Lake Union used to be a bit of a culinary wasteland, but things are changing (especially in South Lake Union), with big-name chefs such as Tom Douglas and Vikram Vij moving in to cater for the new affluent businesses and residents.

✖ Queen Anne

★5 SPOT   BRUNCH $

Map p234 (1502 Queen Anne Ave N; brunch $8-10; ⊙8:30am-midnight; 👪; ☐2) Top of the hill, top of the morning and top of the brunch charts; the queues outside 5 Spot at 10am on a Sunday testify to a formidable late breakfast. The crowds inspire a great atmosphere, and the hearty menu, which has perfected French toast, huevos rancheros and plenty more American standards, will shift even the most stubborn of hangovers.

QUEEN ANNE CAFÉ   NORTHWEST $

Map p234 (☎206-285-2060; 2121 Queen Anne Ave N; breakfast $8-10; ⊙7am-9pm Mon-Fri, 8am-9pm Sat, 8am-2:30pm Sun; 👪; ☐13) Locals flock to this trendy neighborhood spot for traditional comfort food, including broiled pork chops and various sandwiches, but the place really shines at breakfast. Expect a bit of a wait for weekend brunch.

DICK'S DRIVE-IN   BURGERS $

Map p234 (☎206-285-5155; www.ddir.com; 500 Queen Anne Ave N; burgers from $1.25; ⊙10:30am-2am; ☐13) If you're down to your last few dollars and dying for something to eat, don't panic! Dick's is calling you. Welcome to the only fast-food joint in Seattle where you can still buy a burger for $1.25, along with $1.50 fries (hand cut, no less) and $2.15 milkshakes (made with 100% ice cream, of course).

Gourmet it isn't, but as quintessential only-in-Seattle experiences go, it's up there with the Space Needle (and a lot cheaper).

★TOULOUSE PETIT   CAJUN $$

Map p234 (☎206-432-9069; 601 Queen Anne Ave N; mains $13-17; ⊙8am-2am; ☐13) Something of a Seattle phenomenon, Toulouse Petit is hailed for its generous happy hours, cheap brunches and rollicking atmosphere – it's perennially (and boisterously) busy. Somewhere underneath all this cacophony is the specialty food, which pays more than a

passing nod to the Big Easy (aka New Orleans). Soak up your cocktails with plates of gumbo, po'boys, catfish, and the like.

HOW TO COOK A WOLF   ITALIAN $$

Map p234 (☎206-838-8090; www.ethanstowell restaurants.com; 2208 Queen Anne Ave N; pasta $16-18; ⊙5-11pm; ☐13) 🍴 Despite its scary name, the Ethan Stowell–run HTCAW has nothing to do with roasting wild fauna over your campfire. Rather the name is poached from a book written by MFK Fisher during wartime rationing about how to make the most of limited ingredients. Though times have changed, Stowell embraces the same philosophy.

The food is simple but creative Italian nosh listed on a single sheet of paper and served in a small den-like restaurant. If they ever invent a culinary genre called 'Pacific Northwest Italian' HTCAW will be its archetype.

PESO'S KITCHEN & LOUNGE   MEXICAN, BRUNCH $$

Map p234 (☎206-283-9353; www.pesoskitchen. com; 605 Queen Anne Ave N; breakfast $7-10, dinner $10-15; ⊙9am-2am; ☐13) A place that wears many sombreros, Peso's serves fine Mexican food in the evenings amid a cool, trendy scene that is anything but Mexican. But the trump card comes the next morning, after the beautiful people have gone home, with an acclaimed egg-biased breakfast.

GRUB   AMERICAN $$

Map p234 (☎206-216-3628; www.letsgogrub. com; 7 Boston St; mains $14-17; ⊙11am-9pm Tue-Thu, 11am-10pm Fri, 8am-10pm Sat, 8am-3pm Sun; 👪; ☐13) Sounds like an old greasy spoon, but, on the contrary, Grub is clean, fresh and new. Playing to the Queen Anne posh family demographic, it offers hearty, healthy spins on classic American dishes. The interesting salads are singled out for praise and the kids menu is one of the best in the city.

PARAGON BAR & GRILL   AMERICAN $$

Map p234 (☎206-283-4548; 2125 Queen Anne Ave N; mains $12-22; ⊙11:30am-2am Mon-Sat, 10am-2am Sun; ☐13) The Paragon is a bastion of American regional cooking, specializing in grilled fish and updated classics. Try the baby back ribs or a plate of fried green tomatoes. There's an open fireplace and a lively bar scene (the bar's open until 2am).

LOWER QUEEN ANNE

Hungry tourists from the Seattle Center bump into affluent young techies on their lunch breaks in Lower Queen Anne, the thin strip at the bottom of the 'counterbalance' that strikes a less haughty (and more economical) pose than its eponymous neighbor up on the hill. A northern extension of Belltown, Lower Queen Anne – or 'Uptown' as it's sometimes known – is locally renowned for its eclectic mix of restaurants, most of which are quick, casual and above all easy on the wallet. Concert-goers and sports fans from the nearby Intiman Theater and Key Arena naturally gravitate here after performances and games (Queen Anne Ave N and Roy St are the main drags), while downtown is only two minutes away on the monorail. As a neighborhood, Lower Queen Anne has more in common with Belltown than Queen Anne, with new condos slowly snuffing out remnants of its erstwhile seediness.

Most nights there's live music or DJs playing everything from indie rock and hip-hop to funk and soul.

CANLIS NORTHWEST, AMERICAN **$$$**
Map p234 (☑206-283-3313; 2576 Aurora Ave N; mains $36-96; ☺5:30pm-late Mon-Sat) This place is old school enough for either prom night or your grandma's birthday dinner. The traditional, classic food and service are both top notch, and you can rest assured that none of the style is affected. Canlis has been around since 1950 and its authenticity shows. The view is lovely, too. Reservations are recommended, especially for weekends.

🍴 Lake Union

BLUE MOON BURGERS BURGERS **$**
Map p234 (☑206-652-0400; www.bluemoon burgers.com; 920 Republican St; burgers $6-10; ☺11am-8pm Mon-Fri, noon-8pm Sat & Sun; 🚃Westlake & Mercer) One in a trio of local burger joints (the others are in Fremont and Capitol Hill), Blue Moon has brought locavore ethics to fast food, sourcing its buns from Pioneer Square's Grand Central Bakery and their grass-fed beef from local farms. Not that this makes its humungous 'snacks' any healthier. Then again, that's not the point.

SERIOUS BISCUIT BISCUITS **$**
Map p234 (☑206-436-0050; www.serious piewestlake.com; 401 Westlake Ave N; biscuits $6-11; ☺7am-3pm Mon-Fri, 9am-3pm Sat & Sun; 🚃Westlake & Thomas) After Serious Pie comes Serious Biscuit, Tom Douglas' first bite at the South Lake Union cookie that has lured so many new restaurants into the neighborhood in the last couple of years. The buttery biscuits (the savory American

rather than sweet British variety) serve as flaky bases to a variety of brunch-worthy toppings – the 'zach' (fried chicken, gravy, bacon and egg) is a perennial favorite.

Bear in mind that this is a typical Douglas domain with shared tables and limited seating. Upstairs, he operates another of his Serious Pie pizza joints in the evenings.

SERAFINA ITALIAN **$$**
Map p234 (☑206-323-0807; www.serafina seattle.com; 2043 Eastlake Ave E; starters $5-12, pastas $12-18, mains $19-28, prix fixe lunch $14.95; ☺brunch Sun, lunch Mon-Fri, dinner to midnight daily; 🚃70) This lovely neighborhood restaurant in Eastlake specializes in Tuscan-style cooking, with simply prepared meat and fish as well as pastas that can be ordered as a first or a main course. A gorgeous leafy deck area behind the restaurant now doubles as the entryway to **Cicchetti**, Serafina's new sibling that serves Mediterranean snacks. Reservations are recommended.

SHANIK INDIAN, FUSION **$$$**
Map p234 (☑206-486-6884; www.shanik restaurant.com; 500 Terry Ave N; mains $16-27; ☺11:30am-2pm & 5:30pm-late Mon-Fri, 5:30pm-late Sat; 🚃Terry & Mercer) Vancouver culinary institution Vikram Vij brought his internationally lauded Indian-fusion food south in 2012, saving countless driving miles for the loyal stream of Seattleites who regularly used to head north to Canada in order to taste his famous spice-encrusted lamb popsicles (yes, they are *that* good).

Shanik is run by Vij's wife, Meeru, and promises more of that clever crossover cuisine that marries the flavors of the subcontinent with western style and presentation. It'll stay etched in your memory for months.

🍷 DRINKING & NIGHTLIFE

When it comes to drinking, this neighborhood is all over the map. Pleasantly sleepy Queen Anne has everything from traditional beer halls and dives to swanky jazz bars. South Lake Union is full of new corporate bars where the password is Amazon.

🍷 Queen Anne

★ EL DIABLO COFFEE CO. CAFE

Map p234 (www.eldiablocoffee.com; 1811 Queen Anne Ave N; ⏰5:30am-8pm Mon-Fri, 6:30am-8pm Sat & Sun; 🚌13) Anyone for a *café cubano*? While the US trade embargo against Cuba prevents the sale of Cuban coffee beans, you can at least enjoy your coffee Cuban-style (ie strong, short, black and loaded with sugar) in this colorful little cafe on Queen Anne Hill.

UPTOWN ESPRESSO BAR CAFE

Map p234 (☎206-285-3757; 525 Queen Anne Ave N; ⏰5am-10pm Mon-Thu, 5am-11pm Fri, 6am-11pm Sat, 6am-10pm Sun; 🚌13) Competing with Starbucks for generous opening hours, Uptown has been around since the early 1980s and is famous for the 'velvet foam' that embellishes its lattes. The original and best cafe – there are now eight locations – is this neighborhood nexus in Lower Queen Anne, an oasis of casual elegance.

MECCA CAFÉ DIVE BAR

Map p234 (☎206-285-9728; 526 Queen Anne Ave N; burgers $8.75; ⏰7am-2am; 🚌13) The Mecca has been called – by dudes who know – the best bar in Seattle. Half of the long, skinny room is a diner, but all the fun happens on the other side, where decades worth of scribbles on beer mats line the walls, the jukebox still works the way a jukebox should, the bartenders know the songs on it better than you do, and you can get waffles with your beer until 3pm or so.

MCMENAMINS QUEEN ANNE BREWPUB

Map p234 (www.mcmenamins.com; 200 Roy St; ⏰11am-1am; 🎸; 🚌13) Portland's microbrewing McMenamin brothers have extended their franchise to Seattle using their ever-successful interior-design formula: a blend of psychedelia meets art nouveau meets

wood-paneled gentlemen's club. But the real draw is the beer, including the classic Hammerhead pale ale, loaded with Oregon hops. There's good food and it's kid-friendly.

CAFFE LADRO CAFE

Map p234 (www.caffeladro.com; 2205 Queen Anne Ave N; ⏰5:30am-10pm; 🚌13) 🅿 With an Italian name that translates as 'coffee thief,' apparently because it set out to nick business from Starbucks, Ladro has subsequently established its own small Seattle-only chain (13 branches and counting). This is the original, dating from 1994. Not only do they roast their own beans, they do their own baking.

HILLTOP ALE HOUSE PUB

Map p234 (☎206-285-3877; 2129 Queen Anne Ave N; ⏰11:30am-11pm Sun-Thu, to midnight Fri & Sat; 🚌13) Hilltop is a comfy neighborhood hangout on Queen Anne Hill, sister to the 74th Street Ale House. It has a friendly vibe and a large selection of microbrews, served in proper 20oz pints, and the menu is well above your standard pub fare.

🍷 Lake Union

BRAVE HORSE TAVERN PUB

Map p234 (www.bravehorsetavern.com; 310 Terry Ave N; ⏰8am-midnight Mon-Fri, 10am-midnight Sat & Sun; 🚌Terry & Thomas) With this place, posing as a kind of German beer hall meets Wild West saloon, Tom Douglas has made his (inevitable) lunge into the world of pubs. Brave Horse sports two dozen draft beers (local amber ales are well represented) and the place even bakes its own pretzels in a special oven.

With the Amazon HQ around the corner, the crowds are predictably Amazon-ish, though there's plenty of intermingling at the shuffleboard tables.

☆ ENTERTAINMENT

☆ Queen Anne

ON THE BOARDS THEATRE

Map p234 (☎206-217-9888; www.ontheboards.org; 100 W Roy St; 🚌13) *The* place for avant-garde performance art, the nonprofit On

the Boards makes its home at the intimate Behnke Center for Contemporary Performance and showcases some innovative and occasionally weird dance and music. Some of it has an international flavor, while the rest focuses primarily on regional topics and talent.

SIFF CINEMA UPTOWN CINEMA
Map p234 (✆206-285-1022; 511 Queen Anne Ave N; 🚇13) The Uptown is joint HQ for the Seattle International Film Festival (SIFF), meaning its three screens get an intelligent and varied turnaround of movies.

TEATRO ZINZANNI CIRCUS SHOW
Map p234 (www.dreams.zinzanni.org; 222 Mercer St; 🚇13) Welcome to the zany world of the 'circus dinner show,' a sort of vaudeville meets Vegas meets Cirque de Soleil. Sit back in an improvised big top for a night of jugglers, jokers, trapeze artists, music and more. The Teatro has been running since 1998 and became a permanent fixture in 2002. Tom Douglas designed the multicourse dinner menu.

☆ Lake Union

EL CORAZON LIVE MUSIC
Map p234 (✆206-381-3094; www.elcorazonseattle.com; 109 Eastlake Ave E; 🚌70) Formerly the Off-Ramp, then Graceland, El Corazon has lots of history echoing around its walls – and lots of sweaty, beer-drenched bodies bouncing off them. Save your clean shirt for another night, and don't expect perfect sound quality at every show. The gutsy bands play loud, presumably to drown out the traffic noise from I-5 just outside the door.

The venue is etched in grunge-era mythology. Pearl Jam, then going under the name of Mookie Blaylock, played their first ever gig here in October 1990.

🏠 SHOPPING

With its own climbing wall, artificial rainstorms and a simulated mountain trail, the state-of-the-art REI megastore has become a tourist destination in its own right.

🏠 Queen Anne

QUEEN ANNE BOOKS BOOKS
Map p234 (✆206-283-5624; 1811 Queen Anne Ave N; ⏰10am-7pm, to 5:30pm Sat & Sun; 🚇13) This quiet little nook is a charming neighborhood bookstore, with frequent special events and a nice selection of children's materials. The adjoining El Diablo coffee shop has a lovely little patio where you can sip a coffee sand pore over your latest book purchase.

ONCE UPON A TIME CHILDREN
Map p234 (✆206-284-7260; 1622 Queen Anne Ave N; ⏰10am-6pm; 🚇13) This children's store stocks top international brands like Baby Bjorn for savvy parents who like to dress their renaissance tots in labels from around the world. You'll find everything from the practical to the simply adorable: strollers, knit toys, train sets, books, games, little socks and hats, and more.

🏠 Lake Union

SOUL WINE WINE
Map p234 (www.soulwineseattle.com; 401 Westlake Ave N; ⏰11am-7pm Mon-Fri, 10am-6pm Sat, 10am-2pm Sun; 🚌Westlake & Thomas) Strategically situated next to Tom Douglas' Serious Biscuit restaurant (which often requires a wait for tables), this is a wine retail store with tastings ($5 for three wines). They mix local vintages with 'old world' wines, with a strong bias toward Italy. Staff are highly knowledgeable and congenial.

FEATHERED FRIENDS OUTDOOR EQUIPMENT
Map p234 (✆206-292-2210; www.featheredfriends.com; 119 Yale Ave N; ⏰10am-8pm Mon-Fri, 9am-7pm Sat, 11am-5pm Sun; 🚌70) Near REI, Feathered Friends stocks high-end climbing equipment, made-to-order sleeping bags and backcountry ski gear. Products made with down are the specialty.

PATRICK'S FLY SHOP OUTDOOR EQUIPMENT
Map p234 (✆206-325-8988; www.patricksflyshop.com; 2237 Eastlake Ave E; ⏰10am-6pm, to 3pm Sun; 🚌70) Located near Lake Union, this shop has been around as long as anyone can remember. It offers workshops on fly-fishing, sells equipment and gives advice.

🏃 SPORTS & ACTIVITIES

🏃 Queen Anne

SIERRA CLUB WALKING
(www.sierraclub.org; 🚌62) Leads day-hiking and car-camping trips on weekends; most day trips are free.

🏃 Lake Union

CHESHIAHUD LOOP TRAIL
Map p234 Recently inaugurated to tie in with the landscaping of Lake Union Park, this 6-mile route that circumnavigates Lake Union has been criticized by some locals for being little more a gelling together of existing trails, sidewalks and paths – and it's true; there's little new here except for some handy signposts and an official name (which comes from a Native Duwamish chief who once headed a lakeside village).

Nonetheless, if you're an out-of-towner (or a local), this is a good way to keep away from busy roads while traveling through at least five Seattle neighborhoods.

REI OUTDOORS
Map p234 (🖉206-323-8333; 222 Yale Ave N; ⊘9am-9pm Mon-Sat, 10am-7pm Sun; 🚌70) As much an adventure as a shopping experience, this state-of-the-art megastore has its own climbing wall – a 65ft rock pinnacle to the side of the store's entryway. The wall is open for scrambling at various times daily, except Tuesday, when it's reserved for private groups. (You can climb free of charge, but be prepared to wait your turn.) You can also check out the rain-proofing of various brands of gear by entering a special rainstorm shower, or road test hiking boots on a simulated mountain trail. REI also rents various ski packages, climbing gear and camping equipment – call for daily and weekly rates.

MOSS BAY ROWING & KAYAK CENTER ROWING
Map p234 (🖉206-682-2031; www.mossbay.net; 1001 Fairview Ave N; kayak/sailboat rental per hr $13/35; ⊘8am-8pm summer, 10am-5pm Thu-Mon winter; 🚢Fairview & Campus Dr) Moss Bay offers rentals, extensive lessons and tours (from $45 per person) on Lake Union.

NORTHWEST OUTDOOR CENTER INC KAYAKING
Map p234 (www.nwoc.com; 2100 Westlake Ave N; kayaks per hr $14-22; 🚌62) On Lake Union, rents kayaks and offers tours and instruction in sea and white-water kayaking.

SEATTLE SCUBA DIVING
Map p234 (🖉206-284-2350; www.seattlescuba.com; 2000 Westlake Ave N, No 210; ⊘11am-6pm Mon & Wed-Fri, 9am-5pm Sat & Sun; 🚌62) Offers beginners open-water dive courses from $420. Qualified divers can take part in organized excursions. Dive boats go out into Puget Sound for weekend day trips; prices start at $110 (four-person minimum).

Capitol Hill & First Hill

CAPITOL HILL | FIRST HILL

Neighborhood Top Five

1 Strolling along the **Pike–Pine corridor** (p113), stopping off at bars, brunch stops, music venues or restaurants and watching the fashionable theater of life on the Hill.

2 Seeing a name band at legendary live-music venue **Neumo's** (p115).

3 Climbing the **water tower** (p107) in Volunteer Park to admire dazzling vistas of Seattle and Mt Rainier.

4 Gazing jealously at the **mansions on 14th Avenue** and seeing how the top 2% live.

5 Coming up for air after an afternoon of lazy literary immersion at **Elliott Bay Book Company** (p116).

For more detail of this area, see Map p236 ➡

Lonely Planet's Top Tip

In Capitol Hill, restaurants, bars and cafes usually put quality over quantity. Thus the neighborhood abounds with specialist micro- or (even smaller) nano-businesses. Look out for microbreweries (beer), micro-roasteries (coffee), micro-distilleries (spirits) and micro-creameries (ice cream).

✖ Best Places to Eat

➡ Cascina Spinasse (p112)

➡ Sitka & Spruce (p112)

➡ Poppy (p112)

➡ Oddfellows Cafe (p111)

For reviews, see p110 ➡

🍷 Best Places to Drink

➡ Espresso Vivace at Brix (p113)

➡ Victrola Coffee Roasters (p113)

➡ Elysian Brewing Company (p114)

➡ Tavern Law (p114)

For reviews, see p113 ➡

🍷 Best GLBT Places

➡ R Place (p115)

➡ Wildrose (p115)

➡ Neighbours (p115)

➡ Crypt (p116)

For reviews, see p115 ➡

Explore: Capitol Hill & First Hill

To decipher Seattle's most diverse, spirited and downright cool neighborhood it's useful to understand a little of its geography. There are three main commercial strips worth exploring in Capitol Hill – Broadway (the main drag), 15th Ave, and the ultra-cultural Pike–Pine corridor – all of which are refreshingly walkable. Geographically the strips are gelled together by Capitol Hill's residential grid, a mixture of cheap apartment buildings, large grandiose houses and the green expanses of Volunteer Park. This weird but never caustic juxtaposition of rich/poor and chic/scruffy is one of the neighborhood's biggest allures. Herein lives Seattle's wildest assortment of people.

If you're walking up from downtown crossing I-5 on E Pine St, you'll enter the neighborhood close to Melrose Market at the western end of the Pike–Pine corridor. This stretch of aging brick warehouses and former 1950s car dealerships made over into gay bars, live-music clubs, coffeehouses, record stores and fashionable restaurants is Seattle's nightlife central. Explore it by night on foot.

Running perpendicular to Pike–Pine is Capitol Hill's main commercial street, Broadway, while several blocks east is the quieter business district of 15th Ave E. This is where some of the city's wealthiest residents live in the grand old mansions that embellish tree-lined streets such as 14th Ave (aka Millionaires Row). Gawp at the opulence as you make your way up to Capitol Hill's peak, Volunteer Park, home to the Asian Art Museum, a conservatory and a water tower.

More genteel First Hill is best accessed from the bottom of Pike–Pine.

Local Life

➡**Espresso Vivace at Brix** Check out next month's fashion and the latest in facial hair at hipster-ville's (and possibly Seattle's), best coffee roasters.

➡**Cal Anderson Park** On warm summer evenings this is the place to come to watch bike polo, office-versus-office baseball games and tattooed bodies picking up a tan.

Getting There & Away

➡**Bus** Metro bus 43 travels between downtown and the U District via Capitol Hill. Bus 10 goes to downtown (Pine and 5th); bus 8 goes to the Seattle Center. To reach First Hill, catch bus 2 on the western side of 3rd Ave downtown and get off at the Swedish Medical Center.

➡**Streetcar** A new line is coming in 2014, from Pioneer Square up through First Hill to Broadway in Capitol Hill.

➡**Walk** Capitol Hill can be reached from downtown by walking up E Pine St.

◉ SIGHTS

◉ Capitol Hill

SEATTLE ASIAN ART MUSEUM   MUSEUM

Map p236 (www.seattleartmuseum.org; 1400 E Prospect St; adult/child $7/5, 1st Thu & Sat of month free; ⊙10am-5pm Wed-Sun, to 9pm Thu; **P**; 🚌10) In stately Volunteer Park, this outpost of the Seattle Art Museum houses the extensive art collection of Dr Richard Fuller, who donated this late-art-deco gallery (a fine example of Streamline Moderne architecture) to the city in 1932.

Spread over one floor and beautifully presented in uncluttered, minimalist rooms, the collection is notable for its Japanese hanging scrolls, some of which date from the 1300s and have been skilfully restored (the restoration process is detailed along with the art). Also of interest are the Indian stone sculptures in the foyer and some remarkably intricate Chinese bronzes dating from around 1600 BC.

VOLUNTEER PARK
CONSERVATORY   CONSERVATORY

Map p236 (☑206-684-4743; 1400 E Galer St; day pass adult/reduced $4/2; ⊙10am-4pm Tue-Sun; 🚌10) The conservatory is a classic Victorian greenhouse built in 1912. Filled with palms, cacti and tropical plants, it features five galleries representing different world environments. Check out the creepy corpse flower.

JIMI HENDRIX STATUE   MONUMENT

Map p236 (1600 Broadway E; 🚌Pike-Pine) Psychedelic guitar genius of the late 1960s and Seattle's favorite son, Jimi Hendrix is captured sunk to his knees in eternal rock-star pose in this bronze sculpture by local artist Daryl Smith, created in 1997 and located close to the intersection of Broadway and E Pine St.

Hendrix fans often leave flowers and candles at the statue's base, and it's not unusual to find a half-burnt cigarette stuck between his lips.

ST MARK'S CATHEDRAL   CHURCH

Map p236 (☑206-323-0300; 1245 10th Ave E; ⊙performances 9:30pm Sun; 🚌49) Go north on Broadway (as the dandyish boutiques turn to well-maintained houses with manicured lawns) until it turns into 10th Ave E and you're within a block of Volunteer Park. At the neo-Byzantine St Mark's Cathedral, various choirs perform for free on Sunday, accompanied by a 3944-pipe Flentrop organ.

LAKEVIEW CEMETERY   CEMETERY

Map p236 (🚌10) One of Seattle's oldest cemeteries and the final resting place of many early settlers, Lakeview Cemetery borders Volunteer Park to the north. Arthur Denny and his family, Doc and Catherine Maynard, Thomas Mercer and Henry Yesler are all interred here. This is also the grave site of Princess Angeline, the daughter of Duwamish Chief Sealth, after whom Seattle was named.

Most people, however, stop by to see the graves of martial-arts film legends **Bruce and Brandon Lee**. Flowers from fans are usually scattered around Brandon's red and Bruce's black tombstones, which stand side by side in a tiny part of the cemetery. The graves are not easy to find: enter the cemetery at 15th Ave E and E Garfield St; follow the road in and turn left at the Terrace Hill Mausoleum. At the crest of the hill you'll see the large Denny family plot on your left. Look a little further along the road, and you'll find the Lees. Even if you're not usually into graveyards, you'll at least enjoy the beautiful views at this one.

LOUISA BOREN LOOKOUT   VIEWPOINT

(15th Ave E, at E Garfield St; 🚌10) Outside the Volunteer Park boundaries, the Louisa Boren Lookout provides one of the best views over the university and Union Bay. The small park is named after the longest-surviving member of the party that founded Seattle in 1851.

WATER TOWER
OBSERVATION DECK   LANDMARK

Map p236 (1400 E Prospect St; 🚌10) It's practically obligatory to climb the 107 steep steps to the top of Volunteer Park's 75ft water tower. Built in 1907, it provides wonderful vistas of the Space Needle, Elliott Bay and – should it be in the mood – Mt Rainier. Explanatory boards in the covered lookout detail the history and development of Volunteer Park.

◉ First Hill

First Hill, just south of the Pike–Pine corridor, is scattered with traces of Seattle's pioneer-era glory, including a few magnificent old mansions and some excellent examples

Art & Culture

You don't have to go to a gallery to see Seattle's art. Creativity is everywhere: on walls, under bridges, in parks and on hatch covers. Join an art walk, organize an 'art attack' or just wait around in neighborhoods like Fremont and Capitol Hill for the local Picassos to show up.

JOHN ELK / GETTY IMAGES ©

4

ANNE C DOWIE / GETTY IMAGES ©

1. Chihuly Garden & Glass (p78)
This new attraction provides a spectacular homage to Dale Chihuly, the master of glass art.

2. Seattle Asian Art Museum (p107)
A late-art-deco gallery that's home to a beautifully presented collection of Asian art.

3. Fremont Public Art (p141)
Residing under the Aurora Bridge is the colossal Fremont Troll, by sculptor Steve Badanes.

4. Hammering Man (p47)
The 48ft-high *Hammering Man*, by Jonathan Borofsky, guards the entrance to the Seattle Art Museum.

3

LONELY PLANET / GETTY IMAGES ©

THE PUBLIC-TRANSPORTATION REVOLUTION

There's a public-transportation revolution going on in Seattle at the moment and its nexus is Capitol Hill. The giant hole in the ground that has lain gaping like Mt St Helens' summit crater on the corner of Denny Way and Broadway since 2008 should have been filled in by the time you read this. In its place will rise Capitol Hill Station, an interchange for two massive transportation projects: the **First Hill streetcar** and the **University Link Light Rail** line. The former is the second stage of Seattle's ambitious streetcar project (complementing the existing South Lake Union streetcar), whose new line will stretch 2.5 miles from Pioneer Square up through First Hill and its medical facilities to Broadway and Denny Way. The line will have 10 stops and be in operation by mid-2014. The second project is vastly more expensive, costing $1.9 billion to construct an underground light-rail link that will connect existing Westlake Station with Capitol Hill and the U District. It is an extension of the Sea-Tac Airport–Downtown line that opened in 2009 and is due for completion in 2016.

of early Seattle architecture. If you're going to break a leg, do it here: First Hill is nicknamed 'Pill Hill' because it's home to three major hospitals. There's also a good museum and a historic hotel worth visiting.

FRYE ART MUSEUM   MUSEUM
Map p236 (🕿206-622-9250; www.fryemuseum.org; 704 Terry Ave; ⊙11am-5pm Tue-Sun, to 7pm Thu; 🅿; 🚇First Hill South) **FREE** This small museum on First Hill preserves the collection of Charles and Emma Frye. The Fryes collected more than 1000 paintings, mostly 19th- and early-20th-century European and American pieces, and a few Alaskan and Russian artworks.

If this inspires a stifled yawn, think again. Since its 1997 expansion, the Frye has gained a hipness that it once lacked, with fresh ways of presenting its artwork, music performances, poetry readings and interesting rotating exhibits from traveling painters to local printmakers.

SORRENTO HOTEL   HISTORIC BUILDING
Map p236 (900 Madison St; 🚇64) This grand working hotel located on First Hill is a fine example of Italian Renaissance architecture. Built in 1909 by a Seattle clothing merchant, the Sorrento was one of the first hotels designed to absorb the crowds of prospectors journeying through town on their way to Alaska in search of gold.

Don't miss a chance to nose around the interior opulence.

STIMSON-GREEN MANSION   HOUSE
Map p236 (🕿206-624-0474; www.stimsongreen.com; 1204 Minor Ave; tours $10, registration required; ⊙1-2:30pm 2nd Tue each month; 🚇64) One of the first homes on First Hill, the baronial Stimson-Green Mansion is an English Tudor-style mansion completed in 1901 by lumber baron and real-estate developer CD Stimson. Built from brick, stucco and wood, this stately home is now owned by Stimson's granddaughter and used for private catered events such as weddings and themed dinners.

The interior rooms are decorated to reflect the different design styles popular at the turn of the 20th century. To register for a tour, call the **Washington Trust for Historic Preservation** (🕿206-624-9449).

ST JAMES CATHEDRAL   CHURCH
Map p236 (www.stjames-cathedral.org; 804 9th Ave; 🚇64) Seattle's beautiful Italian Renaissance–style Catholic cathedral was built in 1907. The original dome collapsed in 1916, the result of a rare Seattle snowstorm, but the two impressive towers remain. Inside, the altar is located unusually in the church's center.

✖ EATING

Ninety-five percent of the best eating choices are in Capitol Hill.

✖ Capitol Hill

The scene on Capitol Hill is almost as much about style as food: it's no use enjoying a fabulous dinner if no one can see how chic you look while you're eating it. Then again, great ambience hardly detracts from a fine-dining experience, so who's complaining? The restaurants along Broadway and 15th

Ave and the Pike–Pine corridor offer the full range of Seattle dining options.

MAMNOON
MIDDLE EASTERN $

Map p236 (✆206-906-9606; www.mamnoon restaurant.com; 1508 Melrose Ave; takeout $3-8; ☺11am-10pm Tue-Thu & Sun, to 11pm Fri & Sat; ▣10) If you're working your way around the world in one neighborhood, Mamnoon is Capitol Hill's token Middle Eastern stop – with strong Syrian and Lebanese inflections. The chic new perch is in the 'Melrose Triangle,' already sequestered by the slavishly locavore Melrose Market.

Slink inside for an unusual and wonderfully memorable voyage to the culinary Levant where you'll be immersed in fragrant flatbreads and perfumed dips that are complemented by some fine meat kebabs. Prices are reasonable and there's a handy take-out window upfront offering crispy falafels.

ARABICA LOUNGE
CAFE, BRUNCH $

Map p236 (✆206-347-6093; www.arabicalounge. com; 1550 E Olive Way; brunch $9-14; ☺7:30am-3pm Mon-Fri, 9am-6pm Sat & Sun; ▣43) With the once iconic Bauhaus coffee bar moving to Ballard, the Hill's hipsters have had to seek out new places to cross-fertilize their retro fashion ideas. Small and beautiful Arabica Lounge fits the bill, with mismatched chairs and worn wood mixing with candelabras, edgy art and the *New York Times*.

The coffee's smooth, and they also serve a casual brunch daily from 9am to 2pm.

HONEYHOLE
SANDWICHES $

Map p236 (✆206-709-1399; 703 E Pike St; sandwiches $5-12; ☺10am-2am; ▣Pike-Pine) Cozy by day, irresistible at night, the Honeyhole has a lot to recommend it: big, stuffed sandwiches with funny names (Luke Duke, the Texas Tease), greasy fries, a full bar, DJs and a cool cubbyhole atmosphere after sunset.

BLUEBIRD
MICROCREAMERY
ICE CREAM, BAR $

Map p236 (www.bluebirdseattle.blogspot.com; 1205 E Pike St; ice cream from $3; ☺noon-10pm; ▣Pike-Pine) We've witnessed the birth of the microbrewery, the micro-roastery and the micro-distillery, so it was only a matter of time before someone came up with the micro-creamery. Bluebird has gone further than other small-scale ice-cream makers by serving beer and espresso in the same space, either separately (ie in a cup or glass) or mixed in as an ice-cream flavor.

Ask for a tasting spoon and get your head (and tongue) around stout-flavored ice cream made using the stout from Elysian brewery next door.

BIMBO'S CANTINA
MEXICAN $

Map p236 (✆206-329-9978; www.bimbos cantina.com; 1013 E Pike St; burritos $5.50-7.50; ☺noon-2am; ▣Pike-Pine) Bimbo's slings fat tacos, giant burritos and juicy quesadillas until late. The space is bordello kitsch with velvet matador portraits, oil paintings with neon elements and a hut-style thatched awning. The best feature of the restaurant is its subterranean bar, the Cha-Cha Lounge.

MOLLY MOON'S
ICE CREAM $

Map p236 (✆206-708-7947; www.mollymoon icecream.com; 917 E Pine St; ice cream $3-5; ☺noon-11pm; ▣Pike-Pine) 🍃 So what flavor will it be today? The chamomile blossom with 'vegan cold' topping, the Stumptown coffee, or the salt licorice? Choices can be confusing at Molly Moon's, where lines stretch out the door and the whole place smells enticingly of waffles. Nursing locavore sensibilities, Molly gets its cream from hormone-free Washington cows. Its original location is in Wallingford.

CAFÉ PRESSE
FRENCH $

Map p236 (✆206-709-7674; www.cafepresse seattle.com; 1117 12th Ave; mains $14; ☺7am-2am; ▣12) This dreamy cafe, opened by the owners of cute French bistro Le Pichet, specializes in unfussy dishes the likes of which you'd find once upon a time in a terrace cafe around Saint-Germain-des-Prés. The croque monsieur and madame are huge slabs of creamy goodness, steak frites are perfectly cooked and filling, and the vegetables are fresh and crisp.

ODDFELLOWS CAFE
MODERN AMERICAN $$

Map p236 (✆206-325-0807; www.oddfellows cafe.com; 1525 10th Ave; mains $14-18; ☺8am-late; ▣Pike-Pine) 🍃 A trendy dude dressed in '70s retro gear welcomes you at the door and puts your name on the list. The wait's 10 minutes, long enough to take in the decor (historic meeting hall reborn as rustic-meets-urban restaurant) and the clientele (dressed mostly like the guy at the door).

The food, when it comes, is just what your taste buds were craving, especially the brunch, a smorgasbord of flaky biscuits, fluffy eggs and well-dressed salads.

CAPITOL HILL & FIRST HILL EATING

RIONE XIII
ITALIAN $$

Map p236 (📞206-838-2878; www.ethanstowell restaurants.com; 401 15th Ave E; mains $15; ⏰5-11pm; 🚌10) 🍴 The secret of Roman food lies in two words 'simple' and 'effective.' That's its inherent beauty. Local legend Ethan Stowell probably guessed as much when he opened Rione XIII on cool 15th Ave in 2012. Come here for epic *caccio e pepe* (spaghetti with four ingredients), Roman street pizzas, fried artichokes and the popular four-cheese taster plate (spoiler: they're all mozzarella).

Otherwise, Rione exhibits the usual Stowell hallmarks: modern-rustic decor, evening-only opening, and a single-page, ever-changing menu.

COASTAL KITCHEN
NORTHWEST $$

Map p236 (📞206-322-1145; www.coastalkitchen seattle.com; 429 15th Ave E; mains $9-19; ⏰8am-midnight; 🚌10) This longtime favorite turns out some of the best food in the neighborhood – it has an eclectic mix of Cajun, Mayan and Mexican inspirations, and an Italian-language instruction tape running in the bathroom, if that gives a clue about influences. Menus rotate by theme, but constant favorites include roast chicken, pork chops and all-day breakfast.

Fish dishes are startlingly fresh and always interesting. Pasta lunch specials are also highly recommended.

ANNAPURNA CAFE
NEPALESE $$

Map p236 (📞206-320-7770; www.annapurna cafe.com; 1833 Broadway E; mains $9-13; ⏰noon-10pm; 🚇Capitol Hill) One of the Hill's best ethnic places is this subterranean Nepalese restaurant on Broadway whose extensive menu mixes in a few Indian and Tibetan varietals as well. There are soups, thalis, curries, breads and plenty of vegetarian options. It's busy (good sign), but service is quick and efficient.

OSTERIA LA SPIGA
ITALIAN $$

Map p236 (📞206-323-8881; www.laspiga.com; 1429 12th Ave; pastas $15; ⏰11:30am-2:30pm & 5-10pm; 🚇Pike-Pine) Italian restaurants in Pike–Pine aren't labeled 'Italian'; instead, their names are regionalized. Hence, La Spiga describes itself as 'Emilia-Romagna,' specializing in the food of the Bologna and Parma region – arguably Italy's finest.

The *'osteria'* moniker doesn't really fit (the restaurant is large and contemporary), but the food – *tagliatelle al ragú* and the

authentic Romagna bread called *piadina* – shouldn't disappoint Italians or recent visitors to Italy. All pasta is homemade.

R & L HOME OF GOOD BAR-B-QUE
SOUTHERN $$

(📞206-322-0271; 1816 E Yesler Way; mains $10-15; ⏰11am-9pm Tue-Sat; 🚌27) You can't get within a block of this little neighborhood joint without drooling from the smell of barbecue. The storefront looks a little unpromising, but inside there's a wood-paneled cafeteria with curtained windows, a few tables and a counter for take-out orders.

★CASCINA SPINASSE
ITALIAN $$$

Map p236 (📞206-251-7673; www.spinasse.com; 1531 14th Ave; 2-course meal $40; ⏰5-10pm Sun-Thu, to 11pm Fri & Sat; 🚌11) Behind the rather fussy lace curtains hides what is possibly the finest new restaurant in Seattle. Spinasse specializes in cuisine of the Piedmont region of northern Italy. This means delicately prepared ravioli, buttery risottos (enhanced with stinging nettles, no less), rabbit meatballs and roasted artichokes. The impressive wine menu is dominated by fine Piedmontese reds including Barolo, available by the glass.

★SITKA & SPRUCE
NORTHWEST $$$

Map p236 (📞206-324-0662; www.sitkaand spruce.com; 1531 Melrose Ave E; small plates $8-24; ⏰11:30am-2pm & 5:30-10pm; 🚌10) Now in a new location in the Capitol Hill 'hood, this small-plates fine diner has won acclaim for its casual vibe, constantly changing menu, good wine selection and involved chef-owner (he'll be the guy who brings bread to your table). All the ingredients are obtained from local producers, and the idea is to assemble a meal out of a bunch of different taster-size dishes.

Only a few reservations are accepted each night, and the wait can be long, so grab yourself a beer and spend some time studying the chalkboard menu until it's your turn.

POPPY
NORTHWEST $$$

Map p236 (📞206-324-1108; www.poppyseattle. com; 622 Broadway E; 7/10-item thali $26/32; ⏰5:30-11pm; 🚌60) A thali is an Indian culinary tradition whereby numerous small taster dishes are served on one large plate. At Poppy they've cleverly applied the same principle to a broader list of Seattle/

THE PIKE–PINE CORRIDOR: A VILLAGE WITHIN A VILLAGE

The Pike–Pine corridor, a sinuous urban strip on the eastern edge of Capitol Hill, is Seattle's factory of hip, a village within a village where the city's most fashionable offspring come to party like bright young things in a latter-day F Scott Fitzgerald novel.

Once a huddle of auto showrooms (only a couple remain), the area underwent a metamorphosis in the early 21st century when an influx of artists and young entrepreneurs snapped up the vacant car lots and transformed them into unique community-run boutiques, cafes, restaurants, clubs and bars.

A fast-evolving scene was quickly established as Pike–Pine garnered a reputation as the best place in Seattle to buy back your grandma's sweaters, bar crawl with Kurt Cobain's ghost, get your hair cut like Phil Oakey from the Human League or merely pull up a street-side chair and watch life go by.

And what a colorful life it is. Style in Pike–Pine is edgy and ephemeral. Typical interior design juxtaposes old high-school desks and sofas rescued from junkyards with chandeliers, ethnic antiques and post-Pollack art. Even more voguish is the neighborhood's retro-cool fashion scene, which marries beatnik beards and 1980s indie-pop hairstyles with ironic tattoos, natty headgear and Simone de Beauvoir's old dress collection. Tolerance is widespread. This is the epicenter of Seattle's gay life and a haven for every alternative philosophy this side of San Francisco. In the space of half a dozen blocks you'll find a lesbian pub, an anarchist coffee bar, an apothecary, a shop selling sex toys, countless indie coffee shops and Seattle's finest bookstore.

To experience Pike–Pine in all its glamorous glory, start at Melrose Market near I-5 in the early afternoon, then walk up E Pike St to Madison Ave and come back down E Pine St. There are enough interesting distractions to keep you occupied until at least midnight – the next day!

Northwest specialties, meaning that instead of chicken korma you get small portions of halibut, black-eyed peas and orange pickle. It's as good as it sounds.

✕ First Hill

Full up with health-care facilities and educational establishments, First Hill doesn't offer much in the way of restaurants, unless you like hospital food.

HUNT CLUB NORTHWEST $$$
Map p236 (✆206-343-6156; www.hotelsorrento.com; Sorrento Hotel, 900 Madison St; starters $8-16, mains $19-30, afternoon tea $35; ☺7am-10pm Sun-Thu, to midnight Fri & Sat; ☐64) The Hunt Club ought to be on the shortlist if you're looking for a special-occasion, top-end restaurant. The setting is ultra posh and absolutely beautiful: an intimate mahogany-paneled dining room shimmering with candles and decked with flowers. The food is equally stellar, featuring local lamb, fish and steak from sustainable farms, accentuated by inventive sauces and regional produce. Reservations are recommended.

🍷 DRINKING & NIGHTLIFE

Capitol Hill is *the* place to go out for drinks, whether you want a fancy cocktail, a cappuccino or a beer. It's also where 90% of the city's gay bars are located.

🍷 Capitol Hill

★ESPRESSO VIVACE AT BRIX CAFE
Map p236 (www.espressovivace.com; 532 Broadway E; ☺6am-11pm; ☐60) Loved in equal measure for its no-nonsense walk-up stand on Broadway and this newer cafe (a large retro place with a beautiful Streamline Moderne counter), Vivace is known to have produced some of the Picassos of latte art. But it doesn't just offer pretty toppings: many of Seattle's coffee experts rate its espresso shots as the best in the city.

VICTROLA COFFEE ROASTERS CAFE
Map p236 (www.victrolacoffee.com; 310 E Pike St; ☺6:30am-8pm Mon-Fri, 7:30am-8pm Sat & Sun; ☐10) With its main cafe and roasting room occupying an old car showroom in Capitol Hill's factory of hip, the Pike–Pine corridor,

Victrola is something of a trendsetter. The roasting room is quite a spectacle, staffed by bearded boffins who walk around like Q in a James Bond film brandishing earmuffs and clipboards.

You can't argue with the product, though – pure, unadulterated coffee. Come for the free cupping with a coffee expert on Wednesday at 11am.

ELYSIAN BREWING COMPANY
BREWPUB

Map p236 (www.elysianbrewing.com; 1221 E Pike St; ⊙11:30am-2am; ⊡Pike-Pine) On E Pike St, the Elysian's huge windows are great for people-watching – or being watched. This is one of Seattle's best brewpubs (they also run the Tangletown Pub near Green Lake), loved in particular for its spicy pumpkin beers.

SUN LIQUOR DISTILLERY
BAR, DISTILLERY

Map p236 (www.sunliquor.com; 514 E Pike St; ⊙11am-2am; ⊡10) More trendsetting on the Hill. Sun is a micro-distillery that makes its own gin and vodka behind the same bar where they're served (in cocktails, mainly). Even better, the place also offers a full food menu, making it pretty unique in the US; could this be the first in a long line of gastro-distilleries?

Opened in 2011, the distillery is the brainchild of the same guy who co-founded Top Pot Hand-Forged Doughnuts.

BLACK COFFEE
CAFE

Map p236 (www.blackcoffeecoop.com; 501 E Pine St; ⊙8am-midnight; ⊡10) 'And now for something completely different' is not a line you hear often in Capitol Hill, where off-the-wall passes for normal, but Black Coffee pushes the boat out further than most with this new workers co-op/anarchist coffee bar. Come for the big, open windows, vegan muffins, good coffee, mini-library and avant-garde music (think John Cale crossed with Bjork).

TAVERN LAW
COCKTAIL BAR

Map p236 (☑206-322-9734; www.tavernlaw.com; 1406 12th Ave; cocktails $9, dishes $9-15; ⊙5pm-2am; ⊡12) Named for the 1832 law that legalized drinking in public bars and saloons and sparked the golden age of cocktails, Tavern Law is a mandatory stop for those making the rounds of the best drinks in Seattle. Drinks are crafted by star local bartender David Nelson.

The food menu consists of whatever's written on the chalkboard that day; if you're lucky, it will say 'provolone pork belly cheeseburger.'

CAFFÉ VITA
CAFE

Map p236 (www.caffevita.com; 1005 E Pike St; ⊙6am-11pm; ⊡Pike-Pine) The laptop fiend, the date, the radical student, the homeless person, the philosopher, the business guy on his way to work: watch the whole neighborhood pass through this Capitol Hill institution (one of four in Seattle), whose on-site roasting room is visible through a glass partition.

HIGH LINE
BAR

Map p236 (☑206-328-7837; www.highlineseattle.com; 210 Broadway E; ⊙11am-2am Mon-Fri, 9am-2am Sat & Sun; ⊡Capitol Hill) From the guys who ran the late and much-lamented Squid & Ink vegan cafe in Georgetown comes this bar-restaurant hybrid (mostly a bar, but with the distinct advantage of serving hearty food until 1am). As the door guy put it, 'We have lots of games, cheap booze and a full vegan menu' – he strongly recommends the biscuits and gravy for brunch. There's also live music.

STUMPTOWN ON 12TH
CAFE

Map p236 (☑206-323-1544; www.stumptowncoffee.com; 1115 12th Ave; ⊙6am-11pm Mon-Fri, 7am-10pm Sat & Sun; ⊡12) There's a tug of loyalties with Stumptown, Portland's coffee pioneers founded in 1999 by Duane Sorenson, who hails from Puyallup near Seattle. Stumptown practically defined the new third-wave coffee movement when it opened its first cafe in downtown Portland, selling fair-trade, single-origin, home-roasted coffee with an emphasis on taste rather than cup size.

The ethics served to inspire just about every other indie coffee roaster in the US, so it's hardly surprising you'll still find a sizable contingent of Stumptown loyalists, especially among the Seattleites who congregate in this busy nook, one of two Stumptowns in Capitol Hill.

BALTIC ROOM
CLUB

Map p236 (☑206-625-4444; www.thebalticroom.net; 1207 Pine St; free or cover; ⊡Pike-Pine) Classy and high ceilinged, with wood-paneled walls, paper lanterns and an elegant balcony, this Capitol Hill club hosts an excellent mix of local and touring DJs in a range of genres, from reggae and house to drum-and-bass.

BARÇA
COCKTAIL BAR

Map p236 (☑206-325-8263; www.barcaseattle.
com; 1510 11th Ave; ⊙5pm-2am; ⬚Pike-Pine) Velvet couches, filmy curtains, plush booths, a
serpentine bar – this is one sexy, decadent
lounge. Settle in among the other pretty
people for seduction or quiet conversation.

LINDA'S TAVERN
DIVE BAR

Map p236 (☑206-325-1220; www.lindastavern.
com; 707 E Pine St; happy-hour microbrews $3;
⊙4pm-2am Mon-Fri, 10am-2am Sat & Sun, happy
hour 7-9pm; ⬚Pike-Pine) The back patio here
is an excellent place to observe the nocturnal habits of *Hipsterus Northwesticus*.
Linda's is one of the few joints in town
where you can recover from your hangover
with an Emergen-C cocktail and a vegetarian brunch while taxidermied moose heads
stare at you from the walls.

It's also – supposedly – the last place
where Kurt Cobain was seen alive.

R PLACE
GAY

Map p236 (☑206-322-8828; www.rplaceseattle.
com; 619 E Pine St; ⊙4pm-2am Mon-Fri, 2pm-
2am Sat & Sun; ⬚Pike-Pine) Weekend cabaret
performances, amateur strip shows, go-go
boys and DJs – there's something entertaining going on every night of the week at this
welcoming gay bar. Relax with a beer on the
deck or dance your ass off.

Three floors of dancing to hip-hop and
R&B DJs and plenty of sweaty body contact
make this club a blast for pretty much everyone who isn't terribly uptight. If you're feeling brave, take a shot at winning a hundred
bucks in the all-male wet-undies contest.

COMET
DIVE BAR

Map p236 (☑206-323-9853; 922 E Pike St;
⊙noon-2am; ⬚Pike-Pine) Gulp... Unlike all of
those other carefully configured dive bars
on Pike-Pine, Comet really *is* a dive bar,
everything from the tattily dressed, liberally tattooed clientele to the lingering aroma of last week's spilled beer is real. Dive
in and enjoy it while it's still there.

WILDROSE
LESBIAN

Map p236 (☑206-324-9210; 1021 E Pike St;
⊙5pm-midnight Mon, 3pm-1am Tue-Thu, 3pm-
2am Fri & Sat, 3pm-midnight Sun; ⬚Pike-Pine)
This small, comfortable lesbian bar has
theme nights (dykes on bikes, drag-king
shows) as well as a light menu, pool, kara-
oke and DJs. On weekends it gets packed, so
figure on a bit of a wait to get in.

NEIGHBOURS
GAY

Map p236 (www.neighboursnightclub.com; 1509
Broadway Ave E; ⬚Pike-Pine) Check out this
always-packed dance factory for the gay
club scene and its attendant glittery
straight girls.

CANTERBURY ALE & EATS
PUB

Map p236 (☑206-322-3130; 534 15th Ave E;
⊙11am-2am Mon-Fri, 10am-2am Sat & Sun; ⬚10)
If you can get past the suit of armor guard-
ing the door, you'll find that everything else
about this Old English–style pub in a pretty
black-and-white building makes for a cozy
hangout, from the snugs and the tapestried
booths to the fireplace and friendly service.

CENTURY BALLROOM
CLUB

Map p236 (☑206-324-7263; www.centuryball
room.com; 915 E Pine St; ⬚Pike-Pine) Dance lessons ($15 to $20 for drop-ins) followed by
an everyone-out-on-the-floor dance free-
for-all makes a night at the Century the
perfect combination of spectating and
participating. Dance nights include everything from the lindy hop to salsa. Check
the website for a schedule of events.

☆ ENTERTAINMENT

☆ Capitol Hill

NEUMO'S
LIVE MUSIC

Map p236 (www.neumos.com; 925 E Pike St;
⬚Pike-Pine) A punk, hip-hop and alterna-
tive-music venue that counts Radiohead
and Bill Clinton (not together) among its
former guests, Neumo's (formerly known
as Moe's) fills the big shoes of its original
namesake. Yes, it can get hot, and yes,
mid-show it's a long walk to the toilets; but
that's rock and roll.

The club's latest addition is the Barboza
Lounge, a more intimate downstairs music
venue.

CHOP SUEY
LIVE MUSIC

Map p236 (www.chopsuey.com; 1325 E Madison
St; ⬚12) Chop Suey is a dark, high-ceilinged
space with a ramshackle faux-Chinese motif and eclectic bookings – indie, hip-hop
and rock are staples – although its Jai Ho
nights with Bollywood-Bhangra dancing
led by Mumbai native and DJ Prashant
have become riotously popular.

NORTHWEST FILM FORUM CINEMA

Map p236 (www.nwfilmforum.org; 1515 12th Ave; ⓐPike-Pine) A film arts organization whose two-screen cinema offers impeccable programming, from restored classics to cutting-edge independent and international films. It's in Capitol Hill, of course!

ANNEX THEATER THEATER

Map p236 (☎206-728-0933; www.annextheater. org; 1100 E Pike St; ⓐPike-Pine) Seattle's main experimental-fringe theater group is the Annex, whose 99-seat theater (with bar) inhabits the Pike–Pine corridor. The highlight for many is the 'Spin the Bottle' nights on the first Friday of every month (11pm), a riot of comedy, music and variety.

HARVARD EXIT CINEMA

Map p236 (www.landmarktheatres.com; cnr E Roy St & Harvard Ave E; ⓐ60) Built in 1925 as HQ for a pioneering women's group called 'The Women's Century Club,' this building was converted into Seattle's first independent theater in 1968, although the club still meets here. It specializes in independent and foreign-language films.

RICHARD HUGO HOUSE COMMUNITY CENTER

Map p236 (☎206-322-7030; www.hugohouse. org; 1634 11th Ave; ⓧhouse noon-6pm Mon-Fri, to 5pm Sat, zine archive 4-8pm Wed, 1-5pm Thu & Sat; ⓐPike-Pine) Established in honor of famed Northwest poet Richard Hugo, and the nexus of Seattle's literary community, the Hugo House hosts readings, classes and workshops, as well as offering various events around town. Writers-in-residence keep office hours at this 1902 house (a former mortuary), during which they're available for free consultations about writing projects.

The extensive zine library invites all-day lingering, and there's also a library, a conference room, a theater and a cafe with a small stage.

GAY CITY LIBRARY READINGS, TALKS

Map p236 (☎206-860-6969; 517 E Pike St; ⓧ11am-8pm Mon-Fri, to 5pm Sat; ⓐ10) This library was set up in 2009 by Gay City, a community organization, and has already collected 5000 volumes on LGBT topics. There are regular readings and a queer book group that meets on the second Saturday of each month.

🛍 SHOPPING

Shopping on Capitol Hill makes you instantly hipper; even just window-shopping is an education in cutting-edge popular culture. This is the place to find great record stores, unusual bookstores, vintage clothing shops and risqué toy stores.

🏛 Capitol Hill

ELLIOTT BAY BOOK COMPANY BOOKS

Map p236 (www.elliottbaybook.com; 1521 10th Ave; ⓧ10am-10pm Mon-Fri, to 11pm Sat, 11am-9pm Sun; ⓐPike-Pine) Perish the day when ebooks render bookstores obsolete. What will happen to the Saturday-afternoon joy of Elliott Bay, where 150,000 titles inspire author readings, discussions, reviews and hours of serendipitous browsing?

BABELAND ADULT

Map p236 (www.babeland.com; 707 E Pike St; ⓧ11am-10pm Mon-Sat, noon-7pm Sun; ⓐPike-Pine) Remember those pink furry handcuffs and that glass dildo you needed? Well, look no further.

CRYPT ADULT

Map p236 (☎206-325-3882; 1516 11th Ave; ⓧ11am-11pm; ⓐPike-Pine) Now in a bigger space after moving from its cavernlike original location, the Crypt sells clubwear and leather clothing (mostly but not entirely for guys), DVDs, sex toys and novelties.

TWICE SOLD TALES BOOKS

Map p236 (☎206-324-2421; 1833 Harvard Ave; ⓧ10am-9pm, to 10pm Fri & Sat; ⓐCapitol Hill) Twice Sold Tales' Capitol Hill location has moved, but it's still a cozy den full of very-well-priced used books, stacked haphazardly along narrow aisles. A book 'happy hour' discount kicks in after 6pm. A bunch of aloof cats roam the shop, actively ignoring everybody.

DILETTANTE CHOCOLATES FOOD & DRINK

Map p236 (☎206-329-6463; www.dilettante. com; 538 Broadway E; ⓧ5pm-1am Mon-Fri, 11am-1am Sat, 11am-11pm Sun; ⓐCapitol Hill) If you have a sweet tooth to satisfy, try the confection truffles here. There's a great selection of desserts, too. You can taste chocolates in the shop, along with good coffee and other snacks, or pick up a box to take home. The

European-style chocolates are made in-house.

THROWBACKS NW CLOTHING

Map p236 (www.throwbacksnw.com; 1205 E Pike St; ⊙11am-8pm Mon-Sat, noon-6pm Sun; 🚇Pike-Pine) Vintage sports gear of once-great sports teams that are no longer quite so good.

APRIE CLOTHING

Map p236 (☑206-324-1255; 310 Broadway E; ⊙11am-8pm Mon-Sat, to 6pm Sun; 🚇Capitol Hill) A small boutique with a well-curated selection of trendy tops, dresses and skinny jeans from brands too hip to list here (I mean, if you don't know, *I'm* not gonna tell you). Aprie is a miniparadise for fashionistas.

CROSSROADS TRADING CO CLOTHING

Map p236 (www.crossroadstrading.com; 325 Broadway E; ⊙10am-8pm Mon-Sat, 11am-7pm Sun; 🚇Capitol Hill) This used-clothing store is less expensive than others in the area but also generally less hipster-chic, which is nice if you just want to shop for basics without having some too-cool clerk stare down her nose at your khaki slacks. There's another branch in the **U District** (Map p242; ☑206-632-3111; 4300 University Way NE).

WALL OF SOUND MUSIC

Map p236 (☑206-441-9880; 315 E Pine St; ⊙11am-7pm Mon-Sat, noon-6pm Sun; 🚇10) One of the coolest record stores in town, this smart shop stocks music you've never heard of, from obscure noise artists to gypsy folk songs, but nothing the owners and staff wouldn't listen to at home. The wall of magazines, comics and small-press books is top-notch, too.

RED LIGHT CLOTHING

Map p236 (☑206-329-2200; www.redlight vintage.com; 312 Broadway E; ⊙11am-8pm Sun-Thu, to 9pm Fri & Sat; 🚇Capitol Hill) Red Light carries stylish, painstakingly selected vintage clothing, organized by decade or sometimes by color. It's a cool shop...maybe too cool. Rest assured: you will be judged by your purchases. There's also a branch in the **U District** (Map p242; ☑206-545-4044; 4560 University Way NE).

URBAN OUTFITTERS CLOTHING

Map p236 (☑206-322-1800; 401 Broadway E; ⊙10am-9pm Sun-Thu, to 10pm Fri & Sat; 🚇Capitol Hill) Urban Outfitters in the Broadway Market sells clothing geared toward young folks looking to score points on the hip scale without having to think too hard about putting together a look.

🏃 SPORTS & ACTIVITIES

🏃 Capitol Hill

SAMADHI YOGA YOGA

Map p236 (www.samadhi-yoga.com; 1205 E Pike St; 🚇Pike-Pine) Drop-in yoga studio with downstairs boutique (selling clothing) and art gallery. Classes are $15.

Seattle Outdoors

Maybe it's the lure of lofty snowcapped Mt Rainier or the sight of calm, kayak-able Lake Union – Seattle has the unnerving habit of turning traditionally sedentary office stiffs into fleece-donning, Lycra-wearing athletes. Wake up and smell the pine needles. They don't call it the Emerald City for nothing.

MINT IMAGES - MICHAEL HANSON / GETTY IMAGES ©

KARL WEATHERLY / GETTY IMAGES ©

1. Running (p33)
There are good trails for runners, in the urban landscapes and the many city parks.

2. & 4. Mt Rainier National Park (p176)
Outside the city are boundless opportunities, including hiking and cycling in the Cascade mountain range.

3. Discovery Park (p151)
Discovery Park offers 534 acres of urban wilderness and plenty of ways to get windswept.

5. Kayaking from Alki Beach (p167)
Take to the water to explore the Alki Beach area.

KARL WEATHERLY / GETTY IMAGES ©

The CD, Madrona & Madison Park

MADISON PARK | CD | MADRONA

Neighborhood Top Five

1 Following the old trolley route down E Madison St to original Seattle seaside resort **Madison Park Beach** (p129) for a game of Frisbee, a brave dip in the lake, and some wholesome restaurant food.

2 Learning about Seattle's little-known African American heritage in the CD's **Northwest African American Museum** (p122).

3 Finding a French flavor in the bakeries and bistros of **Madison Valley** (p127).

4 Tree-spotting and bird-watching in the **Washington Park Arboretum** (p122).

5 Seeking out great African food in the CD's **Little Ethiopia** (p127).

For more detail of this area, see Map p240 ➡

Explore: The CD, Madrona & Madison Park

While individually distinct, the three neighborhoods sandwiched between Capitol Hill and Lake Washington don't really form a coherent whole. Although they can be explored together, most nonresidents come here for a specific reason: eg the beach at Madison Park, brunch in Madrona, or French food in Madison Valley.

Running down the east slope of First Hill, the Central District (CD) represents the heart of Seattle's African American community and is relatively easy to reach from downtown. The neighborhood's slightly down-at-heel arteries are 23rd Ave and Martin Luther King Jnr Way, but it lacks any real nexus and can feel semi-abandoned after Capitol Hill. You can initiate a stroll of its quiet streets in search of soul food and Ethiopian cuisine starting from the top of the Pike–Pine corridor.

Keep walking east through the CD and you'll hit Madrona, one of Seattle's more ethnically diverse neighborhoods that is being gradually gentrified with some positively opulent mansions overlooking Lake Washington. Madrona is worth a trip to indulge in one of Seattle's most popular brunch places, the Hi Spot Café, followed by a walk along the lakefront.

If the weather's good, Madison Park merits a separate visit for its cute beach, genteel neighborhood vibe and the Madison Park Conservatory, a lauded sustainable restaurant. It is best reached on bus 11 along E Madison St, following an old trolley line that once bussed in knackered lumber workers for some weekend R & R. About a mile before you reach the beach it's worth stopping in tree-lined Madison Valley, aka 'Little France,' for buttery croissants and a quick stroll in the Washington Park Arboretum.

Local Life

➡ Hi Spot Café One of those neighborhood brunch spots that lures in people from all over town, this is where sleepy Madrona wakes up, especially on Sunday.

➡ Madison Park Beach Some say 'the Park' is snooty, but it ain't true, at least not on sunny days, when the whole neighborhood hits the small lakeside beach.

Getting There & Away

➡ Bus Metro bus 11 runs from downtown along Pike and E Pine Sts to Capitol Hill and then along E Madison St all the way to Madison Park. Bus 8 goes from the Seattle Center via Capitol Hill to the CD, where it runs north–south through the neighborhood along Martin Luther King Jr Way. Bus 2 connects downtown with Madrona Beach via Capitol Hill.

Lonely Planet's Top Tip

Madison Valley, the 'other' (fourth) neighborhood in this rather disparate chapter, is worth a visit in its own right. Enjoy some fine French food from one of half a dozen eating places before taking a peek at the tree collection at the Washington Park Arboretum.

✖ Best Places to Eat

➡ Rover's (p127)

➡ Voila! (p127)

➡ Hi Spot Café (p128)

➡ Cafe Selam (p127)

For reviews, see p123 ➡

🍷 Best Places to Drink

➡ Tougo Coffee (p128)

➡ Attic Alehouse & Eatery (p128)

➡ Cortona Cafe (p128)

For reviews, see p128 ➡

◉ Best Parks

➡ Washington Park Arboretum (p122)

➡ Madison Park (p129)

➡ Madrona Park (p129)

➡ Howell Park (p122)

For reviews, see p122 ➡

◉ SIGHTS

◉ Madison Park

WASHINGTON PARK ARBORETUM PARK
Map p240 (🗖11) This wild and lovely park offers a wide variety of gardens, a wetlands nature trail and 200 acres of mature forest threaded by paths. More than 5500 plant species grow within the arboretum's boundaries. In the spring **Azalea Way**, a jogger-free trail that winds through the arboretum, is lined with a giddy array of pink- and orange-flowered azaleas and rhododendrons.

Trail guides to the plant collections are available at the **Graham Visitors Center** (Map p240; 2300 Arboretum Dr E; ⊙10am-4pm). Free guided tours of the grounds take place at 1pm on Saturday and Sunday from January to November.

FOSTER ISLAND WETLANDS TRAIL TRAIL
Map p240 (🗖25) The northern edge of Washington Park Arboretum includes this wonderful woodchip-paved trail around Foster Island in Lake Washington's Union Bay, a picnic spot that once was a burial ground for Union Bay Native Americans. The waterfront trail winds through marshlands and over a series of floating bridges to smaller islands and reedy shoals.

Bird-watching is popular here, as are swimming, fishing and kayaking. It's just too bad that the busy, elevated Hwy 520 roars above the island.

DENNY BLAINE PARK PARK
Map p240 (🗖2) South of Madison Park toward the tail of Lake Washington Blvd is Denny Blaine Park, found at the end of a looping tree-lined lane. This predominantly lesbian beach is surrounded by an old stone wall, which marked the shoreline before the lake level was dropped 9ft during construction of the shipping canal.

VIRETTA PARK PARK
Map p240 (🗖2) Just a little further southwest of Denny Blaine Park, you'll find the two-tiered Viretta Park, from which you can see the mansion once owned by Nirvana's Kurt Cobain and Courtney Love – it's the house on the north side of the benches. Cobain took his life with a shotgun in the mansion's greenhouse in April 1994.

The greenhouse is long gone and Love no longer owns the house, but Nirvana fans still make the pilgrimage to this small park to pay tribute and scribble messages on the benches in the lower part of the park.

JAPANESE GARDEN GARDENS
Map p240 (☎206-684-4725; adult/senior & student $6/4; ⊙10am-7pm Apr-Sep, to dusk Oct-Mar; 🗖11) At the southern edge of Washington Park Arboretum, this 3.5-acre formal garden has koi pools, waterfalls, a teahouse and manicured plantings. Granite for the garden's sculptures was laboriously dragged in from the Cascades. Tea-ceremony demonstrations are frequently available. Call for a schedule.

HOWELL PARK PARK
Map p240 Just south of Viretta Park is a small beachfront called Howell Park. It is usually less crowded due to the lack of parking. If you're on foot, look for a small sign and trailhead that leads to the beach.

◉ CD

NORTHWEST AFRICAN AMERICAN MUSEUM MUSEUM
(NAAM; ☎206-518-6000; www.naamnw.org; 2300 S Massachusetts St; adult $6; ⊙11am-4:30pm Wed & Fri, to 7pm Thu, to 4pm Sat, noon-4pm Sun; 🗖60 from Capitol Hill) Small, concise and culturally valuable, NAAM opened in 2008 after over 30 years of planning. It occupies the space of an old school that until the 1980s educated a large number of African American children in the Central District. After the school closed, it was occupied for a while by community activists who prevented it from being demolished.

Inside, the museum's main exhibits map the story of black immigration to the Pacific Northwest, especially after WWII. Details are given of some of the leading African American personalities, including George Washington Bush (the first black settler in Washington state), Manuel Lopes (Seattle's first black resident), Quincy Jones (the record producer who grew up in Seattle) and Jimi Hendrix (no introduction required). One of the prize exhibits is a hat Hendrix wore at a 1968 concert in LA. A separate room is given over to temporary exhibitions (an interesting one about

LITTLE ETHIOPIA

The Central District has a history of reinventing itself to incorporate successive waves of new immigrants. In the 1910s it was a primarily Jewish neighborhood, pre-WWII it welcomed Japanese settlers, and postwar it became Seattle's main African American enclave, a characteristic it partly retains. However, since the 1970s the neighborhood has seen an increasing number of African immigrants moving in, particularly from Ethiopia.

The first Ethiopians arrived in 1974 after the country's Derg takeover provoked a massive exodus. In 1970 there were no more than 20 Ethiopians in Seattle; today the region counts approximately 25,000, one of biggest communities in the US. The East African flavor is most prevalent along E Cherry St, where you'll see taxi businesses, grocery stores selling local Amharic-language newspapers, and a slew of Ethiopian restaurants (five alone color the crossroads of E Cherry St and Martin Luther King Jnr Way). Not surprisingly, the name 'Little Ethiopia' is sometimes used to describe the area. In 2013, Joseph W Scott and Solomon A Getahun published a book about the diaspora called *Little Ethiopia of the Pacific Northwest*.

novelist James Baldwin was showing at last visit).

JIMI HENDRIX PARK PARK
(www.jimihendrixparkfoundation.org; 2400 S Massachusetts St; ☐60 from Capitol Hill) Dedicated to Hendrix in 2006, the park abuts the Northwest African American Museum just north of the Beacon Hill neighborhood. At the time of research, it was just a grassy expanse, but ambitious development plans have been approved. Proposals include rain drums, a butterfly garden and a performance area.

MOUNT ZION BAPTIST CHURCH CHURCH
Map p240 (☑206-322-6500; 1634 19th Ave, at E Madison St; ☐11) One of the cornerstones of this neighborhood is Mount Zion Baptist Church, a 2000-member congregation with a choir that has reached national acclaim through its gospel recordings. The church is over a century old.

◉ Madrona

COLMAN PARK PARK
(☐27) Head south along Lake Washington Blvd E through the very upscale Madrona Park neighborhood and you'll end up at Colman Park. The entire lakefront stretch between here and Seward Park is parkland. This is an especially good area for bike riding. On the weekends the boulevard is closed to cars.

✗ EATING

Ethiopian restaurants enliven the CD, especially along E Cherry St, while Madison Valley has established itself as a gourmet Gallic quarter with half a dozen French-run establishments. Other small restaurant huddles punctuate Madison Park and Madrona. The brunches are legendary.

✗ Madison Park

INÈS PATISSERIE FRENCH, BAKERY $
Map p240 (☑206-992-5186; www.inespatisserie -seattle.com; 2909 E Madison St; baked goods from $1.50; ☺9am-5:30pm Tue-Sun; ☐11) Combine the words 'French' and 'bakery' and you've already got enough ammunition to make the trip out to the Gallic culinary outpost of Madison Valley. If that doesn't swing it for you, the smell of fresh buttery croissants should.

★VOILA! FRENCH $$
Map p240 (☑206-322-5460; www.voilabistrot. com; 2805 E Madison St; mains $14-23; ☺11:30am-close; ☐11) Cozy French-style bistro where half the deal is in creating an exotic Euro-flavored atmosphere that is as fine-honed as the food. 'Les Plats,' as the menu announces them, consist of well-known Gallic standards from paté to pork chops, and even some escargot it you're lucky.

Only in Seattle

Turn your chewing gum into communal art, sneer back at a grimacing statue of Vladimir Ilyich Ulyanov (aka Lenin), watch fishmongers play catch with giant halibut, and meet *Star Trek* nerds in a futuristic museum that's all about sci-fi...and rock and roll. And you thought Seattle was normal?

1. Monorail & Seattle Center (p76)
The monorail runs by the EMP Museum on its journey between the Westlake Center and Seattle Center.

2. Gum wall (p43)
Seattle's colorful wall of well-chewed morsels resides in Pike Place Market.

3. Lenin statue (p141)
A bronze statue of Lenin finds an unlikely home among the sculpture and street art of Fremont.

4. Rachel the market pig (p43)
This life-size piggy bank is the de facto mascot of the legendary Pike Place Market. .

MUSIC PILGRIMAGES

The CD and its affiliated neighborhoods are of sketchy interest to regular city sight-seers, but, to music geeks, the chance to walk in the hallowed footsteps of some of Seattle's (and the world's) erstwhile musical legends carries a poignant allure.

Ray Charles & Quincy Jones

It's hard to envision today, but, in the late 1940s, Seattle possessed one of the most fervent jazz scenes in the nation. Much of the nocturnal action was centered on S Jackson St in today's International District, which hosted in excess of 30 clubs belting out bebop. But, with many of Seattle's jazz musicians claiming African American roots, the CD proper also had its fair share of sleazy bars.

The fertile West Coast music scene soon began attracting untested new talent. Lured to Seattle because it was the most distant city from his native Florida, the then unknown Ray Charles arrived in town in 1948 aged just 17. Describing the city's music scene as 'really open and smokin',' he took up residence on 20th Ave and hung around the still segregated jazz clubs, where he made the acquaintance of a precocious 15-year-old trumpet player named Quincy Jones.

Though born in Chicago, Jones had arrived in the Seattle area with his family as a young boy. Educated at Garfield High School in the CD (the school now has a Quincy Jones Performance Center named in his honor), he lived for a while on 22nd Ave and, despite grinding poverty, soon graduated to playing hot local jazz venues such as the legendary Washington Social Club on 23rd Ave and E Madison St, and the E Madison YMCA just up the road, where Charles, Jones and African American singer Ernestine Anderson once allegedly played on the same set (oh, to have been there!). The Social Club is now an astrologer's shop, but the Y is still around and continues to host the odd low-key jazz show. Charles and Jones ultimately left Seattle and went on to achieve almost unimaginable musical success elsewhere (Quincy Jones produced the greatest-selling record of all time, Michael Jackson's *Thriller*), but they never forgot the city that had inspired them long before the advent of Hendrix and grunge.

Jimi Hendrix

Born in the suburb of Renton in 1942, but forever linked to the music scene of swinging London, Jimi Hendrix's association with Seattle was ephemeral and curiously under-appreciated, at least until after his death. For a brief period when Jimi was between the ages of 10 and 13 the cash-strapped Hendrix family lived at 2603 S Washington St in the CD. The young Jimi attended Garfield High School (like Quincy Jones before him) and learned to play tunes on a ukulele with one string. Hendrix left Seattle in 1961 having barely played a gig, but he returned a few times after he became famous, performing memorably at Washington State Coliseum (now the Key Arena) in 1969. His CD house has long been demolished, but there's a statue of him in Capitol Hill, a park named after him in the CD (which is currently being refurbished with a memorial garden), plus the EMP Museum that was largely inspired by his legacy. He is buried in Greenwood Cemetery in Renton close to where he was born.

Kurt Cobain

The grunge era always resonated more strongly in Capitol Hill and Belltown than in the city's eastern neighborhoods, but serious Kurt Cobain fans usually pay their most poignant respects to the Nirvana front man in a simple park that abuts the house where the singer killed himself in 1994. Viretta Park, on the shores of Lake Washington just south of Madison Park proper, has no monument to Cobain. Instead, in the true spirit of the DIY 1990s, two ordinary park benches have been commandeered by fans and turned into graffiti-strewn memorials.

HARVEST VINE   BASQUE **$$**

Map p240 (☎206-320-9771; www.harvestvine.com; 2701 E Madison St; mains $18-22; ☺5-10pm, plus brunch 10am-2pm Sat & Sun; ☑11) Themed on what many consider to be the world capital of food – the Basque region – the Harvest Vine mixes Spanish roots with a French overlay. Jumping out of the menu is foie gras, grilled lamb with sauteed artichokes, cured ham, and blue sheep's cheese. It's in Madison Valley, Seattle's 'Little France.'

CAFÉ FLORA   VEGETARIAN **$$**

Map p240 (☎206-325-9100; www.cafeflora.com; 2901 E Madison St; starters & sandwiches $4-12, mains $13-18; ☺9am-10pm, to 9pm Sun; ✍; ☑11) A longtime favorite for vegan and vegetarian food, Flora has a gardenlike feel and a creative menu, with dinner treats like seitan spring rolls and breaded coconut tofu dipped in chili sauce, a portobello French dip, caprese pizza and black-bean burgers. Or go for the hoppin' John fritters or tomato asparagus scrambles at brunch.

CACTUS   TAPAS, MEXICAN **$$**

Map p240 (☎206-324-4140; www.cactus restaurants.com; 4220 E Madison St; dinner $10-18; ☺11am-10pm, to 11pm Fri & Sat; ☑11) Instantly cheery, this Mexican-Southwest restaurant – with branches in Kirkland and Alki Beach – is a fun place to go and pretend you're on a sunny vacation even if it's pouring with rain. A margarita and a king-salmon torta or butternut squash enchilada will scare off the grayest clouds, and the jaunty staff and fun music do the rest.

ROVER'S   FRENCH **$$$**

Map p240 (☎206-325-7442; www.thechefinthe hat.com; 2808 E Madison St; set menus $55-135; ☺lunch Fri, dinner daily; ✍; ☑11) Many locals consider this Seattle's best restaurant. Chef Thierry Rautureau ('the Chef in the Hat') offers three prix-fixe menus a day (one vegetarian), as well as á la carte items. The food is upscale French with a Northwest twist – Oregon quail, for example, or Copper River salmon with morels.

The cozy space is one of the few in Seattle where you'll want to dress up, and reservations are definitely advised.

MADISON PARK
CONSERVATORY   NORTHWEST **$$$**

Map p240 (☎206-324-9701; www.madisonpark conservatory.com; 1927 43rd Ave E; mains $19-27;

BIENVENUE À MADISON VALLEY

Once considered a sleepy hollow on the way to Madison Park and its beach, Madison Valley has recently dusted off its image and established its raison d'être: being French. The key is in the food. Along a tree-lined, detectably Hausmann-esque stretch of E Madison St between 27th Ave E and 29th Ave E there are four French restaurants, two Parisian-style bakeries and a creperie, with most of the businesses owned by immigrant *français*. The Francophile reputation has led people to apply the moniker 'Little France' or 'Petite Paris' to Madison Valley, and in 2012, the neighborhood inaugurated its first **Bastille Bash** – held on the nearest Saturday to Bastille Day (July 14th) – a celebration of food, troubadour music, street performance and general joie de vivre. To get to Madison Valley take metro bus 11 from downtown, disembark around 27th and Madison, and follow the aroma of freshly baked croissants.

☺5:30-10pm Tue-Sat, 5-9pm Mon; ☑11) ✦ The Conservatory opened in 2010 and caused an instant buzz (including being name-checked in the *New York Times*), thanks to locavore chef Cormac Mahoney who has worked at Sitka & Spruce and cemented his reputation with a pop-up taco truck.

The deviled eggs with Dungeness crab head a menu full of locally reared surprises, and even some of the furniture is foraged from Craigslist.

✕ CD

CAFE SELAM   ETHIOPIAN **$**

Map p240 (☎206-328-0404; www.cafeselam.com; 2715 E Cherry St; mains $9-10; ☺10am-9pm Tue-Sun; ☑3) The windows could do with a scrub and the table's a bit wobbly, but you don't come to Selam in the CD's proverbial 'Little Ethiopia' for interior design. Ethiopia is home to Africa's spiciest cuisine, with dishes such as *foul* (a fava-bean concoction that's not at all foul) and *fir fir* (injera bread, yogurt and lamb), and it's all done to perfection here.

The only catch is the lack of knives and forks. In true local style you must scoop up your beans, lamb, okra etc using torn-off bits of bread. Selam even roasts its own coffee, the product so beloved by Seattleites that was first 'discovered,' legend has it, by an Ethiopian goat-herder.

CATFISH CORNER   SOUTHERN $

Map p240 (206-323-4330; www.mo-catfish.com; 2726 E Cherry St; catfish dinners $6-12; 11am-8pm Mon-Fri, noon-9pm Sat, to 7pm Sun; 3) For traditional, inexpensive Southern-style fare, head to this no-frills corner hangout. Catfish strips are the specialty, and you can accessorize them with all the trimmings, including collard greens or red beans and rice, while meeting the neighbors and catching up on all the local gossip.

EZELL'S FAMOUS CHICKEN   SOUTHERN $

Map p240 (206-324-4141; www.ezellschicken.com; 501 23rd Ave; meals $6-10; 10am-10pm, to 11pm Fri & Sat; 3) There's fast food and then there's fast food. This is the good kind. Ezell's dishes out crispy, spicy chicken and equally scrumptious side dishes like cole-slaw and sweet-potato pie. This place experienced a boom after Oprah Winfrey hyped the fried chicken here as some of the best in the country.

✖ Madrona

CAFE SOLEIL   AMERICAN, ETHIOPIAN $

Map p240 (206-325-1126; 1400 34th Ave; mains $10; 5:30-9pm Wed-Fri, 8:30am-2pm & 5:30-9pm Sat & Sun; 2) Surprise! It looks likes an American diner and serves a hearty American brunch (and is less crowded that Hi Spot around the corner), but Cafe Soleil's real specialty is Ethiopian food – it's like a becalmed offshoot from 'Little Ethiopia' in the CD. The bright, light-filled room is an excellent place to dip your injera (bread) in spicy African stews.

★HI SPOT CAFÉ   BREAKFAST $$

Map p240 (206-325-7905; www.hispotcafe.com; 1410 34th Ave; mains $10-14; 7am-4pm Mon-Fri, 8am-4pm Sat & Sun; 2) The cinnamon rolls here are bigger than your head, and that's no exaggeration. It's a comfy little space in an old craftsman-style house where you can either get a sit-down meal (brunch is best) or a quick espresso and pastry to go.

🍷 DRINKING & NIGHTLIFE

🍷 Madison Park

ATTIC ALEHOUSE & EATERY   PUB

Map p240 (206-323-3131; www.atticalehouse.com; 4226 E Madison St; burgers $7-9; 11am-late Mon-Fri, 8:30am-late Sat & Sun; 11) Decades ago, according to legend, the Attic was a shooting gallery–bowling alley combo. It first became a restaurant in the mid-1930s, then became a tavern in the'50s. The current building dates from 1967 – it's a friendly neighborhood pub and a good spot to watch a game of footy while you have a beer and perhaps a handmade burger.

🍷 CD

TOUGO COFFEE   CAFE

Map p236 (www.tougocoffee.com; 1410 18th Ave; 6am-6pm Mon-Fri, 7am-6pm Sat & Sun; 2) When CD-based Tougo almost went under in 2011, the local community dipped into its collective pocket and helped raise the $10,000 necessary to keep it afloat. A cafe worth fighting for. Enough said.

CORTONA CAFE   CAFE

Map p240 (www.cortonacafe.com; 2425 E Union St; 6am-5pm Mon-Fri, 8am-5pm Sat, to 3pm Sun; ☎; 2) Cortona opened in 2009 in a quiet residential part of the CD. It's a small but attractive cafe with a loft space upstairs that has become known for its sweet breakfast waffles.

🛍 SHOPPING

Local one-of-a-kind boutiques can be found in the small business clusters that characterize Madison Valley and Madison Park.

ORIGINAL CHILDREN'S SHOP   CLOTHING

Map p240 (www.theoriginalchildrensshop.com; 4216 E Madison St; 10am-5:30pm Mon-Sat; 11) A piece of the Madison Park furniture, this family-run business has been operating since 1952 selling children's apparel and also functioning as a kids hair salon.

HENRIETTA'S HATS HATS

Map p240 (2707 Madison St; ⊘noon-5pm Tue-Sat; 🚌11) Selling handmade headgear for a quarter of a century on the Madison Valley strip, Henrietta's is the rock that anchors the neighborhood.

⚡ SPORTS & ACTIVITIES

MADISON PARK BEACH BEACH

Map p240 (🏊; 🚌11) A riotously popular place in the summer with a grassy slope for lounging and sunbathing, two tennis courts, a swimming raft floating in the lake, and lifeguards on duty from late June to Labor Day. The park has been a lure for townies since the early 20th century, when a trolley route was built from downtown to bus everyone in.

MADRONA PARK BEACH PARK, BEACH

Map p240 (🏊; 🚌2) Madrona Park Beach, down from the business district in Madrona Park, is one of the nicest along the lake. In clear weather the views of Mt Rainier are fantastic. Swimming is only for hardy souls, however, as the water's icy cold, even in summer. Further south, past the yacht moorage, is **Leschi Park**, a grassy green space with a children's play area.

U District

Neighborhood Top Five

1 Reliving (or living) your cerebral undergraduate years on the leafy, architecturally attractive campus of the **University of Washington** (p132) with its art galleries, neo-Gothic library and tree-studded quad.

2 Reliving the non-cerebral part of your undergraduate days in the pubs and bars of **'the Ave'** (p136).

3 Saving money in cheap, cheerful **ethnic eateries** (p133).

4 Paddling around Lake Union in a **kayak** (p138).

5 Plying the **Burke-Gilman Trail** (p133) to Wallingford for a picnic lunch in Gas Works Park.

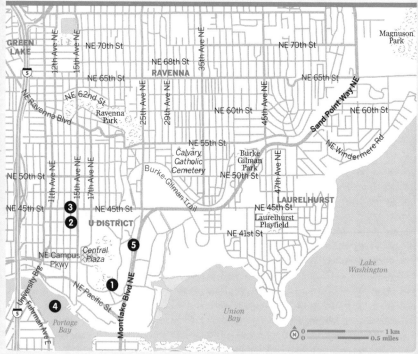

For more detail of this area, see Map p242 ➡

Explore: U District

Head east off I-5 north of Lake Union and suddenly you'll feel as if you're no longer in Seattle. The U District, named for 'U Dub' (what locals call the University of Washington, or UW), feels like its own little college town. Just like you, most of the people here are visitors – they're merely staying a bit longer (several semesters or more).

Nearly everyone gets oriented in the U District on 'the Ave' (University Way, roughly between 40th and 50th Sts), an atmospheric main drag full of tiny cheap eateries, thrift stores, record stores, secondhand bookstores, tattoo parlors, bars and coffee shops full of deadline-chasing, laptop-gazing students. Everyone on the sidewalks around here seems to be between the ages of 18 and 24, but these kids know where it's at. Read fly-posters on lampposts, eavesdrop on conversations in coffee bars and follow the action on 'the Ave' and you'll soon feel 23 again (if you aren't already).

The number of cheap places to eat, especially Indian and Asian, makes the Ave the best place to find an inexpensive meal. Another place to lose your youth is the cavernous University Bookstore, which takes up an entire city block.

Reserve a sunny day to explore the adjacent UW campus, a veritable arboretum–architectural showcase with a couple of top-notch museums focusing on art and natural history. The campus is made for people-watching (or, more specifically, student-watching) and you can enter many of the buildings unannounced, including the Suzzallo Library and the Hub (student union).

Another great way to explore the university is on a bicycle: the Burke-Gilman Trail follows the south side of campus, providing easy access. Further exercise can be procured on water: the campus abuts the shores of Lake Union and is one of the best places in Seattle to hire a kayak.

Local Life

→ **The Quad** On a warm day in spring or summer, students loaf alfresco under the quad's gnarly cherry trees, exchanging gossip, study notes and Facebook photos.

→ **The Ave** Hang around on University Ave anywhere between 40th and 50th Sts and follow the crowds.

Getting There & Away

→ **Bus** Several Metro buses, including buses 70, 72 and 66, run frequently to the U District from downtown Seattle. Bus 43 heads up to Capitol Hill.

Lonely Planet's Top Tip

To avoid parking hassles or public-transportation meltdowns, incorporate a visit to the U District with a trip to Fremont or Lake Union. Simply use the arterial Burke-Gilman Trail to breeze in by bike or on foot.

U DISTRICT

✕ Best Places to Eat

→ Portage Bay Cafe (p135)
→ Ristorante Doria (p135)
→ Pam's Kitchen (p136)
→ Thai Tom (p133)

For reviews, see p133 ➡

🍷 Best Places to Drink

→ Zoka Coffee (p136)
→ Big Time Microbrew & Music (p136)
→ Blue Moon (p136)
→ Café Allegro (p136)

For reviews, see p136 ➡

☉ Best Places to Study

→ Suzzallo Library (p132)
→ Zoka Coffee (p136)
→ Cafe Solstice (p135)
→ Café Allegro (p136)

For reviews, see p132 ➡

◉ SIGHTS

UNIVERSITY OF WASHINGTON   UNIVERSITY
(www.washington.edu; ▣70) Founded in 1861,
Seattle's university is almost as old as the
city itself and is highly ranked worldwide
(the prestigious *Times Higher Education*
magazine listed it 24th in the world in
2013). The college was originally located in
downtown on a 10-acre site now occupied
by the Fifth Avenue Theater (the university
still owns the land), but with both university and city outgrowing their initial confines, a new site was sought in 1895.

The present-day 700-acre campus that
sits at the edge of Lake Union about 3 miles
northeast of downtown is flecked with
stately trees and beautiful architecture,
and affords wondrous views of Mt Rainier
framed by fountains and foliage. Roughly
34,000 students and 13,000 staff enjoy the
noble setting, making 'U Dub' easily the
largest university in the state. The core of
the campus is Central Plaza, known as Red
Sq because of its terracotta-brick base rather than its Marxist-Leninist inclinations.
Close by you can pick up information and a
campus map at the **visitor center** (Odegaard
Undergraduate Library; ⊘8am-5pm Mon-Fri).

The university is ideal for gentle strolls,
people-watching, and exercise on the
Burke-Gilman Trail. The campus also hosts
two decent museums, fine sports facilities,
a theater, a library, and a student-union
building where leaflet-filled noticeboards
advertize the kinds of outré, spontaneous
events that typically color student life.

HENRY ART GALLERY   MUSEUM
Map p242 (www.henryart.org; cnr 15th Ave NE &
NE 41st St; adult/child $10/6, Thu free; ⊘11am-
4pm Wed, Sat & Sun, to 8pm Thu & Fri; ▣70) At
the corner of NE 41st St and 15th Ave is a sophisticated space centered on a remarkable
permanent exhibit by light-manipulating
sculptor James Turrell, featuring various
temporary and touring collections. Expos
here are modern, provocative and occasionally head-scratching. Think of replayed
black-and-white home movies, twittering
bird noises, and loose piles of bricks.

BURKE MUSEUM   MUSEUM
Map p242 (www.burkemuseum.org; cnr 17th Ave NE
& NE 45th St; adult/child $10/7.50; ⊘10am-5pm;
▣70) The best museum of natural history in
the Northwest is situated near the junction
of NE 45th St and 16th Ave. The main collec-

tion has an impressive stash of fossils including a 20,000-year-old sabre-toothed cat. The
Burke's other tour de force is its focus on 17
different Native American cultures.

Of note is the Pacific Northwest bas-
ketry collection, but tribes from all around
the Pacific Rim are represented, including
groups from Asia and Micronesia.

SUZZALLO LIBRARY   LANDMARK
Map p242 (▣70) The architecturally minded
will be interested in the University of Washington's Suzzallo Library. Designed by Carl
Gould around 1926, this bibliophile's dream
was inspired by Henry Suzzallo, UW's president at the time. Suzzallo wanted it to look
like a cathedral, because 'the library is the
soul of the university.' Unfortunately for
him, his bosses disagreed; on reviewing the
building, they deemed it too expensive and
fired Suzzallo for his extravagance.

However, the dream was partially real-
ized in the grand neo-Gothic entrance lobby and the truly beguiling **reading room**
with its massive cathedral-like windows
that, on fine days, cast filtered sunlight
onto the long reading pews.

CENTRAL PLAZA (RED SQUARE)   SQUARE
Map p242 (▣70) The center of campus is
more commonly referred to as Red Sq because of its base of red brick. It's not the
coziest plaza, but it fills up with students
cheerfully sunning themselves on nice days
and it looks impressive at night. *Broken
Obelisk,* the 26ft-high stainless-steel sculpture in the square, was made by noted
color-field painter Barnett Newman.

Just below Red Sq is a wide promenade
leading to lovely **Rainier Vista**, with spectacular views across Lake Washington to
Mt Rainier.

DRUMHELLER FOUNTAIN   FOUNTAIN
Map p242 (▣70) Drumheller Fountain sits
inside what was originally known as Geyser
Basin (now 'Frosh Pond'), one of the few remaining pieces leftover from the 1909 expo
that beefed up the university.

QUAD   LANDMARK
Map p242 (▣70) The lovely Quad is home
to some of the original campus buildings, many of them built in a Collegiate
Gothic style reminiscent of New England.
On sunny days you can relax on the grass
amid Frisbee throwers, sunbathers dodging
seminars, earnest politics undergraduates

LOCAL KNOWLEDGE

HIGHLIGHTS OF THE BURKE-GILMAN TRAIL

Cutting a leafy vehicle-free path through multiple north Seattle neighborhoods, including a large segment of the U District, the Burke-Gilman Trail gets busy with human-powered traffic on sunny days at weekends, when cyclists overtake joggers, and skaters weave in and out of walkers and strollers. The asphalt trail was first laid out in 1978 along the path of a former railroad pioneered by two Seattle attorneys, Thomas Burke and Daniel Gilman, in 1885 (the railway ceased operation in 1971). Initially extending for 12 miles, the route has since been lengthened and now runs almost 20 miles from Kenmore on the northeast shore of Lake Washington to Golden Gardens Park in northwest Ballard. There is a 'missing link' in Ballard between 11th Ave NW and Hiram M Chittenden Locks, though it's easy to navigate through the relatively quiet streets and reconnect. The Burke-Gilman has plenty of pretty sections, many of them surrounded by foliage and close to water, but to get a real taste for the neighborhoods through which it passes (U District, Wallingford, Fremont and Ballard), you need to wander off and explore a little. The places below make good pit stops. For bike hire look no further than Dutch Bike Co (p158) in Ballard or Recycled Cycles (p138) in the U District.

Best for a Coffee Break

Zoka Coffee (p136) in the U District

Fremont Coffee Company (p147) in Fremont

Dutch Bike Co (p158) in Ballard

Best for a Picnic

Gas Works Park (p148) in Wallingford

Hiram M Chittenden Locks (p153) in Ballard

Golden Gardens Park (p152) in Ballard

Best Eating

Portage Bay Cafe (p135) in the U District

Pie (p145) in Fremont

Lockspot Cafe (p154) in Ballard

---

discussing Obamacare, and young love blossoming under the cherry trees.

RAVENNA PARK   PARK
Map p242 (🚇74) Just north of the U District is Ravenna, a residential neighborhood that's home to a lot of professors and university staff. At its heart is Ravenna Park, a lush and wild park with two playgrounds on either side of the mystery-drenched ravine carved by Ravenna Creek. Escape the clamor of the city – briefly.

EATING

This is one of the best districts in Seattle for cheap and authentic ethnic food, and it's also easy to find vegan and vegetarian options. When you're browsing for lunch or dinner, don't be put off by unappetizing-looking storefronts; some of the most interesting food comes from places that have the outward appearance of rundown five-and-dime stores. The adventurous will be rewarded.

THAI TOM   THAI $
Map p242 (🚇206-548-9548; 4543 University Way NE; mains $7-10; ⏰11:30am-9:30pm; 🚌72) About as wide as a train carriage with permanently steamed-up windows, an open-kitchen lunch counter, and flames leaping up from beneath the constantly busy pans on the stoves, Thai Tom feels like some backstreet Bangkok hole-in-the-wall. Yet, many hail its simple Thai food as the best in the city.

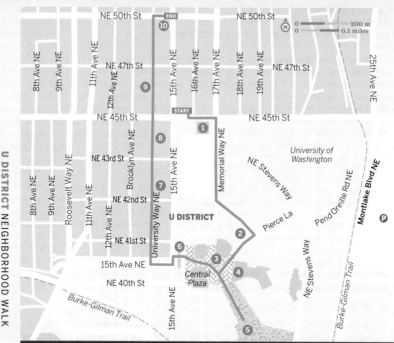

Neighborhood Walk
U District

START BURKE MUSEUM
FINISH THE AVE, OR GRAND ILLUSION CINEMA
LENGTH 2 MILES; ONE HOUR

Start this tour at the **1 Burke Museum** (p132), which you may choose to visit now (this will add at least an hour to the tour time) or simply note to check out later. Its collection of Northwest native art is not to be missed. From here, walk along NE 45th St to Memorial Way NE – take a left and amble into campus through the university's north gate.

Cut behind the Department of Anthropology, cross Denny Yard and enter **2 the Quad** (p132), the campus' prettiest nook. From here a straight path cuts southwest to central **3 Red Square** (p132), full of crisscrossing students rushing to lectures.

Red Sq is dominated by the gorgeous, cathedral-like **4 Suzzallo Library** (p132). Admire it from the inside and out, then take a sharp left when you exit. Descend the stairs and walk straight ahead toward **5 Drumheller Fountain** (p132), which

spews out of the circular pool known as 'Frosh Pond.' Along the pathway leading to the fountain, you'll be stunned (if it's a clear day) by the views from what is appropriately named the Rainier Vista.

Head back toward Red Sq, and bear left at the library. This will lead you to the **6 Henry Art Gallery** (p132), one of the best contemporary galleries in Seattle. After being blinded by modern art, head over to bustling University Way NE, aka 'the Ave.' If you're harboring caffeine-withdrawal symptoms duck into **7 Café Allegro** (p136). Opened in 1975, this (not Starbucks) is Seattle's oldest surviving espresso bar. Continue wandering up the Ave, peeking into shops and cafes along the way. Put your hunger on hold while you investigate the **8 University Bookstore** (p137), then cross the road and squeeze into **9 Thai Tom** (p133) for Bangkok street food. The tour concludes at the intersection with NE 50th St, where you may want to check out what's showing at the arthouse **10 Grand Illusion Cinema** (p137).

Push in among the elephant heads, dark-brown walls and elbow-to-elbow crowds to find out. Cash only.

AGUA VERDE CAFÉ
MEXICAN $

Map p242 (☑206-545-8570; 1303 NE Boat St; starters $2-6, 3 tacos from $9.75; ☺11am-9pm Mon-Sat, 9am-8pm Sun; ▣72) On the shores of Portage Bay at the southern base of University Ave, Agua Verde Café is a little gem that overlooks the bay and serves fat tacos full of lemony cod, shellfish or portobello mushrooms, plus other Mexican favorites.

There's usually a wait for a table, but you can have a drink and wait on the deck, or order from the walkup window. You can rent kayaks in the same building, in case you want to work off your dinner.

FLOWERS
VEGETARIAN, CAFE $

Map p242 (☑206-633-1903; 4247 University Way NE; lunch buffet $8, mains $7-15; ☺11am-2am; ☑; ▣72) One of the most stylish places in the U District, Flowers has a vegetarian buffet served until 5pm, and dinners include meat choices. The lunch menu includes 20 sandwiches, each around $5. After hours, it becomes an inviting place to sip a cocktail, munch on an appetizer and 'do homework' with a promising study partner.

CHACO CANYON CAFÉ
VEGAN $

Map p242 (☑206-522-6966; www.chacocanyon cafe.com; 4757 12th Ave NE; juices $3-5, sandwiches $7-12; ☺7am-9pm Mon-Fri, 9am-9pm Sat & Sun; ☑; ▣66) ✿ Now in a new location, this super-Northwest cafe has a menu that's all vegan, 90% organic and almost half raw food. If you're a newbie to the raw-food movement (it's pretty much what it sounds like), try the spicy Thai grinder or the gluten-free kiwi lime tart.

There's also a long list of vegan sandwiches, smoothies and juices, coffee and tea, and a little window by the entrance where you can pick up vegan, gluten-free, wheat-free baked treats from the Flying Apron organic bakery on your way in or out.

CAFE SOLSTICE
CAFE $

Map p242 (☑206-675-0850; 4116 University Way NE; mac 'n' cheese $5; ☺6:30am-9pm Mon-Fri, 7am-9pm Sat & Sun; ☑; ▣72) This coffee shop has a nice wooden outdoor patio on the Ave and a comfy organic vibe – lots of vegan and bran-heavy snacks – and is so laid-back you have to wonder if anyone here is actually drinking the coffee. The interior is well-worn dark wood and much bigger than it looks from outside. There are also panini, salads, beer and wine.

SCHULTZY'S SAUSAGES
MEAT $

Map p242 (☑206-548-9461; 4142 University Way NE; brats $7-8; ☺10am-2am Mon-Fri, 11:30am-2am Sat, 11:30am-midnight Sun; ☑; ▣72) This former hole-in-the-wall has doubled in size, which serves as a warning to all who overindulge in Schultzy's meaty goodness. Its claim to fame is straightforward and simple: bratwurst, burgers and beer. There are also veggie dogs, but come on, seriously – you can eat vegan food practically everywhere else in the U District.

ORANGE KING
BURGERS $

Map p242 (☑206-632-1331; 1411 NE 42nd St; burgers $2-5; ☺10am-9pm Mon-Fri, 11am-7pm Sat; ▣72) At this tiny, old-fashioned greasy spoon just off the Ave, you can – miraculously – still get a burger and fries for less than $5. It's not gourmet, but it's fast, cheap and, in its own way, charming.

★PORTAGE BAY CAFE
NORTHWEST, BRUNCH $$

Map p242 (☑206-547-8230; www.portagebay cafe.com; 4130 Roosevelt Way NE; brunch $10-13; ☺7:30am-2:30pm; ▣66) Hugely popular brunch spot and for good reason. Aside from the usual suspects (eggs, bacon, pancakes), there's a help-yourself breakfast bar loaded up with fresh fruit, cream, syrup, nuts and the like (all local, of course), waiting to be spread on your doorstep-thick slices of French toast. Arrive early or after 1pm at weekends to avoid the rush.

CEDARS RESTAURANT
INDIAN, MIDDLE EASTERN $$

Map p242 (☑206-527-5247; 4759 Brooklyn Ave NE; mains $8-15; ☺11:30am-10pm Mon-Sat, 1-9pm Sun; ☑; ▣72) Cedars serves enormous curries and vindaloos so smooth and creamy you want to dive into them. Eat here just once and you will dream about it later. There's also a great selection of Mediterranean specialties like shish kebabs, falafel and gyros, much of which is vegetarian. The covered wooden patio is a cool hangout in nice weather.

RISTORANTE DORIA
ITALIAN $$

Map p242 (☑206-466-2380; www.ristorante doria.com; 4759 Roosevelt Way NE; pasta $14-16; ☺4-9:30pm; ▣66) Doria applies the U District stencil of non-budget-breaking, plentiful salt-of-the-earth food to Italian cuisine. There is nothing nouveau about the food or service. Instead, the owner (from Milan) regularly works the tables just as they do in the old country, checking that you like your gnocchi, calamari or chicken parmigiano.

PAM'S KITCHEN
TRINIDADIAN **$$**

Map p242 (☎206-696-7010; www.pams-kitchen.com; 5000 University Way NE; mains $14-16; ⊗5:30-10pm Tue-Thu & Sun, noon-3pm & 5:30-11pm Fri & Sat; ⊜72) In among its Asian noodle houses and vegan sandwich bars, the U District does some interesting niche cuisine. Case in point: Pam's Kitchen, where hot, spicy food from the Caribbean island of Trinidad will have metaphoric flames coming out of your ears in seconds. There are several must-tries here, including the jerk chicken, stuffed roti bread and homemade ginger beer.

🍷 DRINKING &
⚓ NIGHTLIFE

Explore the Ave and surrounding streets for some of the city's most mellow coffee shops, a literary landmark and some lively watering holes.

CAFÉ RACER
BAR

(☎206-523-5282; 5828 Roosevelt Way NE; ⊗9am-1am Thu-Tue; ⊜66) Conspicuously friendly to two-wheeled transport, this tiny bar-cafe has a rec room upstairs where you can lounge on couches and watch movies from the bar library on the bar TV. Downstairs there's a counter, a few tables and a microscopic open kitchen, and decor includes the occasional taxidermied gazelle poised above a MotoGuzzi gas tank. And, um, there's a hair salon inside.

Live music most nights.

CAFÉ ALLEGRO
CAFE

Map p242 (☎206-633-3030; 4214 University Way NE; drinks from $2; ⊗6:30am-10:30pm; ⊜72) You can dispel a few urban myths in Café Allegro. It is this place, not Starbucks, that is the oldest functioning coffee bar in Seattle. Founded in 1975, it was a bona fide espresso bar when Starbucks was still just a store that sold coffee beans and machinery.

Stuffed into a back alley between NE 42nd and NE 43rd Sts, the cafe hasn't changed much since its pioneer days. Bevies of industrious students still drop by to scribble over papers or moon over profes-

sors, although nowadays they're frequently distracted by their iPhones.

BIG TIME MICROBREW & MUSIC
BREWPUB

Map p242 (☎206-545-4509; 4133 University Way NE; ⊗11:30am-2am; ⊜72) A fun hangout, this expansive brewpub is quiet and casual in the daytime but gets hopping at night. During the school year, it can be crowded with students still testing out their alcohol limits.

ZOKA COFFEE
CAFE

(www.zokacoffee.com; 2901 NE Blakeley St; ⊗6am-10pm Mon-Fri, 7am-10pm Sat & Sun; ⊜74) Aside from its desirable coffee (home roasted, of course), Zoka is *the* place to go for a marathon laptop session. Don't feel guilty about lingering: the staff actively encourage you to stay with plenty of plug-in points scattered around a vast wooden interior full of students all seemingly on the same deadline.

UGLY MUG
CAFE, SANDWICHES

Map p242 (☎206-547-3219; 1309 NE 43rd St; bagels $1.50-3; ⊗8am-11pm Mon-Fri, 10am-10pm Sat; ⊜72) Good soups, sandwiches and the atmosphere of a cozy living room make this coffee shop just off the Ave worth a peek. It also serves excellent coffee, as is standard for any Seattle coffee shop.

BLUE MOON
DIVE BAR

Map p242 (712 NE 45th St; ⊗2pm-late; ⊜66) A legendary counterculture dive near the university that first opened in 1934 to celebrate the repeal of the prohibition laws, the Blue Moon makes much of its former literary patrons: doyens Dylan Thomas, Allen Ginsberg and Tom Robbins get mentioned a lot.

These days, it's unlikely you'll meet anyone quite so erudite, though it's still good for impromptu poetry recitations, jaw-harp performances and inspired rants.

MONKEY PUB
DIVE BAR

Map p242 (☎206-523-6457; www.myspace.com/monkeypub; 5305 Roosevelt Way NE; ⊗5pm-1:45am; ⊜66) This unironic U District dive is one of the few places in town where you can slug pitchers of cheap beer, shoot pool and catch a live punk show on a weekend night without having to do any planning whatsoever. If the band sucks, it'll be over soon and did we mention the beer's cheap?

Slices from the pizza shop next door are available, or you can pop over to eat and play video games between sets.

⭐ ENTERTAINMENT

⭐ GRAND ILLUSION CINEMA   CINEMA

Map p242 (☑206-523-3935; www.grand illusioncinema.org; 1403 NE 50th St; 🚇72) Totally unique! Far from being a reincarnated gilded-age movie house, the Grand Illusion sits in an old dentist's office. Run by volunteers and passionately not-for-profit, it has a cherished national reputation among independent movie guerrillas for its director retrospectives and other cool, under-the-radar series. It also hosts its own film festival, facetiously called STIFF (Seattle's True Independent Film Festival).

NEPTUNE THEATER   LIVE MUSIC

Map p242 (www.stgpresents.org; 1303 NE 45th St; 🚇72) Providing an ideal pulpit for young indie bands and smirking comedians sharpening their teeth on the university-gig circuit, the Neptune, a historic theater originally dating from the silent-movie era, reopened its doors in 2011 as a performing arts venue (it formerly functioned purely as a cinema).

Run by the not-for-profit Seattle Theater Group, the 800-capacity venue filled a hole in U Dub's nightlife as well as gifting Seattle with an elusive midsize (but relatively intimate) live venue. Alt-rock and alt-comedy predominate.

VARSITY THEATRE   CINEMA

Map p242 (☑206-632-3131; www.landmark theatres.com/market/seattle/varsitytheatre. htm; 4329 University Way NE; 🚇72) Independent and international arthouse films are shown at this 1940 cinema, the scene of many an undergraduate date night.

🛍 SHOPPING

Bookstores and record stores are the main thing here, although everyone should make time to explore the bins at Hardwick's Hardware Store. The Ave is the main shopping drag.

⭐ UNIVERSITY BOOKSTORE   BOOKS

Map p242 (☑206-634-3400; 4326 University Way NE; ⊙9am-9pm Mon-Fri, 10am-7pm Sat, noon-5pm Sun; 🚇72) University Bookstore is vast and all-purpose, though lacking the timeworn charm of many of Seattle's other, quirkier bookstores. It does have absolutely

FARMERS MARKET

In a city that produced Pike Place Market, it's not surprising that there is a rich stash of other weekly farmers markets where you can sniff out the freshest veg. The largest and oldest (and best in the eyes of many) is the **U District Farmers Market** (Map p242; cnr 50th St NE & University Way NE; ⊙9am-2pm Sat), which has been held every Saturday in the vicinity of the university year round since 1993. Faithful to the spirit of farmers markets, the U District is a food-only affair – all of its displayed produce comes from an alliance of 60-plus stallholding farmers and is grown 100% in Washington state. Products of note include spot prawns (May and June), cheeses, Washington wines and apples (over 30 varieties). Market Bites is a collection of small take-out stalls designed for hungry shoppers on the go. In August look out for Ready, Set, Go...Cook!, a popular cooking competition where chefs are permitted to use only market ingredients.

everything, though, including textbooks and highlighter-abused secondhand books.

SCARECROW VIDEO   DVDS, VIDEOS

Map p242 (☑206-524-8554; www.scarecrow. com; 5030 Roosevelt Way NE; ⊙11am-10pm Sun-Thu, to 11pm Fri & Sat; 🚇66) In an era when video stores appear to have befallen the same fate as the *Tyrannosaurus rex*, Scarecrow soldiers on: it's the largest video store in the country, with over 100,000 films in stock, many of them rare. A true community resource.

MAGUS BOOKS   BOOKS

Map p242 (☑206-633-1800; www.magusbooks seattle.com; 1408 NE 42nd St; ⊙10am-8pm, to 10pm Fri & Sat; 🚇72) Magus is a great used-book store, the kind of place where you can literally spend hours getting lost in the crooked, narrow aisles on the hunt for that obscure title you're not sure you can even remember any more.

BUFFALO EXCHANGE   CLOTHING

Map p242 (☑206-545-0175; www.buffalo exchange.com; 4530 University Way NE;

U DISTRICT ENTERTAINMENT

⊙10am-9pm Mon-Sat, 11am-8pm Sun; ⊒72) This secondhand-clothing store is comfortable to browse in but can be hit-and-miss in terms of good finds. Some of its merchandise is on the square side – which doesn't, ironically, make it any easier to sell your old clothes here: staff are notoriously picky.

PITAYA
CLOTHING

Map p242 (✆206-548-1001; 4520 University Way NE; ⊙11am-9pm Mon-Sat, to 8pm Sun; ⊒72) This is a cute little clothing boutique with carefully selected dresses, hipster jeans and cool accessories.

HARDWICK'S HARDWARE STORE
JUNK

Map p242 (✆206-632-1203; 4214 Roosevelt Way NE; ⊙8am-6pm Mon-Fri, 9am-6pm Sat, later hours in summer; ⊒66) Locals in the know come to Hardwick's to explore the rows and rows of buckets filled with bizarre little gadgets and gizmos. Some people probably know what these objects are for, but most shoppers are looking for things to use in their art projects. It's a hive of a place that's fun just to explore.

BULLDOG NEWS & ESPRESSO
NEWSSTAND

Map p242 (✆206-632-6397; 4208 University Way NE; ⊙8am-9pm; ⊒72) The newsstand of choice at the university, this place has pretty much every magazine or newspaper you might want, from imports and big glossies to stapled-together zines. Good coffee, too.

🏃 SPORTS & ACTIVITIES

HUSKY STADIUM
STADIUM

Map p242 (⊒43) With room for 72,500, the Husky is Seattle's largest sports stadium, though a $250-million 2013 renovation may drop the capacity slightly. It is home to the successful Washington Huskies college football team and also hosts athletics events. Games are well known for being noisier than a Nirvana gig.

AGUA VERDE PADDLE CLUB
KAYAKING

Map p242 (✆206-545-8570; 1303 NE Boat St; single/double kayak per hr $17/22; ⊙10am-dusk Mon-Sat, to 6pm Sun Mar-Oct; ⊒72) On Portage Bay, near the university, you can rent kayaks from this friendly place right at the edge of the water. Stand-up paddleboards are also available (one/two hours $20/34). When you get back from your paddle, be sure to visit the cafe upstairs to eat fish tacos on the covered deck.

RECYCLED CYCLES
CYCLING

Map p242 (✆206-547-4491; www.recycled cycles.com; 1007 NE Boat St; ⊙10am-8pm Mon-Fri, to 6pm Sat & Sun; ⊒66) Recycled Cycles, at the bottom of the U District along Lake Union, sells used and consignment bikes. More importantly, it rents bikes ($30 a day), meaning out-of-towners can hit the adjacent Burke-Gilman Trail and explore out as far as Fremont, Ballard and Discovery Park without touching road. Kids chariots and trail-a-bikes are also available.

UW WATERFRONT ACTIVITIES CENTER
CANOEING

Map p242 (✆206-543-9433; canoe & rowboat per hr weekday/weekend $9/11; ⊙10am-7pm, closed Nov-Jan; ⊒43) A good way to explore the waters surrounding the university grounds is to rent a canoe or rowboat from the UW facility. You need a current driver's license or passport. The center is in the southeast corner of the Husky Stadium parking lot.

Fremont & Green Lake

FREMONT | GREEN LAKE

Neighborhood Top Five

1 Walking around Seattle's most irreverent neighborhood in search of its peculiar sculptures and **public art** (p141) as well as keeping an eye out for any spontaneous pieces that have popped up since this book was written.

2 Exploring one of the US's best animal projects at **Woodland Park Zoo** (p144).

3 Joining the walking, running, skating, cycling mass of humanity powering around beautiful **Green Lake Park** (p144).

4 Soaking up the liberating essence of the summer **Fremont Street Fair** (p21).

5 Watching the wackily attired audience (and the film) at the **Fremont Almost Free Outdoor Cinema** (p147).

For more detail of this area, see Map p244 and p245 ➡

Lonely Planet's Top Tip

If you've had your fill of police sirens, panhandlers and the frenetic pace of downtown Seattle, consider staying over in Fremont's new hotel, the affordable Hotel Hotel Hostel, for a more laid-back, under-the-radar look at one of the city's most interesting neighborhoods.

Best Places to Eat

➡ Pie (p145)

➡ Paseo (p145)

➡ Hunger (p145)

➡ Tangletown Pub (p145)

For reviews, see p145 ➡

Best Places to Drink

➡ Fremont Brewing (p146)

➡ George & Dragon Pub (p146)

➡ Hale's Ales Brewery (p146)

For reviews, see p146 ➡

Best Public Sculpture

➡ Statue of Lenin (p141)

➡ Fremont Troll (p141)

➡ Fremont Rocket (p142)

➡ Apatosaurs (p143)

For reviews, see p141 ➡

Explore: Fremont & Green Lake

Set your watch back five minutes, turn your brain setting to 'ironic' and cross the Fremont Bridge into the self-proclaimed 'People's Republic of Fremont.'

Weirder than Ballard and more self-deprecating than Capitol Hill, Fremont's essential business is its public sculpture. Most of its outlandish statues and monuments lie clustered around a few square blocks on the southern edge of the neighborhood close to the bridge, making viewing easy. Here you'll also find the bulk of the cheap eating places and Fremont's only hotel.

Fremont's a great neighborhood for getting a taste for local life, especially in summer, when festivals and regular outdoor movies send the locals positively delirious. With good bus connections and a bike-friendly intra-urban trail, it can easily be incorporated with visits to the adjacent neighborhoods of Ballard and Wallingford.

Just north of Fremont lies Green Lake, a small natural lake that's the hub of a large park complex and a pleasant low-key neighborhood punctuated by detached craftsman-style houses. The lake is packed with crowds in summer, but it's even better in fall, when the leaves are changing, or on a rare rain-free day in winter. Any time of the year, it's a great spot for a walk or a run, or just to sit back on a bench and watch the rowers on the water.

Below Green Lake, Woodland Park Zoo is a must-see. And don't neglect to head further up to Phinney Ridge, the hilltop neighborhood north of the zoo along Phinney Ave N, for some good pubs and restaurants.

Local Life

➡ **Outdoor Movies** The best time to meet Fremonters in their element is on summer evenings in the parking-lot-turned-movie-theater better known as Fremont Almost Free Outdoor Cinema. The sight of locals relaxing in beach chairs while dressed up as zombies, wizards or Clint Eastwood is far more interesting than the movie itself.

➡ **Green Lake Park Exercisers** Meet the 75-year-old marathon runner, the hyperventilating weight watcher, the in-line skater on his cell phone, and the lawyer from Phinney Ridge getting bullied by his personal trainer.

Getting There & Away

➡ **Bus** Metro bus 26 runs frequently from downtown to Green Lake via Fremont. Bus 5 runs from downtown via Fremont to Woodland Park Zoo. Buses 28 and 40 connect Fremont with Ballard. Buses 31 and 32 link Fremont with the U District.

TOP SIGHT
FREMONT PUBLIC SCULPTURE

Long known for its wry contrarianism, Fremont does bizarre like the rest of the world does normal. For proof, look no further than its public sculpture, an eclectic amalgamation of the scary, the politically incorrect and the downright weird. The five most famous pieces are scattered around four square blocks in the southern part of the neighborhood abutting the Lake Washington Ship Canal.

Statue of Lenin

Fremont's provocative bronze **statue of Lenin** (Map p244; cnr N 36th St & Fremont Pl N) was salvaged from the people of Poprad, Czechoslovakia, in 1993 who, having suffered for 40 years under communism, were probably glad to see the back of the bearded curmudgeon. It was unearthed by a resident of Issaquah, WA, named Lewis Carpenter, who had found it unloved and abandoned in a junkyard while working in Czechoslovakia as an English teacher soon after the Velvet Revolution. Carpenter forked out $13,000 to purchase the fierce 16ft-tall recreation of the wily Bolshevik leader and then put up another $41,000 (by remortgaging his home) to ship it to the US. After Carpenter's death in 1994, the statue turned up – where else? – in Fremont. It still belongs to the Carpenter family and is allegedly 'for sale' for $300,000.

Fremont Troll

Just when you thought you had returned to planet earth, up sprouts the **Fremont Troll** (cnr N 36th St & Troll Ave), a 13,000lb steel and concrete sculpture of a troll crushing a Volkswagen Beetle in its hand that resides under the Aurora Bridge and does a good job of scaring off skateboarders, drug dealers and any passing billy goats. The sculpture was the winner of a 1989 Fremont Arts Council competition to design some thought-provoking public art. It took seven weeks to make.

DON'T MISS...

➡ Fremont Troll
➡ Statue of Lenin
➡ *Waiting for the Interurban*

PRACTICALITIES

➡ Map p244
➡ btwn N 34th St, N 36th St, Aurora Ave N & Evanston Ave N
➡ 🚌26

ART ATTACKS

There are two types of art attack in Fremont. The first targets existing monuments: decorating the *Interurban* is one example; sticking drag on the Lenin statue is another. The second type of attack is to concoct brand-new urban art exhibits. Most of these pieces are temporary and appear anonymously overnight. There have been many classics over the years, including papier-mâché cows, an 8ft-long steel pig, and an enormous spider suspended over a parking lot. The bulk of these inspired creations are quickly removed, though some have entered local folklore and been allowed to stay.

Fremont's newest statue, dedicated in 2008, is a study of two clowns, arms interlinked, striding off in opposite directions. It honors the characters JP Patches and Gertrude, who appeared daily on the children's *JP Patches Show* on Seattle TV during the 1960s and '70s. Located a mere 250yd east of *Waiting for the Interurban,* it has been humorously christened *Late for the Interurban.*

Fremont Rocket

Fremont has adopted this phallic and zany-looking **rocket** (Map p244; cnr Evanston Ave & N 35th St) sticking out of a shoe shop as its community totem. Constructed in the 1950s for use in the Cold War, the rocket was plagued with difficulties and never actually went anywhere, leaving the engineering team with the unfortunate problem of not being able to get it up. Before coming to Fremont, the rocket was affixed to an army surplus store in Belltown. When the store went out of business, the Fremont Business Association snapped it up in 1994.

Waiting for the Interurban

Seattle's most popular piece of public art, **Waiting for the Interurban** (Map p244; cnr N 34th St & Fremont Ave N), sculpted in recycled aluminum, depicts six people waiting for a train that never comes. The train that once passed through Fremont stopped running in the 1930s, and the people of Seattle have been waiting for a new train – the Interurban – ever since (a new train connecting Seattle with Everett opened in 2003 but doesn't stop in Fremont). The sculpture is prone to regular art attacks, when locals lovingly decorate the people in outfits corresponding to a special event, the weather, someone's birthday, a Mariners win – whatever. Rarely do you see the sculpture undressed. Take a look at the human-faced dog peeking out between the legs of the people. That face belongs to Armen Stepanian, one of the founders of today's Fremont and its excellent recycling system. Sculptor Richard Beyer and Stepanian had a disagreement about the design of the piece, which resulted in Beyer's spiteful yet humorous design of the dog's face.

The Guidepost

This whimsical **guidepost** (Map p244; cnr Fremont Ave N & Fremont Pl N) that points in 16 different directions – including the Troll, the Lenin statue and the Milky Way – appeared anonymously on Fremont Ave in 1995, the result of one of the neighborhood's periodic art attacks. Unlike other ephemeral sculptures, the guidepost stayed put and quickly became a neighborhood symbol. Originally made out of cedar wood, the rotting signpost was replaced in 2009 by a better-quality one made out of pressure-treated wood. At the same time, the artist revealed himself to be Maque DaVis, a resident of nearby Ballard, but a Fremonter in spirit. The signpost advertises itself as 'the center of the known universe,' a phrase that has since been adopted as a popular Fremont slogan.

FREEDOM TO BE PECULIAR

Coined the 'Artistic Republic of Fremont' by irreverent locals who once symbolically voted to secede from the rest of Seattle, the neighborhood of Fremont has always marched eccentrically to its own bongo – albeit with its tongue stuck firmly in its cheek. Where else in the US can you find an un-desecrated statue of Vladimir Lenin, a colorful chunk of the Berlin wall, an annual nude cyclists parade, and a sculpted troll crushing a Volkswagen Beetle under a bridge? Even Fremont's vandals are creative. The neighborhood's famous statue *Waiting for the Interurban*, a study of six commuters waiting for a train that never comes, is regularly decorated by audacious art guerrillas who dress the figures up in clothes, hats and ties, or cover them with amusing placards.

Some of Fremont's counter-cultural spirit comes from its history: it was a separate city until 1891, and still is in the minds of many of its residents. 'Set your watch back five minutes' reads a sign on Fremont Bridge as you cross over from the stiffer, less self-deprecating neighborhood of Queen Anne. Fremont's idiosyncratic personality resurfaced in the 1970s, when community activism attempted to offset years of economic decline. The Fremont Public Association, today the envy of every neighborhood association in Seattle, was created in 1974 to provide shelter, food and help to disadvantaged residents. Its formation spawned a number of other thriving community associations, including the Fremont Arts Council, and, in 1994, irked by bureaucratic planning and boundary laws, the neighborhood made its token and somewhat humorous secession.

These days, Fremont is showing signs of creeping gentrification. Various software companies including Google have opened offices there since the mid-2000s, and trendy boutiques are starting to compete with the area's legendary junk shops. But the spirit of ludicrousness still resounds, enshrined in the neighborhood's libertine motto: *De Libertas Quirkas* (Freedom to Be Peculiar). Enough said.

◉ SIGHTS

◉ Fremont

FREMONT PUBLIC SCULPTURE MONUMENTS
See p141.

FREMONT BRIDGE BRIDGE
Map p244 (🚌26) Built in 1916 and since dwarfed by the far taller George Washington Memorial Bridge (colloquially known as the Aurora Bridge), the distinctive orange-and-blue Fremont Bridge became necessary after the construction of the Lake Washington Ship Canal linked Lake Union with Puget Sound. It is the busiest drawbridge in the US, opening over 30 times a day to let boat traffic pass through.

FREMONT SUNDAY MARKET MARKET
Map p244 (www.fremontmarket.com; Stone Way & N 34th St; ◷10am-5pm Sun; 🚌26) 🍴 People come from all over town for this market. It features fresh fruit and vegetables, arts and crafts, and all kinds of people getting rid of junk.

THEO CHOCOLATE FACTORY CHOCOLATE FACTORY
Map p244 (☎206-632-5100; www.theochocolate.com; 3400 Phinney Ave N; tours $5; ◷10am-6pm, tours 1pm & 3pm daily plus 11am Sat; 🚌28) Adding a bit of Willy Wonka to Fremont's atypical street life is this chocolate factory on the site of the old Redhood Brewery (now moved to Woodinville, WA). The micro-chocolate producer makes organic chocolate, producing an aroma that permeates half the neighborhood. Follow the smell to the small store, where you can put your name down for a factory tour.

APATOSAURS MONUMENT
Map p244 (🚌28) Along the banks of the ship canal, Fremont Canal Park extends west, following the extension of the Burke-Gilman Trail. Right at the start of the park, at the bottom of Phinney Ave N, you'll see two giant, life-size 'apatosaurs.' These are the world's largest known topiaries, given to Fremont by the Pacific Science Center.

HISTORY HOUSE MUSEUM
Map p244 (☎206-675-8875; 790 N 34th St; admission $1; ◷noon-5pm Wed-Sun; 🚌26) The History House contains rotating exhibits

TOP SIGHT
GREEN LAKE PARK

A favorite hunting ground for runners, personal trainers and artistically tattooed sunbathers, scenic Green Lake Park surrounds a small natural lake created by a glacier during the last ice age. In the early 1900s, city planners lowered the lake's water level by 7ft, increasing the shoreline to preserve parkland around the lake. After the lowering, however, Ravenna Creek, which fed the lake, no longer flowed through. Green Lake became stagnant and filled with stinky green algae. Massive dredging efforts to keep it a navigable lake continue, although the lake remains prone to algae blooms.

Two paths wind around the lake, but these aren't enough to fill the needs of the hundreds of joggers, power-walkers, cyclists and in-line skaters who throng here daily. In fact, competition for space on the trails has led to altercations; the city government now regulates traffic on the paths. With this in mind, beware the synchronized roller-skating couples holding hands; they're not dangerous, but they may induce nausea.

Green Lake also has a soccer field, bowling green, baseball diamond, basketball and tennis courts, plus boat, bike and in-line-skate rentals. Two sandy swimming beaches line the lake's northern end.

DON'T MISS...

➡ Walking path
➡ Beaches
➡ Boat rentals

PRACTICALITIES

➡ Map p245
➡ 🚌26

focused on the history of the city's neighborhoods. It's a good place to see photos of early Seattle. The building's colorful metal fence is another piece of public art, built by blacksmith and welder Christopher Pauley. The fence features brightly colored houses with open doors, a reflection of Fremont's welcoming attitude.

◉ Green Lake

GREEN LAKE AQUA THEATER   LANDMARK
Map p245 (🚌26) The lonely-looking grandstand at the southern end of Green Lake is all that remains of the former 5500-capacity Green Lake Aqua Theater, an outdoor auditorium overlooking the lake (where the stage once was) that stood here from 1950–70.

Back in the day, the theater's big crowd-puller was its annual summer *Aqua Follies* show, a kind of kitschy water ballet, but it also staged opera, jazz and, towards the end of its tenure, a couple of legendary rock performances by Led Zeppelin and the Grateful Dead. Newer, dryer venues built for the World's Fair in 1962 eventually put the theater out of business and it closed in 1970.

BATHHOUSE THEATER   THEATER
Map p245 (🚌5) The Bathhouse Theater, on the western side of the lake, is a 1928 bathing pavilion that was converted to a live-performance venue in 1970.

WOODLAND PARK ZOO   ZOO
Map p245 (📞206-684-4800; www.zoo.org; 5500 Phinney Ave N; adult/child Oct-Apr $12.50/8.75, May-Sep $18.75/11.75; ⊗9:30am-4pm Oct-Apr, to 6pm May-Sep; 🚼; 🚌5) In Woodland Park, up the hill from Green Lake Park, the Woodland Park Zoo is one of Seattle's greatest tourist attractions, consistently rated as one of the top 10 zoos in the country. It was one of the first in the nation to free animals from their restrictive cages in favor of ecosystem enclosures, where animals from similar environments share large spaces designed to replicate their natural surroundings.

Feature exhibits include a tropical rain forest, two gorilla exhibits, an African savanna and an Asian elephant forest.

SEATTLE ROSE GARDEN   GARDEN
Map p245 (⊗7am-dusk; 🚌5) **FREE** The 2.5-acre Seattle Rose Garden, near the entrance road to the zoo off N 50th St, was started

in 1924 and contains 5000 plants, including heirloom roses and a test garden for All-America Rose Selections.

EATING

Fremont's restaurant scene is a regularly shuffled pack of cards with a few jokers thrown in. There have been some welcome new faces recently and a few relocations. Locavore food is a big deal, wait staff are chatty and informality rules.

Green Lake has an everybody-knows-each-other neighborhood feel to it, and the cafes and restaurants consequently tend to be welcoming and casual.

✕ Fremont

★PIE   PIES $
Map p244 (☑206-436-8590; www.sweetand savorypie.com; 3515 Fremont Ave N; pies $5.95; ⊘9am-9pm Mon-Thu, to 2am Fri & Sat, 10am-6pm Sun; ☐26) 🍴 It's as simple as P-I-E. Bake fresh pies daily on site, stuff them with homemade fillings (sweet and savory), and serve them in a cool, bold-colored Fremont cafe. The pies are ideal for a snack lunch or you can double up and get a sweet one for dessert too. Broccoli cheddar and peanut butter cream go down a treat.

PASEO   CUBAN $
(www.paseoseattle.com; 4225 Fremont Ave N; sandwiches $6-9; ⊘11am-9pm Tue-Fri, to 8pm Sat; ☐5) Proof that most Seattleites aren't posh (or pretentious) is the local legend known as Paseo, a Cuban-style hole-in-the-wall located in a nondescript part of Fremont which people alter their commute drive to visit. The fuss centers on the sandwiches, in particular the Midnight Cuban Press with pork, ham, cheese and banana peppers, and the Cuban Roast (slow-roasted pork in marinade). Grab plenty of napkins.

HOMEGROWN   SANDWICHES $
Map p244 (☑206-453-5232; www.eathome grown.com; 3416 Fremont Ave N; half/full sandwiches $7/12; ⊘8am-8pm; ☐26) 🍴 Slavishly sustainable, this newish sandwich bar proves that green doesn't have to be tasteless. Bread is baked daily in-house and filled with unique ingredients such as split-pea pesto and pork loin rubbed in Stump-town coffee that's been laced with cayenne. Now that's what you call creative.

HUNGER   MEDITERRANEAN $$
Map p244 (☑206-402-4854; www.hungerseattle. com; 3601 Fremont Ave N; mains $10-18; ⊘11am-11pm; ☐26) Recently relocated, Hunger splits its menu four ways: Spanish, Portuguese, Italian and French, highlighting dishes such as paella, cornbread, and dates stuffed with bacon and chorizo. A curvaceous bar and simple tables keep the atmosphere casual.

REVEL   KOREAN, FUSION $$
Map p244 (☑206-547-2040; www.revelseattle. com; 403 N 36th St; rice dishes $12-15; ⊘10am-close; ☐26) Fusing Asia food (this time Korean) with Northwest ingredients is what Seattle does best. People rave about Revel's pancakes, dumplings, and albacore tuna and rice.

✕ Green Lake

MIGHTY-O DONUTS   CAFE $
Map p245 (☑206-547-5431; www.mightyo.com; 2110 N 55th St; doughnuts from $1.50; ⊘6am-5pm Mon-Fri, 7am-5pm Sat & Sun; 🛜🚸; ☐16) 🍴 Going up against Top Pot Hand-Forged Doughnuts is a tall order, but Mighty-O isn't so bothered about the competition, knocking out its vegan doughnuts from this light-filled cafe in the Tangletown district on the cusp of Green Lake and Wallingford. Forget any preconceived ideas you might have about veganism. These sweet creations are sugary and decadent; they just happen to be devoid of animal fat too.

TANGLETOWN PUB   NORTHWEST $
Map p245 (☑206-547-5929; 2106 N 55th St; mains $7-12; ⊘11am-midnight; ☐16) This outpost of the Elysian Brewing Company quickly made friends in the neighborhood, despite having taken over the space that was once the worshipped Honey Bear Bakery. It's a more child-friendly space than Capitol Hill's Elysian brewery, and the building itself is gorgeous: when afternoon sunlight comes streaming into the leaded-glass windows and hits those burgundy walls, look out!

Glorified pub food (chicken wings, an eggplant panini) and Elysian beer carry the day.

BETH'S CAFÉ   BREAKFAST $
Map p245 (☑206-782-5588; 7311 Aurora Ave N; omelets $6-12; ⊘24hr; ☐358) The best – or

---

ℹ️ FREMONT ON FOOT

With its tree-lined waterfront and offbeat statues, Fremont is a highly walkable neighborhood. To help outsiders infiltrate its wacky underbelly, a group of enterprising locals have instituted the **Fremont Tour** (www.thefremonttour.com; adult/child $20/free), a 90-minute neighborhood stroll accompanied by outlandishly costumed guides with names like Rocket Man or Crazy Cat Lady. If you'd rather not suffer overzealous superheroes accosting innocent passersby, you can go it alone. Nearly every local business stocks a handy free *Walking Guide to Fremont* leaflet (with map) or you can download it from the community's official website (www.fremont.com).

---

at least biggest – hangover breakfast in the world is at Beth's, and you can get it all day long. Key words: all-you-can-eat hash browns. You can't smoke in here any more, which, depending on your view, either ruins everything or makes it possible to enjoy Beth's infamous 12-egg omelet while breathing.

Feel free to contribute a piece of scribbled artwork to the wall.

PETE'S EGG NEST   BREAKFAST $

Map p245 (📞206-784-5348; 7717 Greenwood Ave N; breakfast $8-10; ⊘7am-3pm; 🚌5) This Greek-leaning breakfast joint is famous for humongous portions of the satisfying standards – omelets, biscuits and gravy, and mountainous hash browns. Seasonal specials are recommended.

RED MILL BURGERS   BURGERS $

Map p245 (📞206-783-6362; www.redmillburgers.com; 312 N 67th St; burgers $4-10; ⊘11am-9pm Tue-Sat, noon-8pm Sun; 🚌5) This place is constantly collecting accolades for grilling the best burger in town, and it also fries up the fattest, yummiest onion rings. There's usually a line out the door, but it moves along quickly. Cash only.

NELL'S   CONTINENTAL $$

Map p245 (📞206-524-4044; www.nellsrestaurant.com; 6804 E Green Lake Way N; mains $19-29, tasting menu $48; ⊘5:30-10pm; 🚌16) For fine dining near Green Lake, Nell's serves up classic European dishes with North-

western flair. It inhabits the space formerly occupied by Saleh al Lago, and it actually maintains one of that beloved eatery's dishes – the calamari with aioli – to widespread critical acclaim. Opt for seafood dishes, and don't skip dessert.

🍷 DRINKING & NIGHTLIFE

Low-key, residential Fremont is home to a nice variety of bars, taverns and brewpubs. The Green Lake area is all aflutter with new bars and restaurants. Some highlights are below, but make sure to wander further afield if you have time.

🍺 Fremont

⭐FREMONT BREWING   BREWPUB

(www.fremontbrewing.com; 3409 Woodland Park Ave N; ⊘11am-7pm Mon-Wed, to 8pm Thu-Sat, to 6pm Sun; 🚌26) No conventional bar (this, after all, is Fremont!), this new brewery inaugurated in 2008 has what is called an 'Urban Beer Garden': you sit at a couple of communal tables in the brewery and enjoy samples of what are quickly being hailed as some of the finest microbrews in the city.

Pets and kids are welcome and you can bring your own food.

HALE'S ALES BREWERY   BREWPUB

(www.halesbrewery.com; 4301 Leary Way NW; ⊘11:30am-11pm; 🚌40) Hale's makes fantastic beer, notably its ambrosial Cream Ale. Its flagship brewpub in Fremont feels like a business-hotel lobby, but it's worth a stop. There is a self-guided tour leaving near the entrance.

GEORGE & DRAGON PUB   PUB

Map p244 (www.georgeanddragonpub.com; 206 N 36th St; ⊘11am-2am; 🚌40) Attracting every Brit within a 10-mile radius, the George & Dragon is a definitive English boozer where the 'football' on TV is that 11-a-side game you play with your feet, 'chips' are rectangular and fried and not remotely French, and Tetley's is a dark, warm beer as opposed to a brand of tea.

BROUWER'S   PUB

Map p244 (400 N 35th St; ⊘11am-2am; 🚌40) This dark cathedral of beer in Fremont has rough-hewn rock walls and a black metal grate in the ceiling. Behind an epic bar are tantalizing glimpses into a massive beer fridge.

FREMONT COFFEE COMPANY   CAFE

Map p244 (www.fremontcoffee.net; 459 N 36th St; ⊗6am-8pm Mon-Fri, 7am-8pm Sat & Sun; 🚇26) Coffee shop in an old Craftsman-style house with art-adorned rooms, and wicker chairs on a wraparound porch. The clientele is hip meets hippie – Fremont in a bottle.

🍷 Green Lake

EL CHUPACABRA   BAR

Map p245 (✆206-706-4889; 6711 Greenwood Ave N; ⊗11am-2am Mon-Fri, 2pm-2am Sat & Sun; 🚇5) The patio is where it's at for sipping margaritas at this kitschy neighborhood hangout. Be warned: service can be slow when the place is crowded.

74TH STREET ALE HOUSE   PUB

Map p245 (✆206-784-2955; 7401 Greenwood Ave N; pints $4-5, gumbo $5, dinner specials $12-14; ⊗11:30am-11pm Sun-Thu, to midnight Fri & Sat; 🚇5) A sibling to the Hilltop Ale House in Queen Anne, this is the kind of place that, if you lived nearby, you'd find yourself in several times a week. It's immediately comfortable, to the point that you feel like an instant regular – plus there are dozens of outstanding beers on tap, and the food is miles above usual pub standards.

☆ ENTERTAINMENT

☆ Fremont

FREMONT ALMOST FREE
OUTDOOR CINEMA   CINEMA

Map p244 (www.fremontoutdoormovies.com; 3501 Phinney Ave N; ⊗Jul & Aug; 🚇40) Some come dragging sofas, others arrive dressed as cowboys or zombies from *Shaun of the Dead*. Every summer, Fremonters take over this small parking lot for evening movies that quickly turn into frivolous community events with food carts, fancy dress and harmless high jinks. The large projected screen is flanked by iconic images of Bogart and Bergman.

HIGH DIVE   LIVE MUSIC

Map p244 (www.highdiveseattle.com; 513 N 36th St; ⊗5pm-2am; 🚇26) A bit of a dive – but a not unpleasant one – this is one of two local live-music stalwarts. It hosts rock primarily for small-name bands on their way up. Strong drinks and BBQ food provide the accompaniment.

NECTAR   LIVE MUSIC

Map p244 (✆206-632-2020; www.nectarlounge. com; 412 N 36th St; 🚇40) A small, comfortable rock venue that has grown out of its humble beginnings to become a well-established, scenester-approved club, Nectar hosts everything from reggae and dub to funk to Americana, as well as DJ nights.

☆ Green Lake

LITTLE RED HEN   LIVE MUSIC

Map p245 (✆206-522-1168; www.littleredhen. com; 7115 Woodlawn Ave NE; ⊗9am-2am; 🚇16) This is Seattle's primary (or only) venue for authentic, live country music. Nightly entertainment includes country karaoke and good-time honky-tonk bands – or you can make like Billy Ray Cyrus with weekly line-dancing lessons.

🛍 SHOPPING

Once a warren of junk shops and craft-supply stores frequented by granola crunchers, Fremont has become more of a soccer-mom neighborhood. Still, it's a fun place to browse regardless of whether you're in the mood to spend money.

🛍 Fremont

JIVE TIME RECORDS   MUSIC

Map p244 (www.jivetimerecords.com; 3506 Fremont Ave N; ⊗11am-9pm Mon-Sat, to 7pm Sun; 🚇26) A vinyl collector's dream come true full of rarities and secondhand bargains encased in a diminutive interior.

OPHELIA'S BOOKS   BOOKS

Map p244 (www.opheliasbooks.com; 3504 Fremont Ave N; 🚇26) Like an indie record store for bibliophiles, Ophelia's is full of rare, yellowing, story-filled books that possess bags more character than electronic i-readers.

WORTH A DETOUR

WALLINGFORD

The best reason to visit sleepy, residential Wallingford, sandwiched like a tangy relish in between Fremont and the U District, is that no one else does – apart from the several thousand people who call it home. Welcome to a neighborhood bereft of any real tourist 'sights' where you can while away an afternoon slumped in an unpretentious cafe and quietly imbibe a side of Seattle that one million annual visitors to the Space Needle never get to see. Wallingford's arterial road, NE 45th St, supports an eclectic parade of local businesses ranging from the homespun to the bizarre, with moth-eaten bookstores, one-off tearooms, French bakeries and exotic restaurants (Afghan cuisine, anyone?). About a mile to the south, the car-free Burke-Gilman Trail bisects the neighborhood east–west along the northern shores of Lake Union. Stop, if you have time, amid the post-industrial landscape of **Gas Works Park** (Meridian Ave, at N Northlake Way) where a rusting disused power plant contrasts sharply with the surrounding greenery. It remains a favorite spot for lakeside kite-flyers and rock album cover shoots.

NE 45th St is full of interesting places to eat, drink and browse. Don't miss the following:

Wide World Books & Maps (☎206-634-3453; 4411 Wallingford Ave N; ⊙10am-9pm Mon-Sat, 11am-6pm Sun) If you thought guidebooks were dead, visit this multifarious travel emporium staffed by a team of seasoned globetrotters.

Kabul (☎206-545-9000; 2301 N 45th St; starters $4-7, mains $10-20; ⊙dinner) Fine-tune your international tasting palate with Afghan food, including stewed eggplant, lamb kebabs, yogurt, and mild, creamy curry.

Boulangerie (☎206-634-2211; 2200 N 45th St; pastries $2-5; ⊙7am-2:30pm) Reason alone to visit Wallingford is this bread-friendly bastion of Frenchness.

Teahouse Kuan Yin (☎206-632-2055; 1911 N 45th St; cup/pot of tea $2/8; ⊙9am-10pm Sun-Thu, to 11pm Fri & Sat) In Seattle's burgeoning tea scene, Kuan Yin is a leading light. It's usually stuffed with laptop campers until late evening.

🛍 Green Lake

PICNIC
WINE, FOOD

Map p245 (www.picnicseattle.com; 6801 Greenwood Ave N; ⊙11am-6pm Wed-Sat; 🚌5) Like a Euro deli crossed with a Californian wine store, Picnic provides ample justification to put together a gourmet outdoor meal (Green Lake Park beckons). It specializes in locally produced, hard-to-find products (cheese, cured meat, honey, chocolate) and also has a small cafe with wine tastings.

FROCK SHOP
CLOTHING

Map p245 (☎206-297-1638; www.shopfrockshop.com; 6500 Phinney Ave N; ⊙11am-7pm Tue-Sat, to 4pm Sun; 🚌5) Get gorgeous in style with flirty little dresses you can try on in front of movie-star mirrors.

🏃 SPORTS & ACTIVITIES

GREEN LAKE SMALL CRAFT CENTER
BOATING

Map p245 (☎206-684-4074; 7351 W Green Lake Way N; 🚌16) Green Lake's still waters help keep beginner kayakers calm, though the crowds might also keep you waiting. Run by **Seattle Parks & Recreation** (☎206-684-4075; www.cityofseattle.net/parks), the center offers classes in rowing, sailing, canoeing and kayaking. It doesn't rent boats, but you can rent kayaks, canoes, rowboats and paddleboats from March to October from **Green Lake Boat Rental** (Map p245; ☎206-527-0171; rentals per hr $18; ⊙11am-dusk May-Sep) on the eastern shore of the lake.

Ballard & Discovery Park

Neighborhood Top Five

1 Watching birds, fishing boats, motor yachts, kayaks and salmon negotiating **Hiram M Chittenden Locks** (p153) on a sunny summer's evening from the grassy banks of Carl English Jr Botanical Gardens.

2 Making a coffee-and-croissant pilgrimage to local baking legend **Cafe Besalu** (p153).

3 Leaving the city (almost) and exploring on foot inside the verdant ocean-side oasis of **Discovery Park** (p151).

4 Imbibing Ballard's cool, self-contained **bar and music scene** (p156) along Ballard Ave NW on a weekend evening.

5 Enjoying Sunday brunch followed by a visit to the **Ballard Farmers Market** (p152).

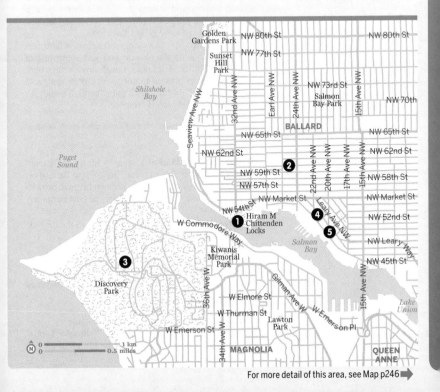

For more detail of this area, see Map p246 ➡

Lonely Planet's Top Tip

Don't miss the unconnected western section of the recreational Burke-Gilman Trail that stretches from Hiram M Chittenden Locks out to Golden Gardens Park (1.75 miles) and takes in a different, quieter side of Ballard that faces the open Sound.

✕ Best Places to Eat

➡ Bastille Cafe & Bar (p153)

➡ Walrus & the Carpenter (p154)

➡ Cafe Besalu (p153)

For reviews, see p153 ➡

🍷 Best Places to Drink

➡ Tractor Tavern (p157)

➡ Noble Fir (p156)

➡ Sexton (p156)

For reviews, see p156 ➡

◉ Best Waterside Attractions

➡ Hiram M Chittenden Locks (p153)

➡ Fishermen's Terminal (p152)

➡ Discovery Park (p151)

➡ Golden Gardens Park (p152)

For reviews, see p152 ➡

Explore: Ballard & Discovery Park

Though just a bridge away from its big metro brother, Ballard is probably the most distinct and independent of Seattle's neighborhoods, whatever libertine Fremonters or Capitol Hillers might say. There's a self-contained music and drinking scene here and a tangible neighborhood identity, forged out of Ballard's history as a separate city. Founded by hard-working Swedish, Norwegian and Danish fishermen, it was incorporated in 1890 and annexed by Seattle in 1907.

Though the neighborhood's now quite spread out, the heart of old Ballard is contained within Ballard Ave NW. This is where you'll find Ballard's notable live-music venues – the Tractor Tavern and Sunset Tavern – and some eclectic bars and pubs where you can warm up first. Seven redbrick blocks have been named a Historic Landmark District, but fortunately the buildings have not been thoughtlessly glamorized: the structures in this district are old, not 'olde.' Pick up a copy of the *Historic Ballard Ave Walking Tour* pamphlet for background on the buildings.

NW Avenue is the other main drag, with a good stash of boutique shops and one-off restaurants, but you've really only seen half of Ballard unless you head west to the Hiram M Chittenden Locks, a beautiful melding of fine engineering and watery Pacific Northwest beauty. Continue on the Burke-Gilman Trail to Golden Gardens Park for more expansive Elliott Bay views.

Discovery Park is 534 acres of urban wilderness northwest of downtown Seattle and just southwest of the mouth of Chittenden Locks. Locals love to come here to escape the ever-present manicure of city gardens and get windswept along the park's many trails. Though it's easy to reach, it feels utterly remote.

Local Life

➡**Sunday Farmers Market** The savvy hit the U District Farmers Market on Saturday and breeze into Ballard on Sunday. Do as they do and grab a cheap brunch, browse the stalls and eavesdrop about where the best bargains are to be found.

➡**Fisherman's Terminal** Pampering little to the tourist dollar, the home of Seattle's fishing fleet is all about hard work, fresh catch, sea air, and age-old working practices. Drink it in.

Getting There & Away

➡**Bus** RapidRide D-Line is the fastest bus into downtown. Metro bus 44 connects to Wallingford and the U District. Metro bus 40 goes direct to Fremont.

TOP SIGHT
DISCOVERY PARK

A former military installation that has been transformed into a wild coastal park, Discovery Park is a relatively recent addition to the city landscape; it wasn't officially inaugurated until 1973. The largest green space in Seattle at 534 acres, the park boasts cliffs, meadows, dunes, forest and beaches, all of which provide welcome breathing space for hemmed-in Seattleites.

DON'T MISS...
→ Loop Trail
→ West Point Lighthouse

PRACTICALITIES
→ Map p246
→ 🚌33

Fort Lawton

The peninsula occupied by the park was originally Fort Lawton, an army base established in 1897 to protect Seattle from unnamed enemies. Fort Lawton didn't see much action until WWII, when it was used as barracks for troops bound for the Pacific. Over the course of the war it held up to 1400 German and Italian prisoners. When the fort was declared surplus property in the 1960s, the City of Seattle decided to turn it into a park, but various historic buildings from the fort remain.

Orientation & Trails

For a map of the park's trail and road system, stop by the **Discovery Park Environmental Learning Center** (Map p246; 📞206-386-4236; 3801 W Government Way; ⏱8:30am-5pm) near the Government Way entrance. Here you can organize educational programs including Saturday nature walks, day camps for children and bird-watching tours. The main walking trail is the 3-mile-long **Loop Trail**, part of a 12-mile network of marked paths that includes the shoreline-hugging North and South Beach Trails. About a mile off the Loop Trail is the still-functioning **West Point Lighthouse**, a great spot for panoramic views of the Sound and mountains to the west. Seventeen acres in the north of the park are Native American land and home to the **Daybreak Star Indian Cultural Center**, a community center for Seattle-area Native Americans. Visitor facilities are limited, but the spot offers one of the best vistas of the Sound.

⊙ SIGHTS

DISCOVERY PARK   PARK
See p151.

NORDIC HERITAGE MUSEUM   MUSEUM
Map p246 (☑206-789-5707; www.nordicmuseum.
org; 3014 NW 67th St; adult/child $6/4; ☺10am-
4pm Tue-Sat, noon-4pm Sun; ☐17) This museum preserves the history of the northern
Europeans who settled in Ballard and the
Pacific Northwest, as well as bringing in
special exhibits of new work by contemporary Scandinavian artists. It's the only
museum in the USA that commemorates
the history of settlers from all five Scandinavian countries.

A permanent exhibit, with one room for
each country, features costumes, photographs and maritime equipment, while a
second gallery is devoted to changing exhibitions. The museum also offers Scandinavian language instruction, lectures and
films.

FISHERMEN'S TERMINAL   DOCKS
Map p246 (cnr 18th Ave & W Nickerson St; ☐Rapid-
Ride D-Line) Seattle's fishing fleet resides at
Fishermen's Terminal, in a wide recess in
the ship canal called Salmon Bay on the
south side of the Ballard Bridge. Fishermen's Terminal is a popular moorage spot
because the facility is in freshwater, above
the Chittenden Locks; freshwater is much
less corrosive to boats than salt water.

It's great fun to wander the piers, watching crews unload their catch, clean their
boats and repair nets. Many of these fishing boats journey to Alaska in summer and
return to dry dock while they wait out the
winter. Outdoor interpretive displays ex-
plain the history of Seattle's fishing fleet,
starting with the native inhabitants who
first fished these waters in canoes. A statue,
the bronze **Seattle Fishermen's Memorial** at the base of the piers, commemorates
Seattle fishers lost at sea. This memorial is
also the site of the ceremonial blessing of
the fleet, held annually on the first Sunday
in May.

In the two terminal buildings are some
good restaurants specializing in the freshest seafood in Seattle, a tobacconist, a ship
chandler and a charts and nautical gifts
store. Stop at the **Wild Salmon Seafood
Market** (p158) to buy the freshest pick of
the day's catch.

BERGEN PLACE PARK   LANDMARK
Map p246 (cnr NW Market St & Leary Ave NW;
☐17) In case you forget where you are or
the origin of the people to whom Ballard
owes its existence, a quintet of flags fly
over diminutive Bergen Place Park: those
of Norway, Sweden, Denmark, Iceland and
Sweden, the five so-called Nordic countries.
The park was inaugurated by King Olaf V
of Norway in 1975 and sports five 'Witness
Tree' sculptures.

The community noticeboard gives details of the latest Nordic-themed events –
Mrs Lundqvist's meatball cook-off and the
like.

CENTER ON CONTEMPORARY ART   GALLERY
Map p246 (COCA; ☑206-728-1980; www.coca
seattle.org; 6413 Seaview Ave NW; ☺9am-5pm
Mon-Fri; ☐61 from Ballard) **FREE** This gallery
has been a force in Seattle's contemporary
art scene for two decades. After moving
around a lot, it has opened a new branch
in **Belltown** (Map p230; 2721 1st Ave) as well
as this primary space in the Shilshole Bay
Beach Club.

GOLDEN GARDENS PARK   PARK
(8498 Seaview Pl NW; ☐61 from Ballard) Golden
Gardens Park, established in 1904 by Harry
W Treat, is a lovely 95-acre beach park with
sandy beaches north of Shilshole Bay Marina. There are picnic facilities, restrooms,
basketball hoops, volleyball nets, gangs of
Canadian geese, lots of parking and plenty
of space to get away from all the activity.

Rising above Golden Gardens is **Sunset
Hill Park** (NW 77th St & 34th Ave), a prime
perch for dramatic sunsets and long views.

SHILSHOLE BAY MARINA   MARINA
Map p246 (Seaview Ave NW; ☐61 from Ballard)
The Shilshole Bay Marina, about 2 miles
northwest of the locks along Seaview Ave
NW, offers nice views across Puget Sound
and, as Seattle's primary sailboat moorage,
a glittery collection of boats. Inside the marina, you can rent sailboats or take classes
at **Windworks** (Map p246; ☑206-784-9386;
7001 Seaview Ave NW).

BALLARD FARMERS MARKET   MARKET
Map p246 (☺10am-3pm Sun; ☐17) Seattle's
most popular Sunday market is a genuine
produce-only farmers market that sets up
in Ballard Ave NW.

TOP SIGHT
HIRAM M CHITTENDEN LOCKS

Seattle shimmers like an impressionist painting at the Hiram M Chittenden Locks. Here, the freshwater of Lake Washington and Lake Union that flows through the 8-mile-long Lake Washington Ship Canal drops 22ft into salt-water Puget Sound. Construction of the canal and locks began in 1911; today 100,000 boats a year pass through. Situated a half-mile west of Ballard, off NW Market St, the locks act as a pedestrian bridge across the canal.

On the southern side of the locks, the **fish ladder** was built in 1976 to allow salmon to fight their way to spawning grounds in the Cascade headwaters of the Sammamish River, which feeds Lake Washington. Visitors can watch the fish from underwater glass-sided tanks or from above (there are nets to keep salmon from overleaping and stranding themselves on the pavement). The best time to visit is during spawning season, from mid-June to September.

On the northern entrance to the lock area is the **Carl English Jr Botanical Gardens**, a charming arboretum and specimen garden. Trails wind through gardens filled with flowers and mature trees, each labeled. Flanking the gardens is a small museum and **visitor center** documenting the history of the locks.

DON'T MISS...

➡ Locks
➡ Fish ladder
➡ Carl English Jr Botanical Gardens

PRACTICALITIES

➡ Map p246
➡ 3015 NW 54th St
➡ ⊙locks 24hr, ladder & gardens 7am-9pm, visitor center 10am-6pm May-Sep
➡ 🚌62

BALLARD & DISCOVERY PARK EATING

🍴 EATING

Ballard offers a growing number of reputable places to eat and drink. It's an ever-changing scene, meaning you can have fun testing out the latest start-ups.

⭐**CAFE BESALU** BAKERY, CAFE **$**
Map p246 (📞206-789-1463; www.cafebesalu.com; 5909 24th Ave NW; pastries from $2.30; ⊙7am-3pm Wed-Sun; 🚌40) Once off the itinerary of Ballard's weekend visitors, who traditionally stick to Ballard Ave, Besalu has started to cause a stir from its isolated perch on 24th Ave with its French-style baked goods (in particular the croissants and quiches), which some bloggers have hailed as 'better than Paris.'

FRESH FLOURS BAKERY, CAFE **$**
Map p246 (📞206-706-3338; www.freshfloursseattle.com; 5313 Ballard Ave NW; pastries $3.50; ⊙7am-5pm; 📶; 🚌17) With Stumptown Coffee (imported from Portland, OR) and almond croissants so flaky they can seriously damage your laptop, Fresh Flours is a leading player in a strong field of Ballard cafes. The tiny tea cookies hint at a Japanese influence.

LA CARTA DE OAXACA MEXICAN **$**
Map p246 (📞206-782-8722; www.lacartadeoaxaca.com; 5431 Ballard Ave NW; mains $7-12; ⊙11:30am-3pm & 5-11pm Tue-Sat, 5-11pm Mon; 🚌17) Mexican restaurants are often duds in Seattle, but then you walk into the Oaxaca, the Mexican city famous for its black *mole* sauces – try the *mole negro Oaxaqueno*, a house specialty. You can sample the same stuff on tamales or go for a combination of various small plates.

Seating is mostly picnic-style, and there's a full bar – handy considering there's usually a wait for a table.

⭐**BASTILLE CAFE & BAR** FRENCH **$$**
Map p246 (www.bastilleseattle.com; 5307 Ballard Ave NW; mains $17-24; ⊙4:30pm-midnight, to 1am Fri & Sat, brunch 10am-3pm Sun; 🚌17) 🌿 French but not at all faux, Bastille could easily pass for a genuine Parisian bistro if it weren't for the surfeit of American accents. First there's the decor: beautiful white tiles juxtaposed with black wood, mirrors and chandeliers. Then there's the menu: *moules* (mussels), *frites* (real French fries), rabbit paté, oysters and steak (all sourced locally).

WALRUS & THE CARPENTER   SEAFOOD $$

Map p246 (☏206-395-9227; www.thewalrusbar.com; 4743 Ballard Ave NW; dishes $8-12; ⏱4pm-close; 🚌17) Puget Sound waters practically bleed oysters and – arguably – there isn't a better place to knock 'em back raw with a glass of wine or two than the Walrus, a highly congenial oyster bar named not after a Beatles song but a poem by Lewis Carroll in *Through the Looking Glass*. The accolades (like the customers) keep flying in.

LOCKSPOT CAFE   SEAFOOD, DIVE BAR $$

Map p246 (☏206-789-4865; www.thelockspotcafe.com; 3005 NW 54th St; mains $10-15; ⏱8am-late; 🚌62) The Lockspot is a throwback to Old Ballard, before the attempted gentrification. Sit down with the potty-mouthed fishermen and antediluvian grandpas for classic greasy-spoon fare. Even better, order fish and chips from the walk-up window outside and take them over to Hiram M Chittenden Locks to watch the boats go by.

LA ISLA   PUERTO RICAN $$

Map p246 (☏206-789-0516; 2320 NW Market St; starters from $4, mains $12-17; ⏱11:30am-2am; 🚌40) What started as a food stand at Fremont Sunday Market has become this always-packed little cafe, offering possibly the only Puerto Rican cuisine in the area. As a starter, try the empanadillas ($4; little fried dough pockets filled with your choice of shrimp, pulled pork, garlicky potatoes, cheese, tofu, chicken or beef).

Better yet, the enormous *pernil* (pulled pork) platter ($15) has a huge pile of juicy meat alongside saucy rice, beans, avocados and cheese, plus a couple of piquant sauces. It's hard to beat – you'll be eating it for hours and still be sad when it's gone.

RAY'S BOATHOUSE   SEAFOOD $$$

Map p246 (☏206-789-3770; www.rays.com; 6049 Seaview Ave NW; mains $24-39; ⏱5-9:30pm; 🅿; 🚌17) OK, so it's a cliché, but Ray's offers views over the Olympics, nautical decor and an exhaustive fresh-fish menu. It offers tourists everything they imagine when they think about a nice dinner out in Seattle. Reservations are required; if you can't get in for dinner, at least come for a drink on the sundeck: the bar's open until midnight.

CHINOOK'S AT SALMON BAY   SEAFOOD $$$

Map p246 (☏206-283-4665; 1900 W Nickerson St; mains $6-30; ⏱11am-10pm Mon-Fri, 7:30am-10pm Sat & Sun; 🚌RapidRide D-Line) Across the

---

🏃 Neighborhood Walk
Old Ballard

START PORTLAND BUILDING
FINISH GOLDEN GARDENS PARK
LENGTH 2.5 MILES; 90 MINUTES TO TWO HOURS

Redbrick Old Ballard is a fetching low-rise version of Pioneer Square and dates from the same era (1890s to 1910s). A great example of the decorative brickwork that graces many of the buildings along Ballard Ave, the ❶ **Portland Building** (5403-5407 Ballard Ave NW) has housed all kinds of businesses since its construction, including taverns and dry-goods stores. It was renovated in 1985.

Continue along Ballard Ave, noting the cute wood-frame building at 5341 Ballard Ave – this particular building was rescued and brought here from the International District (rumor says it was once a bordello), but it's in the same style as most of this street's early buildings. The ❷ **GS Sanborn Building** (5323 Ballard Ave) is Ballard's only example of Richardsonian Romanesque architecture, a style that was popular on the East Coast in the 1880s. It has a sandstone face and a 3rd-story arch, and housed some of Ballard's key businesses in the early 1900s, including a department store.

At 5301 Ballard Ave is the adorable little ❸ **Ballard Savings & Loan Building**, with the helpful motto 'thrift' carved into the roofline. This neoclassical building housed the local Savings & Loan, which was notable for doing comparatively well during the Great Depression.

Across the road is the Second Empire Baroque–style ❹ **Scandinavian American Bank Building** (5300 Ballard Ave), a nice example of the early-1900s tendency to flatter by imitation: its concrete surface is treated to look like stone. You can still see the 'Bank Building' sign embedded in the top corner. The building became the Starlight Hotel and now holds the headquarters of the ❺ **Ballard Farmers Market** (p152).

Continue past the intersection of 20th Ave NW. On your left is one of Seattle's oldest still-operating taverns; its first liquor license was granted in 1902, when

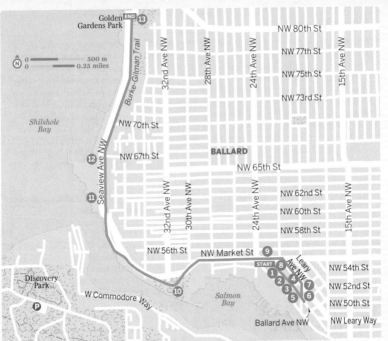

it was called the Owl. Now called ⑥ **Conor Byrne** (p157), it still has the original mahogany bar.

Retrace your steps to the intersection and turn right. On your right is the ⑦ **Cors & Wegener Building** (5000-5004 20th Ave NW). Once the offices of the early local broadsheet *Ballard News*, it's still one of the most impressive buildings in the area. One of the first in Ballard to be revitalized, it's now mostly shops, apartments and office space.

Continue to Leary Ave NW, turn left and head to NW Market St. On the corner of this street and Ballard Ave is a commemorative ⑧ **Bell Tower**. This corner is the original location of Ballard City Hall, sometimes called 'Hose Hall,' which also contained the jail and the fire department hose company (hence the nickname). Weakened by a series of earthquakes, the building was demolished in 1965, but the columns and bell were saved and made into this little landmark.

Back on NW Market St, you'll see the ⑨ **Ballard Building** (2208 NW Market St). Ballard's only major terra-cotta structure, it was built in the 1920s by the Fraternal Order

of Eagles. It once held a community hospital and now houses the *Ballard News-Tribune*.

To really *get* Ballard, you have to prise yourself away from its historic core and digest a bit of its seafaring spirit. Continue west on NW Market St before veering left on NW 54th St. Here you'll find the entrance to ⑩ **Hiram M Chittenden Locks** (p153), as much engineering marvel as waterside attraction, with an interesting visitor center. Back outside the locks and its park, you can pick up the western segment of the Burke-Gilman Trail and follow it to where the ship canal opens out into Puget Sound. If hunger pangs attack, stop off at ⑪ **Ray's Boathouse** (p154) for excellent seafood and equitable views. A little further is the Ballard outpost of the ⑫ **Center on Contemporary Art** (p152), a good place to see what's current on the art scene. Pass Shilshole Bay Marina to the Burke-Gilman's and this walk's end point, ⑬ **Golden Gardens Park** (p152), with its gorgeous sandy beach.

FRELARD

What do you get when you cross offbeat Fremont with Scandinavian-flavored Ballard? Frelard, according to some facetious Seattleites – or, in the words of the *Seattle Times*, an area 'so hip it defies definition.' Seattle neighborhoods have always been indistinct, lacking official borders, and this ambiguity is no more apparent than in the warehouse district where western Fremont dissolves into eastern Ballard. Leary Way NW around 43rd and 45th Aves is where the demarcation gets a bit sticky, with some businesses claiming they're in Fremont, others saying they're in Ballard, and a significant portion in the middle say they don't really know – or care. Hale's Ales, one of Seattle's finest microbreweries, is a classic case. TripAdvisor puts it in Fremont, Yelp claims it's in Ballard, while, sitting diplomatically on the fence, the Hale's Ales Twitter account lists itself as being in Fremont/Ballard. All hail the new neighborhood!

Ballard Bridge in the Fisherman's Terminal, Chinook's is where fish practically leap out of the water and into the kitchen. You can't get it much fresher than this, and the selection of fish and range of preparations is vast. Watch the fishing fleet coming in from the massive restaurant windows.

🍷 DRINKING & NIGHTLIFE

The cat's out of the bag: Ballard, in the minds of many, is the city's most buzzing neighborhood for drinks and live bands, with plenty of variation. New bars and restaurants seem to pop up in the space of a lunch break, while plenty of stalwarts have weathered the recession.

★ NOBLE FIR   BAR
Map p246 (🕿206-420-7425; www.thenoblefir. com; 5316 Ballard Ave NW; ⊗4-11pm Mon-Wed, to 1am Thu-Sat, noon-11pm Sun; 🚍17) Possibly the first bar devoted to the theme of wilderness hiking, the Noble Fir is a bright, shiny new Ballard spot with an epic beer list that might just make you want to abandon all your plans for outdoor adventure. Should your resolve begin to flag, head to the back corner, where there's a library of activity guides and maps that will re-inspire you.

Bonus: Magners Irish cider on tap!

COPPER GATE   BAR
Map p246 (www.thecoppergate.com; 6301 24th Ave NW; ⊗5pm-midnight; 🚍40) Formerly one of Seattle's worst dives, the Copper Gate in Ballard is now an upscale bar-restaurant focused on meatballs and naked ladies. A Viking longship forms the bar, with a peep-show pastiche for a sail and a cargo of helmets and gramophones.

KING'S HARDWARE   BAR
Map p246 (🕿206-782-0027; 5225 Ballard Ave NW; ⊗4pm-2am Mon-Fri, noon-2am Sat & Sun; 🚍17) King's Hardware has a hunting-lodge-meets-Old-West-game-room feel. There's pinball and Skee-Ball towards the rear wooden booths, and taxidermied jackalopes propped between bottles of liquor behind the bar. The spacious hangout also has a good jukebox and, in case you're feeling shaggy, easy access to Rudy's Barbershop (it's attached).

HATTIE'S HAT   BAR
Map p246 (🕿206-784-0175; 5231 Ballard Ave NW; ⊗11am-2am Mon-Fri, 9am-2am Sat & Sun; 🚍17) A classic old divey bar that's been revived with new blood without losing its charm, Hattie's Hat is a perfect storm of stiff drinks, fun-loving staff and cheap greasy-spoon food.

This might be the best place in town to make that ever-so-delicate transition from weekend breakfast to dinner and drinks – you can get coffee with eggs and toast all day long, and nobody will find it odd when you switch to beer, even if it's not quite noon yet.

SEXTON   BAR
Map p246 (www.sextonseattle.com; 5327 Ballard Ave NW; ⊗5pm-2am Tue-Sat, 11am-2am Sun; 🚍17) This new player on Ballard's fertile bar scene has a drinks menu with a strong bourbon and cocktail bias (it's a little pricey, so come during happy hour: 5pm to 7pm). The interior sports intentionally worn wood and an offbeat bar top made out of old cassettes. Creative small food plates soak up the whiskey.

JOLLY ROGER TAPROOM
BREWPUB

(206-782-6181; www.maritimebrewery.com; 1111 NW Ballard Way; 11am-11pm Mon-Sat; RapidRide D-Line) A secret treasure tucked away off busy Leary Way, Maritime Pacific Brewing's Jolly Roger Taproom is a tiny, pirate-themed bar with a nautical chart painted onto the floor. Though lately it's gone less scurvy-barnacle and more placid-yachtsman, the beer's still tops – and served in 20oz pints. The food's not bad either; try a chef's special or a mess of clams and mussels.

There are about 15 taps, all serving Maritime Pacific brews. The strong winter ale, Jolly Roger, is highly recommended.

CONOR BYRNE
PUB

Map p246 (206-784-3640; 5140 Ballard Ave NW; Guinness $4; 4-7pm; 17) A friendly pub notable primarily for its gorgeous, original mahogany bar, it has live music most nights, leaning mostly toward old-timey and blues, plus trivia and comedy events.

⭐ ENTERTAINMENT

Ballard claims two of Seattle's most hallowed medium-small live-music venues.

TRACTOR TAVERN
LIVE MUSIC

Map p246 (206-789-3599; www.tractortavern. com; 5213 Ballard Ave NW; 17) The premier venue for folk and acoustic music, the elegant Tractor Tavern also books local songwriters and regional bands such as Richmond Fontaine, plus touring acts like John Doe and Wayne Hancock. It's a gorgeous room, usually with top sound quality.

SUNSET TAVERN
LIVE MUSIC

Map p246 (206-784-4880; www.sunsettavern. com; 5433 Ballard Ave NW; 17) The Sunset is a Ballard bar that books great dirty-rock shows of local and touring bands, and frequently has free movie nights, including a series of B-grade kung-fu films most weeks.

🛍 SHOPPING

Ballard is a fun place to browse, especially right along the core of Market St, where there's a little cluster of interesting shops, including a branch of indie record store Sonic Boom.

⭐ BOP STREET RECORDS
MUSIC

Map p246 (www.bopstreetrecords.com; 2220 NW Market St; noon-8pm Tue-Wed, to 10pm Thu-Sat, to 5pm Sun; 17) Probably the most impressive collection of vinyl you're ever likely see lines the heavily stacked shelves of Bop Street Records. The collection of half a million records covers every genre – they even have old-school 78s. No wonder rock stars and other serious musicians make it their first Seattle port of call.

CARD KINGDOM
GAMES

Map p246 (www.cardkingdom.com; 5105 Leary Ave NW; 10am-midnight; 17) Attracting poker players, *Dungeons & Dragons* geeks, kids, board-game enthusiasts and tourists on the rebound from Vegas, Card Kingdom is the games emporium you've been dreaming about. There are plenty of organized activities here, including an on-site games parlor, but you can drop by any time it's open to browse the shelves or play a hand.

The attached Cafe Mox is a popular nook for coffee-sipping chess players.

MONSTER ART & CLOTHING
ART, CLOTHING

Map p246 (www.monsterartandclothing.com; 5000 20th Ave NW; 10:30am-6:30pm; 17) Local art and clothing shop that sometimes combines both in inspired screen-printed T-shirts.

WILD AT HEART
ADULT

(206-782-5538; 1111 NW Leary Way; noon-7pm Mon-Sat, to 5pm Sun; RapidRide D-Line) This women-owned shop sells sex toys, fetish-wear, clubwear, lingerie and DVDs. Heavy drapes on the windows keep out prying male eyes.

SECRET GARDEN BOOKSHOP
BOOKS

Map p246 (206-789-5006; www.secretgarden books.com; 2214 NW Market St; 10am-8pm Mon-Sat, 11am-5pm Sun; 17) The children's collection, especially the fiction, is excellent at this bookstore, and the staff will order you anything they don't have.

BUFFALO EXCHANGE
CLOTHING

Map p246 (206-297-5920; 2232 NW Market St; 11am-7pm, to 6pm Sun; 17) Usually rewarding for the patient browser, this used-clothing store has an unpretentious selection and non-intrusive salespeople.

WILD SALMON SEAFOOD
MARKET   SEAFOOD

Map p246 (📞206-283-3366; 1900 W Nickerson St; 🚌RapidRide D-Line) At Wild Salmon Seafood Market – in the Fishermen's Terminal on the south side of the Ballard Bridge, which is technically Magnolia, but still – you can buy fresh salmon and shellfish directly from the fishermen who caught it. The market will also ship fresh fish at reasonable prices.

🏃 SPORTS & ACTIVITIES

STONE GARDENS:
THE CLIMBERS GYM   ROCK CLIMBING

Map p246 (📞206-781-9828; 2839 NW Market St; ⏱6am-11pm Mon-Fri, 9am-10pm Sat & Sun; 🚌62) This is a full climbing gym with 14,000 sq ft of climbing surface on more than 100 routes. The gym also has weights, lockers and showers. Courses, from beginner climber to belaying, are also offered. The drop-in rate is $16 ($12 for children).

DUTCH BIKE CO   CYCLING

Map p246 (📞206-789-1678; www.dutchbike seattle.com; 4741 Ballard Ave NW; ⏱11am-7pm; 🚌17) Perfectly positioned at the western end of the Burke-Gilman Trail, this is one of the few bike-rental places within shouting distance of the trail itself. You'll pay $12 an hour or $60 per day for a sturdy bike. There's also a cafe on site – ideal for a pre- or post-ride coffee or a glass of wine.

Georgetown & West Seattle

GEORGETOWN | WEST SEATTLE

Neighborhood Top Five

1 Seeing how *Homo sapiens* got from the Wright Brothers to the Concorde in the space of just 66 years at the illustrious, entertaining and subtly educational **Museum of Flight** (p161).

2 Slowing down the rhythm a notch on a weekend summer's afternoon on **Alki Beach** (p163).

3 Settling down for an afternoon of serious drinking in a redbricked **Georgetown bar** (p165).

4 Hanging out in the bakeries and record shops of **the Junction**, West Seattle's diminutive downtown.

5 Investigating Georgetown's bohemian inclinations in its monthly **Art Attack** (p164).

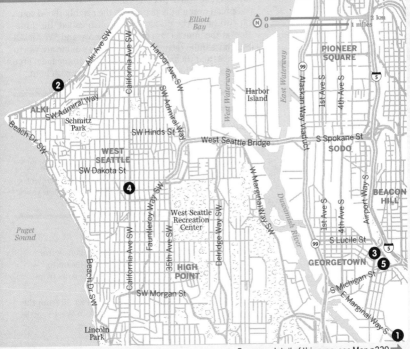

For more detail of this area, see Map p239 ➡

Lonely Planet's Top Tip

Even Seattle's most rain-hardened brethren would admit that West Seattle is best saved for a sunny day. Visit this hilly, beach-embellished neighborhood in spring or summer and join in the high jinks on ebullient Alki Beach.

✕ Best Places to Eat

➡ Bakery Nouveau (p164)

➡ Square Knot Diner (p164)

➡ American Pie (p163)

➡ Spud Fish & Chips (p165)

For reviews, see p163 ➡

☕ Best Places to Drink

➡ Jules Maes Saloon (p165)

➡ Nine Pound Hammer (p165)

➡ All City Coffee (p165)

➡ Elliott Bay Brewery & Pub (p165)

For reviews, see p165 ➡

🔒 Best Independent Shops

➡ Easy Street Records & Café (p166)

➡ Fantagraphics Bookstore & Gallery (p166)

➡ Georgetown Records (p166)

For reviews, see p166 ➡

Explore: Georgetown & West Seattle

Located south of downtown and Pioneer Square, the neighborhoods of Georgetown and West Seattle feel more detached, cut off from the city center by the glassy expanse of Elliott Bay and the boxy warehouse district of SoDo. Since transport connections to and from downtown are better than those between the neighborhoods themselves, they're often visited separately. Georgetown can be incorporated with a visit to the Museum of Flight, while West Seattle works as a pleasant summer weekend beach sortie.

Located 3 miles south of Seattle proper, Georgetown is an old neighborhood with a scrappy yet independent artistic sensibility that's recently been deemed cool. Once you get here (regular buses from downtown take 25 minutes), navigation is easy. Most of Georgetown's pubs, hip bars, funky shops and restaurants are clustered on Airport Way S.

There are plenty of Seattleites who would more likely visit Hawaii than spend a day catching rays in West Seattle. But, although this island-like enclave might feel as if it's halfway to Honolulu in the minds of many, it's actually only – ahem – 15 minutes from downtown by water taxi. Not that everyone dismisses it. Indeed, among a certain type of Seattleite, West Seattle beckons like a proverbial Coney Island, courtesy of sandy Alki Beach, the city's best excuse to get undressed in public and pretend you're in California.

Spread over a hilly peninsula, the neighborhood spins on two hubs: the de facto downtown called 'the Junction' at the intersection of California Ave and SW Alaska St, whose indie record store and bakery alone are worth the visit, and the famous beach and its promenade. Free shuttles from the water-taxi dock connect with both.

Local Life

➡ **Alki Beach** When the sun's out, the beach and its adjacent promenade become Seattle's communal backyard and a good place to play 'guess which neighborhood they're from' with the passing faces.

➡ **Jules Maes Saloon** Crusty pub that's been a collector and spreader of Georgetown gossip for – oh – 126 years.

Getting There & Away

➡ **Bus** Metro buses 106 and 124 run frequently from downtown to Georgetown. The 124 carries on to the Museum of Flight. RapidRide C-Line runs from downtown to West Seattle.

➡ **Water Taxi** Hourly water taxis leave Pier 50 from the downtown waterfront to Seacrest Park in West Seattle. There's no weekend service in the winter.

◉ TOP SIGHT
MUSEUM OF FLIGHT

This clever amalgamation of several hanger-sized galleries is way more than an afternoon sojourn for geeky plane-spotters. It relates the detailed history of anything human-made that has defied gravity, including V2 rockets, lunar modules and gliders.

Great Gallery

The centerpiece of the museum is a humungous gallery filled with historic aircraft that overhang chronological exhibits on the history of flight. If you're short on time, jump-cut to **The Tower**, a mock-up of an air traffic control tower overlooking the still operational Boeing Field. Another must-see is a replica of the Wright Brothers' original 1903 *Wright Flyer*. Nearby, X-Pilot simulators pitch you into a WWII dogfight; they cost an extra $8 per person.

Red Barn

Saved in the 1970s when it was floated upriver from its original location 3km away, this two-story barn dating from 1909 was Boeing's original manufacturing space. It is filled with the early history of flight, with a strong bias toward the Boeing business.

Airpark & Space Gallery

The outdoor Airpark, accessible via a bridge over E Marginal Way, displays half a dozen iconic planes. You can walk through two: a British Airways **Concorde** and the first jet-powered **Air Force One**, used by Presidents Eisenhower, Kennedy, Johnson and Nixon. The adjacent Space Gallery was built in 2012 to house the decommissioned **Full Fuselage Trainer** of the Space Shuttle (it's $30 extra to explore the crew compartment).

DON'T MISS...

➡ *Air Force One*
➡ X-Pilot simulator
➡ 1903 *Wright Flyer*

PRACTICALITIES

➡ ☎206-764-5720
➡ www.museumof flight.org
➡ 9404 E Marginal Way S, Boeing Field
➡ adult/child $18/10, 5-9pm 1st Thu each month free
➡ ⊙10am-5pm Fri-Wed, to 9pm Thu
➡ 🚌124

WORTH A DETOUR

SODO

Giving a neighborhood an acronym is often seen as giving it a green light to become hip, repurposed and tastefully gentrified. In the case of Seattle's SoDo (the name originally meant SOuth of the defunct KingDOme but now means SOuth of DOwntown), the trendy makeover has yet to materialize. A sketchy warehouse district built on reclaimed tidal flats near the mouth of the Duwamish River, SoDo's raison d'être has long been industrial; freight companies, scrap-metal merchants and small factories overlook the ugly tangle of South Seattle's endless rail yards here, though the landscape is slowly changing. Starbucks maintain its HQ in the impressive 1912 former Sears building, now called the Starbucks Center, on Utah Ave S (yes, there's a café!), and ambitious internet start-ups have moved in nearby, lured perhaps by the close-to-downtown location – or the acronym! Nonetheless, SoDo, unlike Georgetown further south, still struggles to tempt many curious visitors. If you come here, it will probably be for a ball game at CenturyLink Field or Safeco Field, or a live gig at **Showbox SoDo** (Map p228; www.showboxpresents.com; 1700 1st Ave S), the sister venue to the original Pike Place Showbox that hosts middle-range rock acts. SoDo's iffy restaurant scene has improved slightly in recent years. Check out **Cafe con Leche** (206-682-7557; 2901 1st Ave S; sandwiches $8-9; 11am-4pm Mon-Wed, to 7pm Thu & Fri), a kind of Cuban 'food cart' that has sprung roots and knocks out some decent pork sandwiches, or go for a drink at the industrial-chic Pyramid Ale House (p73).

⊙ SIGHTS

⊙ Georgetown

MUSEUM OF FLIGHT   MUSEUM
See p161.

OXBOW PARK   PARK
Map p239 (6400 Corson Ave S; 124) This public park in a quiet residential part of Georgetown contains a community pea patch and is home to the giant, carefully restored, bright orange and blue Hat 'n' Boots, a beloved pair of relics from a quirky roadside service station.

This attention-grabbing landmark was built in 1955 and moved here in 2003 – you paid for your gas under the hat, and peed in the boots. Photo opportunity!

GEORGETOWN ARTS
& CULTURAL CENTER   ARTS CENTER
Map p239 (206-851-1538; www.georgetown artcenter.org; 5809 Airport Way S; 11am-5pm Mon, 10am-4pm Tue & by appointment; 124) A former dance studio, this community-friendly arts center hosts rotating exhibitions as well as studio space, classes and workshops. It's one of several key stops along the route of the Art Attack, George-town's monthly art walk. Stop by on a Wednesday night from 6pm to 9pm for its open life-drawing class ($12).

GEORGETOWN STEAM PLANT   LANDMARK
Map p239 (206-763-2542; 6605 13th Ave S; 124) FREE The Georgetown Steam Plant, built in 1906, has one of the last working examples of the large-scale steam turbines that doubled the efficiency of electricity production and shifted the public's view of electricity from a luxury to a standard part of modern living. The plant ceased operations in 1972 and in 1980 was declared a Historic American Engineering Record site.

It's now an education-oriented **museum**, with exhibits as well as classes in steam engineering. However, it was temporarily closed at the time of research for some renovations. Call ahead for updates (visiting hours were traditionally limited to once a month or by appointment).

TOTALLY BLOWN
GLASSWORKS   GLASSWORKS
Map p239 (206-768-8944; www.totallyblown glass.com; 5607 Corson Ave S; 10:30am-4pm Wed-Fri, to 3:30pm Sat; 124) This glassworks studio and shop makes all its work in-house; if you've never seen a glassblowing demonstration, it's worth checking out. The

studio welcomes spectators whenever it's open and is a popular stop in the monthly Art Attack.

West Seattle

DUWAMISH HEAD   LANDMARK

(🚇775 from Seacrest Dock) Popular for its views of Elliott Bay and downtown, this is the former site of Luna Park. In its days as an over-the-top amusement center, the park covered more than 10 acres and boasted the 'longest bar on the bay.' This grand assertion unfortunately led to claims of debauchery and carousing, and the park was eventually closed in 1913 by the conservative powers-that-were.

ALKI BEACH PARK   BEACH, PARK

(🚇775 from Seacrest Dock) Alki Beach has an entirely different feel from the rest of Seattle: this 2-mile stretch of sand could almost fool you into thinking it's California, at least on a sunny day, except for the obvious lack of...Californians. There's a bike path, volleyball courts on the sand, and rings for beach fires.

Look for the miniature Statue of Liberty, donated by the Boy Scouts (currently removed for repair and replaced by a copy). There's also a pylon marking Arthur Denny's landing party's first stop in 1851, which for some reason has a chip of Massachusetts' Plymouth Rock embedded in its base.

WEST SEATTLE'S MURALS

Following a noble city tradition of free public art, West Seattle's Diego Rivera–like **murals** have become an important part of the neighborhood fabric. The 11 giant paintings are scattered over a relatively small area around the Junction commercial zone and do a good job of relating the important chapters of the neighborhood's pioneer history, depicting lively scenes of old street cars, ferries, beach gatherings and esoteric parades. The murals were commissioned in 1989 and painted by artists from around the country. All are etched onto the sides of buildings, including a post office and a bank. They're kept colorful with periodic touch-ups.

ALKI POINT LIGHTHOUSE   LANDMARK

(🚇206-217-6123; btwn Beach Dr & Point Pl, Alki Beach; 🚇775 from Seacrest Dock) The US Coast Guard maintains this lighthouse. It has limited public hours and you can't just walk up to it, but tours are available by appointment. Call for a current schedule and more information.

LOG HOUSE MUSEUM   MUSEUM

(🚇206-938-5293; www.loghousemuseum.info; 3003 61st Ave SW; suggested donation $3; ⊙noon-4pm Thu-Sun; 🚇775 from Seacrest Dock) A historical curiosity in Seattle's oldest neighborhood, this museum was built in 1903 from Douglas fir trees as a carriage house for a much larger property that once stood on the site. When all around it was moved or demolished to lay out West Seattle, the house miraculously survived and now sits amid a dense urban grid rather than dense forest.

It has been a museum focusing mainly on local history since 1995.

HIGH POINT   LANDMARK

(SW Myrtle St & 35th Ave; 🚇21) This intersection marks the highest point in Seattle, 518ft above sea level.

✗ EATING

Most of the action in West Seattle is found along a short strip across from Alki Beach or along California Ave SW. Georgetown's eating joints line Airport Way S.

✗ Georgetown

AMERICAN PIE   BAKERY, CAFE $

Map p239 (🚇206-708-7813; www.americanpie bc.com; 5633 Airport Way S; pie slices $4; ⊙11am-5pm Mon-Fri; 🚇124) Welcome to the latest in Seattle's nano-industries ('micro' was yesterday's prefix!): freshly baked pies. 'What took them so long?' you'll be asking after lunch at American Pie, where the crusty creations can be taken as a full meal – savory for main and sweet for dessert – or a hearty snack. The vibe is typically Georgetown – unpretentious but cool – and the walls are adorned with guess-the-album-cover art. Three points if you get *Let it Bleed* (The Rolling Stones), *Breakfast in America*

GEORGETOWN SECOND SATURDAY ART ATTACK

Georgetown's industrial art scene pulls together on the second Saturday of each month at the **Georgetown Second Saturday Art Attack**. This is the best time to visit the neighborhood's myriad galleries, some of which have rather sporadic opening hours. Almost the entire commercial strip takes part in the monthly event, which runs from 6pm to 9pm and exhibits work in cafes, pubs, galleries and studios. Complimentary drinks and snacks are often laid on. Unique features include a free 'art ride' bus that runs up and down Airport Way S every 15 minutes between 6pm and 9.30pm, and three-hour-long guided art tours undertaken on foot with a group known as **Heart of the Attack** ($5 suggested donation; book in advance via the Facebook page).

Many of the best galleries inhabit the former Rainier Brewery. **Krab Jab Studio** (Map p239; www.krabjabstudio.com; 5628 Airport Way S) is a shared workspace, gallery and shop specializing in fantasy art. The **Roving Gallery** (Map p239; www.theroving gallery.com; 5268 Airport Way S) is run by four local artists who work with clay, collage, painting and woodcutting. They also offer art classes. Other places worth visiting are the Miller School of Art (p167) and Georgetown Arts & Cultural Center (p162).

(Supertramp) and *Extra Texture* (George Harrison).

SQUARE KNOT DINER
DINER $

Map p239 (206-762-9764; 6015 Airport Way S; breakfast from $6; 24hr; 124) In the middle of the night in Georgetown, life in the small strip fizzles down to this one 24-hour diner equipped with all the classic trappings of cheap American eateries: 1950s decor, cozy booths, a long wraparound bar, cheap, no-nonsense food, and ridiculously large portions. The epic vanilla milkshake is made with Porter beer from the Nine Pound Hammer bar next door.

★ FONDA LA CATRINA
MEXICAN $$

Map p239 (206-767-2787; www.fondala catrina.com; 5905 Airport Way S; tacos & tamales $8; 11am-11pm; 124) When you see the skeleton engravings, you know you've arrived at one of Georgetown's newest innovations, a creative but studiously authentic Mexican restaurant in a city where there has long been a dearth of them. While the skeletons provide the art, beef-tongue tacos and chunky tamales color the menu.

The tortillas are made in-house in full view of the tables, and the nutty *mole* sauce spread over chicken is a giveaway $9.

VIA TRIBUNALI
PIZZA $$

Map p239 (206-464-2880; www.viatribunali. net; 6009 12th Ave S; pizza from $10; 11am-11pm Mon-Thu, to midnight Fri, 4pm-midnight Sat, 3-10pm Sun; 124) This small Seattle-founded chain operates in four of the city's hipper sanctums (including Capitol Hill and Fremont) plus a couple of foreign enclaves (NYC and Portland). It deals not in pizzas but *pizze*: crisp-crusted Italian pies that are true to the food's Neapolitan roots.

The extensive wine list is 90% Italian and offers some good accompaniments to pizza – try the sparkling red Lambrusco. Come during happy hour (4pm to 6pm) for $5 *pizze* and $3 beer.

✕ West Seattle

★ BAKERY NOUVEAU
BAKERY $

(www.bakerynouveau.com; 4737 California Ave SW; baked goods from $1.50; 7am-7pm Sun-Thu, to 9pm Fri & Sat; RapidRide C-Line) No discussion of Seattle's best bakery omits Bakery Nouveau. The crumbly, craggy almond and chocolate croissants are as addictive as other substances far worse for your health.

SUNFISH
SEAFOOD $

(206-938-4112; 2800 Alki Ave SW; fish & chips $5-9; 11am-9pm Tue-Sun; 775 from Seacrest Dock) Locals swear by this fish-and-chips institution. Options include cod, halibut or salmon and chips, fried oysters and clam strips – or combinations thereof. Sit at one of the outdoor tables and enjoy the boardwalk feel.

SPUD FISH & CHIPS
SEAFOOD **$**

(☑206-938-0606; 2666 Alki Ave SW; fish & chips $5-9; ◷11am-9pm; 🖟; 🚍775 from Seacrest Dock) The competition is fierce over which Alki institution has the best fish and chips, here or Sunfish. (Why not try both?) Spud gets the tourist vote, with its crisp, beachy interior, friendly staff and large portions of fried fish, clam strips and oysters.

SALTY'S ON ALKI
STEAK, SEAFOOD **$$**

(☑206-937-1600; www.saltys.com; 1936 Harbor Ave SW; mains from $15; ◷11am-9:30pm Mon-Fri, 8:45am-10pm Sat & Sun; 🚢Seacrest Dock) While many restaurants afford views onto Alki Beach and its strutting revelers, most people drive to West Seattle for the view at Salty's on Alki. This steak-and-seafood house looks across Elliott Bay onto downtown Seattle; at sunset, the spectacle of lights, shining towers and the rising moon is amazing. The food is secondary but still good.

PHOENICIA AT ALKI
MEDITERRANEAN **$$**

(☑206-935-6550; www.phoeniciawestseattle. com; 2716 Alki Ave SW; mains $12-22; ◷5-10pm, to 11pm Fri & Sat; 🚍775 from Seacrest Dock) Mediterranean and Middle Eastern food, particularly artisanal pizza, is the focus at Phoenicia. The owner is Lebanese, but the flavors are pulled from as far afield as Italy and Morocco and combined with a bounty of fresh local seafood.

🍷 DRINKING & NIGHTLIFE

Head to Georgetown to find the preferred drinking holes of those in the know. The former home of Rainier Beer (p166) is a poignant place to sup a pint. West Seattle has the beachy charm of a vacation community and a few good watering holes to explore. It also has a great record store where you can drink a beer while you browse.

🍷 Georgetown

⭐JULES MAES SALOON
BAR

Map p239 (☑206-957-7766; 5919 Airport Way S; ◷11am-11pm, to 1am Fri & Sat; 🚍124) You can pretty much imbibe the beer off the wall-

paper in Seattle's oldest surviving pub: it's been offering liquor since 1888, when the city was a youthful 37 years old. Once a speakeasy and allegedly haunted, it still manages a shaky juxtaposition of traditional saloon (pinball and other vintage games) and modern bar (punk rock and tattoos).

NINE POUND HAMMER
BAR

Map p239 (☑206-762-3373; 6009 Airport Way S; ◷5pm-2am; 🚍124) You can bring your dog to this darkened beer hall. The place is generous with the pours and the peanuts, and the mixed crowd of workers, hipsters, punks and bikers vacillates between energetic and rowdy.

SMARTY PANTS
BAR

Map p239 (☑206-762-4777; 6017 Airport Way S; sandwiches $7.50-8.50; ◷11am-2am Mon-Sat, 10am-3pm Sun; 🚍124) This giant industrial hangout for scooterists and sportbike riders has vintage motorcycles propped up in the windows, a hearty sandwich menu (plus a weekend brunch) and an obvious fondness for two-wheeled mischief of all types. Wednesday is Bike Night, when fans watch the week's recorded races.

ALL CITY COFFEE
CAFE

Map p239 (☑206-767-7146; www.allcitycoffee. com; 1205 S Vale St; ◷6am-7:30pm; 🚍124) This coffee shop, opened by a designer who'd discovered there was nowhere to get a decent latte in the area, looks fantastic and pulls a perfect espresso shot. Plan to linger.

🍷 West Seattle

ELLIOTT BAY BREWERY & PUB
BREWPUB

(☑206-932-8695; 4720 California Ave SW; ◷11am-midnight Mon-Sat, to 11pm Sun; 🚍RapidRide C-Line) 🍴 Long and narrow, with a loft at the back of the room and a beer garden outdoors, this comfortable brewpub makes a nice retreat after a day at Alki Beach. Pub food emphasizes organic, locally sourced ingredients and includes monthly specials. There are always two cask-conditioned beers available.

WEST 5
COCKTAIL BAR

(☑206-935-1966; 4539 California Ave SW; 🚍RapidRide C-Line) A long, skinny space lined with tall, white leather wingback chairs and crowned with neon at the far end, West 5 is an oasis of cool on California Ave.

⭐ ENTERTAINMENT

☆ Georgetown

THE MIX   LIVE MUSIC
Map p239 (www.themixseattle.com; 6006 12th
Ave S; ☐124) Rock venue that's typical
Georgetown – cool, but rough around the
edges.

STUDIO SEVEN   LIVE MUSIC
(☎206-286-1312; www.studioseven.us; 110 S Hor-
ton St; free or cover; ☐Stadium) This all-ages
club is south of Safeco Field, in SoDo, just
off 1st Ave S one block north of Spokane St.
It books local and touring punk and metal
shows.

🛍 SHOPPING

🛍 Georgetown

**FANTAGRAPHICS BOOKSTORE
& GALLERY**   COMICS
Map p239 (☎206-658-0110; www.fantagraphics.
com/bookstore; 1201 S Vale St; ☺11:30am-8pm
Mon-Sat, to 5pm Sun; ☐124) One of the coolest
comic-book publishers around, Fantagraphics is based here in Georgetown,
and it's worth making a pilgrimage if you
have even a passing interest. Don't miss

the Damaged Room, with out-of-print and
steeply discounted books. The store holds
readings and events several times a month;
check online for a schedule.

There's also an exhibition space with
new shows each month.

GEORGETOWN RECORDS   MUSIC
Map p239 (☎206-762-5638; 1201 S Vale St;
☺11:30am-8pm, to 5pm Sun; ☐124) This amazing record store has cool customers (Jeff
Ament and Ben Shepherd, anyone?) and
an even cooler vibe, not to mention a great
selection of new and used CDs and vinyl.
It also hosts in-store performances and is
part of the Georgetown art walk (p164).

**KIRK ALBERT VINTAGE
FURNISHINGS**   FURNITURE, HOMEWARES
Map p239 (www.kirkalbert.com; 5517 Airport Way
S; ☺11am-6pm Wed-Sat; ☐124) Not so much
stocked as curated, this funky, beautiful
store represents the obsessions and tastes
of its owner, a designer with a strongly
original aesthetic. Come to browse and
leave inspired.

🛍 West Seattle

⭐**EASY STREET RECORDS & CAFÉ**   MUSIC
(☎206-938-3279; 4559 California Ave SW; ☐Rap-
idRide C-Line) This place has everything:
rock and roll, coffee, beer, food...and an
open, airy place to hang out while enjoying

A NEIGHBORHOOD BUILT ON BEER

Georgetown's reputation for bohemian bars with blue-collar inclinations rests on
solid foundations. The domineering redbrick building that overlooks the commercial
strip of Airport Way S was once the center of operations for Rainier Beer. Colored by
an illustrious history, the Rainier Brewery was founded in 1883 by John Clanser and
Edward Sweeny, who had noticed how nicely hops thrived in the valley. In the early
days it was staffed mostly by Germans and Belgians, a fact not particularly evident in
the Rainier Beer we drink today, but after Prohibition the nation acquired an insatiable
taste for the cool golden liquid. Rainier quickly morphed into the sixth-largest brewery
in the world and the neon 'R' sign (now on show at the Museum of History & Industry)
became a pre–Space Needle Seattle icon. When the beer industry was consolidated in
the 1970s, the company underwent various takeovers, and the famous brewery closed
in 1999 when production shifted to California. But it wasn't all woe. The closure marked
the inauspicious start of Georgetown's beatnik renaissance. With parts of the brewery
divided up into artist studios, a different kind of drinker started frequenting the neighborhood bars and new businesses opened up to serve them. Nonetheless, some of
Georgetown's old-school bars survive, including Jules Maes Saloon (p165), Seattle's
oldest drinking hole, founded in 1888, where, in among the trendy craft beers and
gastro-pub pretensions, you can still purchase a pint of good ole Rainier – on tap.

all of the above. Any place where you can shop for new-import records, have a beer and then kick back on the couch for a while is bound to attract attention, and you might have to elbow some hipsters out of your way to grab that coveted album – just try not to spill.

 SPORTS & ACTIVITIES

West Seattle

⚐ Georgetown

SCHOOL OF ACROBATICS & NEW CIRCUS ACTS   ACROBATICS CLASSES
Map p239 (☏206-652-4433; www.sanca seattle.org; 674 S Orcas St; drop-ins $15-30; ☝;

☐124) Ever dreamed of running away to join the circus? To prepare yourself, run first of all to Georgetown and book into this innovative school where you can practice the esoteric arts of the high trapeze and juggling. Of interest to visitors are the drop-in classes, especially the two-hour 'Intro to Circus' (2:30pm Saturday, 2pm Sunday; $30).

There's also a slew of kids activities.

MILLER SCHOOL OF ART   ART CLASSES
Map p239 (www.millerschoolart.com; 1226A S Bailey St; ☐124) To tap into Georgetown's artistic sensibilities, join an art class under the auspices of professional artist Mark Miller. He offers beginners and experimental classes plus painting with hired models. Materials are provided. Prices work out at approximately $25 per hour.

⚐ West Seattle

ALKI KAYAK TOURS   CYCLING, KAYAKING
(☏206-953-0237; www.kayakalki.com; 1660 Harbor Ave SW; kayaks/bikes per hr $15/10; ☝Seacrest Dock) You can rent bicycles, in-line skates and kayaks from this outlet next to the water-taxi dock should you wish to explore Alki by human-powered means. You won't be the only one. The Alki Trail promenade traffic is thick in the summer, as are the volleyball games that take over the sandy beach that parallels Alki Ave SW between 53rd and 63rd Sts.

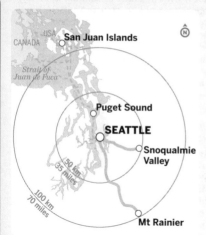

Day Trips from Seattle

Puget Sound p169

These relaxing islands are Seattle's close, rural escape – perfect for wine tasting, fruit picking and exploring by ferry and bike.

San Juan Islands p172

Home to orcas, artist communities and a tangible history. Don't miss the fantasy-novel-worthy nature of one of Washington's most spectacular regions.

Snoqualmie Valley p175

Get nostalgic for the 1990s television show *Twin Peaks* and awed by the massive Snoqualmie Falls before exploring orchards, dairy farms and produce gardens.

Mt Rainier p176

Drive up Washington's iconic, glacial-capped mountain – the highest in the Cascade Range – for the views, rugged hiking and wildflowers in June.

Puget Sound

Explore

The islands of Puget Sound make a fantastic escape from the city. Aside from their scenic beauty – which is very different from the natural landscapes you'll find in and around Seattle, despite their proximity – two activities draw people here: rest and relaxation. These come in many forms, from berry picking or leisurely cycling to wine sampling or lolling on beaches. Reset your internal clock to 'slow' while you take in the gorgeous views of the city and mountains during the ferry ride there, and you'll make the most of a vacation from your vacation. Popular islands to visit very close to Seattle include Bainbridge Island, Vashon Island and Blake Island, or head a little further afield to big and bucolic Whidbey Island.

The Best...

→**Sight** Ferry to Bainbridge Island (p169)
→**Place to Eat** Cafe Nola (p172)
→**Place to Drink** Harbour Public House (p172)

Getting There & Away

All ferries except for Blake Island are run by Washington State Ferries; prices are round trip:

Bainbridge Island Ferry runs hourly from Pier 52 in summer, less frequently in winter. Adult/car and driver: $7.70/16.40.

Vashon Island Frequent daily ferry departures from Fauntleroy in West Seattle. Adult/car and driver: $5/21.

Blake Island Argosy Cruises departs from Pier 55 in Seattle daily late May to early September. Tours adult/child/senior: $79.95/72.95/30; boat fare only adult/child: $40/15.

Whidbey Island Frequent car ferries between Mukileto, 26 miles north of Seattle, and Clinton, Whidbey Island. Adult/car and driver: $4.65/$9.75.

Getting Around

Bike rentals are available on Vashon and Bainbridge Islands and in Langley on Whidbey Island. Expect to pay $25 for two hours or $35 for the day.

Need to Know

→**Area Code** Bainbridge, Blake and Vashon Islands ☏206; Whidbey Island ☏360
→**Location** Bainbridge Island is 9 miles (35 minutes) west of Seattle, Vashon Island is 8 miles (20 minutes) southwest of Seattle, Blake Island is 8 miles (four hours for the entire tour) southwest of Seattle and Whidbey Island is 26 miles (one hour including ferry) north of Seattle
→**Tourist Office Bainbridge Island** (www.visitkitsap.com); **Vashon Island** (www.vashonchamber.com); **Whidbey Island** (www.whidbeycamanoislands.com)

⊙ SIGHTS

BAINBRIDGE ISLAND   ISLAND
(wwwbainbridgeisland.com) Getting to Bainbridge Island really is half the fun. It's a popular destination, largely because it's the quickest and easiest way to get out on the water from Seattle. It's also one of the loveliest. The ferry ride alone provides enough stunning views of Seattle and the Sound to make the trip worthwhile.

Once you get to the island, prepare to stroll around lazily, tour waterfront cafes, taste unique wines, maybe cycle around the invitingly flat countryside, and generally relax.

VASHON ISLAND   ISLAND
(www.vashonchamber.com) Vashon Island has resisted suburbanization – a rare accomplishment in Puget Sound. Much of the island is covered with farms and gardens, and its little towns double as commercial hubs and artists enclaves. There are also unencumbered vistas from Mt Rainier in the south to Mt Baker in the north.

It's a good island to explore by bicycle or car and pick fruit at 'u-pick' gardens or orchards along the way. Plan a hike in one of the county parks.

BLAKE ISLAND   ISLAND
(www.parks.wa.gov) This state park can be approached only by boat. Most people go to the island to visit Tillicum Village, which features the Northwest Coast Indian Cultural Center & Restaurant. A popular tour package includes a traditional salmon bake, dancing and a film about Northwest Native

Seattle Area Ferry Routes

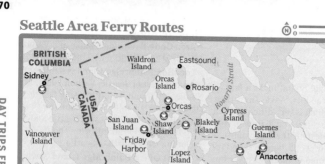

BRITISH COLUMBIA

Waldron Island

Eastsound

Sidney

Orcas Island

Rosario

Rosario Strait

USA
CANADA

Orcas

Cypress Island

Vancouver Island

San Juan Island

Shaw Island

Blakely Island

Guemes Island

Friday Harbor

Lopez Island

Anacortes

Victoria

Fidalgo Island

Skagit Bay

Strait of Juan de Fuca

Whidbey Island

Dungeness Spit

Port Townsend

Keystone

Port Angeles

Admiralty Inlet

WASHINGTON

Whidbey Island

Clinton

Mukileto

Puget Sound

Olympic National Forest

Olympic National Park

Bainbridge Island

Seattle

Hood Canal

Bremerton

Blake Island

Southworth

Fauntleroy

Lake Cushman

Vashon Island

Tahlequah

Point Defiance

Lake Whatcom

Americans. After the meal, there's time for a hike or shopping.

You can also get here by private boat without the formal tour, or watch the performances and skip dinner (or vice versa).

WHIDBEY ISLAND   ISLAND
WHIDBEY ISLAND   ISLAND
(www.whidbeycamanoislands.com) Connected to the mainland by bridge to the north and ferry from the south, this elongated, bucolic isle hosts six state parks, two historic fish-

ing villages, famously good mussels and a thriving artists community. Most visitors try to ignore the US Naval Base that dominates the largest town, Oak Harbor. Hike forests to farm lands, enjoy seafood at an ocean-side historic cafe or kayak off Deception State Park.

Alternatively, check out WWII sites, bird-watch and stroll the beach at Ebey's Landing Historic Preserve.

MAKING SENSE OF SEATTLE FERRIES

Ferries are by far the most fun means of travel in the Seattle area, and a handy way to get to the surrounding islands, but it's not always easy to figure out how to use the system. Schedules are pretty chaotic at first glance – not every ferry goes to every island every day – and the payment system can be confusing, too.

There are two operators: Washington State Ferries and Victoria Clipper. Their services are summarized in the following table, but see each island's listing for more details.

Most of the destinations we cover here are served by **Washington State Ferries** (✆206-464-6400, ferry traffic info 551, in Washington 888-808-7977; www.wsdot.wa.gov/ferries). See the website for online or downloadable schedules for all possible routes. There are also notes about delays or service interruptions. A complicated code, explained in the page's margins, tells you the name of the boat that will be making each run, as well as whether it has disabled access, and specifies that certain routes are only on weekends or only on weekdays.

Then there's a link to the fare information. Fares depend on the length of the route and the size of your vehicle, if you have one. Also, each route seems to have a different way of collecting the fares: some collect on departure, some mid-trip and some when you arrive. These are specified on the website's trip planner.

Note that services to Vashon Island leave from Fauntleroy in West Seattle, while services to the San Juan Islands leave from the Anacortes Ferry Terminal, 85 miles north of Seattle (follow the I-5 north for 65 miles to exit 230, then drive 20 miles west on Hwy 20 to the terminal). There's no charge for journeys back toward Anacortes from Friday Harbor (San Juan Island); the full round-trip fare will have been collected on your way out. Between the San Juan islands, transportation is by inter-island ferries, which travel a circular route exclusively between the four main islands. There is a fee for vehicles (by length) and drivers traveling west-bound only; there is no charge for walk-ons or bicycles.

Victoria Clipper (www.clippervacations.com) operates services from Seattle to Victoria, Canada, and from Seattle to Friday Harbor (San Juan Island).

Destination	Operator	Departs
Bainbridge Island	Washington State Ferries	Pier 52
Blake Island	Washington State Ferries	Pier 55
Lopez Island	Washington State Ferries	Anacortes
Orcas Island	Washington State Ferries	Anacortes
San Juan Island	Washington State Ferries	Anacortes
	Victoria Clipper	Pier 69
Shaw Island	Washington State Ferries	Anacortes
Vashon Island	Washington State Ferries	Fauntleroy
Victoria, Canada	Victoria Clipper	Pier 69
Sidney, Canada (near Victoria)	Washington State Ferries	Anacortes

BAINBRIDGE ISLAND WINERY
WINE TASTING

(✆206-842-9463; ◷tastings 11am-5pm Fri-Sun) This family-owned winery near Winslow is a good destination for cyclists, or for wine-lovers who don't mind a walk – the winery has moved to a place at the edge of its vineyards, about 4 miles north of town on Hwy 305. On Sunday at 2pm there's a winegrower's tour around the vineyards.

✗ EATING & DRINKING

MORA ICED CREAMERY
ICE CREAM $

(✆206-855-1112; www.moraicedcreamery.com; 139 Madrone Lane, Bainbridge Island; single scoop $4.25) Luscious ice creams and sorbets made locally on Bainbridge Island come in cones, cups or pints – and, as a bonus, it's all low fat.

VASHON TEA SHOP
CAFE $

(✆206-463-5202; 17608 Vashon Hwy, Vashon Island; snacks $2-6; ◷9am-6pm Mon-Sat, noon-5pm Sun) A cute little tea shop that also serves gluten-free snacks, brunches and light meals.

CAFÉ NOLA
CAFE $$

(✆206-842-3822; 101 Winslow Way, Bainbridge Island; lunch mains $12-16, dinner mains $16-25; ◷brunch, lunch & dinner) One highlight of a visit to Bainbridge is a meal at this popular bistro, serving a classy blend of Mediterranean and Northwest cooking.

HARBOUR PUBLIC HOUSE
PUB $$

(✆206-842-0969; 231 Parfitt Way, Bainbridge Island; starters $6-12, mains $10-20; ◷11am-midnight) After your bike ride, sit back and quaff microbrews at this public house. Seafood dishes, including the Asian salmon bowl and a calamari appetizer, are recommended.

CHRISTOPHER'S
MODERN $$

(✆360-678-5480; www.christophersonwhidbey.com; 103 NW Coveland St, Whidbey Island; mains $15-23; ◷11:30am-2pm Mon-Fri, midday-2:30pm Sat & Sun, nightly from 5pm) The mussels and clams are the best in town (no mean feat in Coupeville) and the seafood pasta alfredo is wonderfully rich.

San Juan Islands

Explore

There are 172 landfalls in this expansive, magically beautiful archipelago, but unless you're rich enough to charter your own yacht or seaplane, you'll be restricted to seeing the big four – San Juan, Orcas, Shaw and Lopez Islands – all served daily by Washington State Ferries. Communally, the islands are famous for their tranquility, whale-watching opportunities, sea kayaking and seditious nonconformity. A great way to explore the San Juans is by sea kayak or bicycle. Expect a guided half-day trip to cost $45 to $65. Cycling-wise, flat Lopez is tops, San Juan is worthy of an easy day loop, while Orcas offers the challenge of undulating terrain and a steep 5-mile ride to the top of Mt Constitution.

The Best...

➡ **Sight** San Juan Island National Historical Park (p173)

➡ **Place to Eat** Mijita's (p174)

➡ **Place to Drink** Front Street Ale House & San Juan Brewing Company (p174)

Top Tip

Whale-watch from the shore from the west side of Lopez Island, Lime Kiln State Park or the American Camp of the San Juan Island National Historical Park.

Getting There & Away

Airlines serving the San Juan Islands include **San Juan Airlines** (www.sanjuanairlines.com) and **Kenmore Air** (www.kenmoreair.com).

Washington State Ferries (WSF; www.wsdot.wa.gov/ferries) leaves Anacortes for the San Juans; some ferries continue to Sidney, Canada, near Victoria. Ferries run to Lopez Island (45 minutes), Orcas Landing (60 minutes) and Friday Harbor on San Juan Island (75 minutes). Fares vary by season; the cost of the round-trip is collected on westbound journeys only (except those returning from Sidney). To visit all the islands, it's cheapest to go to Friday Harbor first and work your way back through the other islands.

Need to Know

➡️ **Area Code** ☑360

➡️ **Location** San Juan Island is 104 miles (70 minutes) north of Seattle (Anacortes), Orcas Island is 112 miles (70 minutes) north of Seattle (from Anacortes) and Lopez Island is 99 miles north of Seattle

➡️ **Tourist Office Friday Harbor Tourist Information** (☑360-378-6977; Friday Harbor; ⊙10am-4pm)

◉ SIGHTS & ACTIVITIES

◉ San Juan Island

SAN JUAN ISLAND NATIONAL HISTORICAL PARK   HISTORIC SITE
(www.nps.gov/sajh; ⊙8:30am-4pm, visitor center 8:30am-4:30pm Thu-Sun, daily Jun-Sep) 🖊 **FREE**
San Juan Island hides one of the 19th century's oddest political confrontations, the so-called 'Pig War' between the USA and Britain. This curious stand-off is showcased in two historical parks on either end of the island that once housed opposing American and English military encampments. On the island's southern flank, the **American Camp** hosts a small **visitor center** with the remnants of a fort, desolate beaches and a series of interpretive trails. At the opposite end of the island, the **English Camp**, 9 miles northwest of Friday Harbor, contains the remains of the 1860s-era British military facilities.

LIME KILN POINT STATE PARK   PARK
(⊙8am-5pm mid-Oct–Mar, 6:30am-10pm Apr–mid-Oct) 🖊 Clinging to the island's rocky west coast, this beautiful park overlooks the deep Haro Strait and is, reputedly, one of the best places in the world to view whales from the shoreline.

SAN JUAN VINEYARDS   WINE TASTING
(www.sanjuanvineyards.com; 3136 Roche Harbor Rd; tastings per glass $1; ⊙11am-5pm) This unlikely but award-winning winery has a tasting room in an old schoolhouse built in 1896.

Open-minded tasters should try the Siegerrebe and Madeleine Angevine varieties, which are the only estate-grown grapes – other varieties come from the warmer climes of the Yakima Valley. Make sure to at least glance at the camel across the road.

◉ Orcas Island

⭐**MORAN STATE PARK**   PARK
(⊙6:30am-dusk Apr-Sep, from 8am Oct-Mar) This 7-sq-mile park, which has enough attractions to consume the best part of a day, is dominated by 2409ft **Mt Constitution**, the archipelago's highest point and a mountain with the grandeur of a peak twice its size. To say that the view from the summit is jaw-dropping would be an understatement. On a clear day you can see Mt Rainier, Mt Baker, Vancouver's north shore and a patchwork of tree-carpeted islands floating like emerald jewels on a blue crystalline ocean. To see above the lofty firs a 53ft **observation tower** was erected in 1936 by the Civilian Conservation Corp.

For drivers, the mountain has a paved road to the summit, though the view is infinitely better if you earn it via a 4.3-mile hike up from Cascade Lake's North End Campground or a 5-mile cycle that begins just past Cascade Lake. Beginners, beware: the grade is a persistent 7% (7ft vertical rise for every horizontal 100ft) with frequent hairpin turns.

The park's two major bodies of water, **Cascade Lake** and **Mountain Lake**, offer campgrounds, good trout fishing, rentable paddle boats and rowboats, picnic areas and swimming beaches. The lakes are also ringed by hiking trails and linked via a pleasant wooded ramble that passes the spectacular 100ft-high **Cascade Falls**.

Of the more than 30 miles of trails in Moran State Park, about half are open seasonally for mountain biking and one or two for horses. Get a trail map from the park headquarters at the southern end of Cascade Lake.

TURTLEBACK MOUNTAIN PRESERVE   NATURE RESERVE
🖊 Saved from possible development when it was bought for $18.5-million as public land in 2007, Orcas' second mountain

DOWN ON ORCAS

Eddie Bauer, he of the sporting-goods empire, was born on Orcas Island in 1899. As a young man working in an outdoors store he earned a reputation for stringing tennis rackets, even winning a tournament for speed. On a fishing trip on the Olympic Peninsula in 1934, Bauer nearly died of exposure when he took off his wet woolen jacket. Two years later, in Seattle, he invented the down parka. The Skyliner, the quilted down jacket he patented in 1936, became a popular item in the Eddie Bauer store.

(rising to 1519ft) was in private hands for so long that most people had forgotten what was there. The answer: fragile wetlands, Garry oak savannah, spectacular overlooks, wild orchids and acres of solitude. It now has trails open to hikers (daily) and cyclists/horseback riders (alternate days). There are two trailheads; one is on Crow Valley Rd, while the other (best) one is Wild Rose Lane near Deer Harbor and has a steep 1.3-mile trail that leads to Ship's Peak and a view that rivals the one from Mt Constitution.

Horseback trail riding on the mountain is run out of nearby **Turtlehead Farm** (www.turtleheadfarm.com; 231 Lime Quarry Rd; 🐴) for $60 an hour.

◉ Lopez Island

★ SPENCER SPIT STATE PARK   PARK
This is one of only four state parks on the San Juan archipelago. Here two sand spits have formed a marshy lagoon that is a prime spot for various species of waterfowl. It's a good place to kayak, fish, beachcomb and enjoy the unique and stunning scenery. If you've got gear and a shellfish license it's also a popular spot to forage for mollusks.

WATMOUGH HEAD   BEACHES
This scenic area at the island's southeastern extremity holds three trails, the best being the less-than-quarter-mile stroll to Watmaugh Bay, a stunning arc of pebbly sand framed by a sheer rock cliff on its northern side. Young seals may pop their heads up at you from the water as you wander the shore.

LOPEZ ISLAND VINEYARDS   WINE TASTING
(www.lopezislandvineyards.com; Lopez Village; tastings from $5; ☉noon-5pm Fri & Sat May-Sep) This producer has been making wines from grapes grown organically on the island since 1987. Napa Valley it ain't, but you can drop into the Lopez Village tasting room to sample its Madeleine Angevine and Siegerrebe varieties.

🍴 EATING & DRINKING

🍴 San Juan Island

MARKET CHEF   DELI $
(225 A St; ☉10am-6pm) 🌱 Several hundred locals can't be wrong, can they? The 'Chef's' specialty is deli sandwiches and very original ones at that. Join the queue and watch staff prepare the goods with fresh, local ingredients.

DUCK SOUP INN   FUSION $$$
(☎360-378-4878; www.ducksoupinn.com; 50 Duck Soup Lane; mains $29-35; ☉Apr-Oct) 🌱 Duck Soup offers the best island fine dining using its own herb garden to enhance menu items such as oysters, scallops and – best of all – blueberry habanero chicken.

FRONT STREET ALE HOUSE & SAN JUAN BREWING COMPANY   BREWPUB
(1 Front St; mains $10-19; ☉11am-11pm Mon-Thu, to midnight Fri & Sat) San Juan Island's only brewery serves up British-style beers, including Royal Marine IPA, in a real spit-and-sawdust-style pub.

🍴 Orcas Island

★ MIJITA'S   MEXICAN $$
(310 A St, Eastsound; mains $13-22; ☉4-9pm Wed-Sun) Ooh and aah over the Mexican native chef's family recipes like slow-braised short ribs with blackberry *mole* or the vegetarian quinoa cakes with mushrooms, chevre, almonds and pipian.

ISLAND HOPPIN' BREWERY   BREWERY
(www.islandhoppinbrewery.com; 33 Hope Lane, Eastsound; ☉4-9pm Tue-Sun) This is *the* place to go to enjoy six changeable brews on tap while making friends with those islanders

who enjoy beer. There's often live music on weekends.

🍴 Lopez Island

BAY CAFE SEAFOOD $$$
(📞360-468-3700; www.bay-cafe.com; 9 Old Post Rd; mains $14-30) 🍴 Lopez's one and only attempt at fine dining offers romantic sunset views right on the water, with classic fish dishes, including chowder and crab cakes. You could also go bolder with specialties like truffled mac 'n' cheese or rack of lamb paired with wine from the local vineyard.

🛏 SLEEPING

🛏 San Juan Island

There are hotels, B&Bs and resorts scattered around the island, but Friday Harbor has the highest concentration.

WAYFARER'S REST HOSTEL $
(📞360-378-6428; 35 Malcolm St; dm $35, r $65-80; 🛜) The island's only backpackers hostel is a short hike from the ferry terminal. Budget travelers will love its comfortable dorms and cheap private rooms, but beware: it gets busy.

ROCHE HARBOR RESORT RESORT $$
(📞800-451-8910; www.rocheharbor.com; Roche Harbor; r with shared bath $149, 1- to 3-bedroom condos $275-450, 2-bedroom townhouses $499; ❄🛜♿) Located on the site of the former lime kiln and estate of limestone king John McMillin, this seaside 'village' is a great getaway. The centerpiece is the old Hotel de Haro, where the poky rooms are enlivened by the fact that John Wayne once brushed his teeth here.

🛏 Orcas Island

DOE BAY VILLAGE RESORT & RETREAT HOSTEL, RESORT $
(📞360-376-2291; www.doebay.com; dm $55, cabin d from $90, yurts from $120; 🛜) 🍴 Doe Bay has the atmosphere of an artists commune–hippie retreat. Accommodations include sea-view campsites, a small hostel with dormitory and private rooms, and various cabins and yurts, most with views of the water.

OUTLOOK INN HOTEL $$
(📞360-376-2200; www.outlookinn.com; 171 Main St, Eastsound; r with shared/private bath from $79/119; 🛜) The Outlook Inn (1888) is an island institution that has kept up with the times by expanding into a majestic, white (but still quite small) bayside complex. Also on site is the fancy New Leaf Cafe.

Snoqualmie Valley

Explore

East of Seattle's Eastside, the Snoqualmie Valley has long been a quiet backwater of dairy farms, orchards and produce gardens. Although suburbs are starting to take over the valley, there's still plenty of rural, small-town ambience to make for a very pleasant drive or bike ride. The views of forests, pastures, rivers and old farm houses surrounded by incongruously high snow-topped mountains are reason enough to visit.

The Best...

➡**Sight** Snoqualmie Falls (p176)
➡**Place to Eat** Herbfarm (p176)
➡**Place to Drink** Wineries in Woodinville (p176)

Top Tip

Between November and April keep an eye out for herds of elk.

Getting There & Away

Car Follow I-90 east from Seattle. Exit at North Bend (31 miles) and get onto Hwy 202, which follows the Snoqualmie River north.

Need to Know

➡**Area Code** 📞425
➡**Location** 31 miles (30 to 40 minutes) east of Seattle

◎ SIGHTS

NORTH BEND   TOWN
North Bend, on Hwy 202 just off I-90, is *Twin Peaks* country, the setting for David Lynch's surreal TV series from the early 1990s.

SNOQUALMIE   TOWN
Continue along Hwy 202 to the little town of Snoqualmie, where you'll find antique shops and a store devoted to Northwest wines. Just north of town, **Salish Lodge & Spa** (☑425-888-2556, 800-826-6124; www.salishlodge.com; 6501 Railroad Ave; d from $229) is a beautiful resort that sits atop 268ft Snoqualmie Falls. *Twin Peaks* fans know the hotel as the Great Northern; the exterior of the lodge appeared in the opening credits, and an observation point near the parking lot offers the same view. Visitors can also see the falls from the lodge's dining room or hike to them along a winding trail.

CARNATION   TOWN
Hwy 203 branches off from Hwy 202 at Fall City; follow it north to Carnation, where the Snoqualmie and Tolt Rivers meet at John McDonald Park. This is a great place for a riverside picnic, swim or hike. Carnation was once the center of the valley's dairy industry, and several farms here sell fruit and vegetables at roadside stands.

DUVALL   TOWN
Duvall, about 25 miles north of North Bend along Hwys 202 and 203, has a rural small-town atmosphere despite its recent growth spurt. Wander Main St and check out the shops and nurseries.

WOODINVILLE   TOWN
Head west on Woodinville–Duvall Rd for about 10 miles to reach Woodinville, home of several good wineries. There's a trail along the Sammamish River, if you fancy walking it off. From here it's a quick drive along I-405 back to Seattle.

✕ EATING

TWEDE'S   AMERICAN $
(137 W North Bend Way; burgers from $11; ⊙6:30am-8pm Mon-Thu, to 9pm Fri & Sat, to 7pm Sun) The former Mar T's Café, now called Twede's, was the diner with the famous cherry pie and cups of joe in *Twin Peaks*; a fire gutted it in 2000, but it has been rebuilt and is still a good place for lunch or a slice á la mode.

HERBFARM   ORGANIC $$$
(☑425-485-5300; www.theherbfarm.com; 14590 NE 145th St; dinner $179-195; ⊙from 7pm Thu-Sat, from 4:30pm Sun) The legendary Herbfarm is where nine-course dinners are drawn from the gardens and farm itself, as well as small local growers, and matched with locally produced wines.

Mt Rainier

Explore
The USA's fourth-highest peak (outside Alaska), majestic Mt Rainier is also one of its most beguiling. Encased in a 368-sq-mile national park (the world's fifth national park when it was inaugurated in 1899), the mountain's snowcapped summit and forest-covered foothills harbor numerous hiking trails, huge swaths of flower-carpeted meadows and an alluring conical peak that presents a formidable challenge for aspiring climbers.

For information on the park, check out the National Park Service (NPS) website at www.nps.gov/mora, which includes downloadable maps and descriptions of 50 park trails. The most famous is the hardcore 93-mile-long Wonderland Trail that completely circumnavigates Mt Rainier and takes 10 to 12 days to tackle.

The Best...
➡ **Sight** Paradise (p177)
➡ **Place to Eat** Copper Creek Inn (p177)
➡ **View of Rainier** Sunrise

Top Tip
Ask for trail suggestions and maps at the information centers. Depending on the season trails will have different conditions (wildflowers, snow, etc); the rangers will know what's best.

Getting There & Away
Car The park has four entrances: Nisqually, on Hwy 706 via Ashford, near the park's southwest corner; Ohanapecosh, via Hwy

123; White River, off Hwy 410; and Carbon River, the most remote entrance, at the northwest corner. Only the Nisqually entrance is open in winter, when it's used by cross-country skiers.

Tours Evergreen Escapes (www.evergreen escapes.com; 10hr tour $195) runs deluxe and eco-minded guided bus tours from Seattle.

Need to Know

⇒**Park entry** car/pedestrian $15/5

⇒**Location** 95 miles (three hours) southeast of Seattle

⇒**Tourist Office Jackson Visitor Center** (☑360-569-2211, ext 2328; Paradise; ⊘10am-7pm daily Jun-Oct, 10am-5pm Sat & Sun Oct-Dec); Longmire Hiker Information Center (p177) Trail information and backcountry permits.

SIGHTS

◉ Nisqually Entrance

Nisqually, on Hwy 706 via Ashford, near the park's southwest corner, is the busiest and most convenient gate and it's open year-round. Climbs to the top of Rainier leave from the inn; excellent four-day guided ascents are led by **Rainier Mountaineering Inc** (www.rmiguides.com; 30027 SR706 E , Ashford) for $991.

★**PARADISE**　　　　　VISITOR CENTER

FREE 'Oh, what a paradise!' exclaimed the daughter of park pioneer James Longmire on visiting this spot for the first time in the 1880s. Suddenly, the high mountain nirvana had a name, and a very apt one at that. One of the snowiest places on earth, 5400ft-high Paradise remains the park's most popular draw, with its famous flower meadows backed by dramatic Rainier views on the days (a clear minority annually) when the mountain decides to take its cloudy hat off. Aside from hiding numerous trailheads and being the starting point for most summit hikes, Paradise guards the iconic Paradise Inn (built in 1916 and refurbished in 2008) and the massive, informative Henry M Jackson Visitor Center (p177). The center holds a cutting-edge museum with hands-on exhibits on everything from flora to glacier formation and shows a must-see 21-minute film entitled *Mount*

Rainier: Restless Giant. Park naturalists lead free interpretive hikes from the visitor center daily in summer, and snowshoe walks on winter weekends.

LONGMIRE HIKER INFORMATION CENTER　　　VISITOR CENTER

(☑360-569-2211, ext 3317; ⊘summer) **FREE** Worth a stop to stretch your legs or gain an early glimpse of Rainier's mossy old-growth forest, Longmire was the brainchild of a certain James Longmire, who first came here in 1883. Since 1917 the National Park Inn has stood on this site – built in classic 'parkitecture' style – and is complemented by a small store, some park offices, the tiny, free **Longmire Museum** (☑360-569-2211, ext 3314; ⊘9am-6pm Jun-Sep, to 5pm Oct-May) and a number of important trailheads.

 EATING & SLEEPING

✕ Nisqually Entrance

★**COPPER CREEK INN**　　　AMERICAN $$

(www.coppercreekinn.com; 35707 SR 706 E, Ashford; breakfast from $7, burgers $10, dinner mains $12-27; ⊘7am-9pm) This is one of the state's great rural restaurants, and breakfast is an absolute must if you're heading off for a lengthy hike inside the park. Copper Creek has been knocking out pancakes, wild-blackberry pie and its own home-roasted coffee since 1946.

NATIONAL PARK INN　　　HOMESTYLE $$

(mains $16-19; ⊘lunch & dinner) Hearty hiking fare is served at this homely inn-restaurant and – in the absence of any real competition – it's surprisingly good.

PARADISE INN　　　HOMESTYLE $$

(brunch $24, dinner mains $16-23; ⊘breakfast, lunch & dinner Jun-Sep) The huge stone fireplace is the highlight of this dining room and it easily overshadows the food. Buffalo meatloaf and crab mac 'n' cheese are the most enticing options.

WHITTAKER'S MOTEL & BUNKHOUSE　　　HOSTEL $

(☑360-569-2439; www.whittakersbunkhouse.com; 30205 SR 706 E; dm/d $35/90; ☎) Whittaker's is the home base of legendary Northwestern climber Lou Whittaker, who first

CAMPING IN MT RAINIER NATIONAL PARK

There are two campgrounds near Longmire at the southwest corner of the park; for information on all of the area's campgrounds, call ☑360-569-2211 (ext 2304). **Reservations** (☑800-365-2267; www.mount.rainier. national-park.com/camping.htm; reserved campsites $12-15) are strongly advised during summer months and can be made up to two months in advance by phone or online. **Ohanapecosh Campground** (☑360-494-2229; Hwy 123; campsites May-Jun & Sep-Oct $12, late Jun–Labor Day $15) is near the Ohanapecosh Visitors Center and has 188 wooded sites.

summited the mountain at the age of 19 and has guided countless adventurers to the top in the years since. Down-to-earth and comfortable, this place has a good old-fashioned youth-hostel feel with cheap sleeps available in six-bed dorms.

★**PARADISE INN**　　　HISTORIC HOTEL **$$**
(☑360-569-2275; www.mtrainierguestservices. com; r with shared/private bath from $69/114; ☻May-Oct) The historic Paradise was constructed in 1916. Designed to blend in with the environment and built almost entirely of local materials, including exposed cedar

logs in the Great Room, the hotel was an early blueprint for National Park Rustic architecture countrywide.

✗ Other Entrances

The other entrances are **Ohanapecosh**, via Hwy 123 and accessed via the town of Packwood, where lodging is available; **White River**, off Hwy 410 that literally takes the high road (6400ft) to the beautiful viewpoint at the **Sunrise Lodge & Cafeteria** (☑360-569-2425; snacks $5-7; ☻10am-7pm Jun 30-Sep 16); and remote **Carbon River** in the northwest corner, which gives access to the park's inland rainforest.

BUTTER BUTTE　　　CAFE, BAKERY **$**
(105 E Main St, Packwood; ☻7am-5pm) While cops eat doughnuts, park rangers seem to prefer muffins. Stop into this cozy morning spot for the best coffee in town (they roast their own beans), baked goods and perhaps an informative chat with a friendly, khaki-clad officer.

HOTEL PACKWOOD　　　HOTEL **$**
(☑360-494-5431; 104 Main St, Packwood; tw/d with shared bath $38/42, d $54; ☎) A frontier-style hotel with a wraparound verandah, the Packwood ain't fancy, but it's authentic – and at this price, who can argue? There are nine varied rooms in the renovated 1912 establishment, two of which can accommodate four people.

Sleeping

In common with many cities, Seattle's sleeping options are plentiful and varied. Want to drive up to a motor inn and park your car where you can see it through the window? You can do that. Rather slink up in a limo and look down your nose at the overworked bellhop? You can do that too, as well as everything in between.

Room Rates & Fees

Unless otherwise indicated, the prices listed in this book are for a double room, not including tax or extra fees such as parking, breakfast or internet access. Note that the prices quoted are what you can expect to pay in peak season – generally May through August. However, it is important to be aware that prices can vary wildly depending on day of the week and whether there are festivals or events going on in town. Seattle hotel rooms are also subject to a room tax of 15.6% (less for most B&Bs and historical properties) that will be tacked on to the final bill. The rates listed here don't include tax.

Essentially all downtown hotels charge extra for parking, if they have it. It's been said that half the population of Portland, OR, consists of people who couldn't find a place to park in Seattle and, searching in ever-widening circles, eventually wound up in Portland, where they stayed. Many hotels downtown don't offer parking but can direct you to paid lots nearby. Our reviews note whether parking is available; usual rates start at around $20 a night. If there's no icon in the review, you're on your own. Look for street meters and paid parking garages downtown, or off-street parking elsewhere.

FINDING DEALS

Many downtown hotels participate in Seattle Super Saver Packages, a program run by the Convention & Visitors Bureau. Room prices are generally 50% off the rack rates from November through March, with substantial discounts all year, and they come with a coupon book that offers savings on dining, shopping and attractions. For more details, see the website: www.visitseattle.org. Alternatively, the Seattle B&B Association has a searchable list of affiliated B&Bs.

FREE EXTRAS

Everyone likes a freebie. It's par for the course to offer free high-speed wireless internet service in Seattle hotels these days. Most establishments also have a computer terminal available in the lobby for guests to use free of charge. Free city bikes are increasingly available in environmentally conscious hotels. Pineapple Hospitality's four establishments (Five, Maxwell, University Inn and Watertown) all loan out sturdy two-wheeled machines for short journeys. The same quartet also puts out plates of cupcakes and urns of coffee in its lobbies around 5pm daily.

Gyms are available in larger hotels such as the swish Fairmont Olympic Hotel, which has a health club staffed with personal trainers. More common are small cardio rooms and diminutive indoor pools. Last, and most important, you'll find few hotels in Seattle that won't lend you that most useful of Pacific Northwest props – an umbrella.

NEED TO KNOW

Price Ranges

Prices indicated are for a standard double room in high season.

$	less than $100
$$	$101–200
$$$	over $200

Check-In & Check-Out

Check-out times vary but are usually 11am or noon, and check-in usually starts between 2pm and 4pm. Most places are flexible if notified ahead of time; definitely call ahead if you're going to arrive late.

Reservations

Booking ahead is wise at any time of year but essential during summer (June to August) and around the more popular festival times, especially Bumbershoot (Labor Day weekend).

Tipping

It's standard practice to tip your housekeeper by leaving a dollar or two in your room every morning.

Breakfast

Breakfast is not included in the quoted prices, unless specified.

Lonely Planet's Top Choices

Moore Hotel (p184) Location, location, location – and a bit of history too.

Hotel Five (p184) Free city bikes, teatime cupcakes, and interesting retro-design aesthetics.

Edgewater (p182) A piece of rock'n'roll history jutting out over Puget Sound.

Ace Hotel (p184) Seattle's inventors of industrial chic have since exported their brand to New York and London.

Best by Budget

$

Moore Hotel (p184) Cheap, historic and perfectly comfortable option on the cusp of downtown.

Hotel Hotel Hostel (p188) Fremont sprouts its first decent accommodation – a kind of hipster hostel.

City Hostel Seattle (p184) Hostel with private options and good wall art in Belltown.

Green Tortoise Hostel (p182) Seattle's favorite backpacker haunt.

$$

Hotel Five (p184) Bright, funky, hip and in the middle of Belltown.

University Inn (p187) Close to the university, but a long way from austere student digs.

11th Avenue Inn (p187) Cozy ambience and strapping breakfast on Capitol Hill.

Hotel Deca (p187) Art-deco digs in the U District.

$$$

Hotel Monaco (p183) Lavish downtown hotel with refreshingly down-to-earth service.

Edgewater (p182) Led Zeppelin are still banned, but everyone else is welcome.

Alexis Hotel (p182) Comfort plus loads of extras including the beautiful Bookstore Bar.

Arctic Club (p183) Commodious throwback to the age of the gold rush.

Best Pet-Friendly Hotels

Sorrento Hotel (p187) Offers doggie daycare and pet-grooming services.

Alexis Hotel (p182) Visiting dogs are given a bowl of distilled water on arrival, and accommodated in designer doggie beds.

Hotel Monaco (p183) Pets are welcomed at no extra charge and with no size restrictions.

Hotel Vintage Park (p183) Offers pet-sitting services and personalized doggie itineraries.

Best B&Bs

Chambered Nautilus B&B (p188) U District haven of tranquility and good taste.

11th Avenue Inn (p187) Two blocks from Broadway, Capitol Hill's strip of hip.

9 Cranes Inn (p188) New place on Phinney Ridge north of Fremont with a burgeoning reputation.

Gaslight Inn B&B (p186) Something of a Capitol Hill institution.

Where to Stay

Neighborhood	For	Against
Downtown, Pike Place & Waterfront	Highest concentration of hotels of all types; best neighborhood for absolute luxury; fantastic central location	Many places are expensive; driving can be a nightmare and parking usually costs extra
Pioneer Square & International District	Close to sports grounds, downtown and the waterfront	A noisy, rambunctious neighborhood at night that's a bit edgy for some; there's a dearth of non-chain economical hotels
Belltown & Seattle Center	Plenty of economical hotel options within close walking distance of all Seattle's main sights	Noisy at night with a boozy bar scene and some panhandling
Queen Anne & Lake Union	Some great midrange options in Lower Queen Anne a stone's throw from Seattle Center	Lacking accommodation options in Queen Anne proper; Lake Union has a lot of noisy building works and will do for some time yet
Capitol Hill & First Hill	Excellent selection of high-quality, well-run B&Bs; adjacent to Seattle's most exciting nightlife	Lack of any real hotels in Capitol Hill; a little removed from downtown
The CD, Madrona & Madison Park		Despite their proximity to downtown, these largely residential districts are bereft of decent accommodation options
U District	Three fantastic affordable boutique hotels adjacent to the pulsating life of 'the Ave'	A little isolated from the downtown core and other major sights
Fremont & Green Lake	Fun neighborhood to hang out in with plenty of eating options and good bus and walking-trail access	Accommodation options are limited to one budget hotel-hostel and the odd B&B
Ballard & Discovery Park	Lovely spanking-new boutique hotel; exciting but laid-back nightlife and great restaurants	Dearth of choices; isolated from downtown and other neighborhoods
Georgetown & West Seattle	Cheap, motel-style places close to a hip strip	Few options and it's close to nowhere – except Georgetown

🛏 Downtown, Pike Place & Waterfront

GREEN TORTOISE HOSTEL   HOSTEL $

Map p224 (✆206-340-1222; www.greentortoise. net; 105 Pike St; 8-/6-/4-bed dm $32/34/36; @; 🚇Westlake) Seattle's backpacker central – and what a location right across the street from Pike Place Market! Once pretty crusty, the Tortoise moved to the Elliot Hotel Building a few years back and now offers 30 bunk rooms and 16 European-style rooms (shared bath and shower). Free breakfast includes waffles and eggs.

The hostel offers a free dinner three nights a week and there are weekly events such as open-mic nights.

EXECUTIVE HOTEL PACIFIC   HOTEL $$

Map p224 (✆206-623-3900; www.pacificplaza hotel.com; 400 Spring St; r $110-180; P ❄ @ 🛜 🐾; 🚇University St) This reliable but not flashy hotel, located next door to the Seattle public library, has recently been upgraded (with a new cardio room added) and the location makes it a good deal. Rooms are fairly small but functional, with free wi-fi, voice mail and data ports, in-room coffee and tea, and windows that open.

MAYFLOWER PARK HOTEL   HOTEL $$

Map p224 (✆206-623-8700; www.mayflower park.com; 405 Olive Way; r from $199; P ❄ @ 🛜; 🚇Westlake) If you're coming to Seattle to shop, this is the hotel for you. Attached by indoor walkway to the Westlake Center, it's also handy for taking the monorail out to Seattle Center for an event. The lobby bar is a nice hideaway for a drink. High-speed internet access is free throughout the hotel.

PENSIONE NICHOLS   B&B $$

Map p224 (✆206-441-7125; www.pensione nichols.com; 1923 1st Ave; r from $130; @ 🐾; 🚇Westlake) In a town with few cheap hotels and hardly any B&Bs right downtown, Pensione Nichols is a treat. Right in the urban thick of things between Pike Place Market and Belltown, this charmingly remodeled European-style pensione has 10 rooms that share four retro-cool bathrooms, two large suites and a spacious common area that overlooks the market.

Rooms come with a complete and tasty breakfast. There are parking options in a nearby garage.

★EDGEWATER   HOTEL $$$

Map p230 (✆206-728-7000; www.edgewater hotel.com; Pier 67, 2411 Alaskan Way; r 420-750; P ❄ @ 🛜; 🖵13) Fame and notoriety has stalked the Edgewater. Perched over the water on a pier, it was once the hotel of choice for every rock band that mattered, including the Beatles, the Rolling Stones and, most infamously, Led Zeppelin, who took the 'you can fish from the hotel window' advertising jingle a little too seriously and filled their suite with sharks.

These days, the fishing – and Led Zeppelin – is prohibited, but the rooms are still deluxe with a capital D.

★ALEXIS HOTEL   HOTEL $$$

Map p224 (✆206-624-4844; www.alexishotel. com; 1007 1st Ave; r/ste from $280/310; P ❄ @ 🛜 🐾; 🚇University St) Run by the Kimpton Hotel group, the Alexis is a boutique hotel that is positively lavish, with huge rooms, thick carpets, gleaming bathrooms and some luxury extras – a steam room and fitness center, for instance. The hotel's pet-friendly moniker is taken seriously; visiting dogs get bowls of distilled water on arrival.

Thick double-glazed windows keep out the cacophony of downtown just outside the front door.

INN AT THE MARKET   BOUTIQUE HOTEL $$$

Map p224 (✆206-443-3600; www.innatthe market.com; 86 Pine St; r with/without water view $370/255; P ❄ 🛜; 🚇Westlake) The only hotel lodging in venerable Pike Place Market, this elegant 70-room boutique hotel has large rooms, many of which enjoy views onto market activity and Puget Sound. Parking costs $20.

FAIRMONT OLYMPIC HOTEL   HOTEL $$$

Map p224 (✆206-621-1700; www.fairmont.com/ seattle; 411 University St; r from $309; P ❄ @ 🛜 🚼; 🚇University St) Built in 1924, the Fairmont Olympic is listed with the National Register of Historic Places, so it's not too surprising that it feels like a museum of old money. Over the years, remodels to the bathrooms and the main lobby have kept the place functional without destroying the period glamour of its architecture.

With 450 rooms and every imaginable service, this place is certainly a splurge, but it's worth exploring even if you don't stay here – have an oyster at Shuckers, the oak-paneled hotel bar. The palpable decadence of the place has been balanced out lately by earth-friendly policies such as free parking for hybrid cars.

SEATTLE RENAISSANCE HOTEL   HOTEL $$$

Map p224 (☏206-583-0300; www.marriott.com; 515 Madison St; r from $289; P ✸ @ � ≋; ⟐60) With a calming green-and-brown color scheme, this gigantic, 553-room tower (part of the Marriott chain) is one of the city's nicest hotels. Rooms are large, all have views and windows that open, and pets are welcome (nominal fee). Other features include an indoor pool, two restaurants, a bar-lounge, a beauty shop and a spa.

HOTEL MONACO   BOUTIQUE HOTEL $$$

Map p224 (☏206-621-1770; www.monaco-seattle.com; 1101 4th Ave; d/ste $339/399; P @ � ≋; ⟐University St) ✎ Whimsical, with dashes of European elegance, the downtown Monaco is worthy of all four of its illustrious stars. Bed down amid the stripy wallpaper and heavy drapes.

HOTEL VINTAGE PARK   HOTEL $$$

Map p224 (☏206-624-8000; www.hotelvintagepark.com; 1100 5th Ave; r from $310; P ✸ @ � ≋; ⟐University St) The rooms at this wood-paneled, gay-friendly hotel are a little smaller than at some other downtown hotels and they get a bit of street noise, but it's a pleasant place to stay, especially if you get a west-facing room. The theme is wine: rooms are named after Washington vineyards and wineries, and there's wine tasting in the lobby every afternoon.

WESTIN HOTEL SEATTLE   HOTEL $$$

Map p230 (☏206-728-1000; www.westinseattle.com; 1900 5th Ave; r from $329; P ✸ @ � ≋; ⟐Westlake) This impossible-to-miss, two-cylinder luxury business hotel has almost 900 rooms, some of which contain Jacuzzis, CD players or a range of workout equipment. There's a heated pool, an exercise room, a gift shop, internet access (free in the lobby, for a fee in guest rooms) and a business center – not to mention great views and a popular restaurant.

HOTEL MAX   BOUTIQUE HOTEL $$$

Map p230 (☏206-441-4200; www.hotelmaxseattle.com; 620 Stewart St; r from $229; P @ �; ⟐Westlake) Original artworks hang in the small but cool guest rooms, and it's tough to get any hipper than the Max's super-saturated color scheme – not to mention

package deals such as the Grunge Special or the Gaycation. Rooms feature menus for your choice of pillows and spirituality services.

PARAMOUNT HOTEL   HOTEL $$$

Map p224 (☏206-292-9500; www.paramounthotelseattle.com; 724 Pine St; r from $269; P ✸ @; ⟐Westlake) The Paramount has 146 large rooms that, like the lobby areas, are furnished with heavy antiques perhaps meant to give the relatively new hotel an old-world feel. The downstairs restaurant-bar, Dragonfish, has a 'sushi happy hour' and is a convenient place to meet for a drink before hitting the town.

HOTEL 1000   HOTEL $$$

Map p224 (☏206-957-1000; www.hotel1000seattle.com; 1000 1st Ave; r from $429; P ✸ @ �; ⟐University St) If you love the clean lines and simple elegance of IKEA, but you happen to have just won the lottery, you might design a hotel like this. Leather-clad egg chairs cuddle around a concrete-and-steel tube fireplace in the lounge; rooms have bedside tables made of chrome and wood; bathrooms have granite counters and free-standing tubs that fill from the ceiling; beds are curtained off in luxurious earth-toned textiles.

Each room has art reflecting guests' taste (you tell them what kind of art you like when you book or check in and they adjust the art in the room) and a 40in HDTV with surround sound. Some have a private bar, and some are pet-friendly. There is also virtual golf.

ARCTIC CLUB   HOTEL $$$

Map p224 (☏206-340-0340; www.thearcticclubseattle.com; 700 3rd Ave; r from $359; P �; ⟐Pioneer Sq) This plush hotel is housed in a famous downtown building renowned for its carved walrus heads, aka the Arctic Club, a now defunct association for Klondike vets who struck it rich in the 1897 gold rush. Recently taken over by Doubletree hotels, it has been upgraded to lure in equally rich contemporary clients with a wood-paneled gentleman's-club feel not far removed from its original incarnation.

You can relax in rooms adorned with photos of dapper young arctic explorers, or take advantage of the on-site gym and business center. The ground-floor Juno restaurant serves solid Northwest food.

🛌 Pioneer Square & International District

BEST WESTERN PIONEER SQUARE HOTEL
HOTEL **$$**

Map p228 (☎206-340-1234; www.pioneer square.com; 77 Yesler Way; r from $159; P@🛜; 🚇Pioneer Sq) Rooms and common areas at this historical hotel feature period decor and a comfortable atmosphere. The only hotel in the historical heart of Seattle, it can't be beaten for location – as long as you don't mind some of the saltier characters who populate the square in the off hours. Nightlife, restaurants and shopping are just steps from the door.

SILVER CLOUD HOTEL
HOTEL **$$$**

Map p228 (☎206-204-9800; www.silvercloud. com; 1046 1st Ave S; r from $249; P❄@🛜🏊; 🚇Stadium) Sports fans are in luck – this relatively new hotel is smack in the middle of the action, across the street from Safeco Field and next to Qwest Field. Rooms are spacious and modern, with refrigerator and microwave, an iPod dock on the alarm clock, and Aveda bath products.

A free shuttle service takes guests practically anywhere within 2 miles. And in warm weather you can splash around in the rooftop pool.

🛌 Belltown & Seattle Center

Aside from the hotels listed here, Belltown and the Denny Triangle sport some fairly anonymous, motor court–type lodgings from the 1960s, and many of them cater to business travelers – so they're efficient and have all the amenities you might need, if not a lot of character.

★MOORE HOTEL
HOTEL **$**

Map p230 (☎206-448-4851; www.moorehotel. com; 1926 2nd Ave; s/d with shared bath $68/80, with private bath $85/97; 🛜; 🚇Westlake) Old-world and allegedly haunted, the Moore nonetheless has a friendly front desk and a prime location. If that doesn't swing you, the price should. There's a cute little cafe on the premises and the dive-y Nitelite Lounge next door. You can practically hold your breath and walk to Pike Place Market from here.

CITY HOSTEL SEATTLE
HOSTEL **$**

Map p230 (☎206-706-3255; www.hostelseattle. com; 2327 2nd Ave; 6-/4-bed dm $28/32, d $73; @🛜; 🚇RapidRide D-Line) 🍃 Sleep in an art gallery for peanuts – in Belltown, no less. That's the reality in this new 'art hostel,' which will make your parents' hostelling days seem positively spartan by comparison. Aside from arty dorms, expect a common room, hot tub, in-house movie theater (with free DVDs) and all-you-can-eat breakfast.

★HOTEL FIVE
BOUTIQUE HOTEL **$$**

Map p230 (☎206-441-9785; www.hotelfive seattle.com; 2200 5th Ave; r from $165; P❄🛜; 🚇13) This wonderful reincarnation of the old Ramada Inn on 5th Ave in Belltown mixes retro-'70s furniture with sharp color accents to produce something that is dazzlingly modern. And it's functional too. The ultra-comfortable beds could be nominated as a valid cure for insomnia, while the large reception area invites lingering, especially when they lay out the complimentary cupcakes and coffee in the late afternoon.

There's an on-site gym and decent restaurant.

BELLTOWN INN
HOTEL **$$**

Map p230 (☎206-529-3700; www.belltown-inn. com; 2301 3rd Ave; s/d $159/164; P❄@🛜; 🚇RapidRide D-Line) Can it be true? The Belltown is such a bargain and in such a prime location that it's hard to believe it hasn't accidentally floated over from a smaller, infinitely cheaper city. But no: clean, functional rooms, handy kitchenettes, roof terrace, free bikes and – vitally important – borrow-and-return umbrellas are all yours for the price of a posh dinner.

LOYAL INN BEST WESTERN
HOTEL **$$**

Map p230 (☎206-682-0200; www.bestwestern. com/prop_48062; 2301 8th Ave; r from $149; P❄🛜; 🚇Westlake & Denny) More plush than other similarly priced options in the area, this chain hotel is in a convenient location for both Seattle Center and Belltown, and has a Jacuzzi and sauna, a small exercise room and free continental breakfast. Beds are enormous and rooms are relatively spacious; some include mini-refrigerators and microwaves. Self-parking is a reasonable $10 a night.

ACE HOTEL
HOTEL **$$**

Map p230 (☎206-448-4721; www.acehotel.com; 2423 1st Ave; r with shared/private bath $109/199;

P 🛜; 🖵13) Emulating (almost) its hip Portland cousin, the Ace sports minimal, futuristic decor (everything's white or stainless steel, even the TV), antique French army blankets, condoms instead of pillow mints and a copy of the *Kama Sutra* instead of the Bible. Parking costs $15.

BEST WESTERN EXECUTIVE INN   HOTEL $$

Map p230 (📞206-448-9444; www.bestwestern. com; 200 Taylor Ave N; r from $144; P ✳ @ 🛜; Ⓜ Seattle Center) In the shadow of the Space Needle, the Executive Inn has a terrifying, almost brutalist facade but is perfectly decent inside. Pillow-top beds, in-room coffee and tea, microwaves and refrigerators, room service, a fitness room and a sports lounge are available, and it's a pickup point for the Quick Shuttle to Vancouver.

INN AT EL GAUCHO   HOTEL $$$

Map p230 (📞206-728-1133; www.elgaucho.com; 2505 1st Ave; ste from $269; P ✳ @ 🛜; 🖵13) In 18 suites decorated '50s-style, above the type of anachronistic steakhouse that harks back to the good ol' days when vegetarians were eaten by the wealthy as snacks between meals, the Inn at El Gaucho offers a particularly outsized, swaggering American luxury. Plasma-screen TVs, Bose stereo systems, 'Rain System' showers and buttery leather couches grace all the suites.

And if it's too much to leave for even a moment, El Gaucho restaurant will serve you steak in bed.

HOTEL ANDRA   BOUTIQUE HOTEL $$$

Map p230 (📞206-448-8600; www.hotelandra. com; 2000 4th Ave; r from $289; P ✳ 🛜; 🖵 Westlake) It's in Belltown (so it's trendy) and it's Scandinavian-influenced (so it has lashings of minimalist style), plus the Andra's fine location is complemented by leopard-skin fabrics, color accents, well-stocked bookcases, fluffy bathrobes, Egyptian-cotton bed linen and a complimentary shoe-shine. The Lola restaurant next door does room service. Say no more.

WARWICK HOTEL   HOTEL $$$

Map p230 (📞206-443-4300; www.warwickwa. com; 401 Lenora St; r from $289; @ 🛜 🛋; 🖵 Westlake) One of five Warwicks in the US (the most famous is in New York), Seattle's offering looks rather stuffy, but actually it isn't. Rooms, with HBO connection and Lavazza coffee-makers, are airier and more open than the disorientating lobby suggests and

there's a Gallic-accented restaurant on site. In the basement lie a small but useful pool and gym.

🛏 Queen Anne & Lake Union

The Queen Anne hotels are all in Lower Queen Anne, aka 'Uptown,' immediately to the west of Seattle Center, handy for the opera house or Key Arena and a 10-minute walk to the Space Needle.

The shores of Lake Union hold several convenient, business-oriented hotels with easy driving access to the rest of the city and some killer views across the water.

MEDITERRANEAN INN   HOTEL $$

Map p234 (📞206-428-4700; www.mediterranean -inn.com; 425 Queen Anne Ave N; r from $159; P ✳ @; 🖵 RapidRide D-Line) There's something about the surprisingly un-Mediterranean Med Inn that just clicks. Maybe it's the handy cusp-of-Belltown location, or the genuinely friendly staff, or the kitchenettes in every room, or the small downstairs gym, or the surgical cleanliness in every room. Don't try to define it – just go there and soak it up.

SILVER CLOUD INN LAKE UNION   HOTEL $$

Map p234 (📞206-447-9500; www.silvercloud. com; 1150 Fairview Ave N; r/ste from $188/243; P ✳ @ 🛜 🛋; 🖵 Fairview & Campus Dr) This hotel has 184 rooms, some of which have stunning views of Lake Union. There are also a gym, indoor and outdoor pools, laundry facilities and complimentary breakfast, plus a free shuttle service to downtown and free parking – both very handy in this area. On Tuesday evening the hotel hosts a regional beer and wine tasting.

MARQUEEN HOTEL   HOTEL $$

Map p234 (📞206-282-7407; www.marqueen.com; 600 Queen Anne Ave N; r from $175; P ✳ @ 🛜; 🖵 RapidRide D-Line) A classic old-school apartment building (built in 1918), the MarQueen has hardwood floors throughout and a variety of rooms, all with kitchenettes left over from their days as apartments. The neighborhood is an under-visited gem, handy to various attractions. If hill walking isn't your thing, there is a courtesy van to take you to nearby sights.

Children 17 and under stay free with a parent. Note that there are no elevators in this three-story building.

HAMPTON INN
HOTEL $$

Map p234 (206-282-7700; www.hampton innseattle.com; 700 5th Ave N; r from $159; P ✳ @ ⚡; ⌨3) A couple of blocks north of Seattle Center, the Hampton Inn has 198 rooms, most of which have balconies. There's a wide variety of rooms, from standards to two-bedroom suites with fireplaces. A cooked breakfast is included.

INN AT QUEEN ANNE
HOTEL $$

Map p234 (206-282-7357; www.innatqueen anne.com; 505 1st Ave N; r from $109; P ✳ @ ⚡; ⌨RapidRide D-Line) The Inn at Queen Anne is a 1929 apartment building turned hotel in a cool neighborhood. Its 68 rooms come with kitchenettes, complimentary internet access and a free continental breakfast. Weekly and monthly rates are available. Note that there are no elevators in this three-story building.

★ MAXWELL HOTEL
BOUTIQUE HOTEL $$

Map p234 (206-286-0629; www.themaxwell hotel.com; 300 Roy St; r from $179; P ✳ @ ⚡ ⚡; ⌨RapidRide D-Line) Another gorgeous boutique hotel that has recently graced Lower Queen Anne, the Maxwell's huge designer-chic lobby is enough to make anyone dust off their credit card – and it's not too pricey either (if you look out for periodic offers online).

Rooms look like they've just won an HGTV design competition, plus there's a small pool, a gym and free bikes if you're a Seattle outdoor type. The location, one block from the Seattle Center, is ideal for all kinds of entertainment.

COURTYARD MARRIOTT
HOTEL $$$

Map p234 (206-213-0100; www.marriott.com; 925 Westlake Ave N; r from $249; P ✳ @ ⚡ ⚡; ⌨Lake Union Park) Over on the southwest side of Lake Union, the Courtyard Marriott has all the big-hotel amenities you'd expect, including an indoor pool and a restaurant. It's set up to suit the business traveler, but it's comfy enough to justify not getting any work done. There's a small convenience store on site for impromptu snacks.

MARRIOTT RESIDENCE INN
HOTEL $$$

Map p234 (206-624-6000; www.marriott.com; 800 Fairview Ave N; ste from $229; P ✳ @ ⚡ ⚡; ⌨Lake Union Park) A convenient place to settle in for a lengthier stay, the Residence Inn has work-friendly studio suites and family-size two-room suites, all with kitchens.

There's a lap pool, an exercise room and spa, and free breakfast and evening desserts in the lobby. Rooms on the west side of the hotel have good views of Lake Union – rates vary depending on whether you get a view or not.

🛏 Capitol Hill & First Hill

Capitol Hill's B&Bs are all set in beautiful, well-maintained homes on quiet, tree-lined residential streets. These are friendly, welcoming places where you can start your day with a giant breakfast, hear a local's advice on what to see and usually park free of charge on the street. Note, however, that parking becomes much more difficult on weekend evenings as you approach Broadway and the Pike–Pine corridor.

HILL HOUSE B&B
B&B $$

Map p236 (206-720-7161; www.seattlehill house.com; 1113 E John St; r $75-199; P @ ⚡; ⌨Capitol Hill) Close to the hub of Capitol Hill, the guestrooms in this pair of 1903 homes feature queen beds, down comforters, fluffy robes and a range of moods from over-the-top lacy to English gentleman – the eclectic decorating style might not suit everyone's taste, but the place is certainly homey. Some rooms have private bathrooms, and two are large suites with garden and patio access.

BACON MANSION B&B
B&B $$

Map p236 (206-329-1864; www.baconman sion.com; 959 Broadway E; r $104-249; @ ⚡; ⌨49) A 1909 Tudor mansion whose imposing exterior belies the quirky charm of its friendly hosts, this four-level B&B on a quiet residential street just past the Capitol Hill action has a grand piano in the main room that guests are invited to play. The 11 rooms come in a variety of configurations, including a carriage house that's wheelchair-accessible, and include TV and voice mail.

One large suite has a view of the Space Needle, one has a fireplace, and another has an Italian fountain as a backdrop.

GASLIGHT INN B&B
B&B $$

Map p236 (206-325-3654; www.gaslight -inn.com; 1727 15th Ave; s $98-128, d $108-168; @ ⚡ ⚡; ⌨10) In two neighboring homes, the Gaslight Inn has 15 rooms, 12 of which have private bathrooms. In summer, it's refreshing to dive into the outdoor pool or just hang out on the sundeck. No pets: the B&B already has a cat and a dog.

INN AT VIRGINIA MASON HOTEL $$

Map p236 (✆206-583-6453; www.innatvirginia mason.com; 1006 Spring St, First Hill; r from $111; ℗🛜; 🚌64) On First Hill, just above the downtown area near a complex of hospitals, this nicely maintained older hotel caters to families needing to stay near the medical facilities. It also offers a number of basic rooms for other visitors and has a nice rooftop garden with a view from First Hill overlooking the rest of the city.

There are discounts if you are staying at the hotel for family medical reasons.

11TH AVENUE INN B&B $$

Map p236 (✆206-720-7161; www.11thAvenueInn. com; 121 11th Ave E; r $139-199; @🛜; 🚌Capitol Hill) Formerly a boarding house and a dance studio, this 1906 home has been a B&B since 2003. Its facade is not the grandest of Seattle's B&Bs, but you know what they say about judging a book by its cover.

The 11th Avenue Inn has eight rooms, each with eclectic Victorian furnishings, Oriental rugs, handsome headboards, and hand-pressed Egyptian cotton sheets. You won't go hungry here: breakfast is a full-course sit-down affair in the Victorian dining room, and you're invited to help yourself to snacks and drinks throughout the day. There's also a living room with stereo and computer for guest use, or wireless internet if you've brought your own. To complete the historical feeling of the house, there is dark woodwork throughout, surrounding the staircase, doors and windows.

SORRENTO HOTEL HOTEL $$$

Map p236 (✆206-622-6400; www.hotelsorrento. com; 900 Madison St; d from $269; ℗❄@🛜🛝; 🚌64) William Howard Taft, 27th US president, was the first registered guest at the Sorrento, an imposing Italianate hotel known since its birth in 1909 as the jewel of Seattle. The combination of luxurious appointments, over-the-top service and a pervasive sense of class add up to a perfect blend of decadence and restraint.

The hotel's restaurant, the Hunt Club, is worth a stop whether you're staying here or not. Continental breakfast ($11) and a shuttle to the airport ($65) are among the extras on offer.

🛏 U District

Accommodations here are also more likely to include free parking, as real estate is less limited than it is downtown.

COLLEGE INN HOTEL $

Map p242 (✆206-633-4441; www.collegeinn seattle.com; 4000 University Way NE; s/d incl breakfast from $65/75; @🛜; 🚌70) This pretty, half-timbered building in the U District, left over from the 1909 Alaska-Yukon-Pacific Exposition, has 25 European-style guest rooms with sinks and shared baths. There's no elevator.

★UNIVERSITY INN HOTEL $$

Map p242 (✆206-632-5055; www.university innseattle.com; 4140 Roosevelt Way NE; r from $189; ℗❄@🛜🛝; 🚌66) What pushes this spotless, modern, well-located place over the edge into greatness is, believe it or not, the waffles served at the complimentary breakfast. They're amazing. The hotel is three blocks from campus, and its 102 rooms come in three levels of plushness.

All of them offer such basics as a coffee maker, hair dryer and wi-fi; some have balconies, sofas and CD players. There's a Jacuzzi, an outdoor pool, laundry facilities and a guest computer in the lobby. Attached to the hotel is the recommended Portage Bay Cafe, and there's also a free shuttle to various sightseeing areas.

WATERTOWN HOTEL $$

Map p242 (✆206-826-4242; www.watertown seattle.com; 4242 Roosevelt Way NE; r/ste from $179; ℗@🛜; 🚌66) Easy to miss because it looks like one of those crisp new modern apartment buildings, the Watertown has more of an arty-industrial feel than its sister hotel, the University Inn. Bare concrete and high ceilings in the lobby make it seem stark and museum-like, but that translates to spacious and warmly furnished rooms with giant beds, swivel TVs and huge windows.

Thematic 'Ala Carts' (eg a Relaxation Cart, a Seattle Cart or a Game Cart) are delivered free to your room. Guests can borrow bicycles or use the hotel's free shuttle to explore the area.

HOTEL DECA HOTEL $$

Map p242 (✆206-634-2000; www.hoteldeca.com; 4507 Brooklyn Ave NE; r from $160; ℗❄@🛜; 🚌66) The same architect who designed the

Old Faithful Lodge in Yellowstone National Park built this hotel in 1931. Formerly the Meany Tower Hotel, the Deca has since had a $2-million renovation. Its 16 stories offer rooms with either a Cascade view or a downtown view. Rooms also feature flat-screen TVs with DVD players and iPod docks.

There's a workout room, a bar and a restaurant, plus a Tully's coffee shop in the building.

CHAMBERED NAUTILUS B&B INN   B&B $$

Map p242 (✆206-522-2536; www.chambered nautilus.com; 5005 22nd Ave NE; d $109-194; ❋ @ ☎; ☐74) The 1915 Georgian-style Chambered Nautilus has six guest rooms that are decorated with authentic British antiques, as well as an annex with one- and two-bedroom suites. All B&B rooms here come with private bathrooms, down comforters, handmade soaps and a teddy bear. The communal living room has a welcoming fireplace, and the full gourmet breakfast is reason enough to stay.

Across the street they offer four kid-friendly, pet-friendly suites with kitchenettes ($124 to $214).

🛏 Fremont & Green Lake

HOTEL HOTEL HOSTEL   HOTEL, HOSTEL $

Map p244 (✆206-257-4543; www.hotelhotel.co/; 3515 Fremont Ave N; dm $26-30, d with shared/private bath $73/91; ☎; ☐26) Creating something new in a venerable old building replete with exposed brick and chunky radiators, Hotel Hotel is – guess what? – a hostel (with dorms) that also passes itself off as a economical hotel on account of its private rooms (with an assortment of shared and en-suite bathrooms). Sporting industrial-chic decor not unlike Belltown's more established Ace Hotel, it's comfortable without being fancy.

A buffet breakfast is included in the price, and there is a common room and a kitchen.

9 CRANES INN   B&B $$

Map p245 (✆206-855-5222; www.9cranesinn. com; 5717 Palatine Ave N; r $139-229; P ☎; ☐5) A new four-room B&B up on Phinney Ridge near the zoo with sweeping views (if you get the Ballard View room), the 9 Cranes has quickly established a good reputation since its 2012 opening. It inhabits a pleasant self-contained neighborhood near Green Lake that has long lacked good places to stay.

🛏 Ballard & Discovery Park

BALLARD INN   BOUTIQUE HOTEL $$

Map p246 (✆206-789-5011; www.ballardinn seattle.com; 5300 Ballard Ave NW; r $159; ☎; ☐17) Small, intimate hotel with a European feel (the Scandinavian influence?) that offers a far cheaper alternative to the Hotel Ballard next door. The building, dating from 1902, is right on Ballard's main drag. Most rooms share bathrooms.

HOTEL BALLARD   BOUTIQUE HOTEL $$$

Map p246 (✆206-789-5012; www.hotelballard seattle.com; 5216 Ballard Ave NW; d $239; ☎; ☐17) Ballard bags a brand-new designer hotel (opened May 2013), another indication that the neighborhood's on the up. Hotel Ballard has a lovely street profile, with its wrought-iron balconies blending in with the redbricked edifices of yore. Inside, it's even more opulent (upholstered headboards, funky chandeliers, superstreamlined bathrooms) but stays faithful to the neighborhood's Scandinavian heritage with Nordic murals.

Guests get free use of the equally fancy Olympic Athletic Club next door.

🛏 Georgetown & West Seattle

GEORGETOWN INN   HOTEL $

Map p239 (✆206-762-2233; www.georgetown innseattle.com; 6100 Corson Ave; r from $99; P ❋ ☎; ☐124) Your only option in Georgetown is this not unappealing motel-like place just south of the neighborhood's main drag. Bonuses are price, good room size and the buzzing bar and restaurant strip just around the corner.

Understand Seattle

SEATTLE TODAY................................190
Blink and you'll miss something. The evolution of Seattle in the 2010s continues at a blinding pace.

HISTORY 192
A short, action-packed story of yo-yoing fortunes on the way from rambunctious lumber town to high-tech city of the future.

THE WAY OF LIFE 196
A city of latte lunches, cutting-edge culture and outdoor fashion that has modestly produced numerous global brands.

MUSIC 200
Seattle's greatest hits could fill a best-selling album, with Ray Charles, Quincy Jones, Jimi Hendrix, Nirvana, Macklemore and more.

Seattle Today

Ever since the pioneering Denny party felled the trees for their first log cabin on Alki Beach in 1851, Seattle has rarely stood still. Yet, even by its own roller-coaster standards, the recent pace of change has been astronomical. Currently stirring up local debate is a massive public-transportation project, the burying of a 60-year-old freeway, landmark new laws on cannabis and same-sex marriage, and a whole dynamic new neighborhood being hatched on the southern shores of Lake Union.

Best on Film

Sleepless in Seattle (1993) Meg Ryan and Tom Hanks are irresistibly adorable in this riff on *An Affair to Remember*.
Singles (1992) Attractive slackers deal with apartment life and love.
Twin Peaks: Fire Walk with Me (1992) David Lynch rolls his warped eye toward the dark underbelly of the Northwest.
Hype! (1996) An excellent time capsule of the grunge years.

Best in Print

Another Roadside Attraction (Tom Robbins; 1971) Robbins' wacky word carnival imagines Jesus alongside a flea circus at a pit stop.
Waxwings (Jonathan Raban; 2003) Travel writer Raban illuminates Seattle's recent high-tech boom in a novel that tells the parallel stories of two immigrants.
The Terrible Girls (Rebecca Brown; 1992) Experimental collection of short stories about lesbian relationships.
Heavier than Heaven (Charles R Cross; 2001) Moving portrait of Nirvana's Kurt Cobain.

The City that Never Stands Still

If you last visited Seattle in 2010, you could be in for a surprise or three. A number of visible changes have marked the city that never stands still in the last few years, and a couple more are well into the developmental stage. Walkers along the waterfront in the city center can't help but notice a giant Ferris wheel standing sentinel on &Pier 57, a tourist attraction that opened in 2012. Carry on through Belltown to the Seattle Center and you'll see that the Space Needle has a new neighbor, a dynamic glass museum devoted to the work of Tacoma-born artist Dale Chihuly. Also new in 2014 is a handy streetcar from Pioneer Square to Capitol Hill, while coming soon (in 2016) is a light-rail extension through Capitol Hill to the U District. Meanwhile, in the bowels of downtown, the world's largest boring machine, nicknamed 'Bertha,' is busy digging a 2-mile-long tunnel to accommodate soon-to-be-redirected SR 99. When the controversial $3.1-billion tunnel opens in 2016 and the ugly Alaskan Way Viaduct is finally dismantled, 25 blocks between the west edge of downtown and the waterfront will be opened up for redevelopment, a move that will make the city center an infinitely more salubrious place.

A New Amsterdam?

November 2012 was a momentous month for Seattle. As well as returning Barack Obama for a second term at the White House, Washington state voters approved two new social laws by referendum: same-sex marriage and the legalization of cannabis. Both referenda were close but incisive; same-sex marriage edged through with a 53.7% majority, while the cannabis ruling garnered a slightly larger 55.7%. The effects of the first law were immediate. Scores of people started queuing for marriage licenses outside King County administration building in downtown at midnight the day the law came into effect, with more than 140 couples getting married in the first 24 hours alone. The cannabis law still requires some legal wrangling before details regarding the buying and selling of the substance can be mapped out and Seattle starts opening its first Dutch-style 'coffee shops' (an obvious sticking point is Washington's indoor-smoking ban). Nonetheless, the city is all aflutter with aspiring cafe owners discussing the merits of vaporizers over hash cakes, and young entrepreneurs speculating about the lucrativeness of 'pot tourism.' It wasn't long ago that Starbucks and its cohorts cast Seattle as the 'New Vienna' on the coffee bar scene. Could it now be recast as the 'New Amsterdam'?

The Rise of South Lake Union

Amazon.com has already changed the way people buy books. But in 2012 the relocation of the company's main headquarters from Beacon Hill to the former warehouse district of South Lake Union was changing the composition of a whole Seattle neighborhood. Amazon's new $1-billion campus comprises 11 shiny buildings that stretch along Boren Ave N and Terry Ave N for four blocks. With an estimated 9000 employees ultimately set to move in, the area has seen an explosion of shops, cafes and restaurants built to cater for the new workers. Aside from some well-established Seattle mini-chains, including Top Pot Hand-Forged Doughnuts, Blue Moon Burgers and Zoka Coffee, South Lake Union has drawn in name chefs such as Tom Douglas and Vikram Vij. Still up in the air is the nature of the evolving neighborhood's personality. Will it be rakish and hip? Salt-of-the-earth? Corporate white-collar? Watch it develop.

A Taste for Innovation

Away from the headlines, Seattle's industrious army of technologically savvy innovators continues beavering away in garages and bedrooms dreaming up next year's Amazon, Starbucks or Microsoft. Regular visitors to planet earth will have already tasted the city's world-famous coffee and craft beer. But keep your ear to the ground for recent Seattle-fueled crazes including micro-creameries (ice cream), micro-distilleries (whiskey and gin), vegan doughnuts, nano-breweries (pint-sized brewers for ultra-serious beer drinkers), crusty pie shops, and restaurants that forage mushrooms, nettles and wild vegetables from the surrounding countryside.

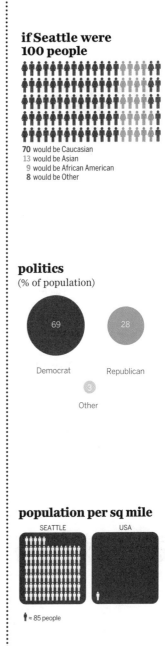

if Seattle were 100 people

70 would be Caucasian
13 would be Asian
9 would be African American
8 would be Other

politics
(% of population)

69
Democrat

28
Republican

3
Other

population per sq mile

SEATTLE   USA

≈ 85 people

History

In the pantheon of world cities, 163-year-old Seattle is still in its kindergarten years. Although native groups have lived in and around Puget Sound for 12 millennia, the region was still covered in thick forest when the first colonial settlers bushwhacked their way through in 1851. And so began a historical trajectory marked by a mixture of bravery, folly, fire, rebirth, bust, boom and an explosion of urban growth almost unparalleled in US history. Hold tight!

Luther Collins staked a land claim near Georgetown on September 14, 1851, two weeks before the Denny party arrived at Alki. Technically, it is he, not Denny, who was Seattle's first settler.

Early Exploration

The first white expedition to explore the Puget Sound area came in 1792, when the British sea captain George Vancouver sailed through the inland waterways of the Straits of Juan de Fuca and Georgia. In the same year, the USA entered the competition to claim the Northwest when Captain Robert Gray reached the mouth of the Columbia River.

The first US settlers straggled overland to the Pacific Northwest in the 1830s on the rough tracks that would become the Oregon Trail. Following in the footsteps of Lewis and Clark, they founded the cities of Portland (1843) and Tumwater (1846) near present-day Olympia and began to look further north.

'New York Pretty Soon'

Arthur and David Denny were native New Yorkers who, in 1851, led a group of settlers across the Oregon Trail with the intention of settling in the Willamette Valley. On the way, they heard stories of good land and deep water ports along Puget Sound. When the Denny party arrived in Portland in the fall, they decided to keep going north. The settlers staked claims on Alki Point, in present-day West Seattle. The group named their encampment Alki-New York (the Chinookan word *alki* means 'pretty soon' or 'by and by'). After a winter of wind and rain, the group determined that their fledgling city needed a deeper harbor and moved the settlement to the mudflats across Elliott Bay. The colony was renamed Seattle for the Duwamish Chief Sealth (pronounced

TIMELINE	9000–11,000 BC	1792	1851
	The ancestors of the Duwamish, Suquamish, Coast Salish and Chinook tribes arrive in Puget Sound.	British sea captain George Vancouver sails through the Straits of Juan de Fuca and Georgia.	The Denny party arrives at Alki Point and settles in Puget Sound, already home to the Duwamish people.

see-aalth, with a guttural 'th' being made up of a hard 't' and an 'h' that's almost a lisp off the end of the word), who was the friend of an early merchant.

Birth of the City

The heart of the young city beat in the area now known as Pioneer Square. Although there was a small but deep harbor at this point in Elliott Bay, much of the land immediately to the south was mudflats, ideal for oysters but not much else. The land to the north and east was steep and forested. The early settlers (whose names now ring as a compendium of street names and landmarks: Denny, Yesler, Bell, Boren) quickly cleared the land and established a sawmill, schools, churches and other civic institutions. From the start, the people who settled Seattle never doubted that they were founding a great city. The original homesteads were quickly plaited into city streets, and trade, not farming or lumbering, became the goal.

Since it was a frontier town, the majority of Seattle's male settlers were bachelors. One of the town's founders (and sole professor at the newly established university), Asa Mercer, went back to the East Coast with the express purpose of inducing young, unmarried women to venture to Seattle. Fifty-seven women made the journey and married into the frontier stock.

Fremont, Ballard and Georgetown were once rival cities to Seattle. They were absorbed by their bigger rival in 1891, 1907 and 1910 respectively.

The Great Fire & the Regrading of Seattle

Frontier Seattle was a thrown-together village of wooden storefronts, log homes and lumber mills. Tidewater lapped against present-day 1st Ave S, and many of the buildings and the streets that led to them were on stilts. No part of the original downtown was more than 4ft above the bay at high tide, and the streets were frequently a quagmire.

On June 6, 1889, an apprentice woodworker accidentally let a pot of boiling glue spill onto a pile of wood chips in a shop on 1st Ave and Madison St. The fire quickly spread through the young city, with boardwalks providing an unstoppable conduit for the flames. By the end of the day, 30 blocks of the city had burned, gutting the core of downtown.

What might have seemed a catastrophe was in fact a blessing, as the city was rebuilt immediately with handsome structures of brick, steel and stone. This time, however, the streets were regraded and ravines and inlets filled in. This raised the new city about a dozen feet above the old. In some areas the regrading simply meant building on top of older ground-level buildings and streets. People had to cross deep trenches to get from one side of the street to another. Buildings were constructed

Seattle History Books

The Good Rain *(1991)*, Timothy Egan

Stepping Westward *(1991)*, Sallie Tisdale

Vanishing Seattle *(2006)*, Clark Humphrey

1889	1897	1910	1932
The Great Fire sweeps through the city, gutting its core and destroying the mostly wooden storefronts and log homes on stilts.	The Klondike gold rush is sparked by the arrival of the ship *Portland*. The city's population doubles by 1900.	Seattle begins to grow up. Its population reaches a quarter million, making it a clear contender for the preeminent city of the Pacific Northwest.	A shantytown called 'Hooverville,' after President Hoover, forms south of Pioneer Square. Made up of lean-tos and shacks, it houses hundreds of unemployed squatters.

KLONDIKE GOLD RUSH

Seattle's first real boom came when the ship *Portland* docked at the waterfront in 1897 with its now-famous cargo: two tons of gold newly gleaned from northern Canadian goldfields. The news spread quickly across the USA; within weeks, thousands of fortune seekers from all over the world converged on Seattle, the last stop before heading north. That summer and fall, 74 ships left Seattle bound for Skagway, AK, and on to the goldfields in Dawson City, Yukon.

In all, more than 40,000 prospectors passed through Seattle. The Canadian government demanded that prospectors bring a year's worth of supplies, so they wouldn't freeze or starve to death midway. Outfitting the miners became big business in Seattle. The town became the banking center for the fortunes made in the Yukon. Bars, brothels, theaters and honky-tonks in Pioneer Square blossomed.

Many of Seattle's shopkeepers, tavern owners and restaurateurs made quick fortunes in the late 1890s – far more than most of the prospectors. Many who did make fortunes in Alaska chose to stay in the Northwest, settling in the thriving port city on Puget Sound.

Seattle grew quickly. The Klondike gold rush provided great wealth, and the railroads brought in a steady stream of immigrants, mostly from Eastern Europe and Scandinavia. Seattle controlled most of the shipping trade with Alaska and increasingly with nations of the Pacific Rim. Company-controlled communities like Ballard sprang up, populated almost exclusively with Scandinavians who worked in massive sawmills. A new influx of Asian immigrants, this time from Japan, began streaming into Seattle, establishing fishing fleets and vegetable farms.

At the height of the gold rush in 1900, Seattle's population reached 80,000, double the population figure from the 1890 census. By 1910, Seattle's population jumped to a quarter million. Seattle had become the preeminent city of the Pacific Northwest.

around the notion that the first floor or two would eventually be buried when the city got around to filling in the trenches.

The sense of transformation inspired by the Great Fire also fueled another great rebuilding project. One of Seattle's original seven hills, Denny Hill, rose out of Elliott Bay just north of Pine St. Its very steep face limited commercial traffic, though some hotels and private homes were perched on the hilltop. City engineers determined that if Seattle's growth were to continue, Denny Hill had to go. Between 1899 and 1912, the hill was sluiced into Elliott Bay. Twenty million gallons of water were pumped daily from Lake Union and sprayed onto the rock and soil. Under great pressure, the water liquefied the clay and dislodged the rock, all of which was sluiced into flumes. Existing homes were simply undercut and then burned.

1942	1954	1962	1975
Japanese Americans are ordered to evacuate Seattle; they are detained under prison conditions in a relocation center for the duration of the war.	Boeing Air Transport, launched 40 years prior and already a pioneer in commercial airline flight, announces production of the 707.	The World's Fair takes place. The headliner on opening night is singer John Raitt. His 12-year-old daughter, Bonnie, holds his sheet music.	Bill Gates and Paul Allen start Microsoft, ensuring the livelihoods of antitrust lawyers for the foreseeable future.

The War Years

Seattle's boom continued through WWI, when Northwest lumber was in great demand. The opening of the Panama Canal brought increased trade to Pacific ports, which were free from wartime threats. Shipyards opened along Puget Sound, bringing the shipbuilding industry close to the forests of the Northwest.

WWII brought other, less positive, developments to Seattle. About 7000 Japanese residents in Seattle and the nearby areas were forcibly removed from their jobs and homes. They were sent to the nearby 'relocation center,' or internment camp, in Puyallup, then on to another camp in Idaho where they were detained under prison conditions for the duration of the war. This greatly depleted the Japanese community, which up to this point had built a thriving existence farming and fishing in Puget Sound. In all, an estimated 110,000 Japanese across the country, two-thirds of whom were US citizens, were sent to internment camps. Upon their release, many declined to return to the homes they'd been forced to abandon.

> Of the 100,000 pioneers who set out for the Klondike gold rush, 40,000 actually arrived, 20,000 worked or prospected and 300 earned more than $15,000, but only 50 kept their fortune.

Boeing & Postwar Seattle

The Boeing Airplane Company, started in 1917, was founded and named by William E Boeing and his partner, Conrad Westervelt. (Boeing tested his first plane, the *B&W*, in June 1916 by taking off from the middle of Lake Union.) For years, Boeing single-handedly ruled Seattle industry. After WWII, the manufacturer diversified its product line and began to develop civilian aircraft. In 1954 Boeing announced the 707, and the response was immediate and overwhelming. The world found itself at the beginning of an era of mass air travel, and Boeing produced the jets that led this revolution in transportation. By 1960, when the population of Seattle topped one million, one in 10 people worked for Boeing, and one in four people worked in jobs directly affected by Boeing.

But the fortunes of Boeing weren't always to soar. A combination of overstretched capital (due to cost overruns in the development of the 747) and a cut in defense spending led to a severe financial crisis in the early 1970s, known as the 'Boeing Bust.' Boeing was forced to cut its workforce by two-thirds; in one year, nearly 60,000 Seattleites lost their jobs. The local economy went into a tailspin for a number of years.

In the 1980s increased defense spending brought vigor back to aircraft production lines, and expanding trade relations with Pacific Rim nations brought business to Boeing, too. But, in September 2001, the world's largest airplane manufacturer, the company as synonymous with Seattle as rain, relocated 50% of its HQ staff to digs in Chicago. However, the Boeing factory has stayed put in Seattle, where the company remains the city's biggest employer with a workforce of 80,000.

> **Seattle's Boom Industries**
> ....
> *Lumber: 1852–89*
> ....
> *Gold: 1897–1905 (Klondike)*
> ....
> *Shipbuilding: 1911–18*
> ....
> *Airplanes: 1945–70 (Boeing)*
> ....
> *Dot com: 1995–2000 (Microsoft)*

1991	1999	2001	2009
The formerly underground style of music known as grunge goes mainstream, with Pearl Jam's *Ten* and Nirvana's *Nevermind* hitting record-store shelves.	Seattle is rocked by the World Trade Organization riots. Microsoft is declared a monopoly and enters into lengthy negotiations over the future of its business.	On February 28, an earthquake measuring 6.8 on the Richter scale hits Seattle, toppling several buildings and causing more than $2 billion in damage.	Generally dismissed as a pipe dream, the long-awaited light-rail line to the airport finally opens.

The Way of Life

Surprisingly elegant in places and coolly edgy in others, Seattle is notable for its technological savoir faire, passion for books, and dedicated army of locavores harboring green credentials. Although it has fermented its own pop culture in recent times, it has yet to create an urban mythology like Paris or New York. But it is the future rather than the past that's more important here. Seattle's lifestyle is organic. Rather than trying to live up to its history, it's defining what happens next.

What is a Seattleite?

To avoid faux pas, don't compare Seattle with Portland, don't say grunge (it's 'the Sub Pop thing'), and don't mention the relocation of the Seattle SuperSonics basketball team to Oklahoma.

Every city has its stereotypes and Seattle is no different. Those who have never been here imagine it as a metropolis of casually dressed, latte-supping urbanites who drive Priuses, vote Democrat, consume only locally grown food, and walk around with an unwavering diet of Nirvana-derived indie rock programmed into their i-players. To the people who live here, the picture is a little more complex. Seattle has a rich multicultural history and is home to Native American, African American, Asian American and growing Ethiopian American populations. Indeed, the city ranks 23rd among the 30 largest US cities in terms of African American population, at 8.4% – higher than every West Coast city except Los Angeles – and its Asian American population (13%) is even higher, 10% above the national average.

Living beneath overcast skies for much of the year, the locals brightened the mood by opening up cafes, reasoning that drinking liberal doses of caffeine in a cozy social environment was more fun than hiking in the rain. Seattleites have reinvented coffee culture, sinking into comfortable armchairs, listening to Ray Charles albums on repeat and nurturing mega-sized locally made coffee mugs large enough to last all day.

Seattle's geographic setting, a spectacular combination of mountains, ocean and temperate rainforest, has earned it the moniker 'Emerald City.' When you look out your office window on sunny days and see broccoli-green Douglas fir trees framing a giant glacier-covered volcano, it's not hard to feel passionate about protecting the environment. The green culture has stoked public backing for Seattle's rapidly expanding public-transportation network and an almost religious reverence for local food.

In contrast to the USA's hardworking eastern seaboard, life out west is more casual and less frenetic. Idealistically, westerners would rather work to live than live to work. Indeed, with so much winter rain, Seattleites will dredge up any excuse to shun the nine-to-five treadmill and hit the great outdoors. The first bright days of summer prompt a mass exodus of hikers and cyclists making enthusiastically for the wilderness areas for which the region is justly famous.

Creativity is a longstanding Northwestern trait, be it redefining the course of modern rock music or reconfiguring the latest Microsoft operating system. The city that once saw one in 10 of its workforce employed at aviation giant Boeing has long been obsessed with creative engineering – and this skill has been transferred to other genres. Rather than making do with hand-me-downs, Seattle's mechanically minded coffee geeks took apart imported Italian coffee machines in the early 1990s and re-invented them for better performance. Similarly, they have experiment-ed boldly with British-style beer, using locally grown hops, and have opened up their own whiskey distilleries. More recently, keen young bakers have started a craze for homemade sweet and savory pies.

Politics & Social Issues

Washington is arguably the most socially progressive state and the only one where same-sex marriage, assisted suicide and marijuana usage are all legal. King County, where Seattle makes up the bulk of the popula-tion, has voted Democrat in presidential elections since the 1980s, with current president Barack Obama enjoying 70% of the popular vote. Sim-ilarly, Seattle has had a Democratic mayor since 1969. The city elected the first female mayor in US history, Bertha Knight Landes, who served from 1926 to 1928. (Ironically, it hasn't elected another woman to the office since.)

Seattle has often stood at the forefront of the push for 'greener' lifestyles, in the form of car clubs, recycling programs, organic restau-rants and biodiesel whale-watching tours. Former mayor Greg Nickels (2001–09) was an early exponent of ecofriendly practices and advocated himself as a leading spokesperson on climate change. Current mayor Michael McGinn is another environmental activist and former state chair of the Sierra Club.

Seattle is one of the country's more gay-friendly cities, with most bars and nightlife centered on Capitol Hill. Journalist and media pundit Dan Savage has long been a high-profile local voice. You can read his weekly column in the *Stranger*, an alternative free newspaper that picked up a Pulitzer Prize in 2012.

Dealing with Success

Despite its achievements and importance to the region, Seattle still has the mellow sense of modesty and self-deprecation that characterizes the Northwest. This dates back to its laid-back origins as 'New York Pretty Soon.' The attitude peaked in the 1950s and '60s, with the wild anti-boosterism of newspaper columnist Emmett Watson (who wrote things like 'Have a nice day – somewhere else' and 'Our suicide rate is one of the highest in the nation. But we can be No 1!'). And it has colored the way the nation perceives Seattle, along with the populariza-tion of the anti-glamorous in the form of grunge, a trend whose fame still seems to mortify the city. Then there was Seattle's naive excitement at being selected to host the 1999 World Trade Organization (WTO) conference and many residents' shock at the resulting fallout.

Seattle has long made a habit of turning its clever homemade inven-tions into global brands. But the city has always had an uncomfortable relationship with the success it has struggled to achieve. Ask an average Seattleite how they rate Starbucks and they might express barely con-cealed pride one minute and tell you they never drink there the next. Similar sentiments are reserved for business behemoths Microsoft, Boeing and Amazon.

Two of Seattle's most successful citizens also happen to be its two largest public figures, Bill Gates and Paul Allen. And they symbolize a certain aspect of the city's contradictory attitude toward its own suc-cess. Both undeniably ambitious and indisputably successful, Gates and Allen are seen simultaneously as points of civic pride and as shameless capitalists who are totally alien to the prevailing Seattle culture.

Seattle is home to 48 micro-breweries and over 200 coffee shops. Seattleites are the biggest coffee consumers in the US.

THE WAY OF LIFE POLITICS & SOCIAL ISSUES

Seattle Brands that Went Global

Amazon

Starbucks

Microsoft

REI

Costco

Nordstrom

Boeing

Arts

Seattle is an erudite city of enthusiastic readers with more bookstores per capita than any other US city. It also produced – and remains HQ to – the world's biggest online retailer, Amazon.com, founded in 1995 as an online bookstore. Not surprisingly, numerous internationally recognized writers gravitate here, among them Tom Robbins, Jonathan Raban and Sherman Alexie. David Guterson – author of the wonderfully evocative *Snow Falling on Cedars* (1994), set on a fictional Puget Sound island – was born in Seattle, graduated from the University of Washington and now lives on Bainbridge Island.

Seattle's visual arts are also dynamic, as its cultural strands (from Native American and Asian to contemporary American) meet and transfuse on canvas, in glass and in sculpture.

Literature

In the 1960s and '70s, western Washington attracted a number of counterculture writers. The most famous of these (and the best!) is Tom Robbins, whose books, including *Another Roadside Attraction* (1971) and *Even Cowgirls Get the Blues* (1976), are a perfect synthesis of the enlightened braininess, sense of mischief and reverence for beauty that add up to the typical mellow Northwest counterculture vibe.

Having, among other things, a fondness for the Blue Moon Tavern in common with Robbins, poet Theodore Roethke taught for years at the University of Washington, and along with Washington native Richard Hugo he cast a profound influence over Northwest poetry.

Raymond Carver, the short-story master whose books include *Will You Please Be Quiet, Please?* (1976) and *Where I'm Calling From* (1988), lived near Seattle on the Olympic Peninsula. Carver's stark and grim vision of working-class angst has profoundly affected other young writers of his time. Carver's second wife, Tess Gallagher, also from Port Angeles and a UW alumnus, is a novelist and poet whose books include *At the Owl Woman Saloon* (1997).

Noted travel writer Jonathan Raban, who lived in Seattle for years then left, only to return recently, has written such books as *Coasting* (1987), *Hunting Mister Heartbreak* (1990) and *Badlands* (1996). His novel *Waxwings* (2003) is an account of two families of Seattle immigrants.

Sherman Alexie is a Native American author whose short-story collection *The Lone Ranger and Tonto Fistfight in Heaven* (1993) was among the first works of popular fiction to discuss reservation life. In 1996 he published *Indian Killer,* a chilling tale of ritual murder set in Seattle, to great critical acclaim. His recent *War Dances,* a collection of poetry and stories, won the 2010 PEN/Faulkner Award for fiction.

The misty environs of western Washington seem to be a fecund habitat for mystery writers. Dashiell Hammett once lived in Seattle, while noted writers JA Jance, Earl Emerson and Frederick D Huebner currently make the Northwest home.

One peculiar phenomenon is the relatively large number of cartoonists who live in the Seattle area. Lynda Barry *(Ernie Pook's Comeek, Cruddy)* and Matt Groening (creator of *The Simpsons*) were students together at Olympia's Evergreen State College. Gary Larson, whose *Far Side* animal antics have netted international fame and great fortune, lives in Seattle. A good number of underground comic-book artists live here, too – among them the legendary Peter Bagge *(Hate),* Jim Woodring *(The Frank Book)*, Charles Burns *(Black Hole)* and Roberta Gregory *(Naughty Bits)*. It could well have something to do with the fact that Fantagraphics, a major and influential publisher of underground comics and graphic novels, is based here.

Seattle's Mini Coffee Chains

Caffe Ladro

Caffè Fiore

Uptown Espresso

Top Pot Hand-Forged Doughnuts

Fuel Coffee

Zoka Coffee

Caffe Vita

Espresso Vivace

Victrola Coffee Roasters

Seattle has two daily newspapers, the *Seattle Post-Intelligencer*, founded in 1863, and the *Seattle Times*, founded in 1993. The *Post-Intelligencer* ended print publication in 2009 but still runs an active website.

VISUAL ARTS

Museums and galleries in Seattle offer a visual-arts experience as varied as the rest of the city's culture. The newly expanded Seattle Art Museum has a substantial European art collection, a range of modern art that's well suited to its new exhibition spaces, and an impressive collection of native artifacts and folk art, especially carved wooden masks. There are also several exhibition spaces around the city devoted to contemporary Native American carvings and paintings. A considerable Asian art collection is located at the Seattle Asian Art Museum in Volunteer Park. More experimental and conceptual art is displayed at the University of Washington's Henry Art Gallery and at the Frye Art Museum.

A specialty of the Puget Sound area is glassblowing, led by maverick artist Dale Chihuly, whose flamboyant, colorful and unmistakable work is now on display at a new museum in the Seattle Center.

Pushing the envelope of contemporary art is the specialty of several younger galleries around town, notably Pioneer Square's Roq La Rue and the Center on Contemporary Art, which has three venues (Ballard, Belltown and Georgetown). These unconventional spaces display provocative, boundary-distorting artwork of all kinds, usually by unknown or underground artists.

Monthly art walks are as common as Starbucks in Seattle. You can wise up on the galleries in Pioneer Square, Georgetown, Fremont or Ballard.

Cinema & Television

Seattle has come a long way as a movie mecca since the days when Elvis starred in the 1963 film *It Happened at the World's Fair,* a chestnut of civic boosterism. Films with Seattle as their backdrop include *Tugboat Annie* (1933); *Cinderella Liberty* (1974), a steamy romance with James Caan and Marsha Mason; and *The Parallax View* (1974) with Warren Beatty. Jessica Lange's movie *Frances,* about the horrible fate of outspoken local actor Frances Farmer (she was jailed on questionable pretenses, then institutionalized for years and eventually lobotomized), was shot here in 1981. Debra Winger's hit *Black Widow* (1986) shows many scenes shot at the University of Washington.

John Cusack starred in *Say Anything* (1989), Michelle Pfeiffer and Jeff Bridges lit up the screen in *The Fabulous Baker Boys* (1989), and Sly Stallone and Antonio Banderas flopped in *Assassins* (1995), all partly filmed in and around Seattle. Horror hit *The Ring* and JLo vehicle *Enough* both had a few scenes shot in Seattle and on local ferries.

The two most famous (until recently) Seattle movies happened when the city was at the peak of its cultural cachet in the '90s: *Singles* (1992), with Campbell Scott, Kyra Sedgwick, Matt Dillon and Bridget Fonda, captured the city's youthful-slacker vibe. (Incidentally, both *Singles* and *Say Anything* were directed by Cameron Crowe, who is married to Nancy Wilson from Seattle rock band Heart.) And then there was *Sleepless in Seattle,* the 1993 blockbuster starring Tom Hanks, Meg Ryan and, perhaps more importantly, Seattle's Lake Union houseboats. As a Seattle-based film phenomenon, however, nothing tops the tween-vampire soap opera *Twilight* and its sequels, set in the town of Forks, WA.

TV's *Northern Exposure,* filmed in nearby Roslyn, WA, and *Frasier* both did a lot to boost Seattle's reputation as a hip and youthful place to live. The creepy, darker side of the Northwest was captured in the moody *Twin Peaks: Fire Walk with Me.* And let's not forget ABC's phenomenally popular hospital drama, *Grey's Anatomy.*

LANGUAGES

Several Native American languages are spoken and taught in Seattle, such as the Duwamish dialect Lushootseed, a branch of the Salishan language family.

Music

Music is as important to Seattle as coffee, computers or airplanes. The jazz era produced Ray Charles, rock delivered Hendrix, and the '70s coughed up crusty hard-rock merchants Heart. Then, in the early 1990s, a generation of flannel-shirted urban slackers tired of being ignored by the mainstream threw away their '80s fashion manuals and turned up the volume on their guitars. Suddenly, the city wasn't just exporting individual artists; it had invented a whole new musical genre: grunge.

The Jazz Age

Born in Texas in 1928, jazz singer Ernestine Anderson moved to Seattle at age 16 and became a product of the fertile jazz scene spearheaded by Ray Charles and Quincy Jones.

At its peak in the 1940s, when many GIs were based in Seattle, S Jackson St – in what is now 'Little Saigon,' an eastern outpost of the International District – and its environs boasted more than 20 raucous bars with music, dancing and bootleg liquor. Although the city never rewrote the jazz songbook with its own genre or style, it provided a fertile performance space for numerous name artists. Charlie Parker, Lester Young and Duke Ellington all passed through and, in 1948, a young, unknown, blind pianist from Florida named Ray Charles arrived to seek his fortune. Later that year, the 18-year-old Charles met 15-year-old trumpeter and Seattle resident Quincy Jones in the Black Elk's Club on S Jackson and the creative sparks began to fly.

Seattle's jazz scene had died down by the 1960s, when S Jackson embraced tight-lipped sobriety, and the young and hip turned their attention to rock and roll (enter Hendrix stage left). Benefiting from regular revivals in the years since, a small jazz scene lives on in Belltown, where two venues – Dimitriou's Jazz Alley and Tula's – still attract international talent.

From Hendrix to Heart

Seattle lapped up rock and roll like every other US city in the late '50s and early '60s, but it produced few rockers of its own, save the Fleetwoods (from nearby Olympia), who had a string of hits from 1959 to 1966. No one took much notice when a poor black teenager named Johnny Allen Hendrix took to the stage in the basement of a local synagogue in the Central District (CD) in 1960. Hendrix's band fired him mid-set for showing off – a personality trait he would later turn to his advantage. Ignored and in trouble with the law, Hendrix served briefly in the US army before being honorably discharged. After a stint in Nashville, he gravitated to New York, where he was 'discovered' playing in a club by Keith Richards' girlfriend. Encouraged to visit London, the displaced Seattleite was invited by bassist Chas Chandler to play in a new nightclub for his mates Eric Clapton and the Beatles, whose jaws immediately hit the floor.

Heart was another band that had to travel elsewhere – in its case, to Canada – to gain international recognition. The band recorded its first album in Vancouver and followed it up with a second, which produced the hard-rock million-seller 'Barracuda.' Enjoying a comeback in the mid-'80s, Heart is probably best remembered for the soft-rock hit 'These Dreams.'

Grunge – Punk's West Coast Nirvana

Synthesizing Generation X angst with a questionable approach to personal hygiene, the music popularly categorized as 'grunge' first dive-bombed onto Seattle's scene in the early 1990s like a clap of thunder on a typically wet and overcast afternoon. The anger had been fermenting for years – not purely in Seattle but also in its sprawling satellite towns and suburbs. Some said it was inspired the weather, others cited the Northwest's geographic isolation. It didn't really matter. Armed with dissonant chords and dark, sometimes ironic lyrics, a disparate collection of bands stepped sneeringly up to the microphone to preach a new message from a city that all of the touring big-name rock acts serially chose to ignore. There were Screaming Trees from collegiate Ellensburg, the Melvins from rainy Montesano, Nirvana from the timber town of Aberdeen, and the converging members of Pearl Jam from across the nation.

Historically, grunge's roots lay in West Coast punk, a musical sub-genre that first found a voice in Portland in the late 1970s, led by the Wipers, whose leather-clad followers congregated in legendary dive bars such as Satyricon. Another musical blossoming occurred in Olympia, WA, in the early 1980s, where DIY musicians Beat Happening invented 'lo-fi' and coyly mocked the corporate establishment. Mixing in elements of heavy metal and scooping up the fallout of an itchy youth culture, Seattle quickly became the alternative music's pulpit, spawning small, clamorous venues where boisterous young bands more interested in playing rock music than 'performing' could lose themselves in a melee of excitement and noise. It was a raucous, energetic scene characterized by stage-diving, crowd-surfing and barely tuned guitars, but, armed with raw talent and some surprisingly catchy tunes, the music filled a vacuum.

A crucial element in grunge's elevation to superstardom was Sub Pop Records, an independent Seattle label whose guerrilla marketing tactics created a flurry of hype to promote its ragged stable of cacophonous bands. In August 1988, Sub Pop released the seminal single 'Touch Me I'm Sick' by Mudhoney, a watershed moment. The noise got noticed, most importantly by the British music press, whose punk-savvy journalists quickly reported the birth of a 'Seattle sound,' later christened grunge by the brand-hungry media. Suitably inspired, the Seattle scene began to prosper, spawning literally hundreds of new bands, all cemented in the same DIY, anti-fashion, audience-embracing tradition. Of note were sludgy Soundgarden, which later went on to win two Grammys; metal-esque Alice in Chains; and the soon-to-be-mega Nirvana and Pearl Jam. By the dawn of the 1990s, every rebellious slacker with the gas money was coming to Seattle to hit the clubs. It was more than exciting.

What should have been grunge's high point came in October 1992, when Nirvana's second album, the hugely accomplished *Nevermind*, knocked Michael Jackson off the number-one spot, but the kudos ultimately killed it. After several years of railing against the mainstream, Nirvana and grunge had been incorporated into it. The media blitzed in, grunge fashion spreads appeared in *Vanity Fair* and half-baked singers from Seattle only had to cough to land a record contract. Many recoiled, most notably Nirvana vocalist and songwriter Kurt Cobain, whose drug abuse ended in suicide in his new Madison Park home in 1994. Other bands soldiered on, but the spark – which had burnt so brightly while it lasted – was gone. By the mid-1990s, grunge was officially dead.

Songs about Seattle

'Frances Farmer Will Have Her Revenge on Seattle,' Nirvana (1993)

'Aurora,' Foo Fighters (1999)

'Belltown Ramble,' Robyn Hitchcock (2006)

'The Town,' Macklemore (2009)

MUSIC GRUNGE – PUNK'S WEST COAST NIRVANA

Green River was an early grunge band whose members went on to bigger things. Mark Arm and Steve Turner started Mudhoney, and Jeff Ament and Steve Gossard set up Pearl Jam.

> **GRUNGE TOP FIVE PLAYLIST**
>
> ➡ *Superfuzz Bigmuff* **(Sub Pop), Mudhoney** Released in 1988; the catchy debut single 'Touch Me I'm Sick' became an instant classic.
>
> ➡ *Nevermind* **(Geffen), Nirvana** Grunge anthem 'Smells Like Teen Spirit' became, and remains, one of the most analyzed singles in the history of rock.
>
> ➡ *Ten* **(Epic), Pearl Jam** The first studio album by one of rock's biggest groups took a while to peak but contained three hit singles.
>
> ➡ *Badmotorfinger* **(A&M), Soundgarden** The hair-metal side of grunge.
>
> ➡ *Facelift* **(Columbia), Alice in Chains** First offering from legendary grunge-metal band with the hidden harmonies.

Indie Music Since the 1990s

These days, one of the surest ways to annoy a Seattle hipster is to ask them where the local grunge bands are playing. Seattle has moved on from the '90s and so has its music. The alternative scene dissipated slightly in the mid-'90s, moving south to Olympia, which embraced feminist punk movement Riot Grrrl, with bands like Bikini Kill and Bratmobile, and north to Bellingham, home of the Posies and Death Cab for Cutie. Post-2000, electronica band the Postal Service gained fresh success for the Sub Pop label, and the advent of KEXP radio gave alternative music a fresh shot of adrenaline. Today, Seattle still produces some interesting musical talent and remains an excellent place to catch up-and-coming live indie acts. Classic surviving 1990s-era venues have been complemented by a revolving stable of newer competition, many of which have widened their repertoire to include hip-hop, electronica or alternative country.

Musical Alumni of Garfield High School

Jimi Hendrix

Quincy Jones

Ernestine Anderson

Macklemore

Hip-Hop

Seattle's hip-hop pioneer was Sir Mix-a-Lot (real name Anthony Ray), whose break-through song 'Posse on Broadway,' released in 1987, describes the intimate geography of Capitol Hill and the CD. The rapper went on to have a massive number one hit with 'Baby Got Back' in 1992.

In recent years hip-hop has successfully infiltrated the indie-rock universe and begun to have serious impact. This is partly thanks to influential radio station KEXP, which adds local hip-hop artists into the mix at all hours. But it's mostly due to the fact that the work coming out of the Pacific Northwest is overwhelmingly high quality and, as befits the region, generally positive and socially conscious. The latest big star, Macklemore (real name Ben Haggerty), proved this point in 2012 with his number one song 'Thrift Shop,' which extolled the virtues of secondhand clothes over the normal rapper uniform (bling). Macklemore, like Hendrix and Quincy Jones before him, is an alumnus of Garfield High School in the CD. He works in tandem with producer and fellow Seattleite Ryan Lewis and their independent 2012 album *The Heist* challenged the boundaries of hip-hop. Other Seattle hip-hop artists to look for include Blue Scholars and Boom Bap Project.

Survival Guide

TRANSPORTATION. .204

ARRIVING IN SEATTLE 204

Sea-Tac
International Airport 204

King Street Station 205

The Piers 205

GETTING AROUND SEATTLE 205

Bicycle 205

Boat 206

Bus 206

Car & Motorcycle 206

Light Rail 207

Streetcar 207

Taxi 207

TOURS 207

DIRECTORY A–Z 208

Customs Regulations ... 208

Discount Cards......... 208

Electricity 208

Emergency 208

Gay & Lesbian Travelers .. 208

Internet Access......... 209

Legal Matters 209

Medical Services 209

Money................. 209

Newspapers & Magazines 210

Opening Hours 210

Post................... 210

Public Holidays......... 210

Telephone 210

Time 211

Tourist Information 211

Travelers with Disabilities.............. 211

Visas.................. 211

Transportation

ARRIVING IN SEATTLE

Seattle is served by the **Sea-Tac International Airport** (SEA; www.portseattle.org/Sea-Tac), located 13 miles south of downtown Seattle. It's one of the top 20 airports in the US with numerous domestic flights and good direct connections to Asia and a handful of European cities, including Paris and London.

Three railway arteries converge in Seattle from the east (the *Empire Builder* from Chicago), south (the *Coast Starlight* from Oregon and California) and north (the *Cascades* from Vancouver, Canada). These land-based journeys through the watery, green-tinged, mountainous Pacific Northwest landscape are spectacular and often surprisingly cheap.

Seattle's main road highway is mega-busy I-5 that flows north–south along the west coast. Points east are best served by cross-continental I-90 that crosses the Cascade Mountains via Snoqualmie Pass. Regular boats arrive in Seattle from Victoria, Canada. It's also possible that you may arrive on a cruise liner.

Sea-Tac International Airport

Sea-Tac International Airport, shared with the city of Tacoma, is the arrival point for 33 million people annually. The options for making the 13-mile trek from the airport to downtown Seattle improved drastically with the completion of the airport light-rail line in 2009 (it's soon to be extended beyond downtown to Capitol Hill and the U District). It's fast and cheap and takes you directly to the heart of downtown as well as a handful of other stops along the way.

There are **baggage storage** (http://kensbaggage.com; suitcases, duffels & backpacks per day $6-10) facilities in the airport as well as currency-exchange services. Car-rental agencies are located in the baggage-claim area.

Light Rail
Sound Transit (www.sound transit.org) runs the Link Light Rail service to the airport. Trains go every 15 minutes or better between 5am and just after midnight. Stops in town include Westlake Center, Pioneer Square, the International District and SoDo. The ride between the two farthest points, Westlake and Sea-Tac, takes 37 minutes and costs $2.75.

Shuttle Bus
Shuttle Express (☑800-487-7433; www.shuttleexpress.com) has a pickup and drop-off point on the 3rd floor of the airport garage; it charges approximately $18 and is handy if you have a lot of luggage.

CLIMATE CHANGE & TRAVEL

Every form of transport that relies on carbon-based fuel generates CO_2, the main cause of human-induced climate change. Modern travel is dependent on airplanes, which might use less fuel per kilometer per person than most cars but travel much greater distances. The altitude at which aircraft emit gases (including CO_2) and particles also contributes to their climate change impact. Many websites offer 'carbon calculators' that allow people to estimate the carbon emissions generated by their journey and, for those who wish to do so, to offset the impact of the greenhouse gases emitted with contributions to portfolios of climate-friendly initiatives throughout the world. Lonely Planet offsets the carbon footprint of all staff and author travel.

Taxi

Taxis are available at the parking garage on the 3rd floor. The average fare to downtown is $42.

Private Vehicle

Rental-car counters are located in the baggage-claim area. Some provide pickup and drop-off service from the 1st floor of the garage, while others provide a shuttle to the airport. Ask when you book your car.

Driving into Seattle from the airport is fairly straightforward – just take I-5 north. It helps to find out whether your downtown exit is a left-hand or right-hand one, as it can be tricky to cross several lanes of traffic at the last minute during rush hour.

King Street Station

Amtrak serves Seattle's King Street Station. Three main routes run through town: the Amtrak *Cascades* (connecting Vancouver (Canada), Seattle, Portland (OR) and Eugene (OR)), the very scenic *Coast Starlight* (connecting Seattle, Oakland (CA) and Los Angeles (CA)) and the *Empire Builder* (a cross-continental roller coaster to Chicago (IL)).

The station is situated between Pioneer Square and the International District right on the cusp of downtown and has good, fast links with practically everywhere in the city.

Streetcar

The brand new streetcar runs up through the International District and First Hill to Capitol Hill every 15 minutes. Fares are $2.50/1.25 per adult/child.

Light Rail

The station is adjacent to the International District/Chinatown Link Light Rail station, from where it is three

---

ARRIVING BY INTERCITY BUS

Various intercity coaches serve Seattle and there is more than one drop-off point – it all depends on which company you are using.

Greyhound (Map p230; www.greyhound.com; 811 Stewart St; ☉6am–midnight) Connects Seattle with cities all over the country, including Chicago (one way $228, two days' journey, two daily), Spokane ($51, eight hours, three daily), San Francisco ($129, 20 hours, three daily) and Vancouver (Canada; $32, four hours, five daily). The company has its own terminal in the Denny Triangle within easy walking distance to downtown.

Quick Shuttle (Map p230; www.quickcoach.com; ☏) Fast and efficient (plus free on-board wi-fi), with five to six daily buses to Vancouver ($43). Picks up at the Best Western Executive Inn in Taylor Ave N near the Seattle Center. Grab the monorail or walk to downtown.

Cantrail (www.cantrail.com) Amtrak's bus connector; runs four daily services to Vancouver ($40) and picks up and drops off at King Street Station.

Bellair Airporter Shuttle (www.airporter.com) Runs buses to Yakima, Bellingham and Anacortes and stops at King Street Station (for Yakima) and the downtown Convention Center (for Bellingham and Anacortes).

---

stops (seven minutes) to the Westlake Center in downtown. Fares are $2.25/1.25 per adult/child.

The Piers

Nearly 200 cruise ships call in at Seattle annually. They dock at either Smith Cove Cruise Terminal (Pier 91), in the Magnolia neighborhood 2 miles north of downtown, or Bell Street Cruise Terminal (Pier 66). The latter is adjacent to downtown and far more convenient. Many cruise lines pre-organize land transportation for their passengers. Check ahead.

The Victoria Clipper ferry from Victoria, Canada, docks at Pier 69 just south of the Olympic Sculpture Park in Belltown. Washington State Ferries services from Bremerton and Bainbridge Island use Pier 52.

Bus

Metro buses 24 and 19 connect Pier 91 in Magnolia with

---

downtown via the Seattle Center. Fares are a flat $2.50.

Shuttle Bus

Shuttle Express links SeaTac airport with the piers ($22) or downtown ($12).

Private Vehicle

If you are driving to Pier 52 for the car ferries leave I-5 at exit 164A (northbound) or exit 165B (southbound).

GETTING AROUND SEATTLE

Bicycle

Many streets downtown have commuter bike lanes. Pick up a copy of the *Seattle Bicycling Guide Map*, published by the City of Seattle's **Transportation Bicycle & Pedestrian Program** (www.seattle.gov/trans portation/bikemaps.htm) and available at bike shops (or

THIS CITY WAS MADE FOR WALKING

Yes the monorail was highly revolutionary in 1962, and the streetcar will bring back pleasant memories of the 1930s if you're over 85, but on a pleasant clear spring day in Seattle, you can't beat the visceral oxygen-drinking act of walking. Because most of Seattle's through-traffic is funneled north–south along one of three main arteries (I-5, the Alaskan Way Viaduct and Aurora Ave N), the central streets aren't as manic as you'd imagine. In Belltown and Pioneer Square your worst hassle is a few innocuous panhandlers, in downtown the hills might slow your progress slightly, while on the waterfront you'll need to watch out for the seagulls – and the tourists! Seattle's most walkable neighborhoods are leafy Capitol Hill and Queen Anne. If you're really adventurous, ditch the car/bus/train and explore the U District, Fremont and Ballard on that entertaining alfresco people-watching bonanza, the Burke-Gilman Trail.

downloadable from the website). The website also has options for ordering delivery the printed map (free of charge).

The best non-motor traffic route is the scenic Burke-Gilman Trail that passes through the northern neighborhoods of the U District, Wallingford, Fremont and Ballard. Other handy bike paths are the Ship Canal Trail on the north side of Queen Anne, Myrtle Edwards Park, Green Lake Park and the Cheshiahud Loop around Lake Union.

Seattle and all of King County require that bicyclists wear helmets. If you're caught without one, you can be fined $30 to $80 on the spot. Most places that rent bikes will rent helmets to go with them, sometimes for a small extra fee. It's also important to make sure your bike has sufficient lights and reflectors attached.

Boat

The most useful inter-neighborhood boat route is the water taxi that connects the downtown waterfront (Pier 50) with West Seattle (Seacrest Park). The water taxi runs hourly every day in summer and weekdays only in winter. The fare is $4 for the 10-minute crossing.

Bus

Buses are operated by **Metro Transit** (www.metro.kingcounty.gov), part of the King County Department of Transportation. The website prints schedules and maps and has a trip planner.

To make things simple, all bus fares within Seattle city limits are a flat $2.50 at peak hours (6am to 9am and 3pm to 6pm weekdays). Off-peak rates are $2.25. Those aged six to 18 pay $1.25; kids under six are free; seniors and travelers with disabilities pay $0.75. Most of the time you pay or show your transfer when you board. Your transfer ticket is valid for three hours from time of purchase. Most buses can carry two to three bikes.

There are four RapidRide bus routes (A to D) with two more coming on board in 2014. Of interest to travelers are lines C (downtown to West Seattle) and D (downtown to Ballard). RapidRide buses are faster and more frequent (every 10 minutes).

Be aware that very few buses operate between 1:30am and 5am, so if you're a long way from home when the bars close, plan on calling a cab instead.

Car & Motorcycle

Driving

Seattle traffic is disproportionately heavy and chaotic for a city of its size, and parking is scarce and expensive. Add to that the city's bizarrely cobbled-together mishmash of skewed grids, the hilly terrain and the preponderance of one-way streets and it's easy to see why driving downtown is best avoided if at all possible.

Rental

Although it can be a hassle in the city, having your own set of wheels can be handy for reaching neighborhoods that are further afield, such as Ballard or Georgetown, and for exploring areas outside of Seattle proper. To rent a car, you need a valid driver's license and a major credit card.

There are rental agencies in Sea-Tac airport, located in the baggage-claim area, with pickup and drop-off service from the 1st floor of the garage. Car-rental agencies within Seattle include the following:

Avis (☑800-331-1212; www.avis.com)

Budget (☑800-527-0700; www.budget.com)

Dollar (☑800-800-3665; www.dollar.com)

Enterprise (☑800-261-7331; www.enterprise.com)

Hertz (☑800-654-3131; www.hertz.com)

Another good option for those who need only limited use of a vehicle is **FlexCar** (☑206-332-0330; www.flexcar.com; membership per year $50, rates per hr/day $7/69). Membership (there's a one-time

$25 application fee) gives you access to a number of car-sharing vehicles distributed throughout the city. Members can make reservations online or by phone for as long as they need the car, then return it to the parking place where they picked it up when they're done. Rules for gas and mileage charges vary depending on which plan you choose.

Light Rail

Sound Transit (www.sound transit.org) operates Link Light Rail. The first – and, as yet, only – Seattle line, Central Link, runs from Sea-Tac airport to Westlake Station in downtown and opened in 2009. There are 13 stations including stops in SoDo, the International District and Pioneer Square. Fares within the city limits are $2.25. From downtown to the airport costs $2.75. Trains run between 5am and 12:30am.

An extension of the Link line, University Link, is under construction and due to open in 2016. It will add two more stations, one in Capitol Hill and one in the U District. By 2021 it is expected that further lines will be built, north to Northgate, and east to Mercer Island and Bellevue.

Streetcar

The revival of the **Seattle Streetcar** (www.seattle streetcar.org) was initiated in 2007 with the opening of the 2.6-mile South Lake Union line that runs between the Westlake Center and Lake Union. There are 11 stops and fares cost a standard $2.50/1.25 per adult/child. Streetcars breeze by every 15 minutes from 6am to 9pm (slightly later on Friday and Saturday). A second 10-stop line will open in 2014 running from Pioneer Square via the International District and First Hill to Capitol Hill.

Roll-out plans for future streetcar lines are extensive, with links earmarked for Fremont, Ballard and the U District.

Taxi

You can hail a cab from the street, but it's a safer bet to call and order one. All Seattle taxi cabs operate at the same rate, set by King County. At the time of research the rate was $2.50 at meter drop, then $2.70 per mile. There may be an additional charge for extra passengers and baggage. Any of the following offer reliable taxi services:

Orange Cab Co (☑206-444-0409; www.orangecab.net)

STITA Taxi (☑206-246-9999; www.stitataxi.com)

Yellow Cab (☑206-622-6500; www.yellowtaxi.net)

TOURS

Seattle offers some first-rate city tours undertaken by various means of transportation. Some tours are neighborhood specific; others cover a particular topic (coffee and beer tours are popular); many pull together the city's best sights.

Argosy Cruises Seattle Harbor Tour (Map p224; www.argosycruises.com; Pier 55; adult/child $23.50/12) Argosy's popular Seattle Harbor Tour is a one-hour narrated tour of Elliott Bay, the waterfront and the Port of Seattle. It departs from Pier 55.

Bill Speidel's Underground Tour (Map p228; ☑206-682-4646; www.under groundtour.com; 608 1st Ave; adult/senior/child $17/14/9; ⊙departs every 30min 11am-4pm Oct-Mar, to 6pm Apr-Sep) Seattle's famous 'underground' tour, which takes you through the tunnels and sidewalks hidden beneath the streets of

Pioneer Square, might get a little corny at times, but it delivers the goods on historic Seattle as a rough and rowdy industrial town. The tour starts at Doc Maynard's Public House, named after one of the city's founding fathers and quite a character. It is massively popular, especially in prime tourist season. No reservations are accepted, so try to arrive half an hour early if you want to be sure you get in.

Ride the Ducks of Seattle (Map p230; ☑206-441-4687; www.ridethe ducksofseattle.com; 516 Broad St; adult/child $28/17; ⊛) This national tour franchise uses amphibious trucks to cart you around Seattle's main sights and takes a dip in Lake Union at the end. Drivers add humor. Good for kids.

Seattle by Foot (☑206-508-7017; www.seattleby foot.com; tours $20-25) Offers a fine quintet of highly rated walking tours, including a coffee crawl, a beer tour and a specific kids tour.

See Seattle Walking Tours (☑425-226-7641; www.see-seattle.com; tours $20; ⊙10am Mon-Sat) See Seattle runs a variety of theme tours, from public-art walks to scavenger hunts. While reservations aren't required for the walking tour that starts at the Westlake Center, they are recommended. A Sunday tour will run if at least six people have signed up.

Tillicum Village (Map p224; ☑206-933-8600; www.tillicumvillage.com; adult/senior/child $79.95/72.95/30; ⊙Mar-Dec) From Pier 55, take a trip to Blake Island, the birthplace of Seattle's namesake Chief Sealth. The four-hour trip includes a salmon bake, a native dance and a movie at an old Duwamish village.

Directory A–Z

Customs Regulations

US Customs allows each person over the age of 21 to bring 1L of liquor and 200 cigarettes duty-free into the USA. US citizens are allowed to import, duty-free, up to $800 worth of gifts from abroad, while non-US citizens are allowed to import $100 worth. If you're carrying more than $10,000 in US and foreign cash, traveler's checks, money orders etc, you need to declare the excess amount. There is no legal restriction on the amount that may be imported, but undeclared sums in excess of $10,000 will probably be subject to investigation. If you're bringing prescription drugs, make sure they're in clearly marked containers. For updates, check www.customs.gov.

Discount Cards

If you're going to be in Seattle for a while and plan on seeing its premier attractions, consider buying a **CityPass** (www.citypass.com/seattle; adult/child aged 4-12yr $74/49). Good for nine days, the pass gets you entry into the Space Needle, EMP Museum, Pacific Science Center, Seattle Aquarium, Argosy Cruises' Seattle Harbor Tour, and Museum of Flight *or* Woodland Park Zoo. You wind up saving about 50% on admission

costs and you never have to stand in line. You can buy one at any of the venues or online.

Electricity

120V/60Hz

120V/60Hz

Emergency

Community Information Line (☑206-461-3200) Information on emergency services, housing, legal advice etc.

Police, Fire & Ambulance (☑911)

Seattle Police (☑206-625-5011)

Washington State Patrol (☑425-649-4370)

Gay & Lesbian Travelers

Seattle is a progressive, left-leaning city with thriving gay and lesbian communities; census data shows that approximately 12.9% of the city's population identifies itself as gay or lesbian, and there doesn't tend to be much sexual-orientation-based hostility among the rest of the population.

At research time, the Seattle LGBT Community Center had been forced to move out of its current location and was looking for a new home.

Some other resources and events to look for:

➡ **Seattle Gay News** (www. sgn.org) A weekly newspaper focusing on gay issues.

➡ **Outcity** (www.outcity.com) A color magazine that focuses on the cities of Seattle, Portland, OR, Vancouver (Canada) and Victoria (Canada).

➡ **Seattle Lesbian & Gay Film Festival** (www.three dollarbillcinema.org) Usually held in the third week of October.

➡ **Seattle Pride** (www.seattle pride.org) Seattle's popular gay-pride parade occurs in June. Seattle Out and Proud, the organization that runs the gay-pride festivities, also serves as an information center.

Internet Access

Seattle seems to be one big wi-fi hot spot. It's free nearly everywhere, in most hotels, many bars and all but a handful of coffee shops. The city had an experiment with free municipal wi-fi beginning in the mid-2000s, but it has recently been discontinued. However, free wi-fi is still provided on some Sound Transit trains, all RapidRide buses and Washington State Ferries (for the latter you must subscribe through Boingo).

Legal Matters

If you're arrested, you have the right to remain silent. There is no legal reason to speak to a police officer if you don't wish to – especially since anything you say 'can and will be used against you' – but never walk away from an officer until given permission. All persons who are arrested have the legal right to make one phone call. If you don't have a lawyer or a family member to help you, call your consulate. The police will give you the number upon request.

Medical Services

As a visitor, know that all hospital emergency rooms are obliged to receive sick or injured patients whether they can pay or not.

Clinics

If you're sick or injured, but not badly enough for a trip to the emergency room, try one of the following options:

45th St Community Clinic (☑206-633-3350; 1629 N 45th St) Medical and dental services.

Harborview Medical Center (☑206-731-3000; 325 9th Ave) Full medical care, with emergency room.

US HealthWorks Medical Group (☑206-682-7418; 1151 Denny Way) Walk-in clinic for nonemergencies.

Money

The US dollar is divided into 100 cents. US coins come in denominations of one cent (penny), five cents (nickel), 10 cents (dime), 25 cents (quarter), the practically extinct 50 cents (half-dollar) and the not-often-seen golden dollar coin, which was introduced in 2000.

Notes come in $1, $2, $5, $10, $20, $50 and $100 denominations.

ATMs

ATMs are easy to find: there's practically one per block in the busier commercial areas, as well as one outside every bank. Many bars, restaurants and grocery stores also have the machines, although the service fees for these can be steep ($2 to $4, plus your own bank's fees). Getting money this way saves you a step – no need to change money from your own currency – and is a safer way to travel, as you only take out what you need as you go.

Changing Money

Banks and moneychangers will give you US currency based on the current exchange rate.

American Express (Amex; 600 Stewart St; ⊙8:30am-5:30pm Mon-Fri)

Travelex-Thomas Cook Currency Services Sea-Tac airport (⊙6am-8pm); Westlake Center (400 Pine St, Level 3; ⊙9:30am-6pm Mon-Sat, 11am-5pm Sun) The booth at the main airport terminal is behind the Delta Airlines counter.

Credit & Debit Cards

Major credit cards are accepted at most hotels, restaurants and shops throughout Seattle, although visitors will find that many smaller cafes and restaurants will tack on an extra 30c or 50c amount for paying with plastic. Places that accept Visa and MasterCard generally also accept (and will often prefer) debit cards, which deduct payments directly from your check or savings account. Be sure to confirm with your bank before you leave that your debit card will be accepted in other states or countries. Debit cards from large commercial banks can often be used worldwide.

If your cards are lost or stolen, contact the issuing company immediately. Toll-free numbers for the main credit-card companies:

American Express (☑800-528-4800)

Diners Club (☑800-999-9093)

Discover (☑800-347-2683)

MasterCard (☑800-627-8372)

Visa (☑800-847-2911)

Traveler's Checks

This old-school option offers the traveler protection from theft or loss. Checks issued by American Express and Thomas Cook are widely accepted, and both offer efficient replacement policies. Keeping a record of the check numbers and the checks you've used is vital when it comes to replacing lost checks. Keep this record in a separate place from the checks themselves.

Bring most of the checks in large denominations. Toward the end of a trip you may want to change a small check to make sure you aren't left with too much local currency. Of course, traveler's checks are losing popularity due to the proliferation of ATMs and you may opt not to carry any at all.

Newspapers & Magazines

Seattle's newspapers and magazines include the following.

Northwest Asian Weekly (www.nwasianweekly.com)

Puget Sound Business Journal (www.bizjournals. com/seattle) Daily.

RealChange (www.real changenews.org) Weekly paper focused on the city's homeless community.

Seattle Daily Journal of Commerce (www.djc.com) Focuses on the region's business world.

Seattle Gay News (www. sgn.org) A weekly newspaper focusing on gay issues.

Seattle Magazine (www. seattlemag.com) A slick monthly lifestyle magazine.

Seattle Post-Intelligencer (www.seattlepi.com) The former morning daily, now online only.

Seattle Times (www.seattle times.com) The state's largest daily paper.

Seattle Weekly (www.seattle weekly.com) Free weekly with news and entertainment listings.

Stranger (www.thestranger. com) Irreverent and intelligent free weekly, edited by Dan Savage of 'Savage Love' fame.

Opening Hours

Banks 9am or 10am to 5pm or 6pm weekdays; some also 10am to 2pm Saturday.

Businesses 9am to 5pm or 6pm weekdays; some also 10am to 5pm Saturday.

Restaurants breakfast 7am to 11am, brunch 7am to 3pm, lunch 11:30am to 2:30pm, dinner 5:30pm to 10pm.

Shops 9am or 10am to 5pm or 6pm (or 9pm in shopping malls) weekdays, noon to 5pm (later in malls) weekends; some places open till 8pm or 9pm.

Post

At time of research, rates for 1st-class mail within the US were 46c for letters up to 1oz and 33c for postcards. For package and international-letter rates, which vary, check with the local post office or with the online postal-rate calculator (http://ircalc.usps.gov). For other postal-service questions, call ☑800-275-8777 or visit the US Post Office website (www.usps.com).

Seattle's most convenient post office locations are:

Main branch (Map p224; 301 Union St; ⊗8:30am-5:30pm Mon-Fri)

University Station (Map p242; ☑206-675-8114; 4244 University Way NE, U District)

Broadway Station (Map p236; ☑206-324-5474; 101 Broadway E)

Queen Anne (Map p234; 415 1st Ave N)

Public Holidays

National public holidays are celebrated throughout the USA. On public holidays, banks, schools and government offices (including post offices) are closed and public transportation follows a Sunday schedule. Plan ahead if you're traveling during many public holidays. Flights are full, highways are jammed and on Christmas and Thanksgiving, many grocery stores and restaurants close for the day.

New Year's Day January 1

Martin Luther King Jr Day Third Monday in January

Presidents' Day Third Monday in February

Easter Sunday March or April

Memorial Day Last Monday in May

Independence Day (Fourth of July) July 4

Labor Day First Monday in September

Columbus Day Second Monday in October

Veterans' Day November 11

Thanksgiving Day Fourth Thursday in November

Christmas Day December 25

Telephone

Phone numbers within the USA consist of a three-digit area code followed by a seven-digit local number. If you're calling long distance, dial 1 plus the three-digit area code plus the seven-digit number. To call internationally, first dial 011 then the country code and phone number.

Phone numbers in Seattle have a 206 area code. Even local calls made to the same area code require you to dial the full 10-digit number (no need to dial 1 first, though).

Toll-free numbers are prefixed with an 800, 877, 866 or 888 area code. Some toll-free numbers for local businesses or government offices only work within the state or the Seattle region, but most can be dialed from abroad. Just be aware that you'll be connected at regular long-distance rates, which could become a costly option if the line you're dialing tends to park customers on hold.

Time

Seattle is in the Pacific Standard Time time zone:

➡ two hours ahead of Hawaii (Hawaii-Aleutian Standard Time)

➡ one hour ahead of Alaska (Alaska Standard Time)

➡ one hour behind Colorado (Mountain Standard Time)

➡ two hours behind Alabama (Central Standard Time)

➡ three hours behind New York (Atlantic Standard Time)

In spring and summer, as in most of the time zones in the US, Pacific Standard Time becomes Pacific Daylight Time. Clocks are reset an hour forward in early spring, and reset an hour back in early fall.

Tourist Information

The main visitor center, **Seattle Visitor Center & Concierge Services** (Map p224; ☑206-461-5840; www. visitseattle.org; Washington State Convention Center, E Pike St & 7th Ave; ⊙9am-5pm) is inside the Washington State Convention and Trade Center. It also operates the useful Citywide Concierge service.

Travelers with Disabilities

All public buildings (including hotels, restaurants, theaters and museums) are required by law to provide wheelchair access and to have appropriate restroom facilities available. Telephone companies provide relay operators for the hearing impaired. Many banks provide ATM instructions in Braille. Dropped curbs are standard at intersections throughout the city.

Around 80% of Metro's buses are equipped with wheelchair lifts. Timetables marked with an 'L' indicate wheelchair accessibility. Be sure to let the driver know if you need your stop to be called and, if possible, pull the cord when you hear the call. Seeing-eye dogs are allowed on Metro buses. Passengers with disabilities qualify for a reduced fare but first need to contact **Metro Transit** (www.metro.king county.gov) for a permit.

Most large private and chain hotels have suites for guests with disabilities. Many car-rental agencies offer hand-controlled models at no extra charge. Make sure you give at least two days' notice. All major airlines, Greyhound buses and Amtrak trains allow guide dogs to accompany passengers and often sell two-for-one packages when attendants of passengers with serious disabilities are required. Airlines will also provide assistance for connecting, boarding and disembarking. Ask for assistance when making your reservation.

The following organizations and tour providers specialize in the needs of travelers with disabilities:

Access-Able Travel Service (www.access-able. com) Packed full of information, with tips on scooter rental, wheelchair travel, accessible transportation and more.

Easter Seals of Washington (☑206-281-5700; http:// wa.easterseals.com) Provides technology assistance, workplace services and camps, among other things.

Society for Accessible Travel & Hospitality (☑212-447-7284; www.sath.org; No 610, 347 Fifth Ave, New York)

Visas

Foreigners needing visas to travel to the US should plan ahead. There is a reciprocal visa-waiver program in which citizens of certain countries may enter the USA for stays of 90 days or less with a passport but without first obtaining a visa. Currently these countries include Australia, Austria, Denmark, France, Germany, Italy, Japan, the Netherlands, New Zealand, Spain, Sweden, Switzerland and the UK. Under this program you must have a round-trip ticket that is nonrefundable in the USA, and you will not be allowed to extend your stay beyond 90 days.

As of January 2009, citizens of the 27 countries in the US Visa Waiver Program will need to register with the government online (https:// esta.cbp.dhs.gov) three days before their visit. The registration is valid for two years.

Other travelers will need to obtain a visa from a US consulate or embassy. In most countries, the process can be done by mail. Visa applicants may be required to 'demonstrate binding obligations' that will ensure their return home. Because of this requirement, those planning to travel through other countries before arriving in the USA are generally better off applying for their US visa while they are still in their home country, rather than after they're already on the road.

The nonimmigrant visitors visa is the most common visa. It is available in two forms: the B1 for business purposes and the B2 for tourism or visiting friends and relatives. The validity period for US visitor visas depends on which country you're from. The length of time you'll be allowed to stay in the USA is ultimately determined by US immigration authorities at the port of entry. Non-US citizens with HIV should know that they can be excluded from entry to the USA.

For updates on visas and other security issues, you can visit the US government's visa page (www. unitedstatesvisas.us), the **US Department of State** (www.travel.state.gov) and the **Travel Security Administration** (www.tsa.gov).

Behind the Scenes

SEND US YOUR FEEDBACK

We love to hear from travelers – your comments keep us on our toes and help make our books better. Our well-traveled team reads every word on what you loved or loathed about this book. Although we cannot reply individually to postal submissions, we always guarantee that your feedback goes straight to the appropriate authors, in time for the next edition. Each person who sends us information is thanked in the next edition – the most useful submissions are rewarded with a selection of digital PDF chapters.

Visit **lonelyplanet.com/contact** to submit your updates and suggestions or to ask for help. Our award-winning website also features inspirational travel stories, news and discussions.

Note: We may edit, reproduce and incorporate your comments in Lonely Planet products such as guidebooks, websites and digital products, so let us know if you don't want your comments reproduced or your name acknowledged. For a copy of our privacy policy visit lonelyplanet.com/privacy.

OUR READERS

Many thanks to the travellers who used the last edition and wrote to us with helpful hints, useful advice and interesting anecdotes:

Richard Becker, Kathleen Drozdowski, Marion Kaempfer, Saskia Kuliga, Kathryn Morris, Laura Sapelly

AUTHOR THANKS

Brendan Sainsbury

Thanks to all the untold bus drivers, tourist-info volunteers, restaurateurs, coffee baristas and indie punk rockers who helped me during my research. Special thanks to my wife, Liz, and seven-year-old son, Kieran, for their company on the road and to Sebastian Simsch for his insights into the Seattle coffee scene.

Celeste Brash

Thanks to my family for helping me research beaches and mountains some days, and getting on at home without me on others. To old friends who I found scattered across Washington and to too many new friends to mention! It was wonderful to work with Suki Gear and from Brendan Sainsbury's excellent base text.

ACKNOWLEDGMENTS

Cover photograph: Seattle skyline at night, Donald E Hall/Getty Images.

THIS BOOK

This 6th edition of Lonely Planet's *Seattle* guidebook was researched and written by Brendan Sainsbury. Celeste Brash wrote the Day Trips chapter. The previous three editions were written by Becky Ohlsen. This guidebook was commissioned in Lonely Planet's Oakland office, and produced by the following:

Commissioning Editor Suki Gear
Coordinating Editors Sarah Bailey, Carolyn Bain
Senior Cartographer Alison Lyall
Coordinating Cartographer David Kemp
Coordinating Layout Designer Jacqui Saunders
Managing Editors Sasha Baskett, Bruce Evans
Senior Editor Catherine Naghten

Managing Layout Designers Chris Girdler, Jane Hart
Assisting Editor Ross Taylor
Cover Research Naomi Parker
Internal Image Research Aude Vauconsant
Thanks to Ryan Evans, Larissa Frost, Genesys India, Jouve India, Trent Paton, Dianne Schallmeiner, Lyahna Spencer, John Taufa, Gerard Walker

See also separate subindexes for:

✕ **EATING P218**

🍷 **DRINKING & NIGHTLIFE P219**

☆ **ENTERTAINMENT P220**

🔒 **SHOPPING P220**

🏃 **SPORTS & ACTIVITIES P221**

🛏 **SLEEPING P221**

Index

A

accommodations 13, 15, 179-88, *see also individual neighborhoods*, Sleeping *subindex*

activities 20-1, 31-3, 118-19, **118**, **119**, *see also individual activities*, Sports & Activities *subindex*

airport 204-5

Alaskan Way Viaduct 13, 59, 67

Alexie, Sherman 198

Alice in Chains 201, 202

Alki Beach 23, 33, 163

Alki Beach Park 163

Alki Point Lighthouse 163

Allen, Paul 82, 194, 197

Amazon 13, 191, 198

ambulance 208

Anderson, Ernestine 200

antiques 74

apatosaurs 143

aquariums 23, 48, **22**

architecture 19

  Ballard 154-5

  downtown 50-1

  Pioneer Square 64, 65, 69

  Queen Anne 96

  Richardsonian Romanesque 65, 70

Arctic Building 48

area codes 210

art

  classes 164, 167

  festivals 21

  galleries 19, 74, 164, 199

Sights 000

Map Pages **000**

Photo Pages **000**

  public art 10, 18, 41, 124-5, 141-2, 163, **10**, **109**, **125**, **141**

  walks 74, 164, 199

arts 29, 198-9, *see also* literature, music

ATMs 209

B

Bainbridge Island 169

Bainbridge Island Winery 172

Ballard & Discovery Park 12, 39, 149-58, **149**, **246-7**

  accommodations 188

  architecture 154-5

  drinking & nightlife 150, 156-7

  entertainment 157

  food 150, 153-4, 156

  highlights 12, 149, 151, 153

  history 154-5

  shopping 157-8

  sights 149, 151, 152, 153

  sports & activities 158

  transportation 150

  walks 154-5, **155**

Ballard Building 155

Ballard Farmers Market 152

Ballard Savings & Loan Building 154

Barry, Lynda 198

bars 27-8, *see also* Drinking & Nightlife *subindex*

baseball 31

basketball 31-2, 92

Bastille Bash 127

Bathhouse Theater 144

Bauer, Eddie 174

beaches 23, 33, 129, 144, 163

beer 27, 166

Bell Tower 155

Belltown & Seattle Center 11, 39, 76-92, **76**, **230-1**

  accommodations 184-5

  children 22

  drinking & nightlife 77, 85, 88-9, 90

  entertainment 77, 85, 90-1

  food 11, 77, 84, 86-8

  highlights 6, 9, 11, 76, 78-82

  history 90

  shopping 91-2

  sights 78-82, 83-4

  sports & activities 92

  transportation 77

  walks 85, **85**

Benaroya Concert Hall 47

Bergen Place Park 152

Best of the Northwest 21

Betty Bowen Park 96

bicycling 32, 205-6

  Burke-Gilman Trail 133

  rental 23, 61-2, 138, 158, 167

  tours 61-2

Bill & Melinda Gates Foundation Visitor Center 13, 83

Blake Island 169, 171

boat tours 23, 207

boat travel 12, 167, 171, 205, 206, **170**, **12**

boating 32, 96-7, 148

Boeing Airplane Company 95, 161, 194, 195

  factory tours 62

Boeing, William E 195

books 190, 193, 198

bookstores 34, 35, *see also* Shopping *subindex*

Borofsky, Jonathan 47

brands 197

brewpubs 27, 28, *see also* Drinking & Nightlife *subindex*

Bumbershoot 21

Burke Museum 132

Burke-Gilman Trail 23, 32, 131, 133, 150

bus travel 205, 206

business hours, *see* opening hours

C

cafes 9, 27-8, **8**, *see also* Eating *subindex*, Drinking & Nightlife *subindex*

camping (Mt Rainier) 178

cannabis legalisation 190-1

canoeing 32, 138, 148

Capitol Hill 9, 39, 105-17, **105**, **236-7**, **8**

  accommodations 186-7

  drinking & nightlife 106, 113-16

  entertainment 115-16

  food 106, 110-13

  highlights 9, 105

  shopping 116-17

  sights 107

  sports & activities 117

  transportation 106

car travel 205, 206-7

Carbon River (Mt Rainier) 178

Carl English Jr Botanical Gardens 153

Carnation (Snoqualmie Valley) 176

cartoonists 198

Carver, Raymond 198

Cascade Falls (Orcas Island) 173

CD, the 39, 120-9, **120**, **240**

  drinking & nightlife 121, 128

  food 121, 127-8

  highlights 120, 121

  history 123

  sights 122-3

  transportation 121

cell phones 14

Center for Wooden Boats 23, 96-7

Center on Contemporary Art (COCA) 152, 199

Central District, *see* CD

Central Plaza 132

Charles, Ray 126, 200

chefs 13, 25

Cherry Blossom & Japanese Cultural Festival 20
Cheshiahud Loop 13, 104
Chihuly, Dale 13, 78-9, 199
Chihuly Garden & Glass 13, 78-9, **78**, **108**
children, travel with 22-3
Children's Museum 83-4
Chinese New Year 20
cinema, *see* films
cinemas 30, *see also* Entertainment *subindex*
CityPass 81, 208
climate 15, 20-1
clubs, *see* Drinking & Nightlife *subindex*
Cobain, Kurt 122, 126, 201
Cobb Building 51
COCA, *see* Center on Contemporary Art
coffee, *see also* Drinking & Nightlife *subindex*
  chains 198
  culture 9, 27, 53, 197, **8**
  Starbucks 57
  tours 49
Collins, Luther 192
Colman Park 123
Columbia Center 52
contemporary art 199
Cornish College of the Arts 83
Cors & Wegener Building 155
costs 14-15, 19, 25, 77, 180, 208
courses
  acrobatics 167
  art 164, 167
  glassblowing 79, 92
credit cards 209
cruise ships 205
culture 190-1, 196-9
currency 14
customs regulations 208
cycling, *see* bicycling

D
Daybreak Star Indian Cultural Center 151
Denny Blaine Park 122
Denny Hill 194
Denny Park 97
Denny party 192
Denny Triangle 84
development 190-1
Dillon, Matt 25, 71
disabilities, travelers with 211

Discovery Park 12, 23, 151, **3**, **12**, **119**, **151**
Discovery Park area, *see* Ballard & Discovery Park
Discovery Park Environmental Learning Center 151
diving 32, 104
Douglas, Tom 13, 25, 86, 87, 88, 101, 102
downtown 39, 40-62, **40**, **224-5**
  accommodations 182-3
  architecture 50-1
  drinking & nightlife 41, 55-6
  entertainment 57-8
  food 41, 50, 52
  highlights 40, 42-6
  shopping 58-9
  sights 42-6, 47-8
  sports & activities 61-2
  transportation 41
  walks 50-1, **51**
drinking & nightlife 27-8, *see also* Drinking & Nightlife *subindex*
drinks, *see* beer, coffee, wine
driving 205, 206-7
Drumheller Fountain 132
Duvall (Snoqualmie Valley) 176
Duwamish Head 163
Duwamish language 199
Duwamish people 192

E
Eagle, The 83
earthquakes 195
economy 190-1, 195
electricity 208
Elephant Super Car Wash 84
emergencies 208
EMP Museum 9, 82, **3**, **9**, **82**, **98**, **124**
entertainment 29-30, *see also* Entertainment *subindex*
Ethiopian community 123
etiquette 196
events 20-1, 127
Everett 62
Experience Music Project, *see* EMP Museum

F
Fantagraphics publishers 166, 198
farmers markets 137, 152

ferries 12, 167, 171, 206, **170**, **12**
Ferris wheels 13, 48, **37**
festivals 20-1, 127
film festivals 21, 29
films 190, 199
fire department 208
Firefighters' Memorial 66
First Hill 39, 105-17, **105**, **236-7**
  accommodations 186-7
  drinking & nightlife 106
  food 106, 113
  highlights 105
  sights 107-10
  transportation 106
Fishermen's Terminal 152
food 13, 24-6, *see also* Eating *subindex*
  children, eating with 22
  costs 25
  farmers markets 137, 152
  innovation 191
  Northwest cuisine 24
  opening hours 25
  restaurant reservations 25
  tours 49
football 31, 75
Fort Lawton 151
Foster Island Wetlands Trail 33, 122
Foster/White Gallery 67
free attractions 19
Freeway Park 48
Frelard 156
Fremont 39, 139-48, **139**, **244**
  accommodations 140, 188
  culture 143
  drinking & nightlife 140, 146-7
  entertainment 147
  food 140, 145
  highlights 10, 139, 140, 141-2
  history 143
  shopping 147
  sights 141-2, 143-4
  tours 146
  transportation 140
Fremont Bridge 143
Fremont Rocket 142, **10**
Fremont Street Fair 21
Fremont Sunday Market 143
Fremont Troll 141, **109**
Frye Art Museum 110, 199
Future of Flight Aviation Center & Boeing Tour 62

G
Gable House 96
Gallagher, Tess 198
galleries 19, 74, 164, 199
gardens 19
Garfield High School 126, 202
Gas Works Park 148
Gates, Bill 13, 83, 194, 197
gay travelers 208-9
  festivals & events 21
  venues 28, 106
Gehry, Frank 82
Georgetown 39, 159-67, **159**, **239**
  accommodations 188
  drinking & nightlife 160, 165, 166
  entertainment 166
  food 160, 163-4
  highlights 10, 159, 161
  history 166
  shopping 160, 166
  sights 161, 162-3
  sports & activities 167
  transportation 160
Georgetown Arts & Cultural Center 162
Georgetown Steam Plant 162
glassblowing 78-9, 92, 162-3, 199
gold rush 66, 194, 195
Golden Gardens Park 152
golf 32
Graham, John Jr 80
Graham Visitors Center 122
Grand Central Arcade 65
Gray, Robert 192
Great Fire 193-4
Green Lake 33
Green Lake Aqua Theater 144
Green Lake area 39, 139-48, **139**, **245**
  accommodations 188
  drinking & nightlife 140, 147
  entertainment 147
  food 140, 145-6
  highlights 139, 144
  shopping 148
  sights 144-5
  sports & activities 148
  transportation 140
Green Lake Park 33, 144
Green River 201
Groening, Matt 198

grunge music 90, 103, 126, 195, 201, 202
GS Sanborn Building 154
guidepost 142
gum wall 43, **3**, **125**
Guterson, David 198
gyms 62, 92

H
Hammering Man 47, **46**, **109**
happy hours 28
Hau Hau Market 68
Heart 200
Hendrix, Jimi 82, 107, 123, 126, 200
Henry Art Gallery 132, 199
High Point 163
hiking 33, 176, 177
Hing Hay Park 68
hip-hop 202
Hiram M Chittenden Locks 23, 153
history 192-5
  Ballard 154-5
  Belltown 90
  CD, the 123
  Fremont 143
  Georgetown 166
  Pioneer Square area 69, 193
History House 143-4
holidays 210
homelessness 72
Hooverville 193
horse riding 174
Howell Park 122
Hugo, Richard 198

I
Icons of Science Fiction 82
immigration 123, 194
innovation 191, 197
International Children's Park 68
International District 39, 63-75, **63**, **228-9**
  accommodations 184
  drinking & nightlife 64, 73
  food 64, 71-2
  highlights 63
  shopping 74-5
  sights 67-8
  transportation 64

Sights 000
Map Pages **000**
Photo Pages **000**

International Fountain 84
internet access 209
internet resources 14, 15, 32, 210
itineraries 16-17

J
Japanese community 20, 195
Japanese Garden 122
jazz 90, 91, 200
Jimi Hendrix Park 123
Jimi Hendrix statue 107
jogging 33
Jones, Quincy 126, 200

K
kayaking 32, 104, 138, 148, 167
Kerry Park 94, 96
KEXP radio station 202
King Street Station 66, 205
Klondike gold rush 66, 194, 195
Klondike Gold Rush National Historical Park 66
Krab Jab Studio 164

L
Lake Union 97
Lake Union area 13, 39, 93-104, **93**, **234-5**
  accommodations 185-6
  drinking & nightlife 94, 102
  entertainment 103
  food 94, 101
  highlights 93, 95, 97
  shopping 103
  sights 95, 96-7
  sports & activities 94, 104
  transportation 94
Lake Union Park 97
Lakeview Cemetery 107
languages 14, 199
Larson, Gary 198
Lee, Brandon 107
Lee, Bruce 107
legal matters 209
Lenin statue 141, **125**
lesbian travelers 208-9
  festivals & events 21
  venues 28, 106
Lewis, Ryan 202
lifestyle 196-7
light rail 15, 110, 204, 205, 207

Lime Kiln Point State Park (San Juan Island) 173
literature 190, 193, 198
Log House Museum 163
Longmire Hiker Information Center (Mt Rainier) 177
Longmire Museum (Mt Rainier) 177
Lopez Island 172-5
Lopez Island Vineyards 174
Louisa Boren Lookout 107
Lower Queen Anne 101

M
Macklemore 202
Madison Park 39, 120-9, **120**, **240**
  drinking & nightlife 121, 128
  food 121, 123, 127
  highlights 120, 121
  shopping 128-9
  sights 122
  sports & activities 129
  transportation 121
Madison Valley 121, 123, 127, 129
Madrona 39, 120-9, **120**, **240**
  drinking & nightlife 121
  food 121, 128
  highlights 120, 121
  sights 123
  sports & activities 129
  transportation 121
magazines 210
manholes 41
maps 38, 222-47
market roll call 45
markets 35, 68, 143
  farmers markets 137, 152
  Pike Place Market 6, 41, 42-5, **6**, **42**, **45**, **125**
McGinn, Michael 197
medical services 209
Mercer, Asa 193
microbrews 27
Microsoft 194, 195
Milepost 31 67
mobile phones 14
Moisture Festival 20
money 14, 25, 35, 180, 208, 209-10
monorail 48, 77, 88, **124**
Moran State Park (Orcas Island) 173
motorcycle travel 205, 206-7
Mount Zion Baptist Church 123

mountaineering 177
Mt Constitution (Orcas Island) 173
Mt Rainier National Park 176-8, **18**, **119**
Mudhoney 201, 202
murals 163
Museum of Flight 10, 23, 161, **11**, **161**
Museum of History & Industry 23, 95, **95**
museums 19, 23, 199
music 98-9, 200-2
  grunge 90, 126, 195, 201, 202
  live music 29, 30
  record stores 34, 35
Myrtle Edwards Park 32, 33, 83

N
Native American art 199
Native American languages 199
newspapers 72, 198, 210
Nickels, Greg 197
nightlife 27-8, see also Drinking & Nightlife subindex
Nirvana 201, 202, see also Cobain, Kurt
Nisqually (Mt Rainier) 177-8
Nordic Heritage Museum 152
North Bend (Snoqualmie Valley) 176
Northwest African American Museum 122-3
Northwest cuisine 24
Northwest Flower & Garden Show 20
Northwest Folklife Festival 20

O
observation decks 81
Occidental Park 66
Occidental Square 66
offbeat Seattle 19, 124-5, **124**, **125**
Ohanapecosh (Mt Rainier) 178
Olympic Sculpture Park 83
opening hours 210
  drinking & nightlife 28
  entertainment 30
  restaurants 25
  stores 35
Orcas Island (San Juan Islands) 172-5

Oregon Trail 192
Oxbow Park 162

P

Pacific Science Center 84
Paradise (Mt Rainier) 177
parks 19
Parsons Garden 96
Pearl Jam 103, 201, 202
picnics 133
Pike Place Market 6, 41, 42-5, **6**, **42**, **45**, **125**
Pike–Pine corridor 113
Pilchuck Glass School 79
pinball 23, 68
Pioneer Building 65
Pioneer Square 65, **65**
Pioneer Square area 39, 63-75, **63**, **228-9**
accommodations 184
architecture 64, 65, 69
drinking & nightlife 64, 72-3
entertainment 73
food 64, 70-1
highlights 63, 65
history 69, 193
shopping 74
sights 65, 66-7
sports & activities 75
transportation 64
walks 69, **69**
Pioneer Square Park 66
planning
budgeting 14-15, 19, 25, 180, 208
children, travel with 22-3
festivals & events 20-1
itineraries 16-17
repeat visitors 13
Seattle basics 14-15
Seattle's neighborhoods 38-9
travel seasons 15, 20-1
websites 14-15
poetry 198
police 208
politics 190-1, 197
population 191, 194
Portland Building 154
postal services 210
Presley, Elvis 88
public art 10, 18, 41, 124-5, **125**
Fremont 141-2, **10**, **109**, **141**
West Seattle 163
public holidays 210

public transportation 15, 110, 205-7
pubs 28, see also Drinking & Nightlife subindex
Puget Sound 12, 169, 171-2

Q

Quad 132-3
Queen Anne 39, 93-104, **93**, **234-5**
accommodations 185
architecture 96
drinking & nightlife 94, 102
entertainment 102-3
food 94, 97-101
highlights 93
shopping 103
sights 96
sports & activities 94, 104
transportation 94
Queen Anne Counterbalance 96
Queen Anne Hill 96
quirky Seattle 19, 124-5, **124**, **125**

R

Raban, Jonathan 198
Rachel the Market Pig 43, **125**
Rainier Beer 166
Rainier Tower 51
Rainier Vista 132
Ravenna Park 133
record stores 34, 35, see also Shopping subindex
Red Square 132
Richardson, Henry 70
Richardsonian Romanesque architecture 65, 70
Robbins, Tom 198
Roethke, Theodore 198
romantic spots 19
Roq La Rue 67, 199
Roving Gallery 164
running 33

S

Safeco Plaza 48
sailing 32, 96-7, 148
SAM, see Seattle Art Museum
Sammamish River Trail 32
San Juan Island National Historical Park 173
San Juan Islands 172-5
San Juan Vineyards (San Juan Island) 173

Scandinavian American Bank Building 154
sculpture 10, 18, 141-2
Seafair 21
seafood 24, 26, **24**
Sea-Tac International Airport 204-5
Seattle Aquarium 23, 48, **22**
Seattle Art Museum 46, 199, **46**
Seattle Asian Art Museum 107, 199, **109**
Seattle Center, see Belltown & Seattle Center
Seattle CityPass 81, 208
Seattle Fishermen's Memorial 152
Seattle Great Wheel 13, 48, **37**
Seattle International Film Festival 21
Seattle Lesbian & Gay Film Festival 21
Seattle Mariners 31, 75
Seattle Metropolitan Police Museum 67
Seattle Pinball Museum 23, 68
Seattle Pride Festival 21
Seattle Public Library 47
Seattle Rose Garden 144-5
Seattle Seahawks 31, 75
Seattle Sounders 32, 75
Seattle Tower 47-8
Seward Park 33
Shilshole Bay Marina 152
shopping 34-5, see also Shopping subindex
Simsch, Sebastian 53
Skid Row 68
Sleepless in Seattle 97, 190, 199
Smith Tower 65
Snoqualmie 176
Snoqualmie Valley 175-6
soccer 32, 75
social issues 72, 190-1, 197
SoDo 162
Sorrento Hotel 110
Soundgarden 201, 202
South Lake Union 13, 94, 100, 191
Space Needle 6, 80-1, **5**, **7**, **80**, **82**
Spencer Spit State Park (Lopez Island) 174
sports 31-3, see also individual sports, Sports & Activities subindex
stadiums 31-2, 75, 138
St James Cathedral 110

St Mark's Cathedral 107
Starbucks company 9, 27, 57, 162, 197
statues 10, 18, 141-2
Steinbrueck, Victor 80
Stimson-Green Mansion 110
Stowell, Ethan 13, 25, 88, 100, 112
streetcars 13, 110, 205, 207
Sub Pop Records 201, 202
Sunset Hill Park 152
Suzzallo Library 132
swimming 33, see also beaches

T

taxes 35
taxis 205, 207
telephone services 14, 210
theater 29, 30, see also Entertainment subindex
Theo Chocolate Factory 143, **17**
Three Piece Sculpture: Vertebrae 48
tickets 30, 32
time 14, 211
Times Square Building 48
tipping 25, 180
Totally Blown Glassworks 162-3
totem poles 66
tourist information 14, 211
tours 49, 207
bicycling 61-2
Boeing factory 62
children 23
coffee 49
food 49
Fremont 146
kayaking 32
Mt Rainier 177
Pike Place Market 49
walking 49, 207
train travel 205
traveler's checks 209-10
travel to Seattle 15, 204-5
travel within Seattle 15, 110, 205-7
Turret House 96
Turtleback Mountain Preserve (Orcas Island) 173-4
TV 199
Twin Peaks 176

U

U District 39, 130-8, **130**, **242-3**

U District continued
  accommodations 187-8
  drinking & nightlife 131, 136
  entertainment 137
  food 131, 133, 135-6
  highlights 130
  shopping 137-8
  sights 132-3
  sports & activities 138
  transportation 131
  walks 134, **134**
Union Station 68
University of Washington 132
Uptown 101
Uwajimaya 67-8, 75

V

vacations 210
Vancouver, George 192
Vashon Island 169
Victor Steinbrueck Park 49
viewpoints 18
Vij, Vikram 25, 101
Viking Days 21
vineyards 56, 172, 173, 174, 176
Viretta Park 122
visas 14, 211
visual arts 199
Volunteer Park Conservatory 107

W

Waiting for the Interurban 142, **141**
walking 206, see also hiking
walks
  art 74, 164, 199
  Ballard 154-5, **155**
  Belltown 85, **85**
  downtown 50-1, **51**
  Fremont 146
  Pioneer Square area 69, **69**
  tours 23, 49, 207
  trails 33, 104, 122
  U District 134, **134**
Wallingford 148
Washington Huskies 138
Washington Park Arboretum 33, 122

Washington State Convention & Trade Center 48
water taxis 167, 206, see also ferries
Water Tower Observation Deck 107
Waterfall Park 67
waterfront 39, 40-62, **40**, **224-5**, **5**
  accommodations 182
  drinking & nightlife 41, 56-7
  entertainment 58
  food 41, 55
  highlights 40
  shopping 60-1
  sights 48-9
  transportation 41
Watmough Head (Lopez Island) 174
weather 15, 20-1
websites 14, 15, 32, 210
West Point Lighthouse 151
West Seattle 39, 159-67, **159**
  drinking & nightlife 160, 165
  food 160, 164-5
  highlights 159
  murals 163
  shopping 160, 166-7
  sights 163
  sports & activities 167
  transportation 160, 167
Westervelt, Conrad 195
Westlake Center 48
whale-watching 172, 173
Whidbey Island 171
White River (Mt Rainier) 178
wine 56
wineries 56, 172, 173, 174, 176
Wing Luke Asian Museum 67
Winterfest 21
Woodinville (Snoqualmie Valley) 176
Woodland Park Zoo 23, 144
World's Fair 80, 88, 194
WWI 195
WWII 195

Y

Yesler Way 67, 68
yoga 117

Z

zoos 23, 144

✕ **EATING**

5 Spot 100
360 Local 86

A

Agua Verde Café 135
American Pie 163-4
Annapurna Cafe 112
Arabica Lounge 111

B

Bakeman's 71
Bakery Nouveau 164
Bar Sajor 71
Barolo Ristorante 87
Bastille Cafe & Bar 153
Bay Cafe (Lopez Island) 175
Beecher's Handmade Cheese 53-4
Belltown Pizza 86
Beth's Cafe 145-6
Bimbo's Cantina 111
Black Bottle 86
Blue Moon Burgers 101
Bluebird Microcreamery 111
Boulangerie 148
Buenos Aires Grill 88
Butter Butte (Mt Rainier) 178

C

Cactus 127
Cafe Besalu 153
Café Campagne 54
Cafe con Leche 162
Café Flora 127
Café Nola (Bainbridge Island) 172
Cafe Paloma 70
Café Presse 111
Cafe Selam 127-8
Cafe Soleil 128
Cafe Solstice 135
Canlis 101
Cascina Spinasse 112
Catfish Corner 128
Cedars Restaurant 135
Chaco Canyon Café 135
Chinook's at Salmon Bay 154, 156
Christopher's (Whidbey Island) 172
Cicchetti 101
Cinnamon Works 54
Coastal Kitchen 112

Copper Creek Inn (Mt Rainier) 177
Crumpet Shop 53
Cutter's Crabhouse 55
Cyber-Dogs 50
Cyclops 86

D

Dahlia Lounge 87
Delicatus 71
Dick's Drive-In 100
Duck Soup Inn (San Juan Island) 174

E

Elliott's Oyster House 55
Etta's Seafood 54-5
Ezell's Famous Chicken 128

F

FareStart Restaurant 86-7
Flowers 135
Fonda la Catrina 164
Fresh Flours 153
FX McRory's Steak, Chop & Oyster House 71

G

Georgian 52
Grand Central Baking Co 70
Green Leaf 71
Grub 100

H

Harbour Public House (Bainbridge Island) 172
Harvest Vine 127
Herbfarm (Snoqualmie Valley) 176
Hi Spot Café 128
Homegrown 145
Honeyhole 111
House of Hong 72
How to Cook a Wolf 100
Hunger 145
Hunt Club 113

I

Il Fornaio 52
Inès Patisserie 123
Ivar's Acres of Clams 55

Jade Garden 71

Kabul 148

La Carta de Oaxaca 153
La Isla 154
La Vita é Bella 86
Le Pichet 54
Lockspot Cafe 154
Lola 87-8
Lowells 54

Macrina 84, 86
Madison Park
  Conservatory 127
Mama's Mexican Kitchen
  86, 90
Mamnoon 111
Market Chef (San Juan
  Island) 174
Matt's in the Market 55
McCormick's Fish House
  & Bar 52
Mee Sum Pastries 54
Mighty-O Donuts 145
Mijita's (Orcas Island) 174
Molly Moon's 111
Mora Iced Creamery
  (Bainbridge Island) 172

National Park Inn
  (Mt Rainier) 177
Nell's 146
New Orleans Creole
  Restaurant 70

Oddfellows Cafe 111
Orange King 135
Osteria La Spiga 112

Palace Kitchen 87
Pam's Kitchen 136
Paradise Inn (Mt Rainier) 177
Paragon Bar & Grill 100-1
Paseo 145

Peso's Kitchen & Lounge
  100
Pete's Egg Nest 146
Pho Bac 71-2
Phoenicia at Alki 165
Pie 145
Pike Place Chowder 54
Pink Door Ristorante 54
Pinxtos 87
Piroshky Piroshky 52-3
Poppy 112-13
Portage Bay Cafe 135
Procopio Gelati 54
Purple Cafe & Wine Bar 52
Purple Dot Cafe 71

Queen Anne Café 100
Queen City Grill 87

R & L Home of Good
  Bar-B-Que 112
Ray's Boathouse 154
Red Mill Burgers 146
Revel 145
Rione XIII 13, 112
Ristorante Doria 135-6
Rover's 127

Salty's on Alki 165
Salumi 70
Schultzy's Sausages 135
Serafina 101
Serious Biscuit 101
Serious Pie 86
Shanghai Garden 72
Shanik 101
Shiro's Sushi Restaurant 87
Sitka & Spruce 112
SkyCity Restaurant 81
Spud Fish & Chips 165
Square Knot Diner 164
Steelhead Diner 54
Sunfish 164
Sunrise Lodge & Cafeteria
  (Mt Rainier) 178

Tamarind Tree 72
Tangletown Pub 145
Taste Restaurant 50
Tavolàta 88

Thai Tom 133, 135
Tilikum Place Cafe 87
Top Pot Hand-Forged
  Doughnuts 84
Toulouse Petit 100
Twede's (Snoqualmie
  Valley) 176

Vashon Tea Shop (Vashon
  Island) 172
Via Tribunali 164
Voila! 123
Von's 1000 Spirits 52

Walrus & the Carpenter 154
Wild Ginger 50

Zaina 70-1

DRINKING & NIGHTLIFE

74th Street Ale House 147
88 Keys Dueling Piano
  Bar 72-3

Alibi Room 56
All City Coffee 165
Athenian Inn 56
Attic Alehouse & Eatery 128

Baltic Room 114
Barça 115
Bedlam 89
Big Time Microbrew &
  Music 136
Black Coffee 114
Blue Moon 136
Bookstore Bar 56
Brave Horse Tavern 13, 102
Brouwer's 146-7

Café Allegro 136
Café Racer 136
Caffe Ladro 102
Caffè Umbria 73
Caffé Vita 114
Canterbury Ale & Eats 115
Central Saloon 73

Century Ballroom 115
Comet 115, 99
Conor Byrne 157
Contour 57
Copper Gate 156
Cortona Cafe 128

El Chupacabra 147
El Diablo Coffee Co. 102
Elliott Bay Brewery &
  Pub 165
Elysian Brewing Company
  114
Espresso Vivace at Brix
  113

Five Point Café 89, 90
Fremont Brewing 146
Fremont Coffee Company
  147
Front Street Ale House
  & San Juan Brewing
  Company (San Juan
  Island) 174
Frontier Room 89
Fuel 73

George & Dragon Pub 146

Hale's Ales Brewery 146
Hattie's Hat 156
High Line 114
Hilltop Ale House 102

Island Hoppin' Brewery
  (Orcas Island) 174-5

J&M Café 73
Jolly Roger Taproom 157
Jules Maes Saloon 165

Kells 57
King's Hardware 156

Last Supper Club 73
Lava Lounge 89
Linda's Tavern 115

M

McMenamins Queen Anne 102
Mecca Café 102
Monkey Pub 136

N

Neighbours 115
Nine Pound Hammer 165
Nitelite Lounge 89
Noble Fir 156

O

Owl & Thistle 55

P

Panama Hotel Tea & Coffee House 73
Pike Pub & Brewery 56
Pyramid Ale House 73

R

R Place 115
Re-Bar 89
Rendezvous 89, 90
Rob Roy 89

S

Seattle Coffee Works 53, 55-6
Sexton 156
Shorty's 88-9, 90
Smarty Pants 165
Starbucks (Pike Place branch) 57
Stumptown on 12th 114
Sun Liquor Distillery 114

T

Tasting Room 56
Tavern Law 114
Teahouse Kuan Yin 148
Tougo Coffee 128
Two Bells Bar & Grill 89

U

Ugly Mug 136
Uptown Espresso Bar 102

V

Victrola Coffee Roasters 113-14, **8**
Virginia Inn Tavern 57

W

West 5 165
Wildrose 115

Z

Zeitgeist 72
Zig Zag Café 56-7
Zoka Coffee 136

⭐ **ENTERTAINMENT**

5th Avenue Theater 58
A Contemporary Theatre 57
Annex Theater 116
Chop Suey 115
Cinerama 91
Comedy Underground 73
Crocodile 90
Dimitriou's Jazz Alley 90
El Corazon 103
Fremont Almost Free Outdoor Cinema 147
Gay City Library 116
Grand Illusion Cinema 137
Harvard Exit 116
High Dive 147
Imax Theater 84
Intiman Theatre Company 91
Jewel Box Theater 89
Little Red Hen 147
Market Theater 58
Mix, The 166
Moore Theater 91
Nectar 147
Neptune Theater 137
Neumo's 115
Northwest Film Forum 116
On the Boards 102-3
Pacific Northwest Ballet 91
Paramount Theater 58
Richard Hugo House 116
Seattle Children's Theater 91
Seattle Opera 91
Seattle Repertory Theater 91
Seattle Symphony 58
Showbox 57-8
Showbox SoDo 162
SIFF Cinema Uptown 103
SIFF Film Center 91
Studio Seven 166

Sunset Tavern 157
Teatro Zinzanni 103
Tractor Tavern 157
Triple Door 58
Tula's Jazz 91
Varsity Theatre 137
Vera Project 91

🛍 **SHOPPING**

A

Alhambra 59
Aprie 117

B

Babeland 116
Barnes & Noble 59
BCBG 60
Bella Umbrella 59
Bop Street Records 157
Brooks Brothers 60
Buffalo Exchange (Ballard) 157
Buffalo Exchange (U District) 137-8
Bulldog News & Espresso 138

C

Card Kingdom 23, 157
Clog Factory 74
Club Monaco 60
Crossroads Trading Co 117
Crypt 116

D

DeLaurenti's 60
Dilettante Chocolates 116-17

E

Easy Street Records & Café 166-7
Elliott Bay Bicycles 92
Elliott Bay Book Company 116
Exofficio 92

F

Fantagraphics Bookstore & Gallery 166, 198
Feathered Friends 103
Fireworks 60
Flanagan & Lane Antiques 74
Frock Shop 148

G

Georgetown Records 166
Glasshouse Studio 74
Golden Age Collectables 61

H

Hardwick's Hardware Store 138
Henrietta's Hats 129

J

J Crew 60
Jive Time Records 147

K

Kinokuniya 74-5
Kirk Albert Vintage Furnishings 166

L

La Buona Tavola 60
Left Bank Books 60
Legacy Ltd Gallery 58
Lush 60

M

Macy's 59
Made in Washington 60, 61
Magus Books 137
Market Magic 23, 60
Metsker Maps 61
Monster Art & Clothing 157

N

Niketown 59
Nordstrom 59-60
Nordstrom Rack 60
North Face 59

O

Old Seattle Paperworks 61
Once Upon a Time 23, 103
Ophelia's Books 147
Original Children's Shop 128

P

Pacific Herb & Grocery 74
Pacific Place 60
Patrick's Fly Shop 103
Peter Miller Architecture & Design Books 91-2
Picnic 148
Pioneer Square Antique Mall 74

Pitaya 138
Pure Food Fish 61

Q

Queen Anne Books 103

R

Read All About It 61
Red Light 117

S

Scarecrow Video 137
Seattle Mystery
  Bookshop 74
Secret Garden Bookshop
  157
Singles Going Steady 90, 92
Souk 61
Soul Wine 103
Sur la Table 61
Sway & Cake 58

T

Tenzing Momo 60
Throwbacks NW 117
Tiffany & Co 60
Twice Sold Tales 116

U

U District Farmers
  Market 137
University Bookstore 137
Urban Outfitters 117
Uwajimaya 67-8, 75

W

Wall of Sound 117
Westlake Center 60
Wide World Books &
  Maps 148
Wild at Heart 157
Wild Salmon Seafood
  Market 158
Williams-Sonoma 60

Y

Ye Olde Curiosity Shop 61

Z

Zanadu 23, 92

SPORTS &
ACTIVITIES

24-Hour Fitness 92
Agua Verde Paddle Club 138

Alki Kayak Tours 167
CenturyLink Field 31, 32,
  75, 162, 31
Cheshiahud Loop 104
Downtown Seattle YMCA
  62
Dutch Bike Co 158
Gold's Gym 62
Green Lake Boat Rental 148
Green Lake Small Craft
  Center 148
Husky Stadium 138
Jefferson Park Golf
  Course 32
Leschi Park 129
Madison Park Beach 129
Madrona Park Beach 129
Miller School of Art 167
Moss Bay Rowing & Kayak
  Center 104
Northwest Outdoor Center
  Inc 104
Rainier Mountaineering Inc
  (Mt Rainier) 177
Recycled Cycles 138
REI 104
Safeco Field 31, 75, 162
Samadhi Yoga 117
SBR Seattle Bicycle Rental
  & Tours 62
School of Acrobatics &
  New Circus Acts 167
Seattle Cycling Tours
  61-2
Seattle Glassblowing
  Studio 92
Seattle Scuba 104
Seattle Sounders 75
Seattle Storm 92
Sierra Club 104
Stone Gardens: The
  Climbers Gym 158
Turtlehead Farm (Orcas
  Island) 174
UW Waterfront Activities
  Center 138
West Seattle Golf Course
  32
Windworks 152

SLEEPING

9 Cranes Inn 188
11th Avenue Inn 187

A

Ace Hotel 184-5
Alexis Hotel 182
Arctic Club 183

B

Bacon Mansion B&B 186
Ballard Inn 188
Belltown Inn 184
Best Western Executive
  Inn 185
Best Western Pioneer
  Square Hotel 184

C

Chambered Nautilus B&B
  Inn 188
City Hostel Seattle 184
College Inn 187
Courtyard Marriott 186

D

Doe Bay Village Resort &
  Retreat (Orcas Island)
  175

E

Edgewater 182
Executive Hotel Pacific
  182

F

Fairmont Olympic Hotel
  182-3

G

Gaslight Inn B&B 186-7
Georgetown Inn 188
Green Tortoise Hostel 182

H

Hampton Inn 186
Hill House B&B 186
Hotel 1000 183
Hotel Andra 185
Hotel Ballard 188
Hotel Deca 187-8
Hotel Five 13, 184
Hotel Hotel Hostel 188
Hotel Max 183
Hotel Monaco 183
Hotel Packwood
  (Mt Rainier) 178
Hotel Vintage Park 183

I

Inn at El Gaucho 185
Inn at Queen Anne 186
Inn at the Market 182
Inn at Virginia Mason 187

L

Loyal Inn Best Western
  184

M

MarQueen Hotel 185
Marriott Residence Inn
  186
Maxwell Hotel 13, 186
Mayflower Park Hotel
  182
Mediterranean Inn 185
Moore Hotel 184

O

Ohanapecosh
  Campground
  (Mt Rainier) 178
Outlook Inn (Orcas Island)
  175

P

Paradise Inn (Mt Rainier)
  178
Paramount Hotel 183
Pensione Nichols 182

R

Roche Harbor Resort
  (San Juan Island)
  175

S

Salish Lodge & Spa
  (Snoqualmie
  Valley) 176
Seattle Renaissance
  Hotel 183
Silver Cloud Hotel 184
Silver Cloud Inn Lake
  Union 185
Sorrento Hotel 187

U

University Inn 187

W

Warwick Hotel 185
Watertown 187
Wayfarer's Rest (San Juan
  Island) 175
Westin Hotel Seattle 183
Whittaker's Motel &
  Bunkhouse (Mt Rainier)
  177-8

Seattle Maps

Map Legend

Sights
- Beach
- Buddhist
- Castle
- Christian
- Hindu
- Islamic
- Jewish
- Monument
- Museum/Gallery
- Ruin
- Winery/Vineyard
- Zoo
- Other Sight

Eating
- Eating

Drinking & Nightlife
- Drinking & Nightlife
- Cafe

Entertainment
- Entertainment

Shopping
- Shopping

Sleeping
- Sleeping
- Camping

Sports & Activities
- Diving/Snorkelling
- Canoeing/Kayaking
- Skiing
- Surfing
- Swimming/Pool
- Walking
- Windsurfing
- Other Sports & Activities

Information
- Post Office
- Tourist Information

Transport
- Airport
- Border Crossing
- Bus
- Cable Car/Funicular
- Cycling
- Ferry
- Monorail
- Parking
- S-Bahn
- Taxi
- Train/Railway
- Tram
- Tube Station
- U-Bahn
- Underground Train Station
- Other Transport

Routes
- Tollway
- Freeway
- Primary
- Secondary
- Tertiary
- Lane
- Unsealed Road
- Plaza/Mall
- Steps
- Tunnel
- Pedestrian Overpass
- Walking Tour
- Walking Tour Detour
- Path

Boundaries
- International
- State/Province
- Disputed
- Regional/Suburb
- Marine Park
- Cliff
- Wall

Geographic
- Hut/Shelter
- Lighthouse
- Lookout
- Mountain/Volcano
- Oasis
- Park
- Pass
- Picnic Area
- Waterfall

Hydrography
- River/Creek
- Intermittent River
- Swamp/Mangrove
- Reef
- Canal
- Water
- Dry/Salt/Intermittent Lake
- Glacier

Areas
- Beach/Desert
- Cemetery (Christian)
- Cemetery (Other)
- Park/Forest
- Sportsground
- Sight (Building)
- Top Sight (Building)

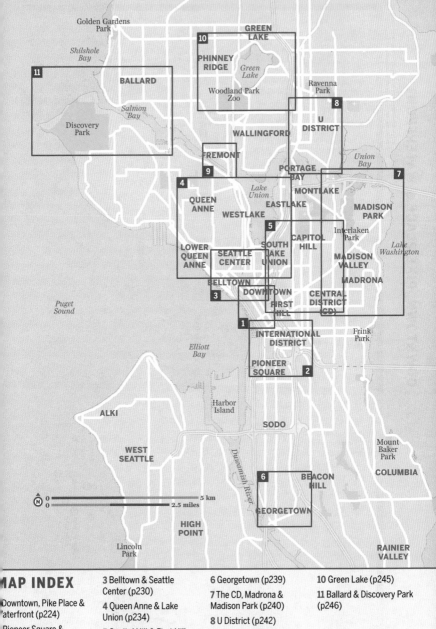

MAP INDEX

Downtown, Pike Place & Waterfront (p224)

Pioneer Square & International District (p228)

3 Belltown & Seattle Center (p230)

4 Queen Anne & Lake Union (p234)

5 Capitol Hill & First Hill (p236)

6 Georgetown (p239)

7 The CD, Madrona & Madison Park (p240)

8 U District (p242)

9 Fremont (p244)

10 Green Lake (p245)

11 Ballard & Discovery Park (p246)

DOWNTOWN, PIKE PLACE & WATERFRONT

Key on p226

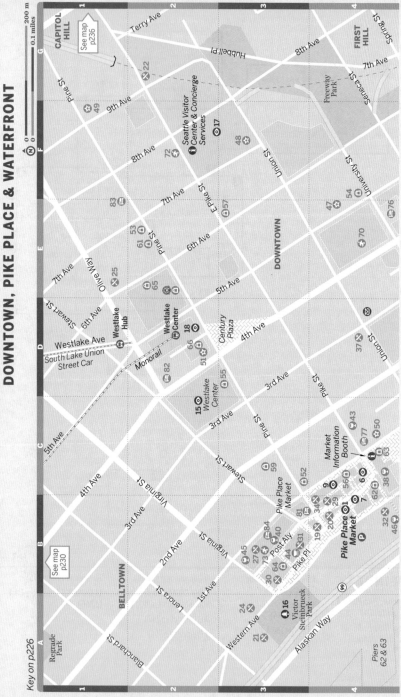

- 0 200 m
- 0 0.1 miles

See map p236

CAPITOL HILL

Terry Ave

Pine St

9th Ave

Hubbell Pl

8th Ave

FIRST HILL

Boren St

7th Ave

Seneca St

Freeway Park

22

49

Seattle Visitor Center & Concierge Services
17

72

8th Ave

48

Union St

University St

54

47

76

7th Ave

E Pike St

57

6th Ave

5th Ave

DOWNTOWN

70

83

53

61

Pine St

25

65

4th Ave

Olive Way

Stewart St

Westlake Hub

Westlake Ave

Westlake Center
18

66

51

82

Monorail

South Lake Union Street Car

Century Plaza

55

37

Union St

3rd Ave

15

Westlake Center

3rd Ave

Pine St

43

77

50

59

Stewart St

Pike Place Market

Market Information Booth

52

9

56

6

63

38

81

34

29

7

62

20

19

31

Pike Pl

Pike Place Market

32

46

45

27

73

64

44

30

84

40

Post Aly

Virginia St

See map p230

BELLTOWN

3rd Ave

2nd Ave

1st Ave

Lenora St

Virginia St

24

16

Victor Steinbrueck Park

21

Western Ave

Blanchard St

Regrade Park

Alaskan Way

Piers 62 & 63

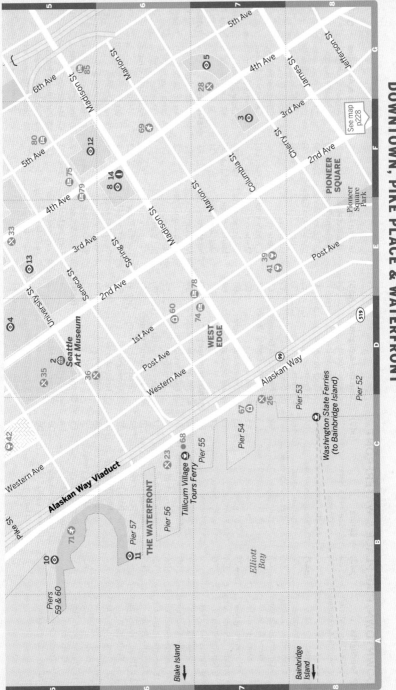

5th Ave

5th Ave

4th Ave

Marion St

6th Ave

Madison St

3rd Ave

James St

Jefferson St

Cherry St

2nd Ave

See map
p228

PIONEER
SQUARE

Pioneer
Square
Park

Columbia St

Post Ave

Marion St

Madison St

Seneca St

Spring St

2nd Ave

1st Ave

Post Ave

WEST
EDGE

Western Ave

Seattle
Art Museum

Alaskan Way

519

Pier 52

Washington State Ferries
(to Bainbridge Island)

Pier 53

Alaskan Way Viaduct

Western Ave

Pike St

Alaskan Way Viaduct

Pier 54

Pier 55

Pier 56

Pier 57

THE WATERFRONT

Tillicum Village
Tours Ferry

Piers
59 & 60

Elliott
Bay

Blake Island

Bainbridge
Island

DOWNTOWN, PIKE PLACE & WATERFRONT

DOWNTOWN, PIKE PLACE & WATERFRONT Map on p224

◎ Top Sights (p42)
1 Pike Place Market...........B4
2 Seattle Art Museum D5

◎ Sights (p47)
3 Arctic Building.................F7
4 Benaroya Concert Hall...D5
5 Columbia Center.............G7
6 Corner & Sanitary
   Market Buildings............C4
   Hammering Man......(see 2)
7 Main & North Arcades.....B4
8 Safeco Plaza...................F6
9 Sanitary Market
   Building........................B3
10 Seattle Aquarium.............B5
11 Seattle Great Wheel........B6
12 Seattle Public Library......F5
13 Seattle Tower.................E5
14 Three Piece Sculpture:
   Vertebrae.....................F6
15 Times Square Building.....C2
16 Victor Steinbrueck
   Park............................A3
17 Washington State
   Convention &
   Trade Center.................F2
18 Westlake Center.............D2

◎ Eating (p49)
19 Beecher's Handmade
   Cheese.........................B4
   Café Campagne......(see 81)
20 Cinnamon Works...............B4
   Crumpet Shop............(see 6)
21 Cutter's Crabhouse..........A3
22 Cyber-Dogs....................G2
23 Elliott's Oyster House......C6
24 Etta's Seafood................A3
   Georgian..................(see 76)
25 Il Fornaio......................E1
26 Ivar's Acres of Clams.......C7
27 Le Pichet.......................B3
   Lowells.....................(see 7)
   Matt's in the Market (see 6)
28 McCormick's Fish
   House & Bar...................G7
   Mee Sum Pastries...(see 20)
29 Pike Place Chowder.........B4
30 Pink Door Ristorante........B3
31 Piroshky Piroshky............B3
32 Procopio Gelati..............B4
33 Purple Cafe & Wine
   Bar.............................E5
34 Steelhead Diner..............B4
35 Taste Restaurant............D5
36 Von's 1000 Spirits............D5
37 Wild Ginger...................D4

◎ Drinking & Nightlife (p55)
38 Alibi Room.....................C4
   Athenian Inn............(see 7)
   Bookstore Bar..........(see 74)
39 Contour........................E7
40 Kells...........................B3
41 Owl & Thistle.................E7
42 Pike Pub & Brewery..........C5
43 Seattle Coffee Works.......C4
44 Starbucks.....................B3
45 Virginia Inn Tavern..........B3
46 Zig Zag Café..................B4

◎ Entertainment (p57)
47 5th Avenue Theater.........E4
48 A Contemporary
   Theatre.......................F3
   Market Theater..... (see 38)
49 Paramount Theater..........F1
   Seattle Symphony......(see 4)
50 Showbox......................C4
51 TicketMaster.................D2
   Triple Door..............(see 37)

◎ Shopping (p58)
52 Alhambra......................C3
53 Barnes & Noble..............E2
   Bella Umbrella........(see 34)
54 Brooks Brothers.............F4
   DeLaurenti's...........(see 38)
   Golden Age
   Collectables...........(see 7)
   La Buona Tavola...(see 20)
   Left Bank Books.....(see 6)
   Legacy Ltd Gallery (see 74)
   Lush.....................(see 66)
55 Made in
   Washington................D3
   Made in
   Washington........(see 66)
   Market Magic.........(see 20)
   Metsker Maps...........(see 7)
56 Niketown......................C4
57 Nordstrom....................E3
58 Nordstrom Rack..............E2
59 North Face...................C3
60 Old Seattle
   Paperworks............(see 7)
61 Pacific Place.................E2
62 Pure Food Fish..............C4
63 Read All About It............C4
64 Souk..........................B3
65 Sway & Cake.................E2
   Tenzing Momo......(see 38)
66 Westlake Center.............D2
67 Ye Olde Curiosity
   Shop..........................C7

◎ Sports & Activities (p61)
68 Argosy Cruises...............C6
   Seattle Harbor
   Tour..........................C6
69 Downtown Seattle
   YMCA..........................F6
70 Gold's Gym....................E4
71 SBR Seattle Bicycle
   Rental & Tours...............B5
72 Seattle Cycling Tours.......F2
73 Tasting Room..................B3
   Tillium Village..........(see 7)

◎ Sleeping (p182)
74 Alexis Hotel..................D7
   Arctic Club..............(see 3)
75 Executive Hotel
   Pacific.......................F5
76 Fairmont Olympic
   Hotel..........................E4
77 Green Tortoise Hostel.....C4
78 Hotel 1000...................E7
79 Hotel Monaco................F5
80 Hotel Vintage Park.........F5
81 Inn at the Market...........B3
82 Mayflower Park Hotel.......D2
83 Paramount Hotel............E1
84 Pensione Nichols............B3
85 Seattle Renaissance
   Hotel..........................G5

PIONEER SQUARE & INTERNATIONAL DISTRICT *Map on p228*

◉ **Top Sights** **(p65)**
1 Grand Central Arcade B2
2 Pioneer Building.. C1
3 Smith Tower C1

◉ **Sights** **(p66)**
4 Foster/White Gallery...............................D2
5 Hau Hau Market...G3
6 Hing Hay Park..E3
7 International Children's Park E4
8 King Street Station...................................D3
9 Klondike Gold Rush National
    Historical Park.......................................C3
10 Milepost 31...B2
11 Occidental Park...C2
12 Occidental Square C2
13 Pioneer Square B2
    Pioneer Square Park ....(see 13)
14 Roq La Rue..B3
15 Seattle Metropolitan Police
    Museum..C3
16 Seattle Pinball Museum............................E3
17 Union Station...D3
    Uwajimaya ....(see 51)
18 Waterfall Park...C2
19 Wing Luke Asian Museum F3
20 Yesler Way B2

✕ **Eating** **(p70)**
21 Bakeman's C1
22 Bar Sajor C3
    Cafe Paloma ....(see 23)
23 Delicatus...B2
24 Fx McRory's Steak, Chop & Oyster
    House C3
    Grand Central Baking Co...................(see 1)
25 Green Leaf F3
26 House of Hong.. F3
27 Jade Garden E3
28 New Orleans Creole Restaurant..............B2
29 Pho Bac H2
30 Purple Dot Café...E3

31 Salumi C2
32 Shanghai Garden.......................................E3
33 Tamarind Tree G2
34 Zaina..B1

◉ **Drinking & Nightlife** **(p72)**
35 88 Keys Dueling Piano Bar.......................C2
    Caffè Umbria....................................(see 12)
36 Central Saloon B2
37 Fuel..C2
38 J&M Café B2
39 Last Supper Club.......................................C2
40 Panama Hotel Tea & Coffee House E2
41 Pyramid Ale House....................................B6
42 Zeitgeist..C3

✪ **Entertainment** **(p73)**
43 Comedy Underground...............................C2
    Seattle Mariners.............................(see 53)
    Seattle Seahawks............................(see 52)
44 Showbox SoDo B7

🛍 **Shopping** **(p74)**
    Clog Factory......................................(see 10)
45 Flanagan & Lane Antiques C3
46 Glasshouse Studio C2
47 Kinokuniya..D3
48 Pacific Herb & Grocery.............................E3
49 Pioneer Square Antique Mall....................C1
50 Seattle Mystery Bookshop.......................C1
51 Uwajimaya..D4

⚙ **Sports & Activities** **(p75)**
    Bill Speidel's Underground Tour ....(see 2)
52 CenturyLink Field C4
53 Safeco Field..C6
    Seattle Sounders.............................(see 52)

🛏 **Sleeping** **(p184)**
54 Best Western Pioneer Square Hotel........B2
55 Silver Cloud Hotel.....................................C5

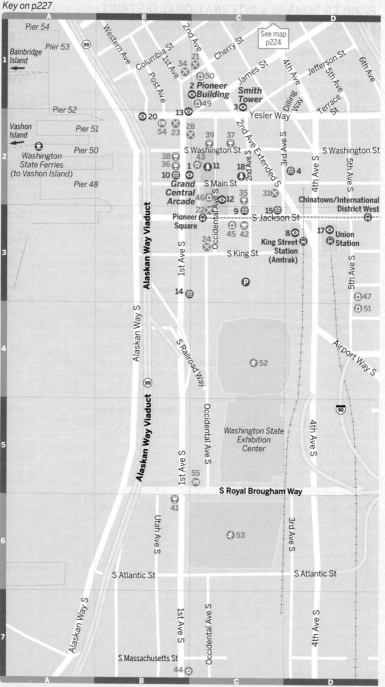

Key on p227

PIONEER SQUARE & INTERNATIONAL DISTRICT

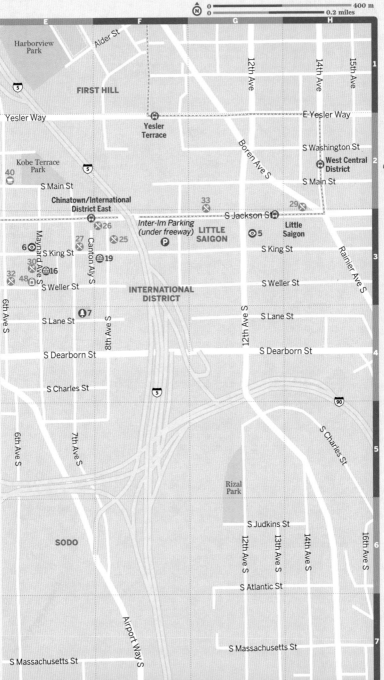

BELLTOWN & SEATTLE CENTER

Key on p232

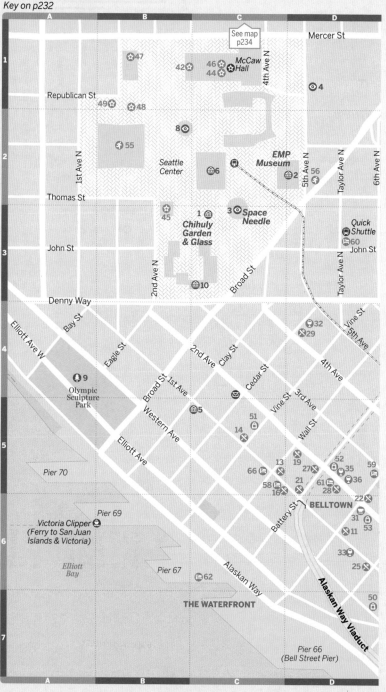

See map p234

Mercer St

McCaw Hall

47

42

46
44

4

Republican St

49

48

4th Ave N

4

Thomas St

55

8

Seattle Center

6

EMP Museum

2

5th Ave N

56

Taylor Ave N

6th Ave N

John St

45

1

Chihuly Garden & Glass

3 Space Needle

10

Broad St

Quick Shuttle

60

John St

Taylor Ave N

Denny Way

Bay St

Eagle St

2nd Ave

Clay St

32

29

Vine St

5th Ave

4th Ave

Elliott Ave W

9

Olympic Sculpture Park

Broad St
1st Ave

Cedar St

Vine St

3rd Ave

Western Ave

5

51

14

Wall St

Elliott Ave

13

19

27

52

35

59

Pier 70

66

58

16

21

61
28

36

BELLTOWN

22

Battery St

31

11

53

Victoria Clipper
(Ferry to San Juan Islands & Victoria)

Pier 69

33

25

Elliott Bay

Pier 67

62

Alaskan Way

50

THE WATERFRONT

Alaskan Way Viaduct

Pier 66
(Bell Street Pier)

A   B   C   D

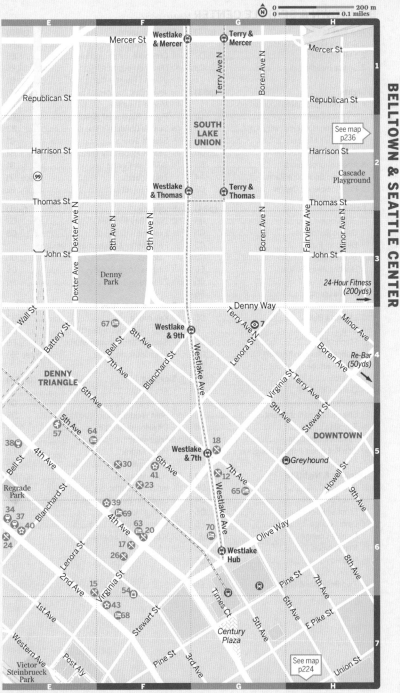

0   200 m
0   0.1 miles

Mercer St

Westlake & Mercer

Terry & Mercer

Mercer St

Terry Ave N

Boren Ave N

Republican St

SOUTH LAKE UNION

Republican St

See map p236

Harrison St

99

Cascade Playground

Harrison St

Westlake & Thomas

Terry & Thomas

Thomas St

Dexter Ave N

8th Ave N

9th Ave N

Boren Ave N

Fairview Ave

Minor Ave N

Thomas St

John St

Dexter Ave

Denny Park

John St

24-Hour Fitness (200yds)

Denny Way

Wall St

Battery St

67

8th Ave

Westlake & 9th

Terry Ave N

7

Minor Ave

DENNY TRIANGLE

Bell St

7th Ave

Blanchard St

Westlake Ave

Lenora St

Boren Ave

Re-Bar (50yds)

6th Ave

Virginia St

Terry Ave

9th Ave

Stewart St

5th Ave

57

64

DOWNTOWN

38

4th Ave

Bell St

30

6th Ave

41

18

Westlake & 7th

7th Ave

12

Greyhound

Howell St

9th Ave

23

65

Regrade Park

34

37

40

Blanchard St

39

4th Ave

69

63

20

70

Olive Way

24

Lenora St

17

26

Westlake Hub

2nd Ave

15

Virginia St

54

Times Ct

Pine St

7th Ave

8th Ave

1st Ave

43

68

Stewart St

Century Plaza

5th Ave

6th Ave

E Pike St

Western Ave

Post Aly

Pine St

3rd Ave

See map p224

Union St

Victor Steinbrueck Park

BELLTOWN & SEATTLE CENTER *Map on p230*

BELLTOWN & SEATTLE CENTER

◉ Top Sights (p78)
1 Chihuly Garden & Glass C3
2 EMP Museum D2
3 Space Needle C3

◉ Sights (p83)
4 Bill & Melinda Gates Foundation
   Visitor Center D1
5 Center on Contemporary Art C5
6 Children's Museum..................................C2
7 Cornish College of the Arts G4
8 International Fountain..............................B2
9 Olympic Sculpture Park...........................A4
10 Pacific Science Center C3

◎ Eating (p84)
11 360 Local D6
12 Barolo Ristorante....................................G5
13 Belltown Pizza C5
14 Black Bottle C5
15 Buenos Aires Grill E6
16 Cyclops..C5
17 Dahlia Lounge..F6
18 FareStart Restaurant G5
19 La Vita é Bella D5
20 Lola F6
21 Macrina D5
22 Mama's Mexican Kitchen.........................D6
23 Palace Kitchen F5
24 Pintxos...E6
25 Queen City Grill D6
26 Serious Pie...F6
27 Shiro's Sushi Restaurant.........................D5
28 Tavolàta D5
29 Tilikum Place Cafe D4
30 Top Pot Hand-Forged Doughnuts F5

◎ Drinking & Nightlife (p88)
31 Bedlam...D6
32 Five Point Café D4
33 Frontier Room..D6
34 Lava Lounge E6
   Nitelite Lounge ....(see 68)
35 Rendezvous D5
36 Rob Roy..D5
37 Shorty's..E6
38 Two Bells Bar & Grill E5

◉ Entertainment (p90)
39 Cinerama F6
40 Crocodile E6
41 Dimitriou's Jazz Alley...............................F5
42 Intiman Theater Company.......................B1
   Jewel Box Theater...........................(see 35)
43 Moore Theater..F7
44 Pacific Northwest Ballet..........................C1
45 Seattle Children's Theater B3
46 Seattle Opera...C1
47 Seattle Repertory Theater B1
48 SIFF Film Center B1
   Tula's Jazz ....(see 37)
49 Vera Project B1

◎ Shopping (p91)
50 Elliott Bay Bicycles..................................D7
51 Exofficio C5
52 Peter Miller Architecture & Design
   Books D5
53 Singles Going Steady...............................D6
54 Zanadu F6

◉ Sports & Activities (p92)
55 Key Arena B2
56 Ride the Ducks of Seattle........................D2
57 Seattle Glassblowing Studio.................... E5
   Seattle Storm..................................(see 55)

◎ Sleeping (p184)
58 Ace Hotel C5
59 Belltown Inn D5
60 Best Western Executive Inn.....................D3
61 City Hostel Seattle D5
62 Edgewater C6
63 Hotel Andra F6
64 Hotel Five...E5
65 Hotel Max G5
66 Inn at El Gaucho.......................................C5
67 Loyal Inn Best Western............................F4
68 Moore Hotel F7
69 Warwick Hotel..F6
70 Westin Hotel Seattle G6

QUEEN ANNE & LAKE UNION *Map on p234*

◎ Top Sights	(p95)
1 Museum of History & Industry	F5

◎ Sights	(p96)
2 Betty Bowen Park	B4
3 Center for Wooden Boats	F5
4 Denny Park	F7
5 Gable House	C4
6 Kerry Park	C4
7 Lake Union	F5
8 Lake Union Park	F5
9 Parsons Garden	A4
10 Queen Anne Counterbalance	C5
11 Turret House	B2

⊗ Eating	(p99)
12 5 Spot	C4
13 Blue Moon Burgers	F6
14 Canlis	E1
15 Dick's Drive-in	C6
16 Grub	C2
17 How to Cook a Wolf	C2
Paragon Bar & Grill	(see 18)
Peso's Kitchen & Lounge	(see 22)
18 Queen Anne Café	C3
19 Serafina	H2
20 Serious Biscuit	F6
21 Shanik	F6
22 Toulouse Petit	C5

◎ Drinking & Nightlife	(p102)
23 Brave Horse Tavern	F6
24 Caffe Ladro	C2
25 El Diablo Coffee Co.	C3

26 Hilltop Ale House	C2
27 McMenamins Queen Anne	D5
28 Mecca Café	C6
29 Uptown Espresso Bar	C6

◎ Entertainment	(p102)
30 El Corazon	G7
31 On the Boards	C5
32 SIFF Cinema Uptown	C6
33 Teatro Zinzanni	D5

◎ Shopping	(p103)
34 Feathered Friends	G7
35 Once Upon a Time	C3
36 Patrick's Fly Shop	H2
Queen Anne Books	(see 25)
Soul Wine	(see 20)

◎ Sports & Activities	(p104)
37 Cheshiahud Loop	F5
38 Moss Bay Rowing & Kayak Center	G4
39 Northwest Outdoor Center Inc.	F3
40 REI	G7
41 Seattle Scuba	F3

◎ Sleeping	(p185)
42 Courtyard Marriott	E5
43 Hampton Inn	E5
44 Inn at Queen Anne	C6
45 MarQueen Hotel	C5
46 Marriott Residence Inn	G5
47 Maxwell Hotel	D5
48 Mediterranean Inn	C6
49 Silver Cloud Inn Lake Union	G4

QUEEN ANNE & LAKE UNION

Key on p233

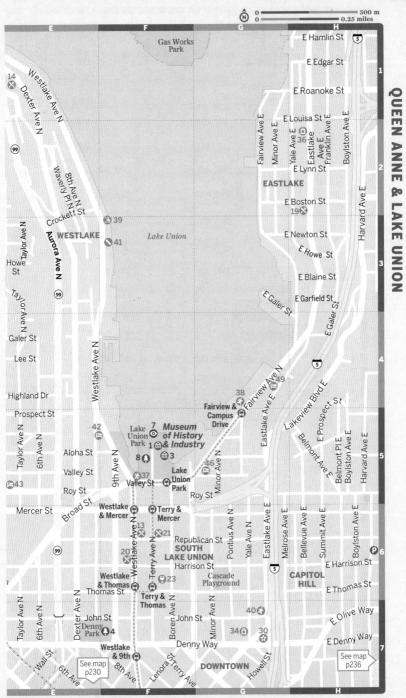

0   500 m
0   0.25 miles

E Hamlin St
E Edgar St
E Roanoke St
E Louisa St E
36
E Lynn St
Gas Works Park
14
Westlake Ave N
Dexter Ave N
99
Fairview Ave E
Minor Ave E
Yale Ave E
Eastlake Ave E
Franklin Ave E
Boylston Ave E
Harvard Ave E

EASTLAKE

E Boston St
19
E Newton St
E Howe St
E Blaine St
E Garfield St

8th Ave N
Waverly Pl N
Crockett St
39
WESTLAKE
41
Lake Union

Taylor Ave N
Aurora Ave N
99
Howe St
Taylor Ave N
Galer St
Lee St
Highland Dr
Prospect St

E Galer St
E Galer St
I-5

Westlake Ave N
42
Lake Union Park
7
Museum of History & Industry
1
3
8
37
Valley St
Lake Union Park
46
Roy St

Fairview Ave N
49
38
Fairview & Campus Drive
Eastlake Ave E
Lakeview Blvd E
E Prospect St
Belmont Pl E
Boylston Ave E
Belmont Ave E
Harvard Ave E

Taylor Ave N
6th Ave N
Aloha St
9th Ave N
Valley St
Roy St
43
Mercer St
Broad St

Westlake & Mercer
13
Terry & Mercer
21
Republican St
SOUTH LAKE UNION
Harrison St

Westlake Ave N
Terry Ave N
Minor Ave N
Pontius Ave N
Yale Ave N
Eastlake Ave E
Melrose Ave E
Bellevue Ave E
Summit Ave E
Boylston Ave E

6

99
20
23
Westlake & Thomas
Thomas St
Terry & Thomas
John St
Denny Park
4
John St
Cascade Playground
40
34
30
Denny Way

CAPITOL HILL
E Harrison St
E Thomas St
E Olive Way
E Denny Way

Taylor Ave N
6th Ave N
Dexter Ave N
Boren Ave N
Minor Ave N
Howell St

Westlake & 9th
See map p230
Wall St
6th Ave
8th Ave
Lenora St
Terry Ave
DOWNTOWN
See map p236

Key on p238

500 m

0.25 miles

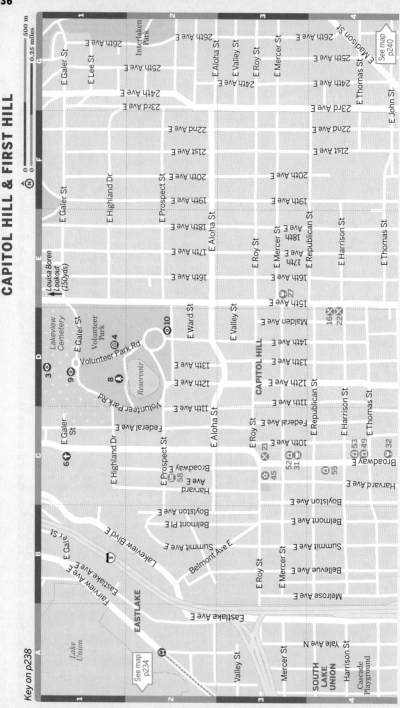

CAPITOL HILL

EASTLAKE

SOUTH
LAKE
UNION

Lake
Union

Lakeview
Cemetery

Volunteer
Park

Reservoir

Interlaken
Park

Cascade
Playground

Louisa Boren
Lookout
(150yds)

See map
p234

See map
p240

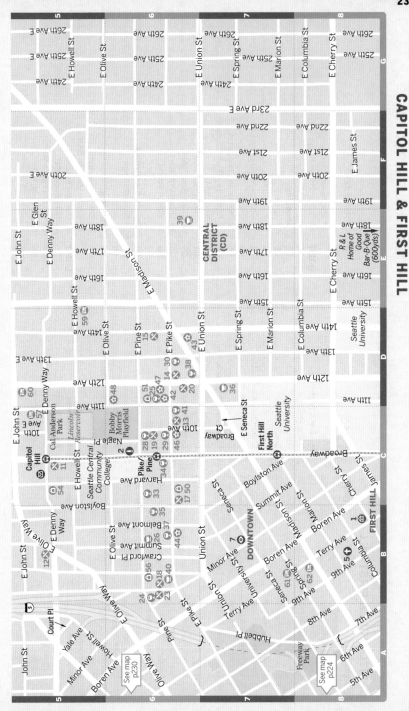

CAPITOL HILL & FIRST HILL *Map on p236*

◎ Sights (p107)
1 Frye Art Museum...B8
2 Jimi Hendrix Statue...C6
3 Lakeview Cemetery...D1
4 Seattle Asian Art Museum...D1
Sorrento Hotel...(see 62)
5 St James Cathedral...B8
6 St Mark's Cathedral...C1
7 Stimson-Green Mansion...B7
8 Volunteer Park...D1
9 Volunteer Park Conservatory...D1
10 Water Tower Observation Deck...D2

◎ Eating (p110)
11 Annapurna Cafe...C5
12 Arabica Lounge...B5
13 Bimbo's Cantina...C6
14 Bluebird Microcreamery...D6
Café Presse...(see 36)
15 Cascina Spinasse...D6
16 Coastal Kitchen...D4
17 Honeyhole...C6
Hunt Club...(see 62)
18 Mamnoon...B6
Molly Moon's...(see 28)
19 Oddfellows Cafe...C6
20 Osteria La Spiga...D6
21 Poppy...C3

22 Rione XIII...D4
23 Sitka & Spruce...B6

◎ Drinking & Nightlife (p113)
24 Baltic Room...B6
25 Barça...D6
26 Black Coffee...B6
Caffé Vita...(see 13)
27 Canterbury Ale & Eats...E3
28 Century Ballroom...C6
29 Comet...C6
30 Elysian Brewing Company...D6
31 Espresso Vivace at Brix...C3
32 High Line...C4
33 Linda's Tavern...C6
34 Neighbours...C6
35 R Place...B6
36 Stumptown on 12th...D7
37 Sun Liquor Distillery...B6
38 Tavern Law...D6
39 Tougo Coffee...E6
40 Victrola Coffee Roasters...B6
41 Wildrose...C6

◎ Entertainment (p115)
42 Annex Theater...C6
43 Chop Suey...D6
44 Gay City Library...C3

45 Harvard Exit...C3
46 Neumo's...C6
47 Northwest Film Forum...D6
48 Richard Hugo House...D6

◎ Shopping (p116)
49 Aprie...C4
50 Babeland...C6
Crossroads Trading Co...(see 53)
51 Crypt...D6
52 Dilettante Chocolates...C3
Elliott Bay Book Company...(see 19)
53 Red Light...C4
Throwbacks NW...(see 14)
54 Twice Sold Tales...C5
55 Urban Outfitters...C4
56 Wall of Sound...B6

◎ Sports & Activities (p117)
Samadhi Yoga...(see 14)

◎ Sleeping (p186)
57 11th Avenue Inn...C5
58 Bacon Mansion B&B...C2
59 Gaslight Inn B&B...D5
60 Hill House B&B...D5
61 Inn at Virginia Mason...B7
62 Sorrento Hotel...B8

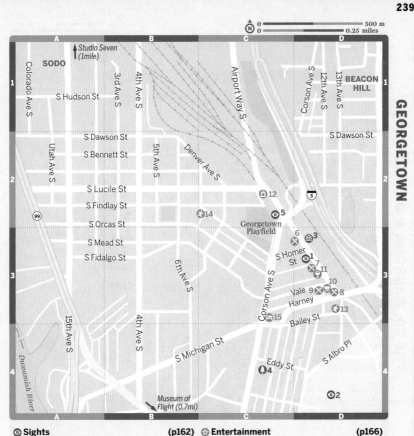

◎ **Sights** (p162)
1 Georgetown Arts & Cultural Center........D3
2 Georgetown Steam Plant D4
 Hat 'n' Boots ....(see 4)
3 Krab Jab Studio.......................................D3
4 Oxbow Park C4
 Roving Gallery ....(see 3)
5 Totally Blown Glassworks.......................C2

✕ **Eating** (p163)
6 American Pie D3
7 Fonda la Catrina.....................................D3
8 Square Knot Diner D3
9 Via Tribunali...D3

🍷 **Drinking & Nightlife** (p165)
10 All City Coffee...D3
11 Jules Maes Saloon D3
 Nine Pound Hammer.........................(see 8)
 Smarty Pants....................................(see 8)

✪ **Entertainment** (p166)
 The Mix ....(see 9)

🛍 **Shopping** (p166)
 Fantagraphics Bookstore &
  Gallery ....(see 10)
 Georgetown Records.........................(see 10)
12 Kirk Albert Vintage Furnishings...............C2

⚽ **Sports & Activities** (p167)
13 Miller School of Art...................................D3
14 School of Acrobatics & New
  Circus Acts C2

🛏 **Sleeping** (p188)
15 Georgetown Inn C3

THE CD, MADRONA & MADISON PARK

U DISTRICT

E Shelby St

E Hamlin St

Marsh Island
2

Foster Island

520

Montlake Park

E Miller St

E Calhoun St

E Mc Graw St

E Lynn St

Graham Visitors Center

Broadmoor Golf Club

E Mc Gilvra St

20th Ave E
23rd Ave E
24th Ave E
25th Ave E
26th Ave E

E Howe St
E Blaine St
Fuhrman Ave E

Lake Washington Blvd E

E Shore Dr

Broadmoor Dr E

Shenandoah Dr E

38th Pl E

39th Ave E

McGilvra Blvd E
41st Ave E
42nd Ave E
43rd Ave E

7

40th Ave E

16
8
20

Madison Park

Interlaken Park

E Crescent Dr

19th Ave E
20th Ave E
21st Ave E
22nd Ave E
23rd Ave E
24th Ave E

Arboretum Dr E

Parkside Dr E

Blenheim Dr E

E Blaine St

E Garfield St

E Galer St

E Lee St

MADISON PARK

37th Ave E
38th Ave E
39th Ave E

E Helen St

E Ward St

E Aloha St

E Aloha St

E Valley St

4

Lake Washington Blvd E

E Madison St

34th Ave E
36th Ave E

E Valley St

McGilvra Blvd E
39th Ave E

See map p236

19th Ave E
20th Ave E
21st Ave E
22nd Ave E
23rd Ave E
24th Ave E
25th Ave E

17
9
18

31st Ave E

E Mercer St

E Ford Pl

E Republican St

E Harrison St

E Thomas St

Lakeview Park

Lake Washington

14

E Arthur Pl

E John St

E Florence Ct

E John St

40th Ave E

1

6

MADISON VALLEY

E Denny Way

E Howell St

E Olive St

E Pine St

19th Ave
20th Ave
21st Ave
22nd Ave
23rd Ave
24th Ave
25th Ave

Martin Luther King Jr Way

29th Ave E

32nd Ave
33rd Ave
35th Ave

37th Ave
38th Ave

Dorffel Dr E

Madrona Pl E

Grand Ave

5

3

5

MADRONA

19
E Union St

26th Ave
27th Ave

30th Ave
31st Ave

35th Ave
36th Ave

15
11

E Spring St

E Marion St

E Columbia St

Madrona Park

Lake Washington Blvd

21

CENTRAL DISTRICT (CD)

E Columbia St

12

E Cherry St

E James St

13

10

27th Ave

E Jefferson St

Fullerton Ave

E James St

THE CD, MADRONA & MADISON PARK

◎ **Sights** (p122)
1 Denny Blaine Park C5
2 Foster Island Wetlands Trail.....................B1
3 Howell Park...C5
4 Japanese Garden......................................B4
5 Mount Zion Baptist Church......................A6
6 Viretta Park...C5
7 Washington Park Arboretum B2

✕ **Eating** (p123)
8 Cactus D2
9 Café Flora...B4
10 Cafe Selam B7
11 Cafe Soleil..C6
12 Catfish Corner..B7
13 Ezell's Famous Chicken A7
14 Harvest Vine...B5

15 Hi Spot Café..C6
Inès Patisserie ....(see 9)
16 Madison Park Conservatory D2
17 Rover's..B4
18 Voila! B5

◎ **Drinking & Nightlife** (p128)
Attic Alehouse & Eatery...................(see 16)
19 Cortona Cafe...A6

◎ **Shopping** (p128)
Henrietta's Hats...............................(see 14)
Original Children's Shop...................(see 8)

◎ **Sports & Activities** (p129)
20 Madison Park Beach..................................D2
21 Madrona Park Beach C7

THE CD, MADRONA & MADISON PARK

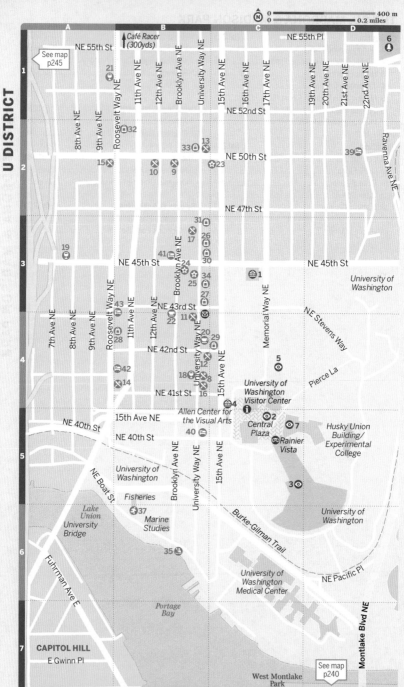

U DISTRICT

CAPITOL HILL

See map p245

See map p240

Café Racer (300yds)

NE 55th St

NE 55th Pl

NE 52nd St

NE 50th St

NE 47th St

NE 45th St

NE 45th St

NE 43rd St

NE 42nd St

NE 41st St

NE 40th St

NE 40th St

15th Ave NE

8th Ave NE
9th Ave NE
Roosevelt Way NE
11th Ave NE
12th Ave NE
Brooklyn Ave NE
University Way NE
15th Ave NE
16th Ave NE
17th Ave NE
19th Ave NE
20th Ave NE
21st Ave NE
22nd Ave NE

7th Ave NE
8th Ave NE
9th Ave NE
Roosevelt Way NE
11th Ave NE
12th Ave NE
University Way NE
15th Ave NE

Brooklyn Ave NE

Ravenna Ave NE

Memorial Way NE

NE Stevens Way

Pierce La

University of Washington

University of Washington

University of Washington

University of Washington Visitor Center

University of Washington Medical Center

Husky Union Building/ Experimental College

Central Plaza

Rainier Vista

Allen Center for the Visual Arts

University of Washington

Fisheries

Marine Studies

Lake Union

University Bridge

NE Boat St

Fuhrman Ave E

Burke-Gilman Trail

NE Pacific Pl

Montlake Blvd NE

Portage Bay

West Montlake Park

E Gwinn Pl

◎ **Sights** (p132)

1 Burke Museum........................ C3
2 Central Plaza (Red
   Square) C5
3 Drumheller Fountain C5
4 Henry Art Gallery C4
5 Quad C4
6 Ravenna Park D1
7 Suzzallo Library C5

◎ **Eating** (p133)

Agua Verde Café..........(see 35)
8 Cafe Solstice........................ B4
9 Cedars Restaurant B2
10 Chaco Canyon Café.............B2
11 Flowers B4
12 Orange King........................... B4
13 Pam's Kitchen B2
14 Portage Bay Cafe B4
15 Ristorante Doria...................A2
16 Schultzy's Sausages B4
17 Thai Tom B3

◎ **Drinking & Nightlife** (p136)

18 Big Time Microbrew &
   Music B4
19 Blue Moon A3
20 Café Allegro B4
21 Monkey Pub........................... A1
22 Ugly Mug B4

◎ **Entertainment** (p137)

23 Grand Illusion Cinema......... C2
24 Neptune Theater...................B3
25 Varsity Theatre B3

◎ **Shopping** (p137)

26 Buffalo Exchange..................B3
   Bulldog News &
   Espresso ....(see 20)
27 Crossroads Trading
   Co...B3
28 Hardwick's Hardware
   Store......................................B4
29 Magus Books...........................C4
30 Pitaya B3
31 Red Light..................................B3
32 Scarecrow Video B2
33 U District Farmers
   Market B2
34 University Bookstore B3

◎ **Sports & Activities** (p138)

35 Agua Verde Paddle
   Club B6
36 Husky Stadium E6
37 Recycled Cycles....................B6
   University of
   Washington
   Huskies ....(see 36)
38 UW Waterfront
   Activities Center E7

◎ **Sleeping** (p187)

39 Chambered Nautilus
   B&B Inn.................................D2
40 College Inn............................B5
41 Hotel Deca............................B3
42 University Inn B4
43 Watertown B3

FREMONT

◎ **Top Sights** (p141)
1 Fremont Public Sculpture D3

◎ **Sights** (p143)
2 Apatosaurs B3
3 Fremont Bridge..D4
4 Fremont Rocket..C3
5 Fremont Sunday Market..............................C3
6 Guidepost C3
7 History House...D3
8 Statue of Lenin...C2
9 Theo Chocolate Factory B2
10 Waiting for the Interurban.........................D3

✗ **Eating** (p145)
11 Homegrown...D3
12 Hunger...C2
13 Pie..C3
14 Revel..B2

◎ **Drinking & Nightlife** (p146)
15 Brouwer's..B2
16 Fremont Coffee Company C2
17 George & Dragon Pub.................................B2

✿ **Entertainment** (p147)
18 Fremont Almost Free Outdoor
   Cinema..B2
19 High Dive...C2
20 Nectar...B2

◎ **Shopping** (p147)
21 Jive Time Records......................................D3
22 Ophelia's Books...D3

◎ **Sleeping** (p188)
23 Hotel Hotel Hostel.....................................C2

GREEN LAKE

◎ **Top Sights** (p143)
1 Green Lake Park................D2

◎ **Sights** (p144)
2 Bathhouse Theater..............C2
3 Green Lake Aqua Theater......C3
4 Seattle Rose Garden............B4
5 Woodland Park Zoo..............B4

✕ **Eating** (p145)
6 Beth's Café......................C2
7 Mighty-O Donuts...............D4
8 Nell's.............................D2
9 Pete's Egg Nest.................A1
10 Red Mill Burgers...............B2
Tangletown Pub.............(see 7)

◎ **Drinking & Nightlife** (p147)
11 74th Street Ale House.........A2
12 El Chupacabra..................A2

◎ **Entertainment** (p147)
13 Little Red Hen.................E2

◎ **Shopping** (p148)
14 Frock Shop.....................B3
15 Picnic...........................A2

◎ **Sports & Activities** (p148)
16 Green Lake Boat Rental.......D2
17 Green Lake Small Craft Center...C3

◎ **Sleeping** (p188)
18 9 Cranes Inn....................A4

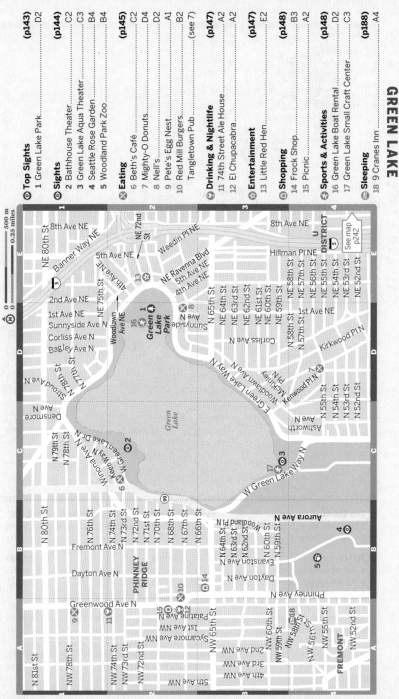

BALLARD & DISCOVERY PARK

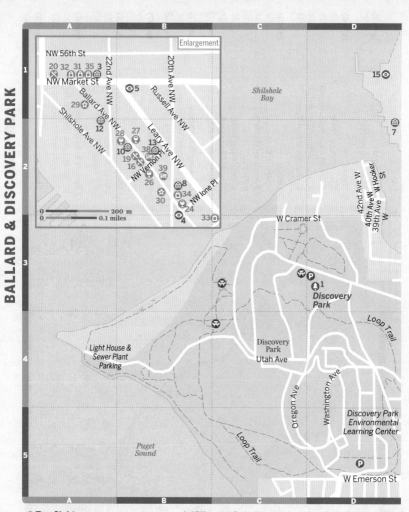

⊚ Top Sights (p151)
1 Discovery Park D3
2 Hiram M Chittenden Locks F3

⊚ Sights (p152)
3 Ballard Building A1
4 Ballard Farmers Market B3
5 Bergen Place Park B1
6 Carl English Jr Botanical Gardens F3
7 Center on Contemporary Art D2
8 Cors & Wegener Building B2
9 Fishermen's Terminal H5
10 GS Sanborn Building B2
11 Nordic Heritage Museum F1
12 Portland Building A2

13 Scandinavian American Bank Building ... B2
14 Seattle Fishermen's Memorial H5
15 Shilshole Bay Marina D1

⊗ Eating (p153)
16 Bastille Cafe & Bar B2
17 Cafe Besalu G2
18 Chinook's at Salmon Bay H5
19 Fresh Flours B2
   La Carta de Oaxaca .... (see 29)
20 La Isla A1
21 Lockspot Cafe F3
22 Ray's Boathouse E2
23 Walrus & the Carpenter H3

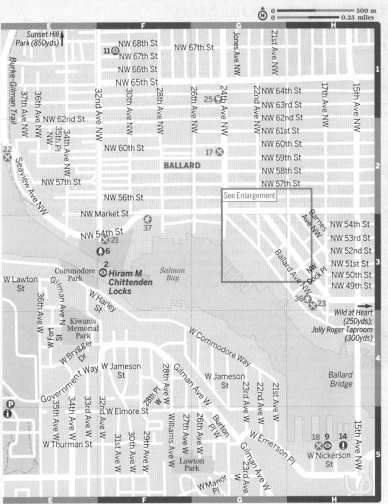

Drinking & Nightlife (p156)
24	Conor Byrne	B2
25	Copper Gate	G1
26	Hattie's Hat	B2
	King's Hardware	(see 30)
27	Noble Fir	B2
28	Sexton	B2

Entertainment (p157)
| 29 | Sunset Tavern | A1 |
| 30 | Tractor Tavern | B2 |

Shopping (p157)
| 31 | Bop Street Records | A1 |
| 32 | Buffalo Exchange | A1 |

33	Card Kingdom	C3
34	Monster Art & Clothing	B2
35	Secret Garden Bookshop	A1
	Wild Salmon Seafood Market	(see 18)

Sports & Activities (p158)
36	Dutch Bike Co	H3
37	Stone Gardens: The Climbers Gym	F3
	Windworks	(see 15)

Sleeping (p188)
| 38 | Ballard Inn | B2 |
| 39 | Hotel Ballard | B2 |

Our Story

A beat-up old car, a few dollars in the pocket and a sense of adventure. In 1972 that's all Tony and Maureen Wheeler needed for the trip of a lifetime – across Europe and Asia overland to Australia. It took several months, and at the end – broke but inspired – they sat at their kitchen table writing and stapling together their first travel guide, *Across Asia on the Cheap*. Within a week they'd sold 1500 copies. Lonely Planet was born.

Today, Lonely Planet has offices in Melbourne, London and Oakland, with more than 600 staff and writers. We share Tony's belief that 'a great guidebook should do three things: inform, educate and amuse'.

Our Writers

Brendan Sainsbury

Coordinating Author, Downtown, Pike Place & Waterfront, Pioneer Square & International District, Belltown & Seattle Center, Queen Anne & Lake Union, Capitol Hill & First Hill, The CD, Madrona & Madison Park, U District, Fremont & Green Lake, Ballard & Discovery Park, Georgetown & West Seattle An expat Brit from Hampshire in England, Brendan first developed an interest in Seattle in the early 1990s when he became entranced with the electric chaos of grunge. He has been a regular visitor to the city ever since moving to Vancouver, Canada, in 2004 and has been posting Seattle reviews for Lonely Planet in its biennial *USA* guide since 2009. When not sampling the latest Guatemalan single-origin coffee beans in a Capitol Hill cafe, Brendan likes running up mountains, traveling to anywhere he hasn't been yet, and teaching his son, Kieran, to play David Bowie songs on the piano.

Celeste Brash

Day Trips Locals have a hard time believing it, but the beauty of the Pacific Northwest is what coaxed Celeste back to the US after 15 years in Tahiti. She was thrilled to explore and imbibe the treasures of her new backyard for this book: hike snowy peaks, look for orcas and get in touch with her cowboy and Indian roots. Find out more about Celeste and her writing at www.celeste brash.com.

Published by Lonely Planet Publications Pty Ltd
ABN 36 005 607 983
6th edition – February 2014
ISBN 978 1 74220 136 8
© Lonely Planet 2014   Photographs © as indicated 2014
10 9 8 7 6 5 4 3 2
Printed in Singapore